BRITISH PROPAGANDA IN THE 20TH CENTURY

International Communications
Series Editor: Philip M. Taylor

This is the first comprehensive series to tackle the fast-expanding subject of International Communications.

This multi-disciplinary subject is viewed as a field of enquiry and research that deals with the processes and impact of the transfer of information, news, data and cultural products as well as other forms of transborder communications between nation-states within the wider context of globalisation. As such it is not only a field of study in its own right but also directly connected to international history, international politics, international affairs and international political economy.

Most writers in these more 'established' fields are agreed that communications have come to play an ever more significant part in relations between states at the political, economic, diplomatic, military and cultural levels. This series will show *how* communications serves to influence those activities from the points of transmission to those of reception.

Enormous breakthroughs in communications technologies – satellite communications, computer mediated communications, mobile personal communications – are now converging, and the possibilities which this might present are forcing a reconsideration of how established patterns of inter-state relations might adapt to, or be influenced by, this latest phase of the information age.

Debates relating to international regulation, censorship, public diplomacy, electronic democracy, cross-cultural communications and even information warfare all reflect the sense that communications are transforming the nature and practice of government, education, leisure, business, work, and warfare. Information has become the lifeblood of this globalising set of patterns.

Books in this series reflect this phenomenon but are rooted in historical method, even when tackling more contemporary events. They are truly international in coverage. The range of books reflects the coverage of courses and teaching in international communications and they are carefully aimed at students and researchers working in this area.

British Propaganda in the 20th Century

Selling Democracy

Philip M. Taylor

Edinburgh University Press

For my students – past, present and future

© Philip M. Taylor, 1999

Edinburgh University Press
22 George Square, Edinburgh

Typeset in Ehrhardt by
Carnegie Publishing, Chatsworth Rd, Lancaster and
printed and bound in Great Britain by
MPG Books Ltd, Bodmin

A CIP catalogue record for this book is available from the British Library

ISBN 0 7486 1040 5 (hardback)
ISBN 0 7486 1039 1 (paperback)

Contents

Preface

This book draws together a variety of articles that I have published in academic journals or as book chapters over the past twenty years. For reasons best known to myself in my youth, I frequently published material in quite obscure places or obscure forms – which meant that it was not particularly accessible except to the most diligent of scholars. Some of those lesser known pieces are revived here, suitably updated and revised to fit this book's format. Together with one or two more centrally placed pieces, also revised and updated here, plus a new final chapter and conclusion, they purport to constitute a coherent analysis of Britain's development of its overseas information services, and, to a lesser extent, its domestic propaganda, from their origins during the First World War to the present day.

When asked to undertake this task in order to launch Edinburgh University Press's new 'International Communications' series, I approached it with a degree of ambiguity. I was curious to revisit earlier work in order to ascertain whether it stood the test of time – and the work of other scholars. But equally, whether it did or not, there was a sense in which I wanted to leave what was done in the past well alone, as a reflection of my own academic development over the past twenty years. To my surprise, however, the process helped me to realise that throughout that period there was a remarkable degree of consistency about the issues I was interested in, regardless of whether they took place at the start of this century or in more recent times. Hence the title of this book reflects my lifelong fascination with why the British have been particularly nervous about something they have demonstrated time after time that they were extremely good at. The British are a remarkable people with some remarkable achievements to their name. But their capacity to make other peoples appreciate this without the appearance of blowing their own trumpet – the famous 'British reserve' or 'stiff upper lip' – was something that always fascinated me.

When I began my research in the mid 1970s, I was told that my interests were peripheral to mainstream historical research. I disagreed, and still do. I do not believe that one can understand our past – or our present – without reference to perception. Most people in the twentieth century have perceived the wider world around them not through personal experience but via the mass media. I was the same, as a child of the last great days of the cinema and as a member of the first generation weaned on television. This would suggest that a tremendous responsibility has been placed on the media to represent events accurately and without prejudice to the 'truth'. That they often fail to do this, while in itself interesting, is entirely understandable given the complexities of our world and the procedures by which the media 'industries' operate. But when one throws into the equation the attempts of propagandists of all persuasions who are deliberately attempting to alter human perceptions for their own purposes, we are getting into the realm of power.

As someone now employed by a 'knowledge industry' (that is, a British University in the 1990s) I have always been interested in the often-made assertion that 'information is power'. Power to do what? Power to persuade people to one's own point of view? Is that the role of education, or is it propaganda? And is there anything wrong with that if one genuinely believes that one perceives the world 'correctly'? But how do people come to perceive that their view of the world is the correct one? What influences them? Parents, experience, religion, politics, culture, economic circumstances, travel, gender, age, the media? Is perception innate or is it created by factors external to our being? If it is the latter, what is the relationship of 'truth' and 'reality' to all those images which dominate the twentieth century, thanks to communications media unknown in any period before it?

I have no answers to these questions. Nor do I know whether they are even the right questions to ask. But they are what drive my historical and contemporaneous curiosity and, I trust, that of my students who, over the years, have chosen to take my courses. I had many arguments with my late father about these issues, including the Second World War, which he was reluctant to talk about but which I was so keen to study. I now take this as a sign that image and reality were quite distinct. His reality and my image of it were very different experiences, a source of debate and disagreement rather than a point of common understanding. Meanwhile, when he as a young man was fighting the Japanese in the Burmese jungle, my mother went to the movies three or four times a week to escape from the bombing that scarred her psychologically as well as physically. Small wonder that I should develop an interest in film as well as in history. The two came together as an interest in the history of propaganda.

Acknowledgements

I would like to thank Nicholas Pronay and Nick Weekes especially for granting their permission to reproduce amended versions of jointly authored articles in this book. I am also grateful to the editors and publishers of the appropriate books and journals for permission to reprint, and to the Controller of HM Stationery Office for permission to quote from Crown copyright records. Anna Claybourne, my copy-editor, was a joy to work with and tolerant of my writing idiosyncracies. My wife, Sue, deserves special mention as always for helping to keep me alive. The staff and students of the Institute of Communications Studies at Leeds help to provide a stimulating environment in which to teach and research, while my friends and colleagues elsewhere contribute more than they can ever know to the successful completion of writing that is, ultimately, conducted in an insular and isolated fashion. To all my sincere thanks.

Propaganda:

'Any information, ideas, doctrines or special appeals disseminated to influence the opinion, emotions, attitudes or behaviour of any specified group in order to benefit the sponsor, either directly or indirectly'. (Current NATO definition)

Public Diplomacy:

'Public Diplomacy – the open exchange of ideas and information – is an inherent characteristic of democratic societies. Its global mission is central to ... foreign policy. And it remains indispensable to ... [the US's] interests, ideals and leadership role in the world'. (US Advisory Commission on Public Diplomacy, 1991 Report)

Psychological Operations:

'Planned psychological activities in peace or war directed at enemy, friendly and neutral audiences in order to influence attitudes and behaviour affecting the achievement of political and military objectives'. (Current NATO definition)

Deception:

'The manipulation, distortion or falsification of evidence addressed at an enemy audience and using whatever channels of communication are considered appropriate to present manipulations, distortions and falsehoods as credible, the aim being to induce the enemy to react in a manner prejudicial to his interests'. (Current NATO definition)

SECTION ONE

The Experience of the Great War, 1914–18

The First World War occupies a special place in the twentieth-century popular psyche. Trenches and mud, barbed wire and gas, mass slaughter, the Somme, Gallipoli, Passchendaele, Lord Kitchener's intimidating finger pointing out that 'Your Country Needs You' – these remain the enduring images of a conflict which few people today would regard as anything remotely like a 'just war'. There is a tendency to forget, however, that the war was in fact immensely popular on its outbreak just about everywhere in Europe and, indeed, that it lasted for four, almost five, Christmasses when it was expected to have been all over before one. The people of Russia, Germany and elsewhere in Central Europe may have eventually risen up in social revolt against the war's continuation by 1917–18, but not in the Allied countries (barring the isolated mutiny or strike). Yet it is in those victorious countries that the Great War now holds a unique position as the milestone by which both the brutality and the futility of industrialised warfare have come to be measured: an 'end of innocence' or a 'rite of passage' to our modern world.

It cannot be stressed too strongly, however, that such a perspective could only have developed largely after the conflict had ended. This is because, quite simply, this was the first modern war in which all the belligerent nations deployed the twin weapons of censorship and propaganda to impose a rigid control over public perceptions *at the time* about how and why the war was being fought. As Lord Rothermere (the brother of Lord Northcliffe) confessed at a private dinner party on 8 November 1917, just as the Canadians were securing their final positions on Passchendaele ridge:

> We're telling lies, we daren't tell the public the truth, that we're losing more officers than the Germans, and that it's impossible to get through on the Western Front. You've seen the [war] correspondents shepherded by [General] Charteris. They don't know the truth, they don't speak the truth, and we know that they don't.[1]

But if the 'truth' – that often-cited first casualty of war – was not being told, does this really mean that someone was lying?

Certainly, it was only when wartime restrictions on the flow of information were released after the war that the sheer extent of the brutality and slaughter became more widely known, discussed and appreciated. And it was then, and only then, that the widespread sense of futility, the iconography and the mythology began to take root. The continuing controversy over General Haig's reputation as a hero, villain or donkey became part of this debate. Popular culture, first in the form of novels (such as *Goodbye to All That*)[2] and then, later, films (such as *Paths of Glory*)[3] and television programmes (such as *Blackadder Goes Forth*),[4] reinforced the continuing sense of injustice and futility tinged with sadness and tragedy. How could what subsequent generations came to know about the war and the way it was fought not be so blatantly apparent to people living through it at the time? After all, wasn't this the first conflict in which the mass media played a significant part in relaying news about the war from the fighting fronts to the public? Given that even the smallest hamlet in England or France seems to contain a memorial to those lost from the community in the Great War, surely the extent of the casualties, the slaughter and the suffering, was self-evident?

The answers to these questions are simple but disquieting. They are what make the propaganda of the Great War so significant. For such was the pervasiveness of the official propaganda and censorship systems that an image-reality gap was created between the people actually fighting the war (the soldiers) and those supporting them (the public). For example, many post-war novels, such as *All Quiet on the Western Front*,[5] refer to disquieting incidents when the soldier home on leave finds himself amidst a civilian population infinitely more bellicose than himself, a bellicosity created by the hate propaganda used to sustain public support on the home front.

The first systematic incursion by the British government into the so-called 'black art' of propaganda between 1914 and 1918 remains, therefore, even to this day, the subject of considerable controversy. Largely neglected by British historians until the early 1980s,[6] this area of enquiry is now flourishing to the point that we can even discern the beginnings of a revisionist school. Most recently, for example, some historians have begun to question whether modern research may have gone too far in suggesting that the film propaganda of the period was anything like as successful as had been assumed previously.[7] Counter-factual historians – currently enjoying a new-found respectability – have long been fond of speculating that if television cameras had been allowed anywhere near the trenches to record the harsh realities of the Western Front, the war would never have lasted as long as it did. Due to the paucity of evidence from this era before public opinion research and polling data, we will, alas, probably never have conclusive answers to either conjecture.

What we do have is sufficient surviving documentation on the evolution of the one propaganda machinery that is felt to have provided the model for others subsequently to follow. Britain's Great War experiment is interesting because it was conducted by an evolving democratic system that was still coming to terms with the idea that the people were becoming political players. With the introduction for the first time ever in Britain of conscription in 1916, the road to a full (male) electorate was probably made inevitable. With increasing access to information thanks to the development of the *mass* media (popular newspapers and films), the people were beginning to matter in both military and political terms, a situation that required increasing attention to the news they received and the views they formed as a result. The Britain that entered the war in 1914 could hardly be described as a fully functioning democracy. At the end of the war, the Representation of the People Act trebled the size of the electorate. In between, the country that boasted the 'Mother of Parliaments' found itself having to sell its ideology in order to justify its actions, not just to its own citizens but to other countries, and especially to that young, admittedly problematic (in terms of its non-white population) democracy, the United States of America.

In the three chapters that follow, these developments are examined in terms that are informed by subsequent scholarship. The idea, for example, that 'the camera never lies' has long been modified by an appreciation of the manipulative powers of mass media such as the cinema. Still silent, cinema was just emerging as a truly mass medium by the time the Great War broke out, and huge advances have been made in our historical understanding of its social and political impact, especially in the run-up to the medium's centenary in 1996. My own early work on British wartime propaganda mentioned film only in passing,[8] although several important works by other scholars quickly rectified this gap.[9] Except where relevant, in this first section of the book, film again receives only cursory attention. This is partly because I have no wish here merely to reiterate the findings of others, but it is also to some extent due to the recurring theme of the book's first section. This is that between 1914 and 1917, British *overseas* propaganda was primarily directed not at the kinds of mass audiences who were flocking to see the movies, but rather at elite audiences whose main sources of information in this period were still literary rather than visual. In 1918, when the emphasis on direct mass propaganda was increased, film was hardly a useful weapon in the psychological warfare techniques described in this book. On the home front, it was quite a different matter and film rightly deserves a central position in any discussion of domestic morale. Indeed, no account of the Great War is complete without reference to the film record of the period, not least because of its role in carving the experience and perceptions of the Great War into the twentieth-century consciousness.

Whoever else may have been guilty of keeping the war's brutal realities away from people with no direct experience of the fighting, it has to be said that the cameras filming aspects of the Great War virtually always lied – but by omission rather than commission. And if ultimately we are unable to track the precise impact of any propaganda campaign upon its target audience in this period, we can at least piece together the thinking and structures behind what was essentially the first experiment by a modern nation state to target propaganda at friendly as well as enemy regimes. In 1914, when the British government opened a Pandora's Box in order to fight its first Total War in which the gap between soldier and civilian narrowed substantially, it scarcely imagined that just over four years later it would prove impossible to put the lid back on, or that the price of selling the very idea of democracy would be actually to deliver it.

Notes and References

1 Lucy Masterman, *C. F. C. Masterman, A Biography* (Cassell, 1929), p. 296. For a more detailed examination of this by this author, see Philip M. Taylor and Steven Badsey, 'Images of Battle: The Press, Propaganda and Passchendaele', in Peter Liddle (ed.), *Passchendaele in Perspective* (Pen and Sword Press, 1997), pp. 371–89.

2 Robert Graves, *Goodbye to All That* (Cassell, 1958).

3 *Paths of Glory*, film, directed by Stanley Kubrick. United Artists, 1957.

4 *Blackadder Goes Forth*, BBC television programme, writted by Richard Curtis and Ben Elton. BBC video, 1995.

5 *All Quiet on the Western Front*, film, directed by Lewis Milestone. Universal, 1930.

6 But not by American social scientists, such as Harold Lasswell, who in the 1920s was the first scholar from any academic discipline to study Great War propaganda.

7 N. Hiley, 'Cinema, spectatorship and propaganda: *The Battle of the Somme* (1916) and its contemporary audience', *Historical Journal of Film, Radio & Television*, 17:1 (1997) 5–28. See also his forthcoming book on *The Power of Film Propaganda: Image or Reality?*, for which I am grateful to Dr Hiley for letting me see an early manuscript. For a published example of recent film scholarship, see K. Dibbets and B. Hogenkamp (eds), *Film and the First World War* (Amsterdam University Press, 1995).

8 M. L. Sanders and Philip M. Taylor, *British Propaganda during the First World War* (Macmillan, 1982).

9 N. Reeves, *Official Film Propaganda during the First World War* (Croom Helm, 1986).

Opening Pandora's Box: The Battle for Control of British Propaganda, 1914–18[1]

Like any new experiment, the British government's first incursion into the scientific conduct of propaganda was riddled with anxieties. Not unnaturally, many of the concerns were philosophical. Yes, the nation was at war, and therefore the gloves needed to come off. But, before long, it was soon apparent that August 1914 heralded a new kind of conflict. This was Total War in which the exigencies of national survival would require the mobilisation of every aspect of the nation's resources – including the morale of the British people and even more intangible assets such as Britain's reputation abroad. What were the 'rules' for this experiment, its possibilities and constraints? What would be the impact on the political, social, economic and cultural configuration of Britain itself? Moreover, in the conduct of inter-state relations, what would be its consequences for the British Empire, at that time the most powerful political, economic and cultural entity on the entire planet?

In July 1918, Lord Northcliffe, pioneer of English popular journalism and owner of the *Daily Mail* and *The Times*, suggested that propaganda and foreign policy were incompatible.[2] Did he mean that pluralistic societies should eschew propaganda as a matter of principle? After all this was a man who once said that 'God made people read so that I could fill their heads with facts, facts, facts – and later tell them whom to love, whom to hate and what to think'.[3] We are not therefore dealing with someone nervous about the rights and wrongs of manipulating human perceptions. Besides, Northcliffe was by then in charge of Britain's Enemy Propaganda Department at Crewe House, and had already been dubbed as the 'Minister for the Destruction of German Confidence' by the German authorities. Why then did he feel this way, and was it a justifiable viewpoint?

By the summer of 1918, Northcliffe had become immensely frustrated with the way traditional government departments, and especially the Foreign Office, seemed to delight in endless bureaucratic battles of attrition with him for control over this most recently created of official responsibilities. On a superficial level, this was simply a power struggle. However, some of the more visionary permanent officials in Whitehall realised that involvement in what we would now term 'official public relations' had the potential to become one of the most significant of governmental activities, not just in the present war but in future peace as well.

In propaganda, image must not lose sight of reality, nor short-term goals lose sight of long-term interests. It seemed to many officials that Northcliffe, by concentrating in both cases on the former, was increasingly in danger of losing touch with the latter. We need to remember that this was an era in which many of the new techniques of persuasion – from commercial advertising to press relations – were being tried and tested for the first time, that psychology as a science was in its infancy, and that the behaviour of individuals and crowds was an object of widespread fascination. The Foreign Office believed it had already found one of the secrets of the new alchemy: that propaganda and (foreign) policy – that image and reality – must ultimately go hand in hand. However, certain fundamental questions remained which plagued the propaganda experiment from the outset of the war. Was it possible to combine the conduct of inter-state relations, traditionally done in private, with public information? If so, what form should British propaganda take? What would be its guiding principles and characteristics? What indeed should be its relationship to policy? Who should be its primary target audiences? On just about every one of these issues, there was a fundamental and perhaps irreconcilable difference of opinion between the men from the relatively new world of publicity and those government officials traditionally responsible for Britain's conduct of its relations with other countries.

1.1 Propaganda and Diplomacy

In February 1918, when Northcliffe accepted the Prime Minister's invitation to take control of directing propaganda against the Central Powers, he established the Enemy Propaganda Department at Crewe House. This appointment, coupled with that of Lord Beaverbrook (owner of *The Daily Express*) as Britain's first Minister of Information, seemed to many to hold out the promise of a new and more spectacular phase in Britain's wartime propaganda. Indeed, for the remaining months of the war, it did. In a nutshell, Beaverbrook and Northcliffe switched the emphasis from elite, indirect propaganda to direct mass propaganda. This means that instead of concentrating on influential groups of opinion-makers – the preferred method of the Foreign Office since the start of the war – they directly targeted public opinion itself.

The Foreign Office did not believe that this was a direction that would ultimately serve the long-term interests of British foreign policy. Indeed, many officials feared that British diplomacy in the final year of the war was being shaped more by propaganda than by policy, rather than the other way round. There is in fact a case to be made that the kind of direct mass propaganda conducted in 1918 was to create significant long-term problems which were to affect adversely British foreign policy for the next two decades, and we shall be returning to this in chapter three. But equally, as we shall see in chapter two, the kind of indirect elite propaganda conducted by the Foreign Office in the first three years of the war was also to create long-term problems – as well, admittedly, as short-term results – especially for Anglo-American relations.

First, however, we need to look at the way the wartime organisation evolved and the reasons why the creation of the two new departments in 1918 produced an intolerable situation for everyone concerned. We shall see that it was not so much a question of whether Foreign Relations and Public Relations were inherently incompatible, but rather an issue of how the two activities, through the wartime experience, could be fused into a new democratic governmental responsibility. In these respects, therefore, we are talking about the genesis of Britain's overseas information services and of a new type of diplomacy for the twentieth century, the century of *mass* communications – and of the mass media.

Part of the Foreign Office's problem was pique. In February 1918, when it had finally been forced to hand over its control of propaganda work to the press barons, the Foreign Office felt slighted. It had fought long and hard to retain that control through three years of bitter inter-departmental rivalry and squabbling with other Whitehall departments. Once it was passed to 'outsiders', however, government departments closed ranks and united behind the Foreign Office in opposition to any further handover of related duties to Fleet Street. Propaganda for the state by the state was one thing, but propaganda for the state by the Third Estate was quite another. It was this power struggle which prompted Northcliffe to conclude that:

> As a people we do not understand propaganda ways ... Propaganda is advertising and diplomacy is no more likely to understand advertising than advertising is likely to understand diplomacy.[4]

This observation therefore says more about the clash of personalities and opinions between Whitehall and Fleet Street about the direction in which British propaganda should go than it does about whether the British were generally incompetent at propaganda overseas. Indeed, as we shall see, nothing could be further from the truth.

If Northcliffe's experience had not been a happy one, Lord Beaverbrook believed his was even worse. Britain's first ever Minister of Information recalled that, in the months following his appointment, he too found himself engaged in 'a remorseless battle ... without compensations',[5] complaining that he had to employ a full-time secretary 'simply and solely for the purpose of conducting the diplomatic correspondence with the Foreign Office, as with a neighbouring and none-too-friendly power'.[6] These criticisms implied that, if British propaganda was at all successful in helping to bring about the end of the war, then little credit for this was due to Whitehall in general, least of all to the Foreign Office.

For many years, this was the accepted view of the wartime record: three years of inadequacy followed by almost a year of qualified success and this, no thanks to Whitehall but with great credit to Beaverbrook and Northcliffe. Again, as we will see, the actual historical record belies this. It was certainly true that the Foreign Office continued to prove unyielding throughout the final months of the war. The newspapermen who were brought into the official machinery to direct propaganda not unreasonably felt they understood the mass audience better than the Whitehall officials; it was after all their business. The diplomats, for their part, felt that mass opinion was neither the most appropriate nor the most likely target audience to generate the kind of results desired. This was a brave new world, fraught with dangers and implications for the relationship between the state and its citizens. Directly appealing to foreign public opinion, for example, bypassing their governments, was simply too novel and too dangerous a precedent to set for the new post-war diplomacy. They felt it far better – and safer – to appeal to movers and shakers in foreign societies who could, if they were duly inclined, speak to their own people on Britain's behalf. To a large extent this stemmed from the contemporary unspoken assumption that elites were like 'us', whereas the mass public were still thought of in terms of 'them'. Yet out of the resultant struggle, the British were to evolve a unique approach to the conduct of propaganda that was to provide a model for others subsequently to adopt and adapt. It was, nonetheless, to prove a legacy with a huge inheritance tax.

The stimulus for such change came from without. The need for Britain to conduct official propaganda in foreign countries was initially recognised as a response to the hostile activities of its enemies. Shortly after the outbreak of the war in August 1914, it became apparent to the Cabinet that a determined effort would be required to counter the detrimental effects of German propaganda upon 'British interests and prestige', particularly in neutral countries.[7] There was, however, neither precedent nor blueprint for such an experiment. Having entered the war completely unprepared for the control and influence of foreign opinion, the government was forced rapidly to improvise the necessary machinery. Nowhere was the British penchant for 'muddling through' to become more apparent.

The initial plans for the conduct of propaganda abroad were tentative and uncertain. The Foreign Office, as the department of state primarily responsible for relations with other countries, simply assumed itself to be the proper authority for the supervision of any propaganda conducted on foreign soil. Among its first cautious steps was the creation of a small section designed to meet the increased demand from the British and overseas newspaper correspondents in London for news and information concerning the war. This section comprised a nucleus staff of two or three permanent officials, and soon came to be known as the News Department of the Foreign Office. It was originally made directly answerable to the Foreign Secretary, Sir Edward Grey, but was, before the end of 1914, placed under the general supervision of the parliamentary under-secretary of state for foreign affairs, at that time Frederick Acland.[8]

Progress was cautious, based on experience gained as the work developed. The people involved were experimentalists and improvisers but in the early stages of the war they received precious little high-level support, perhaps because their work marked a significant departure from established diplomatic tradition and, as such, was viewed with suspicion, even distaste. Besides, the widely held 'short-war illusion' encouraged the belief that it would all be over by Christmas. This was hardly conducive to planning for a long war in which morale would play an increasingly significant role.

Working with some autonomy, the News Department decided upon a preference for 'information' or presswork, concerning itself more with the dissemination of news abroad and the cultivation of relations with British and foreign journalists than with the actual production and distribution of propaganda material such as leaflets and pamphlets. The emphasis, in other words, was on news rather than views. More creative methods of propaganda involving attacks upon the aims and actions of the enemy and the presentation of the British case tended to be left to the various unofficial patriotic committees which seemed to combust spontaneously into existence on the outbreak of war.[9] Apart from these, two semi-official propaganda organisations, the Neutral Press Committee and the War Propaganda Bureau at Wellington House, were to prove especially significant.

These two organisations were established independently of Foreign Office arrangements. The Neutral Press Committee was formed under the auspices of the Home Office on 11 September 1914 in connection with the Press Bureau, the government's principal wartime press censorship organisation.[10] A fortnight later the Neutral Press Committee was placed under the able direction of G. H. Mair, the recently retired assistant editor of the *Daily Chronicle*. His work was essentially concerned with analysing the neutral press, promoting the interchange of news between English and foreign newspapers, the promotion of English newspaper sales in neutral countries, the postal distribution of propaganda articles and, before long, the inauguration of another innovation, a wireless news service.[11]

Meanwhile, earlier in September 1914, Prime Minister Asquith had invited his close friend Charles Masterman, Chancellor of the Duchy of Lancaster and chairman of the National Insurance Commission, to take charge of the production and distribution side of the work, and Masterman began to establish his literary bureau, the War Propaganda Bureau, at Wellington House. Working in strict secrecy under the aegis of the Foreign Office, Wellington House rapidly developed into the most active of all the propaganda departments, arranging for the production and overseas dissemination of books, pamphlets and periodicals as well as photographs, lantern slides and picture postcards.[12] By June 1915 the bureau was producing its own illustrated periodicals printed in foreign languages.[13] Extreme care was taken to disguise the source of all material produced in order to preserve the credibility of the views expressed, a factor which was of particular importance in that most vital of neutral countries, the United States of America (see chapter two).[14]

As Christmas 1914 faded into memory, the work began to expand. It soon became apparent that the Foreign Office would need to establish and maintain close contacts with both the Neutral Press Committee and Wellington House if the views expressed in their material were to stay in tune with foreign policy. Indeed, before long the News Department began to serve as a general co-ordinating centre, furnishing the other bodies with advice, information and material obtained from other government departments that were also now beginning to take an active interest in propaganda work. Apart from its press activities, the News Department began to transmit daily news telegrams to diplomatic and consular missions abroad, with instructions to make use of them for purposes of publication as they thought suitable to local conditions.[15] The missions were further supplied with special news telegrams sent on the occasion of, say, an important speech by a cabinet minister, along with any material produced by the other propaganda agencies. In this way, the diplomatic and consular services acted as the News Department's distribution agents in the field, although special areas required special arrangements. In the United States, for example, great care was taken from an early stage to avoid a sense of exhortation in order to avoid offending American sensitivities any further than German propaganda was already doing.[16] In Russia, the Anglo-Russian Commission was established at Petrograd in December 1915 to receive telegrams, articles and bulletins relayed by the News Department with a view to securing publicity in the Russian press.[17] Elsewhere, local committees of British residents and anglophiles were established to help missions distribute propaganda material in both allied and neutral countries.[18]

The News Department also advised the Press Bureau on all matters of censorship connected with foreign affairs and received any questionable material for final decision.[19] However, this work proved to be time-consuming and the effort required was found to be generally disproportionate to the results achieved. There were, inevitably, some early difficulties that may be put down to inexperience on the part of permanent officials unfamiliar with the demands of journalists at war. Fleet Street, for its part, was inevitably irritated by the new wartime restrictions and, before long, Geoffrey Dawson, editor of *The Times*, was complaining: 'Why in the world the P[ress] B[ureau] or the Foreign Office should always be trying to score off the newspapers, I cannot for the life of me imagine'.[20]

So indeed it must have appeared to a British press unused to routine directives about what it could or could not print. From the other side, the Foreign Office saw the newspapers as both a potential ally and a potential danger. Tension was perhaps inevitable with a government department attempting to utilise the publicity potential and reputation abroad of a medium which cherished liberal traditions of freedom to criticise, while at the same time making sure it didn't provide the enemy with useful information – including critical editorials about the British government's conduct of the war. Any press criticism could be read abroad and interpreted as a lack of unity, a divided nation or a divided alliance. As early as October 1914 the Foreign Secretary had already become alarmed at receiving:

> Almost daily, accumulating evidence of the harm which is done in neutral countries by articles which have appeared in the British Press. He wishes to have the attention of Editors drawn to this evil, which undoubtedly

undoes much of the work which he endeavours to do with a view to
securing a friendly attitude on the part of neutrals.[21]

A missive issued to the press on these lines merely served to make matters
worse, and Fleet Street continued to resent the censorship arrangements until
October 1915[22] when, following the enlightened appeals of Lord Robert Cecil,
the political censorship of all material relating to foreign affairs was discontinued.[23]

This departure heralded a new period of mutual co-operation and trust
between the Foreign Office and the press. It also left the News Department
with more time to concentrate upon propaganda, although it did continue to
advise the chief cable and postal censors at the War Office and the naval censor
at the Admiralty until the end of 1917.[24] Clearly, those responsible for the
military conduct of the war were not quite so willing to risk security for the
sake of publicity.

Given the tentativeness with which the work had begun, and the somewhat
haphazard manner in which the work initially developed, it is hardly surprising
that British propaganda during the first eighteen months of the war was plagued
with innumerable difficulties. Robert Donald[25] subsequently observed:

> The system was started without any policy having been defined, or any
> clear conception arrived at about the way propaganda should be carried
> on. Mr. Mair drifted between the Home Office, Press Bureau and the
> Foreign Office – which began to take an interest in the work without being
> altogether reconciled to it.[26]

Yet if the Foreign Office as a whole remained uneasy about the News Department's growing involvement in propaganda, it was happier to leave the more
direct methods in the hands of the quasi-official organisations, such as Wellington House, provided it retained ultimate control over questions of policy. This
became increasingly more apparent during 1916 and 1917, when in the face of
mounting criticism, the Foreign Office tenaciously fought to retain its control
over the existing system.

1.2 The Bureaucratic Battle for Power

As government departments other than the Foreign Office were increasingly
drawn into greater involvement with the mechanics of wartime propaganda,
problems of overlapping, duplication of effort and a general lack of co-ordination
became more serious. The result was that, before long, the system became
subject to inter-departmental jealousies and rivalry – factors which proved
debilitating in work which required continuity, creativity and speedy action.
This prompted the director of special intelligence, Brigadier-General G. R. Cockerill, to urge on 29 November 1915 that the war of words should now demand
'as much attention as the economic war'.[27] While also being an indication of

the way the war was beginning to impact upon every aspect of British life, this plea sparked off a series of clashes between the Foreign Office and the various Whitehall departments responsible for the Armed Services.

On 10 December 1915 the Army Council signalled its anxiety that 'the multiplicity of organisations concerned and the lack of one central controlling authority prove a serious bar to effective action', and proposed an inter-departmental conference to discuss the means by which the situation could be improved.[28] The War Office had in mind the creation of an executive committee under the leadership of 'a Civil Servant of position and standing'.[29] Hubert Montgomery, who had been involved in the News Department's work from the outset, conceded the need for more co-ordination but dismissed the War Office proposals with some irritation:

> I should have thought the Army Council had plenty of other (from their point of view) more important matters to consider: moreover in the one respect in which they could really have aided us in combating enemy propaganda i.e. in giving facilities for neutral and allied correspondents to visit the front and centres of military interest, and in supplying news, they have signally failed.[30]

Sir Claud Schuster, Masterman's chief executive officer at Wellington House, agreed but was even more sarcastic about the proposals:

> I must say that I find it sickening that the War Office and the Admiralty, after pursuing a policy of deliberate obstruction for about seventeen months, should finally complain that the policy has produced its natural results, and then propose so wholly absurd an expedient as that described in their letter.[31]

Elsewhere, Schuster maintained that if the pro-German press in neutral countries were getting more news from enemy than from Allied sources, then this was not, as the Army Council maintained, due to any lack of effort on the part of the three existing main propaganda bodies. Rather, it was because of the strict censorship insisted upon by the War Office and the Admiralty, combined with their reluctance to comply with continued Foreign Office requests for the extension of greater facilities to the press.[32] This line of argument became the stock reply to all subsequent criticism.

It was, it has to be said, a justifiable retort. The News Department had been trying unsuccessfully since the start of the war to persuade the military authorities to permit journalists to visit the front and report on conditions for themselves rather than having to accept the unsatisfactory coverage provided by the 'official eye-witnesses'.[33] Likewise, the Admiralty was also slow in allowing newspapermen to visit the fleet. This only happened for the first time in October 1915, fourteen months after the outbreak of war.[34] There was a tendency in the armed forces to mistrust the press and especially the relatively new profession of the war correspondent. Stung by press criticism of its performance in the Crimean War,[35] the army inclined to the view that no news for the press was good news for the fighting forces. However, the problem was not merely one of access for, as Schuster recognised:

> In any circumstances the course of military events would have rendered it easier for the Germans than for us to influence neutral opinion through the Press. The early efforts to convince neutrals that we were right were completely successful, partly because the work was, in my opinion, well done, but far more, because we had a good case. Neutral opinion is now interested, not in the cause, but in the probable results of the war, and for obvious reasons, until we have a change in the military situation, it is far more difficult to explain that we are likely to win, than to explain that we were just.[36]

The Foreign Office also recognised that no amount of words, however well-argued, could alter the harsh reality of military events. It nonetheless believed that it was possible to control what we would now call the 'spin' on bad news by a press corps working from the basis of co-operation rather than conflict. In the short term, that is. In the longer term, its work would continue to suffer in the absence of a coherent declaration of British war aims by the government. To date, all the government had really announced was 'the liberation of Belgium'.

'Poor Little Belgium', whose invasion by the Germans had torn up the infamous 'scrap of paper', was hardly a sufficient rallying cry to sustain public support for long. Accordingly, on 14 December 1915 the Foreign Office informed the Army Council that it had already identified the need for improved co-ordination[37] and would make the appropriate changes internally. There was therefore no need for an inter-departmental conference.[38] The terms of the Foreign Office reply sought to check any further incursions by the Service departments into a field which it now considered its own:

> The direction in which both the War Office and the Admiralty can be of the greatest assistance in influencing opinion in neutral and allied countries is in affording as many facilities as possible for newspaper correspondents to visit or accompany the British forces in the field ... and in issuing Military and Naval news as frequently and as fully as military and naval considerations will permit.[39]

The War Office, in particular, resented this allotted subsidiary role, especially at a time when it envisaged greater involvement in the work through the creation of its own special propaganda and censorship division known as MI7, as part of the overall reorganisation of the Imperial General Staff.[40] The Foreign Office's response also jeopardised the conclusions of a pre-war investigation by a Committee of Imperial Defence (CID) planning subcommittee, inspired by a War Office initiative in the wake of the Fashoda Crisis of 1898, which had considered means of preventing the leakage and publication of military and naval information likely to be of use to the enemy in time of war.[41] It was therefore not prepared to let the matter rest here.

Meanwhile, the Foreign Office did set about trying to put its own house in order. On 16 December 1915, Montgomery approached the Home Office about rectifying the anomalous position of Mair's Neutral Press Committee by transferring responsibility for its work into the hands of the Foreign Office. This, he added, would not only provide greater efficiency and economy but would also ensure 'more security that what is done is consistent with the interests of our foreign policy'.[42] The Home Secretary, Sir John Simon, was not keen on this despite his admission that 'We have never considered him [Mair] as in any sense acting under our directions, and in fact, so far as his operations are guided by any Government Department, it is by the Foreign Office.'[43]

Instead, Simon wished to see a return to the original concept of Mair's position whereby he would act on his own responsibility 'and that the government should not be bound by anything he might have done'.[44] This provides a clue as to the covert nature in which most of the work was being conducted. Any views expressed by Mair or Masterman must not be attributable to the government. The government, in other words, did not engage in 'propaganda'; it told the truth. Although he was prepared to discuss this further, the implication of Simon's reply was that, in order to continue the government's policy of secrecy in the conduct of official propaganda and the disguising of the source of any views expressed, the Neutral Press Committee should remain on the Home Office (i.e. Secret Service) Vote.

Cecil was not convinced. He pointed out to Simon that much of Mair's work was identical with that of the News Department and, despite good relations with him, 'as things stand we cannot and have no right to give directions to him as to what exactly he should do and what we should do. The result is a certain want of unity and loss of effort'.[45] He further assured Simon that Mair was not simply a pawn in the dispute with the War Office:

> Nothing is further from my thoughts than to try and filch some work from the Home Office and give it to the Foreign Office, and if it were practicable I should be only too glad to push the whole of propaganda business on to your shoulders, but the difficulty is that, since it affects foreign countries, it necessarily must be done either by us or under our guidance.[46]

While still not seeing the need for an inter-departmental conference, Cecil nonetheless agreed to attend if one were called. He added that there was no point in asking Nicolson, the Foreign Office permanent under-secretary, to accompany him 'because he really does not know or care anything about news or propaganda'.[47] Then, as now, many diplomats remained uneasy about more open government interacting with the publicity world.

On 26 January 1916 Cecil reluctantly attended the long-awaited inter-departmental conference at the Home Office presided over by the newly appointed Home Secretary, Sir Herbert Samuel.[48] The meeting proved to be a shambles and degenerated into a fierce row between the War Office and the Foreign Office. It was eventually agreed that greater co-ordination was a vital prerequisite to further progress; it was the different proposals for achieving that aim which created the tension. However, Cecil successfully resisted a War Office demand for the creation of a separate organisation for the central control of all government propaganda under the direction of a 'responsible head – e.g. Lord Onslow'[49] (a War Office man) and supervised by an advisory committee. He achieved this by convincing those present that the Foreign Office was already in possession of adequate machinery and that the necessary improvements would be made internally.[50]

The degree to which this had now become a power struggle was revealed in a letter from Masterman to Cecil a few days later:

Heartiest congratulations to you and the Foreign Office and Grey [the Foreign Secretary] for having slaughtered your enemies last Wednesday in what I think is the most effective destruction that any Office has given to any of its critics during the eighteen months of war.[51]

Victory, however, proved to be short-lived.

The dispute between the War Office and the Foreign Office essentially centred on their different interpretations of propaganda techniques. Cecil maintained that the problem was simply one of increasing both the quality and the quantity of information about the progress of the war from the various fighting fronts supplied via the News Department for release to the press. On the other hand, Sir Reginald Brade, representing the War Office at the conference, did not consider the Foreign Office approach sufficient to counter the intensive German propaganda. 'The really important thing', he insisted, 'was not the facts, but the way in which they were presented'.[52] This emphasis – which might today seem academic – was alien to the Foreign Office conception, and the insistence on the value of accurate news and information constituted the basic principle on which all subsequent News Department activity was based. But it was a conception that was ultimately to lose the Foreign Office its control over wartime propaganda.

For the moment, however, the Foreign Office was held responsible for the improvement of its existing system. Two days after the Home Office conference, Cecil submitted a scheme for increased efficiency and co-ordination of the available machinery. The main proposal was for the appointment of 'news officers' by the different government departments to help improve the supply of official information to the Foreign Office machinery.[53] The News Department was subsequently reorganised in such a way as to make it an appropriate nucleus for the conduct of British overseas propaganda. Co-ordination with the Press Bureau was also improved, to aid domestic publicity.[54] After some initial reservations caused by fear of losing some of its status,[55] Masterman was reassured that Wellington House would be expected to continue the initiative it had already begun.[56] Mair's committee was at last amalgamated into the News Department.[57] In February 1916 Lord Newton became nominal head of the revamped organisation,[58] and it seems that he was appointed partly 'to lend the prestige of a great name to the work'[59] and partly to appease the War Office desire for a 'responsible head' without actually appointing a War Office man. Nevertheless, with the aid of Montgomery as his capable assistant, and with a wealth of talented permanent officials on his staff, including Miles Lampson (in charge of film propaganda), the poet Alfred Noyes, John Buchan, J. D. Gregory and Stephen Gaselee, Newton expanded the work along more imaginative and proactive lines.[60]

Despite the visible improvement both in organisation and in the range of material produced, the War Office remained dissatisfied with the system which was, it claimed, merely a continuation of the former arrangements on a grander scale but with all the inherent deficiencies remaining. The War Office felt that Cecil's scheme made 'no serious attempt to provide what is required' and fell 'far short of the essential minimum'.[61] Grave doubts were expressed about the Foreign Office's 'very limited conception of the realities of the case':

> Until the idea is grasped of combating enemy propaganda not merely by news, which it is impolitic to fabricate, but also and even mainly by views, which it is quite possible to propagate, it seems hopeless to expect that any progress will be made towards designing an organisation suited to the necessities of the case.[62]

This 'news versus views' issue was to lie at the heart of debates surrounding best practice approaches to propaganda for many years to come.

Following the reorganisation of the General Staff in February 1916, and the improvements made to the War Office propaganda machinery, tension with the Foreign Office continued to mount, with the efficiency of British propaganda the major casualty. The squabbling continued throughout the summer. In July General Charteris identified the essential problem:

> Both the Foreign Office and the War Office are worrying a great deal about propaganda, particularly in France, and there seems to be great confusion at home as to who is responsible ... The trouble about propaganda work at home appears to be that while the Foreign Office wants to publish favourable news, the War Office wants to withhold anything that tends to show that the Germans are hard hit ... To the outside world there is no doubt that we have tended to discourage confidence in ourselves by always holding back that which is favourable.[63]

He also commented on 'a little war within a war between the War Office and the Foreign Office all about films',[64] and concluded that 'the trouble is that the Foreign Office, Home Office, War Office, Admiralty and Masterman's absurd committee are all working separately and each is jealous of the other'.[65]

As criticism of the Foreign Office continued to mount and gain wider currency, so also did the pressure for increased centralisation. But this only made the Foreign Office more determined than ever to retain its control. The situation was not helped by differences of opinion within the Foreign Office itself. For example, Miles Lampson wrote to Montgomery:

> To be quite frank, the situation is *not* in hand at present. I know you

disagree with me: but my opinion remains and *will* remain the same, until some more methodical organisation is working than is now the case.[66]

Montgomery's reply illustrates the impasse reached:

> I am afraid we will have to agree to differ about this. I don't know in what respect the situation is not in hand! It is true that there is no one stately building that one can point to and say 'That is the Maison de la Presse where all these things are done' but *results* are the main point and results are not at all unsatisfactory.[67]

Had the Foreign Office been more prepared to accept that parts of the system were deficient and to rectify the faults, it might have served to disarm the pressure for reform. Instead the inflexible stance adopted, based on the belief that it had already found the secret of success, merely served to reinforce the views of its critics that it was incapable of effective responsibility for propaganda work.

1.3 Enter the Politicians

The dispute reached a dramatic climax in December 1916 when Lloyd George became Prime Minister. Indeed, at the very first meeting of the new War Cabinet, it was decided that the whole question of propaganda required immediate attention.[68] This decision, however, merely provided the signal for a renewed campaign by each of the government departments involved, each striving to secure Cabinet approval for its own particular views on propaganda at the expense of the other. Given Lloyd George's well-known distrust of diplomats, the writing was on the wall at the Foreign Office.

The Admiralty argued that hitherto British propaganda had been too defensive and passive in nature, and advocated greater activity in the United States under the general supervision of the naval attaches.[69] This was a bit rich coming from a department whose attitude to publicity was encapsulated in the nickname of its submariners: the 'silent service'. The War Office once again reiterated its scheme for a central propaganda bureau that would unite under one independent head all the various information sources, producing houses and distributing centres. It further suggested that special officers should be appointed in the various countries in order to relieve the pressure of work on the diplomatic, consular and secret services, particularly as there were certain activities 'which are hardly compatible with the dignity of His Majesty's Representatives abroad, and which, therefore, they cannot carry out satisfactorily'.[70] Was this a recognition on the part of the War Office that disinformation was about to become part of British propaganda strategy? Given the track record so far of both the War Office and Admiralty in suppressing rather than releasing news about the war, it is at least reasonable to deduce that their efforts to take control of propaganda were driven more by considerations of censorship than publicity.

The Foreign Office had to pull out all the stops. Far from constituting a mere apologia for past errors, it presented a thorough and convincing defence of the existing machinery and the methods employed while being, at the same time, a persuasive critique of the proposals to establish a separate propaganda authority, unless of course, that authority was to be placed under the aegis of the Foreign Office. After indicating that the News Department's chief difficulty was the 'tradition of silence [of government departments] only very slowly breaking down', Montgomery wrote:

> A hankering after an institution on the lines of the Maison de la Presse in Paris has from time to time manifested itself in some quarters, but I am convinced, after an experience dating from the early days of the war, that the general control of propaganda in Allied and Neutral countries should continue to rest with the Foreign Office, as it is now. It is that Office which is concerned with most of the current questions about which the foreign, and especially the American correspondents want daily information ... The correspondents ... will come much more freely to the Foreign Office, which is the natural place for them to seek information and facilities from, than they will to an Office known to be established for propaganda purposes.[71]

Moreover, he continued:

> It would be quite unworkable to have our various organisations in foreign countries independent of the Embassies and Legations, which would necessarily be the case if they were placed under the control of a separate authority in London.[72]

Robert Cecil endorsed these views entirely, and in submitting the Foreign Office case to the Cabinet he made five general observations based on his experience of the work conducted so far:

1 Official propaganda known to be such was 'almost useless' with the exception of published documents and State papers;

2 'It is much easier to do harm than good by propaganda', in other words, great care was required at all times;

3 'Our national habit of self-deprecation is a handicap. Moreover, in many countries we are suspected of arrogance and the most moderate criticism of foreign countries is, for this and other reasons, bitterly resented';

4 It remained important to avoid the appearance of propaganda in the United States where the only plan was 'to do good by stealth';

5 'Lastly, in wartime, it is the facts that count, not words. All we can do to help by propaganda is to let foreigners know what is actually happening. If the events are discouraging, they will be discouraged. No doubt we may also offend people by stupid observations, but we can never explain away disagreeable facts'.[73]

Herein lay the guiding principles of the Foreign Office's approach to propaganda.

The War Cabinet was supposed to consider all the different arguments on 24 January 1917.[74] However, the Foreign Office case had already been pre-empted by a Cabinet decision of some three weeks earlier to accept 'in principle' the creation of a new and separate propaganda organisation to take over control of the work.[75] Instead of relying on the bureaucrats, Lloyd George had instead chosen to rely on the 'objectivity' of a man outside the Civil Service and had invited his friend Robert Donald to investigate the entire situation and make his recommendations.[76]

Donald's report was ready a week later. He did not feel that the 'reorganis-ation' of spring 1916 had introduced the necessary improvements, and claimed that there was still a lack of co-ordination. While praising the activities of Wellington House and of several News Department officials, Donald never-theless considered that Lord Newton had not proved a wise choice: 'He is not solely occupied with the work,[77] and he does not profess to have any knowledge of publicity methods'.[78] In short, the report's criticism of the existing arrangements seemed to vindicate the views of the War Office, while also expressing doubts as to the competence of permanent officials at the Foreign Office to supervise an activity for which they had little experience and flair and which required a degree of freedom not always available in Whitehall. 'Personally', he concluded, 'I think the less they have to do with it the better'.

Donald's report further confirmed the War Office belief that the only solution was to establish a separate organisation with an independent head. On Lord Milner's recommendation, John Buchan, the famous author who had served as Newton's liaison officer with GHQ in France, was appointed head of the Department of Information (DoI) established at the end of January 1917.[79] Although independent, the new department was instructed to maintain 'the closest possible association with the Foreign Office in regard to the policy to be pursued'.[80]

Once presented with this *fait accompli*, the Foreign Office changed its tactics in an attempt to salvage as much control over the new department as was possible. Hubert Montgomery insisted that the Foreign Office should command the major share of responsibility for the new organisation because:

> The general policy of propaganda in Allied and Neutral Countries must necessarily run parallel with the work of the Foreign Office and be subject to the Foreign Secretary, and it is essential that the person who is respon-sible for the administration of propaganda work should be in constant touch with the Foreign Secretary and the Minister of Blockade, or with those carrying out their directions.[81]

Eric Drummond, Balfour's private secretary, enlisted top-level support for this view [82] and the Foreign Secretary submitted Montgomery's observations to the War Cabinet, stating that they deserved careful consideration 'before any fundamental severance is effected between those who are responsible for conducting foreign policy and those who are responsible for talking about it'.[83]

The outcome was almost a classic example of compromise. In theory the DoI was an independent, centralised propaganda bureau directly responsible to the Prime Minister but working in close contact with the Foreign Office. In practice, however, the department effectively functioned as an annexe of the Foreign Office. In constructing his new organisation, Buchan was fully aware of his dependence on the facilities and co-operation that would be extended to him by the diplomats.

The department was divided into four main sections: administrative; the literary branch (at Wellington House); the press and cinema division (at the House of Lords); and intelligence (at 82 Victoria Street).[84] Buchan, himself a former News Department official, chose Montgomery as his assistant and as head of the administrative division – the most powerful of the four sections. Buchan further located his headquarters in the Foreign Office building, where the News Department effectively functioned as the administrative division. The Cabinet approved Buchan's scheme on 20 February 1917.[85] A much more significant indication of the Foreign Office's continued influence was that the work abroad remained in the hands of diplomatic missions and local patriotic committees under their supervision. Continuity in personnel and facilities was therefore largely preserved. Indeed, far from constituting any radical departure from previous arrangements, the DoI was, in effect, merely a streamlined version of the original 'model'.

While it is undoubtedly true that the Department of Information did benefit from the lessons of earlier experience to increase efficiency and co-ordination, and generally to improve both the quality and the quantity of Britain's overseas propaganda, it nonetheless ultimately failed to rectify some of the basic deficiencies inherent in the system. For example, the DoI continued to operate from four or five different buildings scattered about Whitehall. The absence of a ministerial head to champion the cause of propaganda in the War Cabinet was also a serious handicap, the more so because Buchan lacked the necessary authority and prestige to deal with other ministries on an equal basis. Moreover, one of Buchan's major innovations, the Advisory Committee to the DoI, proved to be a constant source of criticism, although admittedly this was largely of Buchan's own making. This committee, composed of leading newspapermen and publicity experts such as Robert Donald, C. P. Scott, Lord Burnham and Lord Northcliffe (who was subsequently replaced by Lord Beaverbrook), had originally been appointed to provide Buchan with a 'cabinet'. Buchan chose not to consult it, preferring instead to receive advice on questions of policy from the Foreign Office. Robert Donald soon became dissatisfied with the new arrangements:

The propaganda headquarters are still at the Foreign Office, and are more entrenched there than ever ... Mr. Buchan is under the Foreign Office almost as much, I believe, as if he were an official, and I do not think this is desirable.[86]

Even following the personal intervention of Lloyd George on behalf of the committee[87] – a taste of things to come – the position remained unsatisfactory and criticism of the DoI as a whole continued to mount until the end of the year.[88]

Buchan was well aware that the new arrangements left much to be desired but claimed that, although directly answerable to the Prime Minister, he did not in fact have direct access to him. Accordingly, in September 1917, following constant appeals for ministerial representation for the DoI, the War Cabinet decided that Sir Edward Carson 'should extend his sphere of supervision and act as Minister in charge of all propaganda, whether at home or abroad'.[89] Carson, however, did not prove to be a wise choice; there was little evidence of enthusiasm for his new task.[90] Consequently, Lloyd George once again turned to Robert Donald, who was again invited to examine the situation with a view to finally placing the system on a more professional basis.[91]

Donald advocated a strengthening of the role of the advisory committee[92] and still further centralisation. Indeed, in his second report, produced in December 1917, Donald reiterated many of the criticisms of the first: the system was still dominated by the Foreign Office; lack of unity and co-ordination remained serious problems; Buchan had not taken reorganisation far enough; further centralisation was essential.[93] Indeed, unless changes were immediately introduced, the advisory committee threatened to resign en bloc.[94]

Buchan, for his part, did not deny that the system was imperfect, but he objected to the speed at which Donald had reached his conclusions. Propaganda work was, he claimed, highly complex and required the perpetual analysis of foreign opinion so that it might be tempered in accordance with the fluctuating moods of public opinion abroad. Criticism that little or nothing was being done was unfounded and partly derived from the intense secrecy which surrounded the work. Moreover, he claimed, experience had shown that the most effective approach involved the dissemination of accurate news combined with an honest explanation of Britain's policies, a view fully endorsed by the Foreign Office.[95]

1.4 Enter the Press Barons

By the end of 1917, however, the question was no longer simply that of a strengthened machinery. The changing demands of the military and economic situation, particularly after the treaty of Brest-Litovsk which took Russia out of the war, made a fundamental change of approach in propaganda necessary. With the failure of the more conventional methods of warfare to secure decisive results on the field of battle, alternative methods of breaking the military deadlock were sought. Universal war-weariness and the instability of the internal structure of the Central Powers convinced many observers that the time had come to transform British propaganda into an all-out psychological offensive against the enemy [96] (see chapter three). The emphasis on straight but selective information was no longer considered to be an adequate method of combating enemy activities;[97] what was now required was an adventurous and resolute propaganda campaign. The Foreign Office, followed by the DoI, had been too cautious in its approach, too hesitant to expand and develop earlier activities in accordance with the changing demands of the war, and too casual in its treatment of proposals for change. Moreover, the Foreign Office had concentrated primarily on propaganda for allied and neutral countries; little attention had been given to the subject of propaganda direct into enemy countries, except where pro-British material had reached the enemy public through neutral channels such as Switzerland. Indeed, to many critics it appeared that the Foreign Office had forfeited the right to supervise Britain's overseas propaganda, and the arguments that had been advocated by the War Office since the end of 1915 now held the day. Following the resignation of Carson in January 1918, the way was left clear for the emergence of a full Ministry of Information (MoI), forcing the Foreign Office finally to relinquish its remaining control over propaganda.

It is difficult to avoid the conclusion that this was largely the work of Lloyd George, who had always expressed an active personal interest in publicity and propaganda. He had been responsible for the innovative publicity campaign of 1912 when the Insurance Commission had organised a corps of lecturers, recruited mainly from outside the civil service, to tour the country explaining the intricacies of the new National Insurance Act.[98] It was Lloyd George who, in August 1914, had first suggested the idea of an official propaganda bureau,[99] a proposal which resulted in the establishment of Wellington House. As Secretary of State for War in 1916 he was undoubtedly introduced to the views of his permanent officials concerning the creation of a centralised propaganda organisation, a concept only fully realised when he became Prime Minister at the end of that year. His contacts with influential journalists, such as Robert Donald and Lord Riddell, are as well known as his mistrust of diplomats and his interest in, and flair for, publicity – eventually underlined by his purchase of the *Daily Chronicle* in 1918. A. J. P. Taylor has written that, in contrast to the majority of his contemporaries who disliked propaganda intensely, Lloyd George, 'if anything, rated the influence of propaganda and the press too highly'.[100] The establishment of the Ministry of Information under Lord Beaverbrook in February 1918, and of the Enemy Propaganda Department at Crewe House under the direction of Lord Northcliffe, can thus be seen as the logical outcome of the Prime Minister's personal interest in propaganda, his sensitivity to mounting criticism of the Foreign Office and the increasing pressure for reform of the system as a whole.

The gradual erosion of Foreign Office control over propaganda must further be placed in the wider context of the Prime Minister's increasing personal involvement in diplomacy at the expense of Foreign Office influence in the making of British foreign policy.[101] The creation of the DoI did not seriously threaten the Foreign Office's influence on either policy or propaganda largely because John Buchan chose to work with, rather than against, it. Neither Beaverbrook nor Northcliffe, who were both made directly answerable to the Prime Minister, proved anything like as co-operative. Moreover, once the press barons tried to improve the effectiveness of British propaganda by actually giving it something to say about why Britain was fighting beyond 'poor little Belgium', tension with the Foreign Office was bound to increase.

The propagandists had always wanted a more coherent governmental statement of war aims, the previous absence of which had deprived British propaganda of any real consistency and purpose.[102] The problem was that, at Crewe House, it was believed that to be effective, propaganda 'must be inspired by policy, but at the same time, its varying needs also suggest policy'.[103] It was this latter assertion which was challenged by the Foreign Office throughout 1918. In short, it may have lost its control over propaganda, but it was determined not to allow the same to happen with regard to policy.

The purpose of Crewe House was essentially to reveal to the enemy the futility of their cause and the certainty of allied victory. To this end, Northcliffe considered that it was first necessary for the British government to announce what it was still fighting for so that the propaganda departments of Allied countries could pursue a uniform line. Immediately upon his appointment, he and one of his officials, Henry Wickham Steed,[104] began to try to push Balfour into issuing a definitive statement of war aims towards the 'oppressed nationalities' of Austria-Hungary.[105] Crewe House had selected Austria-Hungary as its initial target because that area offered the greatest prospect of immediate success, but the question was complicated by the problem of minority groups and the overall issue of self-determination.[106] Balfour became anxious at the incursions of both Crewe House and the Ministry of Information into the exclusive realm of foreign affairs, complaining to Lloyd George that their activities extended 'a good deal beyond anything I, at least, have been accustomed to describe as propaganda, using that word even in the widest sense'.[107] One historian has suggested that:

> Had Crewe House been as willing as Wellington House to accept dictation from the Foreign Office on matters of foreign policy there would have been fewer problems ... [but] Northcliffe's innovation was not that he made propaganda consistent with policy, but that he tried to alter foreign policy to make it consistent with propaganda formulated by Seton-Watson and Wickham Steed.[108]

Furthermore, the appointment of special propagandist agents in neutral countries gave the Ministry of Information, as Beaverbrook recognised, the potential to develop into 'a second Foreign Office at home with a new set of representatives abroad'.[109] This was clearly unacceptable to the Foreign Office.[110] The resultant tension proved to be a major hindrance to propaganda work during the last year of the war, and was the root cause of the frustration echoed in the comments of Beaverbrook and Northcliffe quoted at the start of this chapter.

1.5 Intelligence, Propaganda and Foreign Policy

Under the 1918 reorganisation, the News Department of the Foreign Office effectively became the news division of the Ministry of Information. This loss was to some extent offset by the transfer of the DoI's intelligence branch to the Foreign Office, where it was reconstituted as the Political Intelligence Department (PID). The ensuing tussles over the PID were at the heart of the dispute between the Ministry of Information and the Foreign Office. When Beaverbrook was first appointed, he tried to secure the intelligence division for his new ministry. The Foreign Office resisted, maintaining that intelligence work was not solely concerned with propaganda, its function being to compile, principally from diplomatic dispatches and telegrams, periodical summaries of the political situation in foreign countries for the use of the policy-makers.[111] However, because these summaries were also invaluable in propaganda work, Beaverbrook argued that the PID should form an integral part of his ministry.[112] Accurate intelligence was indeed a vital component of propaganda; without it, propaganda lacked its basic raw material. But Beaverbrook's mistake was to assume that political intelligence was only of value to the propagandist. Whitehall saw the loophole in his argument and closed ranks on him. The relevant government departments united in defence of duties for which they had been traditionally responsible. Balfour, the Foreign Secretary, wrote:

> It is quite true that propaganda must be based on knowledge; but the knowledge required covers only a fraction of that involved in the day to day work of the Foreign Office, Admiralty and War Office; and the creation of a new department, which regards it as one of its functions to co-ordinate all the most confidential information which three other departments have collected for their own purposes, is not only indefensible from the point of view of organisation, but would render secrecy even more difficult to maintain than it is at present.[113]

It was also suggested – somewhat dubiously – that Beaverbrook's argument was based upon a fundamental fallacy: 'Propaganda and Intelligence are two entirely different functions; the former depends on the latter for inspiration, but in their inherent nature and method of operation they have nothing in common. Diplomacy and Intelligence have; the one is the essence of the other'.[114] The culture of secrecy was clearly still more deeply imbedded than any requirements of official publicity.

In the face of such opposition, Beaverbrook submitted the dispute to the War Cabinet for arbitration,[115] but the issue was in turn passed on to an inter-departmental conference which convened on 5 March 1918. Here, Beaverbrook succeeded in reversing the initial arrangement: the intelligence division was to be part of his Ministry and not of the Foreign Office.[116] But then, on hearing this decision, the staff of the PID resigned *en bloc*, each member apparently reaching his decision independently of the others (!)[117] Beaverbrook was forced to submit. Better to have an intelligence division in the Foreign Office than none at all. Accordingly, the staff members of the PID were reinstated and became Foreign Office officials.[118]

In this struggle, Whitehall resented the incursions of the upstart Ministry into areas of traditional responsibility and was not prepared to allow an outside, and probably temporary, department to interfere with the cherished duty of collecting and utilising the political information upon which government policy was formulated. The Foreign Office was ultimately prepared to concede that it was not properly equipped or experienced to conduct the new propaganda, and was therefore prepared to surrender the work to a group of press barons that claimed to understand it better. But it was less ready to relinquish a responsibility which predated the propaganda experience and which would remain a vital aspect of its work. To this extent, propaganda was still being regarded as an instrument of warfare, and a distasteful one at that, a temporary expedient made necessary only because of the activities of the enemy. Whatever its future role, established diplomatic practices would continue after the war had ended. There might be serious consequences if a group of temporary officials – particularly those recruited from Fleet Street – were allowed direct access to information which normally would be kept secret from them. Furthermore, once it was fully appreciated, albeit late in the day, that propaganda was dependent for its success upon well-defined policy and accurate intelligence, the Foreign Office unwittingly held the trump card, which it retained so long as its traditional status and duties were preserved. When these issues became clear, and their implications recognised in the winter of 1917–18, the PID became the key to the Foreign Office door. Beaverbrook was permitted a free rein over propaganda partly because the Foreign Office had always preferred to keep such work, if not completely outside the door, then in the back hallway. That he found the door bolted from the inside on the twin issues of policy and intelligence was a reflection of the limited power of the Ministry of Information. Beaverbrook was fully aware of this and it remained a constant source of frustration and irritation to him. Without control over intelligence, he would be forced to accept that 'a Ministry of Information "functioning on its own" was not called for, and that, in fact, all it could do was to function as a Department of the Foreign Office'.[119] Indeed, as the dispute continued, he despairingly informed Balfour:

> If you face the facts the Ministry of Information is not really a Department independent of the Foreign Office, but one subsidiary to it. And what is the case in fact had much better be so in name too, if friction and waste of time are to be avoided.[120]

Yet friction persisted to the end of the war, with periodic threats of resignation from Beaverbrook. The Foreign Office, despite Lloyd George's hostility, usually emerged triumphant.

Having said all this, the Ministry of Information did represent the culmination of that process begun in 1914 whereby the systematic release of targeted information was elevated into a major responsibility of government. The style and character of British propaganda was moulded essentially by a small group of Foreign Office officials who may appear to have lacked the necessary credentials for work which involved considerations generally alien to their traditional concept of foreign affairs. Propaganda therefore developed along highly individual and idiosyncratic lines determined by the particular role that the Foreign Office saw for it during the various stages of wartime diplomacy. It attempted to conduct the work by the honest presentation of facts, albeit after careful selection. A factual basis was thus the foundation of all British official propaganda, a fundamental principle largely continued by Beaverbrook and Northcliffe. By 1917–18, however, the preoccupation with the presentation of the British point of view in allied and neutral countries was becoming less important than the demand for propaganda in enemy countries, as well as at home. Both Beaverbrook and Northcliffe recognised the potential power of propaganda over mass opinion and how it could be used to influence that opinion directly in order to alter events within a society and thereby alter the course of the war.

By July 1918, even officials at the PID had come to realise that:

> There are two ways, and two ways only, in which the Allies can win the war and impose their will on the rulers of Germany. One is by victory in the field. The other is by breaking down the determination of the German people to support their Government in its resistance to the Allies' demands. When that determination, and the patriotic idealism by which it is sustained, has been broken down, when the bulk of the German people has been brought, not necessarily to a spirit of revolt, but to a condition of distrust and passive hostility resembling that of the masses in Austria, the end of the war will be in sight.[121]

Crewe House therefore directed its propaganda to the mass populations of enemy societies in the belief that by convincing ordinary people of the incapacity of their ruling elites to govern, they would force their rulers to sue for peace, or else see them replaced by a government which would. One can readily see why government officials would be uneasy about this. Yet this in turn became the approach adopted by the other Allied propaganda departments – the Americans and the French – which attempted to make it clear that their chief object was:

> The changing of Germany, not the destruction of the German people; and that the German people can hope for an adequate position in the world and for admission into a future society of nations, when they have qualified themselves for partnership with civilised communities by making the

necessary reparations and restorations (primarily in the case of Belgium), and by overthrowing the system known as Prussian militarism, and when they have effectively abandoned all designs of mastery over Europe.[122]

Such was felt to be the power of opinion and the role of propaganda that it was now directed to all levels of society, from soldier to civilian, from civilian to politician, and from politician to potential revolutionary.

1.6 Elite versus Mass Opinion

This type of propaganda could not have been conducted from the Foreign Office, which had neither the heart nor the conviction for such an approach. It threatened to lead policy rather than follow it. It bypassed traditional inter-governmental procedures and, by appealing directly to the masses, it was both unpredictable and dangerous. It was for these reasons that, during the first three years of the war, Foreign Office propaganda had been directed to a much more selective audience. The concept of mass public opinion was generally incomprehensible to the exclusive and sheltered members of the foreign-policy-making elite. Rather, mass opinion was to be influenced only indirectly. Foreign Office-inspired propaganda was directed towards the opinion-makers, such as journalists, publicists and politicians, rather than to the mass of foreign peoples, 'the principle being that it is better to influence those who can influence others than to attempt a direct appeal to the mass of the population'.[123] News issued by the News Department alongside guidance emanating from Wellington House was accordingly directed towards leading personalities in foreign societies. Both placed great emphasis on personal propaganda. Prominent men were invited to see for themselves the merits of the British cause or the extent of Britain's commitment to the allied effort. In this way, it was believed that the confidence and goodwill generated by one elite towards another would ultimately be transmitted to larger numbers of people who might, in turn, express sympathy for Britain in various ways often without realising that their own leaders were acting, in effect, as propagandists for the British government. As one official wrote:

> The importance of secrecy need not be laboured ... The intrusion of a Government, or of persons notoriously inspired by Government, in the sphere of opinion, invariably excites suspicion and resentment ... It is not to be desired that all converts to the British point of view should proclaim their conversion: the object to be aimed at is rather to ensure that opinion in neutral countries shall not be based on imperfect or distorted information regarding the nature of the British case.[124]

The emphasis upon secrecy was thus not simply a device to prevent clean hands from getting dirty, but derived from a genuine belief in the value of disguised, indirect propaganda.

As a consequence, between 1914 and 1917, British propaganda was restrained in character and cautious in approach. Indeed, it was almost academic. The uncritical tone adopted was later considered too defensive. The Foreign Office was, however, always hindered by the lack of any declaration of war aims and the secrecy that surrounded the work. By stimulating and promoting friendly relations with influential foreigners, it was believed that British propaganda would serve the national interest in a constructive, though perhaps invisible manner. However, by the winter of 1917–18, with America in the war, it was felt that:

> Camouflage and the indirect appeal were no longer necessary, and that those who were in charge of the nation's propaganda could now 'speak out loud and bold', developing with special energy the most direct and effective known forms of publicity – personal propaganda, propaganda by film, by wireless and by cable.[125]

Accordingly, it was decided to appoint proven experts in these areas, men who were well versed in dealing with public opinion in its widest sense. The advent of the 'Press Gang', as they were known in Whitehall, made a widening of the audience of British propaganda inevitable.

The Foreign Office did not lose its control over propaganda simply as a result of its previous mistakes or because of professional ineptitude. It was because the requirements of propaganda in 1918 were entirely different from those that had prompted the creation of the system in 1914, requirements for which the Foreign Office lacked the necessary experience and inclination. As T. L. Gilmour, the head of the press and cinema division of the DoI, recognised in 1917:

> The conditions of modern warfare have now so enormously increased the value of the moral[e] factor that it is less a question of armies being arrayed against armies than of nations against nations – so that the civilian front is scarcely, if any, less important than the fighting front.[126]

In short, the Foreign Office was no longer felt to be equipped to supervise propaganda which targeted public opinion on a mass scale as a determinable factor not only in the internal affairs of a country but also in international affairs. As we shall see, this was not an entirely fair judgement. The Foreign Office had been the first to recognise the importance of propaganda and, through its wartime experience, many of its officials had come to see a genuine role for it in the future. But, with the war in its fourth year and with Lloyd George at the helm, its opponents held the day.

Beaverbrook, who considered propaganda to be 'the popular arm of diplomacy',[127] saw the First World War as a struggle in which 'the munitions of the mind become not less vital for victory than fleets or armies'.[128] He argued that since strength for the purpose of war entailed the total strength of each belligerent, and because the war encompassed neutral countries to an unprecedented degree, many of which were potential combatants, it was imperative to cultivate foreign opinion as a military asset. As Beaverbrook explained to Lloyd George:

> Since our appeal lies not to the diplomatic representatives of foreign countries, but to the public opinion of those countries, our methods must be different from those of the Foreign Office. We have a diplomacy of our own – a popular diplomacy – and for this we must have our own special organisation ... The Foreign Office has, however, both in principle and in practice refused to recognise this duty of the new Ministry from its inception. It says in effect that the doctrine of popular diplomacy implied a setting up of a Foreign Office at home with a new set of representatives abroad, and a policy possibly divergent from that of the Foreign Secretary.[129]

It was this fundamental difference of interpretation as to the role of propaganda which prompted Lord Northcliffe's statement that propaganda and diplomacy were incompatible. Indeed they were, but only in so far as the mass propaganda of the Ministry of Information and of Crewe House proved incompatible with the elite approach of the Foreign Office.

Notes and References

1 This chapter's original form appeared as 'The Foreign Office and British propaganda during the First World War', *Historical Journal*, 23, 4 (1980), pp. 875–98.
2 G. Harmsworth and R. Pound, *Northcliffe* (Cassell, 1959), p. 653.
3 Cited in Hugh Cudlipp, *The Prerogative of the Harlot* (London, 1980), p. 82.
4 Northcliffe to C. J. Phillips, 12 July 1918. Cited in Harmsworth and Pound, *Northcliffe*, p. 653.
5 Lord Beaverbrook, *Men and Power, 1917–18* (London, 1956), p. 290.
6 Cited in A. J. P. Taylor, *Beaverbrook* (Simon and Schuster, 1972), p. 145.
7 H. H. Asquith to the King, 31 August 1914, CAB 41/35/38. All references hereafter with prefixes such as CAB[inet Office], F[oreign] O[ffice], INF[ormation Ministry], W[ar] O[ffice] and PREM[ier's Office] are from the Public Record Office in London unless stated otherwise.
8 H. O. Lee, 'British propaganda during the great war, 1914–18', PRO, INF 4/4A. The exact dates remain vague and even this document, the 'official' history written shortly after the war but before the papers relating to First World War propaganda were destroyed in 1920, fails to throw light on the early chronological developments. For a detailed study of the News Department see Philip M. Taylor, '"The projection of Britain"; British overseas publicity and propaganda, 1914–39, with particular reference to the News Department of the Foreign Office', Leeds University Ph.D. thesis, 1978.
9 For an excellent review of the numerous unofficial propaganda bodies see J. D. Squires, *British Propaganda at Home and in the United States from 1914 to 1917* (Harvard University Press, 1935), pp. 16–25.
10 The work of the Press Bureau has been described by Sir Edward Cook in his *The Press in Wartime* (London, 1920), but awaits a modern study.

11 G. H. Mair, 'Report on [the] propaganda of [the] Neutral Press Organisation', undated. PRO, FO 371/2555, 12467: memorandum by J. A. Simon, 'The Neutral Press Committee', 8 Oct. 1915. CAB 37/135/14.

12 'The activities of Wellington House during the great war', undated, unsigned. INF 4/1B.

13 Lee, 'British propaganda during the great war, 1914–18', INF 4/4A.

14 For a more detailed examination of the work of Wellington House see M. L. Sanders, 'Wellington House and British propaganda during the First World War', *Historical Journal*, xviii, 1 (1975), 119–46.

15 Unsigned memorandum on the News Department, 29 January 1915. FO 371/2555, 12467.

16 One official observed in 1914: 'The contumely with which the German propaganda has been visited shows very clearly that Americans dislike any kind of machinery for the manipulation of their public opinion'. A. Willert to G. Robinson, 20 November 1914. Willert MSS, T[he] T[imes] A[rchive].

17 Foreign Office memorandum, 'British propaganda in allied and neutral countries', 20 Dec. 1916. CAB 24/3, G. 102.

18 Ibid.

19 J. Tilley and S. Gaselee, *The Foreign Office* (London, 1933), pp. 279–83.

20 Robinson to Willert, 31 December 1914. Willert MSS, TTA.

21 Unsigned memorandum, 27 October 1914. FO 371/2555, 12467.

22 It was later noted that 'in the early days of propaganda, even Westminster was found to be too far from Fleet Street'. General notes on propaganda, undated, unsigned. INF 4/1B.

23 Cecil, then responsible for the News Department's work in his capacity as parliamentary under-secretary of state for foreign affairs, had insisted that 'the Foreign Office could allow very considerable latitude to journalists, and would even go so far as to abandon any preliminary admission of matter connected with foreign policy at all'. Memorandum by J. A. Simon, 27 October 1935. CAB 37/136/34.

24 For further details see Rear-Admiral Sir Douglas Brownrigg, *Indescretions of the Naval Censor* (London, 1920), ch. 3.

25 Robert Donald: editor, *Daily Chronicle*, 1904–18; appointed by Lloyd George to investigate British propaganda organisations in 1917.

26 Donald to Lloyd George, 9 January 1917. INF 4/4B.

27 A history of the work of M. I. 7, 1914–19. INF 4/1B.

28 Sir R. Brade to Foreign Office, 10 December 1915. FO 371/2579, 188244.

29 Ibid.

30 Minute by Montgomery, 10 December 1915. FO 371/2579, 188244.

31 Schuster to Montgomery, 13 December 1915. FO 371/2579, 190927.

32 Schuster to Sir E. Troup, 13 December 1915. FO 371/2579, 190927.

33 P. Knightley, *The First Casualty; The War Correspondent as Hero, Propagandist and Mythmaker from the Crimea to Vietnam* (Harcourt Brace Jovanovich, 1975), pp. 80–112; Brig-Gen. J. Charteris, *At G. H. Q.* (Cassell, 1931), pp. 79, 94, 114–16; C. Hazlehurst, *Politicians at War* (Cape, 1971), pp. 147–51.

34 Brownrigg described Montgomery and Mair as resembling 'eager bridegrooms, ever pressing and coaxing me, the elusive bride, to grant them more and yet more favours in the shape of permits to visit the fleet'. Brownrigg, *Indescretions of the Naval Censor*, p. 79.

35 Especially William Howard Russell's reports for *The Times*. See Knightley, *First Casualty*.

36 Schuster to Troup, 13 December 1915. FO 371/2579, 190927.
37 This was, in fact, accurate. See Montgomery's proposals of 2 October and 6 December 1915. FO 371/2579, 190927.
38 Maurice de Bunsen to War Office, 14 December 1915. FO 371/2579, 190927.
39 Ibid.
40 A history of the work of M. I. 7, 1914–19. INF 4/1B.
41 Report and proceedings of a standing subcommittee's enquiry regarding press and political censorship in time of war, press censorship, 31 January 1913, CAB 38/23/6. See also P. Towle, 'The debate on wartime censorship in Britain, 1902–14' in B. Bond and I. Roy (eds), *War and Society: a Yearbook of Military History* (Croom Helm, 1975).
42 Memorandum by Montgomery, 6 December 1915, enclosed in Montgomery to S. W. Harris, 16 December 1915. FO 371/2579, 200406.
43 Simon to Cecil, 20 December 1915. FO 371/2579, 200406.
44 Ibid.
45 Cecil to Simon, 22 December 1915. FO 371/2579, 200406.
46 Ibid.
47 Ibid. This statement reveals an important point. In the first half of the war, any reference to the 'Foriegn Office attitude' concerning propaganda really means a small group of officials centred on Montgomery and Cecil. Grey and Nicolson rarely played an active role in the work. Their successors, however, Balfour and Hardinge, were more prepared to involve themselves, although perhaps more by force of circumstance than through personal choice.
48 Samuel had succeeded Simon following the latter's resignation over the issue of conscription on New Year's Day 1916. It appears that he was more amenable than Simon on the transference of Mair to the Foreign Office. See Cecil to Samuel, 21 January 1916. FO 371/2835, 17981.
49 Lord Onslow had been permanent private secretary to Sir Edward Grey and Sir Arthur Nicolson, 1911–13, but was at this time a member of MI7.
50 Record of proceedings of a conference at the Home Office, 26 January 1916, INF 4/9.
51 Masterman to Cecil, 31 January 1916, FO 371/2835, 20631.
52 Record of proceedings of a conference at the Home Office, 26 January 1916, INF 4/9.
53 Memorandum by Cecil, 28 January 1916, FO 371/2835, 17981.
54 E. T. Cook to Montgomery, 31 January 1916 and Montgomery to Cook, 1 February 1916, FO 371/2835, 20630.
55 Masterman to Cecil, 31 January 1916, FO 371/2835, 20631.
56 Montgomery to Masterman, 31 January 1916, FO 371/2835, 20631.
57 Minutes by Cecil, 6 and 7 February 1916, FO 371/2835, 21459.
58 Lord Newton, *Retrospection* (Murray, 1941), p. 218.
59 Squires, *British Propaganda*, p. 33.
60 It is from this point that the administrative records of the News Department begin, and for the remaining two-and-a-half years of the war there exist about 250 volumes in the FO 395 series at the PRO.
61 War Office memorandum on press propaganda, 1 February 1916, INF 4/9.
62 Ibid.
63 Charteris, *At G. H. Q.*, diary entry for 22 July 1916. See also the exchange of letters between Montgomery and Cockerill of 11 and 12 July 1916. FO 371/2835, 136247.

64 Charteris, diary entry for 2 August 1916. Miles Lampson, commenting upon the 'incredible and discreditable' lack of public interest in war films, informed Charteris that 'all the people want to see is Charlie Chaplin'. Ibid. p. 166.

65 Ibid, diary entry for 19 September 1916.

66 Lampson to Montgomery, 28 July 1916. FO 371/2835, 184995.

67 Minute by Montgomery, undated. FO 371/2835, 184995. See also the undated War Office memorandum enclosed in Macdonagh to Newton, 14 September 1916, and Newton's reply (not sent) of 18 Sept. FO 371/2835, 193134.

68 CAB 23/1, 1 (4), 9 December 1916.

69 'British propaganda in allied and neutral countries; Admiralty notes on the use of the press in the United States of America', 20 December 1916. CAB 24/3, G. 101.

70 'Note by the General Staff on the organisation of propaganda', 23 December 1916, CAB 24/5. G. 103.

71 Foreign Office memorandum, 'British propaganda in allied and neutral countries', 20 December 1916, CAB 24/3, G. 102.

72 Ibid.

73 Note by Cecil, 29 December 1916, CAB 24/3, G. 102.

74 CAB 23/1, 43 (7).

75 CAB 23/1 29 (9). 2 January 1917.

76 Lloyd George to Donald, 1 January 1917, INF 4/4 B.

77 Newton was also head of the prisoners of war department of the Foreign Office.

78 Donald to Lloyd George, 9 January 1917, INF 4/4B.

79 Donald to C. P. Scott, 29 May 1917. INF 4/7.

80 CAB 23/1, 43 (7). 24 January 1917.

81 Note by Montgomery, 3 February 1917, PRO, FO 800/384, Pp/17/2.

82 Drummond to Balfour, 3 February 1917, FO 800/384, Pp/17/3; Drummond to Cecil (now minister for blockade), 4 February 1917, FO 800/384, Pp/17/4.

83 Note by Balfour, undated. CAB 24/6, G. T. 2.

84 Note by J. Buchan, 'Propaganda – a department of information', 3 February 1917, CAB 24/3, G. 128.

85 CAB 23/1, 75 (13).

86 Donald to C. P. Scott, 29 May 1917, INF 4/7.

87 Lloyd George to Donald, 6 June 1917; Buchan to Donald, 6 June 1917, INF 4/4B.

88 Northcliffe, for example, wrote: 'We were in high hopes when Mr Buchan was created "Director of Information", a sufficiently comprehensive title. But Mr Buchan turns out to be virtually a subordinate of the Foreign Office where he works. His work, we are sure, is of the greatest national importance. The point is that it is merely that of an addition to the existing "publicity" departments, not that of a supreme co-ordinating centre'. The Times, 7 August 1917.

89 CAB 24/3, 230 (15). 10 September 1917.

90 Beaverbrook, Men and Power, p. 266.

91 Lloyd George to Donald, 19 October 1917, INF 4/4B; H. A. Taylor, Robert Donald (Stanley Paul, undated), pp. 156–7.

92 Donald to Carson, 25 October 1917, INF 4/4B.

93 Robert Donald, 'Inquiry into the extent and efficiency of propaganda: reports on various branches of propaganda work, and recommendations', 4 December 1917, INF 4/4B; CAB 27/18, PAC 3.

94 Burnham, Riddell, Beaverbrook and Donald to Sir Edward Carson, 14 December 1917, INF 4/4B.

95 Buchan to Carson, 28 December 1917, INF 4/5.

96 Memorandum sent to M. P. A. Hankey and covering note by Sir E. Carson, 'A psychological offensive against Germany', 11 December 1917, CAB 24/35, G. T. 2941.

97 See the unsigned memorandum prepared by M. I. 9a entitled 'German propaganda in 1917, some notes on its methods, material and manipulation', INF 1/715.

98 Sir F. Clark, *The Central Office of Information* (Allen and Unwin, 1970), p. 23.

99 H. H. Asquith to the King, 31 August 1914, CAB 41/35/38.

100 A. J. P. Taylor, *Beaverbrook*, p. 137.

101 R. Warman, 'The erosion of Foreign Office influence in the making of foreign policy, 1916–18', *Historical Journal*, 15:1 (1972) 113–59.

102 Note by the intelligence department of the Department of Information, 4 January 1918, CAB 24/38, G. T. 3226.

103 Report of the work of the department of propaganda in enemy countries, undated, unsigned, CAB 24/75, G. T. 6839.

104 Henry Wickham Steed: foreign editor, *The Times*; appointed editor-in-chief, 1919–22.

105 Northcliffe to Balfour, 24 February 1918. FO 889/4, No. 764.

106 For further details see Sir Campbell Stuart's *Secrets of Crewe House: The Story of a Famous Campaign* (Hodder & Stoughton, 1920), ch. 3.

107 Balfour to Lloyd George, 31 July 1918, FO 800/207.

108 K. J. Calder, *Britain and the Origins of the New Europe, 1914–18* (Cambridge University Press, 1976), p. 177.

109 Beaverbrook to Lloyd George, 24 June 1918, enclosed in Northcliffe to Balfour, 7 July 1918, FO 800/212.

110 See, for example, Cecil's views on the subject cited in Taylor, *Beaverbrook*, pp. 148–9.

111 Memorandum by Balfour, 5 February 1918. CAB 24/41, G. T. 3788.

112 Memorandum by Lord Beaverbrook, 'The need for an intelligence department of the ministry of information', 20 February 1918, CAB 24/43, G. T. 3788.

113 Memorandum by Balfour, 28 February 1918. CAB 24/43, G. T. 3788.

114 Foreign Office memorandum, undated, unsigned (but probably by Hardinge), enclosed in a memorandum by Balfour, 28 February 1918, CAB 24/43, G. T. 3788.

115 CAB 23/5, 349 (11), 29 February 1918.

116 Minutes of a conference held in General Smuts' room, 5 March 1918. CAB 24/44, G. T. 3823.

117 Minutes of a conference held in General Smuts' room, 13 March 1918, CAB 24/45, G. T. 3942.

118 FO 366/787, 44472.

119 Enclosure in Balfour to First Lord of the Admiralty, 11 April 1918, FO 800/207.

120 Beaverbrook to Balfour, 21 May 1918, FO 800/207.

121 Memorandum by E. Percy and A. E. Zimmern, 17 July 1918, FO 371/3474, 108951.

122 Report of the policy committee of hte inter-allied conference on propaganda in enemy countries, enclosed in H. K. Hudson to M. P. A. Hankey, 21 August 1918. CAB 24/61, G. T. 5492.

123 Schuster to Robinson, 3 December 1914, INF 4/1B.

124 Enclosure in Schuster to Montgomery, 18 December 1914, FO 371/2207, 88913.

125 H. O. Lee, 'British propaganda during the great war, 1914–1918', INF 4/4A.

126 Cited in G. C. Bruntz, *Allied Propaganda and the Collapse of the German empire in 1918* (Stanford University Press, 1938), p. 8.

127 Taylor, *Beaverbrook*, p. 145.
128 Memorandum by Beaverbrook, 'The organisation and functions of the ministry of information', September 1918, INF 4/5:.
129 Beaverbrook to Lloyd George, 24 June 1918, FO 800/212; also cited in F. Owen, *Tempestuous Journey* (Hutchinson, 1954), pp. 433–4.

2

Targeting Elite Opinion: The War Propaganda Bureau at Wellington House, 1914–17[1]

The War Propaganda Bureau, better known as Wellington House after its accommodation at that now demolished property in London's Buckingham Gate,[2] was Britain's most important official propaganda department for the first two and a half years of the Great War. Its head throughout this period was the writer, Charles Masterman, who served as Chancellor of the Duchy of Lancaster in Asquith's cabinet on the outbreak of war, but who was to prove far more successful as an administrator and as a propagandist than he ever did as a politician.[3] The work of Wellington House was conducted in great secrecy, so much so that few (even in Parliament) were even aware of its existence at the time. This in turn was one of the secrets of its success, although there was a price to be paid for this. Its work was directed primarily at overseas targets, including allied (including the Dominions and Colonies) and neutral countries (especially, until 1917, the United States). As such, it worked under the careful supervision of the Foreign Office. By far its single most important section was its American branch, headed by Sir Gilbert Parker, the Canadian-born writer and MP for Gravesend, who volunteered his services free of charge. Overall the entire Wellington House experiment cost the British taxpayer around £2 million.[4]

2.1 Targeting the American Elite

At first, British propaganda policy was not explicitly designed to get America into the war on the Allies' side. Benevolent neutrality was infinitely preferable to intervention – especially if it was on the side of Britain's enemies! Rather, its objective was to provide American opinion-formers with the material they needed to make up their own minds about the issues. By way of contrast, on war's outbreak, German propagandists on the spot in the US, in the diplomatic corps or in German-American *bunds*, made the mistake of bombarding American public opinion with their propaganda of exhortation. The British, seeing the counter-productive results which this approach appeared to be generating, decided not to appeal directly to mass American public opinion. The decision was therefore made to target the American elite, as people who were in a position to influence other, much larger numbers of their own people, in their own words and in their own accents. This elite – gleaned incidentally from the names contained in such publications as the American *Who's Who* – consisted of policy-makers, academics, teachers, businessmen and newspapermen, and became the primary target of Wellington House's attentions, not mass opinion itself. 'We have determined to present facts and general arguments based on facts',[5] stated the first report on the work of Wellington House.

This required very careful handling. Educated people like to believe that they can spot propaganda when they see it. And, having duly identified it as such, they can readily dismiss it as 'propaganda'. Wellington House therefore had to disseminate material to its target audience that did not appear to be propaganda but rather took the form of reasoned, almost quasi-academic, explanations of the issues involved, with the facts – even if not all the facts – presented in an objective manner and with measured argument. Nonetheless, the very point that such products were emanating from an official propaganda department reinforced the rationale behind the need for secrecy. Today, we would label Wellington House-inspired propaganda at the least as 'grey'[6] or perhaps even as 'black propaganda', which purports to emanate from someone or somewhere other than the true source. For this reason, not only was the publishing operation at Wellington House kept secret, but the material it produced was also distributed under the imprint of commercial publishing houses,[7] such as Hodder and Stoughton, Methuen, John Murray and Macmillan.

If we look at the people summoned to the first two meetings responsible for setting up Wellington House which Masterman convened in September 1914, we get a clue as to how and why this approach was chosen. The first meeting was attended by the likes of J. M. Barrie, Arnold Bennett, G. K. Chesterton, Arthur Conan Doyle, John Galsworthy, Thomas Hardy, Anthony Hope Hawkins, John Masefield, A. E. W. Mason, Gilbert Murray, Henry Newbolt, G. M. Trevelyan and H. G. Wells. This meeting has been described as 'probably the most important gathering of creative and academic writers ever assembled for an official purpose in the history of English letters'.[8] Noticeably absent, however, was Rudyard Kipling.[9] The second meeting was attended by leading editors, such as E. T. Cook, Robert Donald, Geoffrey Dawson, J. L. Garvin, then of the *Pall Mall Gazette*, Sidney Low of *The Standard*, J. A. Spender of the *Westminster Gazette* and J. St. Loe Strachey of *The Spectator*. In other words, the British approach to propaganda was to be based largely upon the prevalent media of the time, namely the written word. In the years that followed, pamphlets produced by the finest writers of the day poured out of Wellington House and through the mailboxes of America's opinion-making elite with no identification that their commissioning body was Britain's principal official propaganda department. To all outward purposes, it merely appeared that Britain's intelligentsia had mobilised itself out of spontaneous patriotism with no motive other than a desire to explain the issues of the war as they saw it from their individual and personal perspectives.

This approach was linked to a further operational ground rule of British propaganda, namely that it should always be based primarily upon so-called neutral facts or objective information. Now, of course, there is no such thing since all facts are selective. But Masterman's principle was to eschew known falsehoods in the correct belief that the truth would invariably out and, if the truth told a different story to that told by the propaganda, it would have a counter-productive effect from a propaganda point of view in that the credibility of the source would be compromised. Unpalatable facts could anyway always be omitted through censorship procedures. And who better to serve as advisers to ensure such principles were carried out than historians? Accordingly, Masterman appointed Arnold Toynbee, Lewis Namier, and J. W. Headlam-Morley as guardians of the Wellington House conscience.

At the heart of the campaign was the personal touch. As Harold Lasswell put it in the first academic study of the subject:

> When a lance was broken in public for the British cause, it was done by an American and not by a foreigner . . . It was the social lobby, the personal conversation, and the casual brush which forged the strongest chain between America and Britain. All countries found that an effective carrier of propaganda for their cause in America was the titled foreigner who said nothing whatever for the public prints, but who talked privately and casually of the War. The sheer radiation of aristocratic distinction was enough to warm the cockles of many a staunch Republican heart, and to evoke enthusiasm for the country which could produce such dignity, elegance and affability.[10]

This personal approach is perhaps best illustrated by the type of individual letter that Gilbert Parker wrote to accompany each specifically directed book or pamphlet. One, from March 1915, went as follows:

Dear Sir,

> I am well aware that American enterprise has made available reprints of the official papers relating to the present European war; but the original British prints of these publications may not be accessible to those persons of influence who would study them for a true history of the conflict. I am venturing to send to you under another cover several of these official documents. I am sure you will not consider this impertinence, but will realise that Britain's desire that their cause may be judged from authoritative evidence.
>
> In common with the great majority of Americans, you have, no doubt, made up your mind as to what country should be held responsible for this tragedy, but these papers may be found useful for reference, and because they contain the incontrovertible facts, I feel that you will probably welcome them in this form.
>
> My long and intimate association with the United States through my writings gives me confidence to approach you and I trust you will not think me intrusive or misunderstand my motive.[11]

Who could be offended at this? A remarkable group of individuals, therefore, leading experts in various fields and the finest writers of the time, were recruited as part of the general mobilisation of British society for Total War.

2.2 The Cult of Secrecy

So what was it like working there? There seems to have been some collective relish, even chic, about the covert nature of the work. This however meant that the government was often criticised for not doing enough in the realm of propaganda – to which Masterman and his colleagues were unable to respond. At the decision-making level, the senior officials and advisers met together several times a week in what they called 'the Moot'. One rare surviving account tells how these generally serious and long affairs would see members raise 'problems and materials for discussion':

> 'Charles', as he was officially known, often sat hunched at his chair silent until suddenly he would intervene with an unanswerable criticism or a final wise decision. Any records that were kept did not record his language, which was usually refreshingly unofficial. The work was not always dull or serious and we got a great deal of fun sometimes. One day we were asked to consider a formal complaint about the badness of our German translations, and on the offending document being called for it was found that it was a German reprint of a charm against bullets – in archaic German made in Germany and sold to the German soldiers.[12]

On a day-to-day basis, the various branches of Wellington House dealing with different geographic regions scrutinised publications, including newspapers, to monitor ebbs and flows of elite public opinion. Appropriate 'information' was then translated into various forms such as pamphlets and leaflets for distribution through the Foreign Office News Department. By June 1915, Wellington House had produced some 2.5 million propaganda items in 17 languages[13] and just over twelve months later was also distributing six fortnightly illustrated newspapers and 4,000 photographs a week. An increasing awareness of the importance of visual material saw Wellington House campaign for war artists to visit the front (Muirhead Bone was the first to go) as well as journalists and film cameramen: and it was Wellington House which produced the documentary film *Britain Prepared*. This was originally intended for neutral audiences but was premiered in London in December 1915. Masterman was also behind the commissioning of the hugely successful film, *The Battle of the Somme*.[14] But Wellington House's major output was directed not at the mass audiences which films were beginning to attract, nor at British audiences, even though there was increasing seepage of its material onto the domestic front. The bulk of its output was the written word, directed at foreign educated professional and influential audiences based upon rational argument rather than emotional appeals. Indeed, such was the success of its policy of disguising the source of its material that several Wellington House pamphlets were actually reviewed in the German press![15]

It was in the United States that Wellington House's invisible achievement
was most evident. Lord Cecil summed up British propaganda there when he
said that Britain must 'do good by stealth'.[16] Greatly helped by a series of
clumsy German mistakes, in essence Gilbert Parker was able to capture the
moral high ground for the British in providing an overall perceptual framework
in which the German invasion of Belgium, their sinking of the *Lusitania* and
the activities of German agents in America came to be seen as examples of
Hunnish barbarism. On the other hand, the British naval blockade, censorship
and even the crushing of the Easter Rising in Ireland came to be viewed as
the necessary actions of an island nation leading a united Empire in a war on
behalf of civilisation and decency against a barbaric enemy. Democracy barely
came into the discussions, and when it did such factors as the female suffrage
were glossed over or dismissed. Propaganda, once again, should not be allowed
to dictate policy.

Of Anglo-Irish descent and married to a wealthy American socialite, Gilbert Parker was singularly well placed to spearhead this campaign which
revolved around lecture tours, a steady stream of pamphlets distributed to a
mailing list that by 1917 numbered 170,000 influential Americans, and other
material which reached over 550 syndicated American newspapers. It was, he
boasted, 'an extraordinarily widespread organisation in the United States, but
which does not know it is an organisation. It is worked entirely by personal
association and inspired by voluntary effort ... the quiet and subterranean
nature of our work has the appearance of a purely private patriotism and
enterprise'.[17]

Wellington House was quick to exploit the *Lusitania* sinking in which 124
of those who lost their lives were Americans. With memories of the *Titanic*
sinking in 1912 already entering popular culture as the first great disaster story
of the twentieth century, the psychological backdrop to the news about the
Lusitania was such that a calculated attempt to deliberately sink a passenger
liner was bound to provoke horror.[18] Indeed, this incident provides a good
example of how the unobtrusive British campaign of stealth was punctuated
by spectacular campaigns revolving around individual German mistakes, the
exploitation of which was vital and at times brilliant.

Timing is critical in a successful propaganda campaign and at the core of
Wellington House's success were its detailed analyses of the foreign papers.
The American press was read daily by Kenneth Durant, a young American
volunteer, who pored his way through more than 60 newspapers per day to
produce the *American Press Resumé* which often found its way to the British
cabinet. On 12 April 1916, the *Daily Review of the Foreign Press* contained an
extract from the *Nieuwe Amsterdammer* which described a bronze medal struck
privately by a German artist to commemorate the sinking of the passenger
liner that, as is now known, was carrying munitions. But when the Germans
claimed that this was the case at the time, such was the extent to which the
British were controlling the flow of information out of Europe that the claim
fell on outraged ears. Moreover, the British seized on this very claim to

demonstrate the bestiality of German actions, focusing the issue back on to the killing through using that time-honoured emotional ploy of 'innocent women and children'. The obverse of the German medal portrayed the artist's impression of the *Lusitania* laden with guns, beneath the words *Keine Bannware!* ('No Contraband'). On the reverse were the words *Geschäft über alles* ('Business before everything') above a depiction of civilians refusing to heed the warnings about the German U-boat campaign while queuing for tickets from a skeleton sitting in the Cunard office. When the Foreign Office managed to secure an actual copy of the medal, photographs were sent to the United States and were published in the *New York Times* on 7 May 1916. They attracted so much attention that Wellington House decided to produce a boxed replica with a leaflet that read as follows:

> This medal has been struck in Germany with the object of keeping alive in German hearts the recollection of the glorious achievement of the German Navy in deliberately destroying an unarmed passenger ship, together with 1198 non-combatants, men, women and children ... The picture seeks apparently to propound the theory that if a murderer warns his victim of his intention, the guilt of the crime will rest with the victim, not the murderer.[19]

Wellington House at first produced 50,000 replicas of the *Lusitania* medal; thereafter, to meet the constant high global demand until the end of the war, Gordon Selfridge of department-store fame assumed responsibility for production and distribution, with profits going to the Red Cross. At one point 10,000 replicas a week were being produced.

That the British version of events generally prevailed, helped by the catastrophic commemorative medal that was typical of German naivity in propaganda matters prior to the age of Hitler and Goebbels, was due in no small part to the creation of a moral framework in which such actions as the sinking of the *Lusitania* came increasingly to be perceived. Perhaps the single most important document laying out the moral parameters whereby round pegs fitted easily into square holes was Bryce's infamous 'Report of the Committee on Alleged German Outrages' in Belgium, published within days of the *Lusitania*'s sinking in May 1915. The author of *The American Commonwealth* (1888), a former British ambassador to Washington (1907–13), a man much respected in Germany and an admirer of Germany over the French, Lord Bryce was bound to command a credibility which rubbed off onto the highly dubious 'evidence' presented in the report which bore his name. There is no need here to rehearse the unchallenged acceptance of testimonies by Belgian refugees who claimed they had seen or heard of the raping of women and children, babies' heads and women's breasts being cut off, the bayoneting of children and the nailing of a child to a farmhouse door.[20] One might just quote some words which raise doubts about much vaunted British judiciary practices long before the Guildford Four, the Birmingham Six and other miscarriages of justice occurred:

When ... we found that things which at first seemed improbable were testified to by many witnesses coming from different places, having had no communication with one another, and knowing nothing of one another's statements, the points in which they all agreed become more and more evidently true ... The force of the evidence is cumulative. Its worth can be estimated only by pursuing the testimony as a whole'.[21]

Not that Bryce was by any means alone. When the British Foreign Secretary, A. J. Balfour, surveyed the 'evidence' surrounding a later German atrocity story, the infamous 'corpse conversion factory', he agreed that the evidence was inconclusive but added that 'there does not, in view of the many atrocious actions of which the Germans have been guilty, appear to be any reason why it should not be true'.[22]

The Bryce Report made front-page news just about everywhere. As Masterman informed Bryce in June 1915:

Your report has swept America. As you probably know, even the most sceptical declare themselves converted, just because it is signed by you. It was a great idea of the P. M.'s to ask you to do this piece of work, which will stand as a historic document – hideous enough, God knows ... I wish, as I have no doubt you have – that you could have disproved the evidence or brought in a verdict of 'Not Guilty'. But as it was true – the world must know it; that it may never occur again.[23]

2.3 The Task Completed

Although the *Lusitania* incident coincided with the appearance of the Bryce Report, it did not bring the Americans into the war. The re-election of President Wilson in November 1916 on a neutrality ticket, however, came at a time when British aims *vis à vis* the United States were changing from keeping it neutral to actively getting it involved. The departure of Asquith and the arrival of Lloyd George as Prime Minister in the following month proved a catalyst that would see British propaganda go through a series of reorganisations. Yet while all the political manoeuvring and departmental in-fighting was going on, the propagandists soon found that they had another propaganda bombshell on their hands. In the early hours of 16 January 1917, the night duty officers in the Admiralty's Room 40 intercepted a telegram from the German foreign minister, Zimmermann, to Count Bernstoff, the German ambassador in Washington. This extraordinary cable proposed the introduction of unrestricted submarine warfare from 1 February and suggested an alliance with Mexico in the event of American intervention. Thanks to the ability of the British since the end of 1915 to crack the German diplomatic codes, most of the Zimmermann telegram was deciphered immediately; enough at least to grasp its meaning and significance. But two major problems remained. The first was how to convince the Americans that it was authentic, especially since American code-breaking at that time was unable to crack the ciphers and thereby verify its content. The second issue was whether to risk publicising it, thereby revealing to the Germans that their code had been cracked, which would inevitably prompt them to change their codes and the British would thus lose an important advantage. Moreover, the telegram had been sent by a variety of routes, including via the American cables, which the British were reluctant to admit they had also been monitoring for fear of antagonising a Washington already sensitive to British censorship practices. While Room 40 and its flamboyant chief 'Blinker' Hall pondered the risks, the Germans, right on schedule, launched their unrestricted U-boat campaign designed to starve the Allies into submission. Then a copy of the telegram was secured from the Mexican end, which the British decided to use as a cover for their other code-breaking activities. Accordingly, on 23 February 1917, Balfour showed the telegram to Walter Page, the American Ambassador in London, and it was published in the United States on 1 March. Not unnaturally, it caused a sensation and then, in an astonishing act of stupidity, Zimmermann admitted two days later that the telegram was genuine. A month after that, President Wilson declared war on Germany and her allies. Although he had already made up his mind to intervene on the Allied side before he heard of the Zimmermann telegram from Page, it undoubtedly helped smooth Wilson's decision with the powerful anti-interventionist lobby that had dictated the President's 'Keep America out of the War' ticket in the elections barely six months earlier. It was as if the British had broken the news of Pearl Harbour in advance to the Americans.

As the involvement of Room 40 in this episode indicates, Wellington House was not the only propaganda department operating in the first half of the war, but it was the most important. The very fact that its role after 1916 was diminished had more to do with the fact that Lloyd George wanted to reduce the role of the Foreign Office, under whose close auspices Wellington House worked, and cultivate press barons such as Beaverbrook and Northcliffe, to whom responsibility for propaganda was handed in 1918, than it did to any failure on the part of Masterman and his colleagues. Moreover, the chief *raison d'être* of Wellington House activity, the United States, disappeared when President Wilson joined the Allies as an Associated Power in April 1917. But by then, both Masterman and Parker were already in declining positions. Parker had visited the United States in January but his health was deteriorating and he resigned the following month. At the same time, Lord Northcliffe was beginning to take an active interest in propaganda in the USA, conducted along quite different lines than that of Wellington House, and he was appointed to replace Balfour as head of the British War Mission in America in May 1917. Masterman's fate was also sealed by the change of government. Lloyd George, Masterman's former boss at the Insurance Commission, was persuaded by Milner to put John Buchan in charge of propaganda when the Department of Information was set up in February 1917. Wellington House survived within the reorganisation, essentially as a printing unit, and Masterman had to suffer the humiliation of watching others take the credit for work he had masterminded

– and at a lower salary. When Beaverbrook and Northcliffe took command in 1918, Masterman was almost a forgotten figure. Moreover, when they publicised their wartime work after the armistice, both Beaverbrook and to a lesser extent Northcliffe deliberately diminished the significance of those who had worked before them, serving to provide an inaccurate impression that propaganda only began to be conducted properly when they took charge of it.

On setting up Wellington House, Masterman had warned his colleagues that when their work was finished 'it was highly probable it would go completely unrewarded and unacknowledged'.[24] Yet the most effective propaganda is that which is conducted in a cumulative fashion, and Wellington House provided the foundations upon which subsequent propagandists were to reap rewards, not just during the war itself but in all effective campaigns conducted ever since.

2.4 The Legacy of Wellington House

The history of Wellington House is remarkable in several ways. It was responsible for conducting the first ever systematically organised official worldwide wartime propaganda campaign, including the pioneering of new communications technologies and media to spread covertly its messages around the globe. This had several long-term ramifications for friends and former foes alike. Rarely and barely mentioned in most mainstream histories of the subsequent inter-war era, the consequences for British foreign policy and indeed for international relations generally were nonetheless significant. For example, after the war, when the sheer extent of Wellington House's work in the United States between 1914 and the American entry into the conflict in 1917 became known, it aroused massive indignation. Inter-war 'isolationist' factions on the other side of the Atlantic quickly seized upon the post-war revelations to 'demonstrate' how the United States had been 'duped' into entering the conflict by skilful, surreptitious and successful propaganda emanating from Masterman, Parker and their colleagues. This in turn generated significant mistrust in Anglo-American relations and reinforced a 'fortress America' mentality which underpinned US reluctance to involve itself in international relations (with the exception of 'dollar diplomacy') right down to December 1941. A glance at one of the earliest historical analyses of the subject, H. C. Peterson's 1939 work *Propaganda for War: the Campaign Against American Neutrality, 1914–17*, reveals the overriding US inter-war American perception; that we may have been duped into the last war by British propaganda but we must be especially on our guard against a repetition in the next one. By the time this book appeared, the Second World War was, of course, only months away for Europe but a still few years away for the United States. And whereas it would be too bold an assertion to suggest that Britain's First World War propaganda in the USA jeopardised American involvement in World War Two, it was not until the Japanese attack on Pearl Harbour in December 1941 that the Americans could finally bring themselves to formally allying with Britain once again.

As a result, in the meantime the British, especially after the fall of France in June 1940, stood alone. The extent to which American mistrust of Wellington House had taken root by 1939 was revealed when *Life* magazine reminded its readers of how British wartime propaganda, 'pressed with relentless skill by Sir Gilbert Parker', had enticed America to send two million men to Europe in the last war.[25] A decade earlier, the American novelist Upton Sinclair had more graphically confessed to being:

> One of the hundred and ten million suckers who swallowed the hook of the British official propaganda, conducted by an eminent bourgeois novelist, Gilbert Parker, who was afterwards knighted for what he did to me.[26]

In the meantime, others maintained that 'the self-respecting American is down on all propagandists as the self-respecting housewife is down on vermin ... especially of the British persuasion'.[27] However widespread these resentments might have been, it was clear that any British propaganda directed at the United States between 1939–41 would have to be even more unobtrusive than it had ever been during the 1914–17 period.[28] And propaganda had become a dirty word.

Of course, one cannot attribute American involvement in either conflict solely to propaganda. On the other hand, one can too readily dismiss the idea in much the same way as others have done with Adolf Hitler's arguments in *Mein Kampf* about Germany not being defeated on the field of battle. Rather, this particular argument ran, the German army had been forced to succumb to armistice negotiations by the collapse of morale at home, a 'stab-in-the-back' fuelled by highly effective British propaganda emanating from another, later, organisation – the Enemy Propaganda Department at Crewe House (see chapter three). Propaganda thus begets propaganda. But, especially in this era of emerging popular party politics, perceptions of the past often count for more than the actual historical record and, in the United States, the perceived legacy of Wellington House was to result in the passing of the 1938 Foreign Agents Registration Act, still in force today, requiring the formal licensing of all foreign publicists operating on American soil.

A second significant legacy of the 1914–17 experiment was that Wellington House officials laid down the operational ground rules which subsequent propagandists, especially those working on behalf of democratic regimes but also people like Hitler, Goebbels and Stalin, ignored at their peril. These are worth reiterating. Perhaps the foremost lesson, encapsulated in the Zimmerman telegram episode, was in the relationship between propaganda, intelligence and censorship. As we have seen in the previous chapter, this lesson was learned through bitter inter-departmental power struggles which involved territorial disputes caused by the new needs of Total War fought against the backdrop of the new conditions created by the communications revolution. Traditional Whitehall departments were simply not geared up for this new fusion, and even the unprecedented establishment of a Ministry of Information in 1918 in an attempt to meet the new conditions was hampered by conservative attitudes to change and fundamental differences of opinion about target audiences.

It is not just a question of what, how, why and when you say something, and to whom, but also of what you decide to leave out. In propaganda, omission is just as significant as commission. Interestingly, because it indicates the almost instinctive British understanding of the connection between positive persuasion (propaganda) and negative persuasion (censorship), some evidence suggests that the person who first urged Lloyd George to raise the issue of propaganda in the Cabinet at the start of the war was none other than T. P. O'Connor. From 1917, O'Connor became President of the British Board of Film Censors.[29] Moreover, in the age of communications, normally if one warring faction decides deliberately to omit certain information, you can be pretty sure that the other side will attempt to publicise it. Enormous effort is therefore required to identify, through intelligence activity, information about the other side. For the propagandist, it becomes essential to monitor and control the flow of raw information at as many points between source and target as possible. The British had learned this through their nineteenth-century development of a global cable communications system, known as the 'All Red Network' connecting all those points on the world map shaded red, with London at the centre.[30] Accordingly, the British started the First World War, before they had even fired a shot, with an action which gave them an enormous advantage in the coming struggle for American hearts and minds. This was the cutting, within hours of the ultimatum to Germany expiring, of the direct transatlantic cables from Germany to the United States by the *Telconia*. Because wireless was still in its infancy and still largely confined to morse code ship-to-shore messages, the cutting of its cables was a significant blow to the German propaganda machine from which it never really recovered. It meant that thereafter all German news, information and opinions about the war, its cause and course, had to reach the USA by indirect routes through cable relay stations in neutral countries in Scandinavia and Iberia – which the British organisations such as the Admiralty's Room 40 were intercepting. They were able to read these transmissions because the various German codes had been cracked.[31] The culmination of the *Telconia's* action was again to be seen in the ability of the British to intercept, decipher and disseminate the infamous Zimmermann telegram in 1917. Hence this joint recognition of the intrinsic relationship between propaganda and censorship and between propaganda and intelligence activities – despite what was said in 1918 in rows over the PID – provided Wellington House with a tremendous advantage in the war of words in that it meant that the vast majority of news reaching America was through British filters, not German. It also established the blueprint for how modern states should go about conducting a global propaganda campaign in a world that was already witnessing what we now call the globalisation of communications. And despite the fact that this censorship issue was almost as irksome to the neutral Americans as the British blockade of their trade with the Central Powers, the British got away with it quite simply because most of it was so unobtrusive that the sheer extent of the censorship operation was unknown.

Part of the reason for this lack of knowledge about Allied activity was due to another operational ground rule adopted by Wellington House relating to the target audience which it identified as being the most likely to bear fruit. Masterman and his colleagues recognised that foreigners did not like being told what to do, let alone what to think, by people from other countries, especially when they have a different accent. One also has to bear in mind the general principle – or 'fiction' as Harold Lasswell perhaps more accurately called it [32] – of international relations at that time that states did not interfere with the internal affairs of other states, and this included public opinion. So, in the United States, despite the advantages of a near-enough common language, Wellington House decided wisely to eschew exhortation in favour of explanation. In typical British understatement, it defined its objective simply to persuade Americans 'to take a right view of the actions of the British government since the commencement of the war'.[33] This essentially was how London, at the heart of the British Empire and of a global communications network, was able to persuade a former colony and emerging superpower that siding with the past was essential for the future. The demonisation of the enemy by the British, all backed up with 'facts' such as those contained in the Bryce Report or in the Zimmermann telegram, was so effective that it became impossible for decent Americans to contemplate siding with the Central Powers. And when the Huns threatened the very shores of America via Mexico, their true bestiality became plain for all to see. It did not matter any more about squabbles with the British over censorship, trade or Ireland, nor did it matter that the British Empire was still a system which cherished different concepts of democracy to those held in Washington. The fact of the matter was that the Germans were worse, or rather were seen to be worse, and hence it was in American interests to send their troops into battle in a faraway war to the death between competing Empires. Once this task had been completed, with Britain's back safeguarded, the British government turned its propaganda attention to its European front and to the question of psychological warfare against its enemies.

Notes and References

1 An earlier version of this chapter, which was first delivered at the 'Leeds International First World War Conference' in 1994, appeared as 'Propagandists at war: working for the Secret War Propaganda Bureau at Wellington House', *Gunfire: A Journal of First World War History*, 34 (1995), 14–25. pp. 14–25.

2 Formerly the home of the pre-war National Insurance Commission, established by Lloyd George in connection with the 1911 National Insurance Act. It can be argued that the Commission served as Britain's first ever official propaganda organisation since it employed a team of civil service lecturers, but mostly used publicists drawn from outside Whitehall to tour the country proselytising the

benefits of the Act to both employers and workers. See Sir Fyfe Clark, *The Central Office of Information* (Allen & Unwin, 1970), p. 23.

3 Author of *In Peril of Change* (publisher unknown 1905) and *The Condition of England* (Methuen, 1910). He was also Chairman of the National Insurance Commission which, so far as I am aware, awaits its historian. Masterman was not however an MP at the time, having failed to secure a seat following his appointment as Chancellor of the Duchy of Lancaster, a source of alienation from his friend and former head, Lloyd George. Masterman had to resign from the Cabinet in February 1915. For further details, see G. S. Messenger, *British Propaganda and the State in the First World War* (Manchester University Press, 1992), chapter 3.

4 According to Lucy Masterman, *C. F. G. Masterman* (Cassell, 1968), p. 294.

5 First report of the work of Wellington House, 7 June 1915, INF 4/5.

6 That is, propaganda emanating from an unidentifiable source.

7 H. O. Lee, 'British propaganda during the Great War, 1914–18', Public Record Office (hereafter PRO) INF 4/4A.

8 P. Buitenhuis, *The Great War of Words: Literature as Propaganda, 1914–18 and After* (Batsford, 1989), p. 14.

9 Despised by Foreign Secretary, Sir Edward Grey, who even threatened to resign if the government backed Kipling's visit to the United States in late 1914. See Messinger, *British Propaganda*, p. 277.

10 H. Lasswell, *Propaganda Technique in the World War* (MIT Press reprint, 1971), p. 157.

11 M. L. Sanders and P. M. Taylor, *British Propaganda during the First World War, 1914–18* (Macmillan, 1982), p. 169.

12 Masterman, *Masterman*, p. 294.

13 First report of the work of Wellington House, 7 June 1915, INF 4/5.

14 *The Battle of the Somme*, official film, 1916.

15 Masterman, *Masterman*, p. 288.

16 Note by Cecil, 29 December 1916, CAB 24/3, G. 102.

17 First report of the work of Wellington House, 7 June 1915, INF 4/5. See also J. C. Adams, *Seated with the Mighty: a Biography of Sir Gilbert Parker* (Borealis Press, 1979), p. 164.

18 Richard Howells, *The Myth of the Titanic* (Macmillan, 1999).

19 This story is recounted in Sanders and Taylor, *British Propaganda*, pp. 130–1.

20 For the context see T. Wilson, *The Myriad Faces of War* (Polity, 1986), p. 186.

21 Report of the Committee on Alleged German Outrages (HMSO, 1915).

22 Minute by Balfour, 26 April 1917, FO 395/147.

23 Cited in Messenger, *British Propaganda*, pp. 74–5.

24 Masterman, *Masterman*, p. 273.

25 J. C. Adams, *Seated with the Mighty*, pp. 174–5.

26 Cited in Messenger, *British Propaganda*, p. 68.

27 J. Nock, 'A New Dose of Britain Propaganda', *American Mercury*, 42 (December 1937) p. 482.

28 N. J. Cull, 'The British Campaign against American "Neutrality": publicity and propaganda, 1939–41', Ph.D. thesis, University of Leeds, 1991, subsequently published as *Selling War: The British Propaganda Campaign against American 'Neutrality' in World War Two* (Oxford University Press, 1995).

29 Masterman, *Masterman*, p 294. On O'Connor's role at the BBFC, see N. Pronay, 'The first reality: film censorship in Liberal England' in K. R. M. Short, (ed.) *Feature Films as History* (Croom Helm, 1981), pp. 122ff.

30 P. M. Kennedy, 'Imperial cable communications and strategy, 1870–1914', *English Historical Review*, 86:3 (1971), 725–52.
31 C. Andrew, *Secret Service* (Heinemann, 1985).
32 Lasswell, *Propaganda Technique*, p. 6.
33 First report of the work of Wellington House, 7 June 1915, INF 4/5.

3

Targeting Mass Opinion: Crewe House, Psywar and British Propaganda against the Central Powers in 1918[1]

Thanks chiefly to the published memoirs of its practitioners, it was long thought that British propaganda directed against the Central Powers during the final year of the Great War proved extremely effective in undermining the morale of the enemy and thereby contributed materially to Germany's defeat. Although the late Michael Balfour attempted to 'demythologise' the work of Crewe House in 1978,[2] and despite the absence of adequate target audience reception data from this era, the testimonies of enemy commanders would at least appear to suggest a genuine and widespread impact. Amongst others, General Ludendorff, in his graphic and often quoted tribute, maintained that 'we were hypnotised by the enemy propaganda as a rabbit is by a snake. It was exceptionally clever and conceived on a great scale. It worked by strong mass suggestion, kept in touch with the military situation and was unscrupulous as to the means it used.'[3] 1918 therefore still remains an essential starting point for any study of modern psychological warfare techniques.

3.1 The Politics of Propaganda

As we have seen, until the final year of the war British propagandists had directed their energies largely towards elite opinion in allied and neutral countries.[4] The original conception of wartime propaganda had been determined first by the need to counter the virulent German campaign in neutral countries, particularly the USA, and then by the need to reassure its allies that Britain was pulling its weight in the combined struggle against the Central Powers. For the former, a news-based approach was adopted by the Foreign Office while the latter required more creative and covert, views-based, methods on the part of organisations like Wellington House. The need to launch a psychological offensive against the actual enemy, however, took a little more time to gain wide acceptance. The creation in February 1918, therefore, of a specific enemy propaganda department designed to 'reveal to the enemy the hopelessness of their cause, and the certainty of Allied victory'[5] may perhaps be said to have been long overdue.

This is not to suggest that little or nothing in the way of psychological warfare operations against the enemy had been undertaken before 1918. As

Adolf Hitler, who claimed to have 'learned enormously from this enemy war propaganda', wrote in *Mein Kampf*:

> With the year 1915 enemy propaganda began in our country, after 1916 it became more and more intensive, till finally at the beginning of the year 1918 it swelled to a positive flood. Now the results of this seduction could be seen at every step. The army gradually learned to think as the enemy wanted it to.[6]

If Hitler was therefore correct in realising that this had been a cumulative campaign, who was doing the work prior to the creation of Crewe House in 1918?

In fact, S. A. Guest, working from Wellington House, had initiated the work. Guest had been drawn increasingly into enemy propaganda work through his activities with Germany's neighbouring neutral states, Holland and Switzerland, and can justifiably be described as the single most important figure in the enemy propaganda campaign prior to the appointment of Lord Northcliffe. Even Northcliffe himself admitted in December 1918:

> I do not think I was quite fair to Mr Guest in suggesting that he should [only] receive a Commandership of the Order of the British Empire. I was not fully aware that Mr Guest had been engaged in this propaganda for more than three years and the culminating success was considerably due to the routes and methods he had devised.[7]

If the balance of historical judgement invariably tends to rest with those who finished the campaign, due credit must also be given – as Masterman and his colleagues at Wellington House would no doubt agree – to those who began it.

This same judgement must also be applied to the work of MI7.[8] The War Office had been comparatively slow to recognise the value of propaganda in war, being more initially preoccupied with censorship (or negative propaganda) as a means of influencing public opinion at home and abroad.[9] However, amongst other things, the successful partnership of propaganda and recruitment prior to the introduction of conscription in 1916 had demonstrated to the military authorities the value of more positive forms of persuasion at the time when they badly needed volunteers to offset the enormous casualties being sustained on the western front. MI7, formed in February 1916 to take charge of all propaganda relating to military matters, was determined to increase the work in military zones and on the battlefields. Does therefore the establishment of Crewe House two years later indicate a condemnation of these previous efforts? After all, neither of the two reports initiated by Lloyd George during 1917 into the conduct and efficiency of British propaganda (the Donald reports) contained any criticism of the way in which propaganda directed against the enemy was being conducted.[10]

Why, then, was the Enemy Propaganda Department established? It seems in fact that the actual decision to establish such a body independent of the newly formed Ministry of Information was sudden and unforeseen. Even Lord

Beaverbrook was initially unaware that enemy propaganda work would not fall within the responsibilities of his new ministry. It was suspected at the time that Lloyd George had issued his invitation to Northcliffe of 13 February 1918 in an attempt to draw the teeth of Fleet Street's most powerful and influential critic of the government. Relations between the two men had always been erratic;[11] the Prime Minister had once quipped that he would sooner take a ride on the back of a grasshopper than a walk in the park with Lord Northcliffe. Lloyd George, who respected the power of the press perhaps far beyond its actual significance,[12] might well have regarded Northcliffe's appointment as an ideal opportunity to curb the criticism of this most recalcitrant of newspapermen. Northcliffe, for his part, had indeed been a constant critic of the government and of its handling of the war but, although he had accepted the post as head of the British War Mission to the United States in 1917, he generally preferred to avoid official appointments for fear that they might restrict his freedom to criticise the authorities if he chose to do so.[13] Accordingly, when Lloyd George offered him a ministerial appointment on his return from the United States, Northcliffe politely turned it down. But the fresh bait of a virtually autonomous enemy propaganda department proved irresistible to a man who had expressed a passionate interest in such work from the early days of the war. Northcliffe himself maintained that the offer came from 'those who are doing the actual fighting in the war'[14] – which presumably meant the War Office. This is, however, curious. Northcliffe had certainly supported the Generals – with some notable exceptions – and he had frequently defended their cause before the government as, for example, during the shell-shortage crisis of 1915. Even so, it nonetheless remains difficult to explain why the military authorities should apparently be so prepared to relinquish control over work in which MI7 had been becoming increasingly involved and for which they had proven their determination to retain during their bitter inter-departmental battles with the Foreign Office.[15] Perhaps, as another source suggests, this anomaly can be explained by the fact that Northcliffe's appointment was proposed by Sir William Tyrrell, head of the Foreign Office's Political Intelligence Department, who had been involved in propaganda since the very beginning of the war.[16] In light of the rivalry which had previously existed between the Foreign Office and the War Office over the question of propaganda, it is not inconceivable that Northcliffe's name was put forward by one department or the other as a convenient means of solving what had become intractable inter-departmental problem.

It does, however, seem unlikely. More probably the idea originated with the Prime Minister himself. Unlike the vast majority of his contemporaries, Lloyd George fully appreciated the role which the new weapon of propaganda could play in wartime. But he did not consider that the Foreign Office, or any other Whitehall department for that matter, possessed the right sort of people who were capable of realising its full potential. From the moment he had become Prime Minister in December 1916, he had displayed considerable determination in his attempt to weaken the grip that the Foreign Office had established on the direction and conduct of British overseas propaganda since the outbreak of war. He felt that British propaganda had been too defensive and cautious, too resistant to proposals for change and that it had been directed towards too narrow a target audience. What was now required was an adventurous and resolute campaign directed against the morale of enemy soldiers and civilians rather than the previous practice of directing propaganda at their governments and ruling elites. He preferred to entrust this work to newspapermen well versed in techniques of news management and mass persuasion.

This was certainly a dangerous ambition. Lloyd George laid himself open to the charge that he was merely attempting to muzzle the press for political reasons. The type of pragmatism which he displayed in wresting away the grip of the Foreign Office over propaganda during 1917 as part of his wider attempt to reduce its influence in the formulation of British Foreign policy[17] was, however, typical of Lloyd George's premiership. It therefore becomes difficult to distinguish between his desire to utilise the particular expertise of men such as Northcliffe and Beaverbrook in their capacity as experts on mass opinion, and his determination to curtail their influence as newspaper owners. Although Lloyd George reassured C. P. Scott, editor of the *Manchester Guardian*, that neither man 'would allow their propaganda work to be determined by their personal views – and would simply take the line which they thought likely to be the most useful in the particular case', Scott commented: 'as this is not very far from being Lloyd George's own state of mind it did not seem much use to argue the matter.'[18]

The formation of the Enemy Propaganda Department amidst a blaze of publicity was thus interpreted by Lloyd George's supporters as a long overdue attempt to find a satisfactory organisational solution to the chaos which had characterised the development of official propaganda since the start of the war. His critics saw the appointments of both Northcliffe and Beaverbrook as Lloyd George's most outrageous attempt to muzzle the British press. The Foreign Office regarded it as another incursion into their traditional role in the making of foreign policy. There is validity in all these interpretations. By the end of 1917, however, the deteriorating war situation demanded more than simply administrative reform. The mutiny of French troops following the ill-fated Nivelle offensive, the Italian defeat at Caporetto in October, the failure of the British offensive towards Passchendaele in November, the critical situation in Russia in the aftermath of the Bolshevik revolution and the German-Russian armistice at Brest-Litovsk, anxieties concerning an impending German offensive and the slow progress of American intervention – all these factors raised serious concerns for the condition of morale throughout the Entente. Even in Britain, where the famous Lansdowne letter published by *The Daily Telegraph* on 29 November 1917 was symptomatic of a mounting tide of pacifist feeling, urgent counter-measures were required. Domestic propaganda, which had largely been left to the jingoistic press and unofficial patriotic committees up to this point, was at last put on a serious official footing with the creation of the unfortunately named National War Aims Committee.[19]

As the war passed through its fourth Christmas, not only had new methods of winning the war to be tried when others had failed, but it was also important that the government was seen to be pulling out all the stops. Lloyd George was finally forced into a public declaration of British war aims in January 1918, thereby providing British propaganda with an essential focus that had been lacking previously. The time had also arrived – for political reasons as much as any other – to launch a psychological offensive against the hearts and minds of the enemy peoples. When all else had failed to break the military deadlock, any new weapon was worth trying.

3.2 Psywar Origins: The Snake

Psychological warfare was first practised by the Germans who initiated leaflet-dropping raids over Allied lines in Nancy during the battle of Grande-Couronne in September 1914.[20] Some leaflets even appear to have been dropped subsequently over Paris.[21] By October 1914 the Germans were publishing the *Gazette des Ardennes* for the benefit of French troops. At first, the British were reluctant to respond. When in September 1914 Lord Northcliffe, acting on his own private initiative, suggested to Sir John French and General Wilson that leaflets should be dropped over German lines by aeroplane, the latter replied that propaganda was 'a minor matter – the thing was to kill Germans'.[22] But when, in response to the Nancy venture, Sir Earnest Swinton, the official 'eyewitness' at the front at a time when journalists were still not allowed, suggested that the Royal Flying Corps could be used to scatter literature over German lines, it was agreed to experiment with this type of warfare. By March 1915, a full-scale 'paper war' had developed under the supervision of General Cockerill at the War Office's Directorate of Special Intelligence.[23] What is less well-known – or appreciated – is that the War Office remained in charge of the production of propaganda material for military zones until 1 September 1918 – six months after the creation of Crewe House – and in fact never lost control over its distribution in the forward areas.

Delivery systems are always a problem for propagandists. This was especially the case for the military on the Western Front once the distribution of propaganda material by aeroplane was brought abruptly to an end at the start of 1918. This was because of an official German announcement in May of the previous year that the dropping of inflammatory literature, especially material directed against the Kaiser, would henceforth be considered a violation of international law. At first, the British ignored the threat but then, on 17 October 1917, four British airmen were captured and tried by court martial 'for having distributed pamphlets containing insults against the German army and Government among German troops in the Western Theatre of War'.[24] Although two of the accused were acquitted due to lack of evidence, and although the German court questioned the ruling concerning violations of international law, the other two officers were sentenced to ten years' imprisonment. The British, meanwhile, who were at first unaware of this judgement, pressed ahead with their plans for a more intensive campaign of aerial propaganda on the Western Front. On 20 December 1917, GHQ in France suggested that a good deal more could be done in view of the apparent success of German propaganda in Russia and France and also because of the mounting German fear concerning the impact of British propaganda. Consequently, on 9 January 1918, the War Office approved the intensification of aerial propaganda and the dropping of its specially produced newspaper, *Le Courier de l'Air*, over occupied zones. Then, on 28 January, German wireless broadcasts contained news of the punishments meted out to the British airmen and the War Office ordered the immediate suspension of aircraft distribution of all British propaganda over German lines. After several protests, the British government eventually threatened reprisals which produced the desired effect as, on 11 March 1918, the eve of reprisals, the Dutch government informed the British that the two airmen were to be pardoned, returned to their camps and treated as normal prisoners of war.[25] Despite this, however, the Air Ministry proved reluctant to risk any more of its men and machines on propaganda raids[26] and the order to suspend the aircraft distribution remained in force on the western front until the end of October 1918.

Instead, the British chose to rely chiefly upon distribution by balloon. The Director of Military Intelligence stated that, in the right conditions, the balloons could reach Germany but 'the bulk of the propaganda was distributed over an area of from 10 to 50 miles behind enemy lines'.[27] This is what essentially led Michael Balfour to challenge the alleged efficiency of balloon propaganda:

> Leaflets could thus only have reached German civilians by the occasional freak balloon, by being brought back by soldiers on leave and by such surreptitious channels as being slipped inside neutral books and papers sent into Germany. It is hard to believe this was how a revolution was set off.[28]

Indeed so. Aircraft distribution was undoubtedly a more effective means of reaching the German civilian population, as Beaverbrook always recognised,[29] but the balloons were capable of reaching the critically important contact areas where fresh troops mingled with soldiers returning home on leave. Moreover, aircraft distribution was resumed during the critical days of early November by which time, as Hitler and Ludendorff recognised, the cumulative effect of a campaign that had been fought over the past three years was beginning to produce decisive results.

3.3 One Rabbit: Germany

The effect of any propaganda designed to undermine the will to fight of enemy soldiers invariably depends, of course, upon the fortunes of war. Victorious troops tend to have high morale precisely because they are victorious, regardless of the harshness involved in the process. They are more vulnerable to propaganda and suggestion in the aftermath of a great offensive that has failed to produce decisive results even if it has not actually resulted in military defeat. Thus when the great German spring offensive of 1918 had been contained by the Allies, British propaganda was provided with a genuinely fertile field in which it could have a significant impact. According to Campbell Stuart, the number of leaflets dropped over and behind enemy lines by balloon totalled 1,689,457 in June and 2,172,794 in July. Hindenburg testified to their successful distribution: 'Our soldiers have delivered to the authorities the following number of hostile handbills: in May 34,000; in June 120,000; in July 300,000.'[30] The number of leaflets handed in can therefore be reasonably assumed to have been but a fraction of those which were not. During August, an average number of 100,000 leaflets a day were being despatched, totalling 3,958,116. But the most remarkable aspect of this work is that these leaflets were actually produced by MI7 at the War Office, and not by Crewe House.

It was not until the end of August 1918 that Crewe House assumed responsibility from MI7 for the production of enemy propaganda leaflets and, as already mentioned, at no time did it take charge of distribution in military zones. But when it did become the principal production agency for this material, producing its first leaflet on 4 September, its output was nonetheless impressive. In September the total number of leaflets dropped over German lines dropped slightly to 3,715,000 but increased to 5,360,000 in October. During the last ten days of the war, an astonishing 1,400,000 leaflets were dropped by balloon and the resumed method of aeroplane drops.[31]

The very fact of being able to drop such large numbers of leaflets with relative impunity was in itself an indication of the changing fortunes of war. It is, for example, noticeable that the various orders issued to German troops forbidding them to read or disseminate the British and French leaflets are largely dated in August 1918 – after the Allied breakthrough but before Crewe House took charge of the work.[32] It was at this time that leaflets appeared describing the collapse of Germany's allies and the arrival of the 'First Million' Americans. Moreover, the failure of the German spring offensive, the impact of the tightening Allied blockade, the increased German submarine losses and military setbacks or defeats were driven home in leaflets depicting the pointlessness and futility of German sacrifices. That prominent Gothic symbol, the skull, made regular appearances in which Death toasted its latest German recruits. The revelations of Prince Lichnowsky,[33] from which 'proof' of aggressive German diplomacy and war aims was extrapolated,[34] were also exploited to great effect; Ludendorff claimed subsequently that 'Prince Lichnowsky shares the gruesome distinction of having undermined the discipline of the army with the Bolsheviks and many others'.[35] If, therefore, British propaganda cannot claim credit for the conditions that led to Germany's collapse in November 1918, it can be said to have exploited and accelerated the process of defeat. And the credit for this must go as much to MI7 at the War Office as it has previously gone to Crewe House.

3.4 Another Rabbit: Austria-Hungary

Far less questionable is Crewe House's record insofar as the campaign against Austria-Hungary was concerned. The Austro-Hungarian section of Crewe House was placed under the direction of Henry Wickham Steed, then foreign editor of *The Times* and a recognised authority on the Dual Monarchy. Steed was assisted by Dr R. W. Seton-Watson, the distinguished Central European scholar. Steed was the natural choice to run the Austro-Hungarian section. A member of Northcliffe's Fleet Street stable, he had served as diplomatic correspondent of *The Times* in Vienna between 1902 and 1913, where he had acquired a wide knowledge and considerable understanding of the Habsburg monarchy. With the outbreak of war in 1914, Steed began to throw his energies into the cause of national self-determination for the 'oppressed nationalities' of the Dual Monarchy. In collaboration with Seton-Watson, Steed was responsible for launching what was, perhaps, the single most important innovation that occurred in British propaganda in 1918, namely the campaign to undermine morale within Austria-Hungary.

In July 1917, Seton-Watson had drawn up a memorandum in which he argued that seven essential themes should be stressed in any campaign of Allied propaganda directed against the Dual Monarchy:

1 The artificial nature and dualistic structure of Habsburg government;

2 The absolutist policies followed by that government in certain parts of the empire before 1914;

3 The oppressive foreign policy of the Vienna cabinet, particularly in the Balkans;

4 The racist ideology and practices of the Magyar ruling oligarchy;

5 The wartime atrocities inflicted upon the smaller communities;

6 The growth of patriotic freedom movements;

7 The question of Bosnia-Herzegovinia, especially the desire of Yugoslavia to amalgamate with Serbia.

However, Seton-Watson also felt that until the British government was prepared to issue a clear statement of its wartime policy towards Austria-Hungary, and concluded that it would be 'far safer and wiser to refrain from all propaganda' that would raise 'false hopes and whose realisation there is no intention of assisting'.[36] In other words, clear policy declarations were an essential prerequisite to any successful propaganda campaign. Steed agreed and wrote that:

> The futility of British propaganda hitherto has been due to its divorce from policy. It is no good dumping down literature in various parts of the world explaining what noble people we are and how immense has been

our contribution to the war. That does not interest people. You have got to make up your mind where and how hard you can hit the enemy hardest and then to get to work and do it without talking about it. For that there must be a policy; and once it has been laid down and sanctioned it must be carried out by every available means.[37]

Such views raised serious problems. That British propaganda hitherto had been hampered by the absence of a coherent statement of British war aims was not the fault of those who were responsible for supervising the work. It was a government problem. Yet it was the propagandists in general, and the Foreign Office in particular, who were bearing the brunt of the mounting chorus of public criticism of the way in which British propaganda was being conducted. Moreover, that criticism was emanating chiefly from Fleet Street and people like Northcliffe and Steed. If responsibility for propaganda were transferred into their hands, the problem of policy would remain.

However, President Wilson led the way to a solution on 8 January 1918 when he proclaimed his 'Fourteen Points' calling, amongst other things, for a readjustment of Italy's frontiers on lines of nationality, autonomous development for the peoples of Austria-Hungary, and the restoration of Romania, Serbia and Montenegro on the principle of self-determination. Clear policy direction at last. The problem was that the weeks that followed witnessed the process by which the Foreign Office was forced to relinquish its three-and-a-half year grip on the direction of British overseas propaganda. The issue then for the Foreign Office was how to prevent the requirements of propaganda being allowed to dictate the course of British foreign policy.

This became apparent from the very moment Crewe House was established. Steed was quite clear in his own mind that Austria-Hungary should constitute the primary target for Britain's enemy propaganda. Following the Russian departure from the war, the situation in Germany seemed to offer less hope of an initial success – so vital to the government and to Crewe House – whereas in Austria-Hungary industrial unrest was mounting to fever pitch. Mass strikes broke out in January 1918 when the government was forced to retain seven combat divisions for internal security purposes.[38] The Austrian Germans and the Magyars, upon whom the German government chiefly relied for stability within the Habsburg Monarchy, had previously been neglected as targets of British propaganda. So too had the non-German and non-Austrian peoples of this vastly heterogeneous empire. Steed believed that if only the 'oppressed nationalities' could be convinced of Allied sincerity as evinced by Wilson and Lloyd George, together with the certainty of Allied victory, 'destabilisation' would increase thereby undermining the fighting power of the Habsburg armies. In short, he believed that the primary objective of Crewe House was to foster the disintegration of the Dual Monarchy through the promotion of internal disaffection and even insurrection among the subject races which, in turn, would weaken Germany's capacity to sustain the fight. The story of how the implications of this policy forced the Foreign Office to resist and obstruct

Crewe House has been told elsewhere.[39] The story of how those implications came home to roost during the Paris Peace negotiations, with all its consequences for European history between the wars, remains to be told.

Between May and October 1918, some 60 million copies of 643 different leaflets in 8 languages, and some 10 million copies of 112 different newspapers in four languages, were distributed in Austria-Hungary.[40] The material was distributed chiefly by aeroplane as the Austrians had foolishly failed to follow the German example in this respect. Having seen the British reaction, which was to stop aeroplane drops over the Western Front, they missed an opportunity to have the same happen on the Southern Front. By October, desertions were taking place on a massive scale and, according to one source, hundreds of thousands of Slav troops surrendered without a fight.[41] Campbell Stuart also boasted of the high rate of desertion as well as the considerable sabotage that took place behind the Austrian lines.[42] Many deserters were found to be carrying Allied propaganda material – despite heavy penalties for so doing if discovered by the Austrian authorities. Crewe House was convinced that its propaganda had been instrumental in helping to stem the Austrian offensive on the Piave in June 1918. Subsequent research has shown, for example, that on one single day of the Piave offensive, 800 leaflets were found on 350 prisoners of war.[43] There can be no doubt, therefore, that this campaign seriously undermined Germany's ability to continue the war. Just as the entry of a new ally in the form of the USA greatly increased Britain's chances of victory, the departure of Germany's ally was a serious blow to Berlin.

3.5 Damned with Faint Praise

On 29 August 1918 a German Army order warned that the British government had 'founded … a special ministry, "The Ministry for the Destruction of the German Confidence", at the head of which it has put the most thorough-going rascal of all the Entente, Lord Northcliffe.'[44] The 'Ministry' to which this order referred was, of course, Crewe House which was not a ministry at all. Yet although the appointment of both press barons provoked a political outcry at home, raising the spectre of Lloyd George's attempts to curb press freedom by making its owners part of the government, by the end of the war barely nine months later tributes to their contribution to war's victory gushed forth freely from the mouths of friends and former foes alike.

Immediate post-war revelations merely served to confirm the impression that Crewe House had performed miracles against the defeated Hun. *The Times History of the War* (vol. 21), written in 1920 while – significantly – Northcliffe was still in command at Printing House Square, provided the first brief but illuminating insight into the work.[45] The details were fleshed out as the inevitable wartime memoirs started to appear. Sir Edward Cook described his wartime censorship activities at the Press Bureau,[46] while Sir Douglas Brownrigg did the same for his period at the Admiralty.[47] But the most influential work relating to the Enemy Propaganda Department was undoubtedly the quasi-autobiographical account written by Lt. Col. Sir Campbell Stuart, Northcliffe's chief administrator and his Deputy Director, entitled *Secrets of Crewe House: The Story of a Famous Campaign*.[48] Because the British government did not commission an official history of this particular wartime activity and, indeed, authorised the destruction in 1920 of the vast majority of the documentation involved, Stuart's best-selling book has remained the most authoritative published account of the activities of Crewe House and remains the first port of call for all subsequent historical evaluations of its impact. However, a substantial less well-known document has somehow survived in the Public Record Office that also provides a significant and detailed account of the work of Crewe House. Although it is unsigned, it is almost certainly the product of Campbell Stuart's pen; it was he who had been appointed Acting Chairman of the British War Mission following Northcliffe's resignation in November 1918, with instructions to close down Crewe House by the end of the year. Originally intended for publication by HMSO as an official report, the document was submitted to the Cabinet in February 1919 as CAB 24/75, GT 6839 and constitutes the most complete official record known to have survived relating to the activities of Crewe House.

The reasons behind the decision not to publish this report are unknown. Nevertheless, close observation will reveal a striking similarity in style, format and content to Campbell Stuart's published account. Indeed it would appear that the report is in fact a much fuller and detailed version of *Secrets of Crewe House*, which could therefore be said to assume the distinction of being tantamount to an official history of the Enemy Propaganda Department. Even so, there are certain aspects to the story which are not explained by either account, aspects which help any revaluation of Crewe House and its alleged success.

Propaganda, by itself, could not defeat the enemy. Actions on the field of battle or in the political arena counted for much more. The continued reluctance of the British government to issue policy statements concerning the Yugoslavs beyond the initial, somewhat vague declarations about 'self-determination' meant that events were eventually to overtake Crewe House. As one historian has stated, the question of Yugoslavia 'was decided by the Southern Slav people themselves, before the British had come to any decision in their favour ... Yugoslavia, despite all the British sympathy for it, had never become a declared British war aim'.[49] Even so, Crewe House was able to push the British government further than it might otherwise have gone concerning its policy towards Austria-Hungary, thereby providing British propaganda with greater clarity of purpose than it had ever before possessed. Steed could thus justifiably claim credit for Crewe House, 'not for the actual break-up, but for very materially accelerating the break-up of Austria'.[50] Propaganda is as much about timing and the identification of the right target as it is anything else. And despite the hyperbole of his newspapers ('Good propaganda probably saved a year of war and ... at least a million lives', claimed the Northcliffe-owned *The Times*)[51] and that of his adversaries ('Ach, diese Propaganda von Northcliffe! Es war

Ko–loss–al!'),[52] Northcliffe himself was always more modest in assessing the overall impact of Crewe House. 'We have', he wrote, 'to some extent hastened the end'.[53]

One further legend is worthy of comment, namely the personal role of Northcliffe in the campaign. Despite his attempts to play down his contribution, Northcliffe's name has become synonymous with Crewe House's success. Chalmers Mitchell, seconded to Crewe House from MI7, believed that Northcliffe was not in fact the principal figure, merely a figurehead, and that Henry Wickham Steed was the real 'ideas man' and Campbell Stuart 'the organisation man'.[54] Northcliffe was certainly ill for long periods during 1918 and he was quite prepared to leave the day-to-day running of his department to his trusted deputies. Nevertheless, it was Northcliffe whom Lloyd George feared and it was Northcliffe's support for the ideas of his officials that enabled Crewe House to nudge British policy much further than many might otherwise have preferred into statements concerning the Central Powers, with profound consequences not only for central and southern Europe but also for Europe as a whole. After all, no matter how vague the concept of 'self-determination' for the oppressed peoples of European empires remained, the very notion raised the question of self-determination for the comparatively freer peoples of the victorious powers.

Notes and References

1   An earlier version of this chapter was first published as an introduction to a document entitled 'Report of the work of the department of propaganda in enemy countries' held in the Public Record Office (CAB 24/75). The introduction and document (which is 71 pages long) were published as a microfiche by the now defunct Oxford Historical Microforms in 1983.

2   M. Balfour, 'The demythologising of Crewe House', the opening chapter of *Propaganda in War, 1939–45* (Routledge & Kegan Paul, 1978).

3   General Erich von Ludendorff, *My War Memories, 1914–18* (2 vols, E. S. Mittler, 1919) I, p. 349.

4   See M. L. Saunders 'Wellington House and British propaganda in the First World War', *Historical Journal*, 18:2 (1975), pp. 119–46; K. Neilson, '"Joy Rides"? British intelligence and propaganda in Russia 1914–17', *Historical Journal*, 24:4 (1981), 885–906.

5   As defined by C. P. Robertson in a memorandum written on 12 September 1935, CAB 16/129, MIC (CC) 2.

6   Adolf Hitler, *Mein Kampf* (Hutchinson, 1969, with an introduction by D. C. Watt), ch. 6.

7   Northcliffe to J. T. Davies 5 December 1918, British Library, Northcliffe papers, vol. V.

8   'A History of the work of MI7, 1914–19', INF 4/1B.

9   See D. Hopkin 'Domestic censorship in the First World War', *Journal of Contemporary History*, 5:2 (1970), pp. 151–69.

10 The first Donald report is enclosed in his letter to Lloyd George, 9 January 1917 and the second 'Inquiry into the extent and efficiency of the propaganda', 4

December 1917 is contained in the same file. INF 4/4B, Arthur Spurgeon, a Treasury official, investigated Wellington House and his report dated 14 November 1917 is also in INF 4/4B.

11 J. M. McEwan, 'Northcliffe and Lloyd George at War, 1914–18' *Historical Journal*, 24:4 (1981), pp. 651–72.
12 A. J. P. Taylor, *Beaverbrook* (Hamilton, 1972), p. 137.
13 R. Pound and G. Harmsworth, *Northcliffe* (Cassell, 1959), ch. 22.
14 Memorandum by Northcliffe, 28 February 1918. The Times Archive, Northcliffe papers.
15 Philip M. Taylor 'The Foreign Office and British propaganda during the First World War', *Historical Journal*, 15:2 (1972), pp. 113–59.
16 H. Wickham Steed, *Through Thirty Years* (2 vols, Heinemann, 1924), vol. 2, pp. 185–6; Steed, *The Fifth Arm* (Constable, 1940), p. 14.
17 R. Warman, 'The erosion of Foreign Office influence in the making of foreign policy, 1916–18', *Historical Journal*, 15:2 (1972), pp. 113–59.
18 T. Wilson (ed.) *The Political Diaries of C. P. Scott, 1911–28* (Collins, 1970) entry for 4 March 1918.
19 There is no adequate history of the NWAC, but for domestic propaganda in general see Cate Haste' *Keep the Home Fires Burning* (Allen Lane, 1977).
20 Hansi (pseudonym for Jean Jacques Waltz) and H. Tonnelat, *A Travers les lignes ennemis* (Floury, 1922), p. 10.
21 J. M. Spaight, *Air Power and War Rights* (Longman, 1924), p. 124.
22 Pound and Harmsworth, *Northcliffe*, p. 468.
23 Sir George Cockerill, *What Fools We Were* (Hutchinson, 1944), pp. 62–3.
24 MI6 report, 'The legal aspect of the distribution of propaganda by aeroplane' 12 April 1918. PRO, WO 32/5140.
25 Ibid.
26 Memorandum by W. A. Robinson, 3 August 1918. PRO, CAB 24/58, GT5323.
27 Campbell Stuart, *Secrets of Crewe House* (Hodder & Stoughton, 1920), p. 60.
28 Balfour, *Propaganda in War*, p. 4.
29 Memorandum by Beaverbrook, 12 July 1918. CAB 24/57 GT 5100.
30 Cited in L. M. Salmon *The Newspaper and Authority* (Oxford University Press, 1923), p. 349.
31 Stuart, *Secrets of Crewe House*, p. 93.
32 See G. C. Bruntz, *Allied Propaganda and the Collapse of the German Empire in 1918* (Stanford University Press, 1938), pp. 209–16.
33 Prince Lichnowsky, *My London Mission* (George H. Doran, 1918).
34 Harry F. Young *Prince Lichnowsky and the War* (University of Georgia Press, 1977).
35 Ludendorff, *War Memories*, II, p. 641.
36 Cited in A. J. May *The Passing of the Habsburg Monarchy 1914–18* (2 vols, University of Pennsylvania Press, 1966), vol. 2, p. 605.
37 Steed, *Through Thirty Years*, II, p. 186.
38 Leo Valiani, *The End of Austria-Hungary* (Secker & Warburg, 1973).
39 M. L. Sanders and Philip M. Taylor, *British Propaganda during the First World War* (Macmillan, 1982).
40 Valiani, *End of Austria-Hungary*, p. 245.
41 E. V. Voska and Will Irwin, *Spy and Counter-Spy* (G. G. Harrap & Co., 1940), pp. 290ff.
42 Stuart, *Secrets of Crewe House*, p. 44.

43 Valiani, *End of Austria-Hungary*, p. 246.
44 General Order of the 18th Army, 29 August 1918. Cited in Ralph Lutz, *The Fall of the German Empire, 1914–18* (Stanford University Press, 1932), p. 162.
45 The author of this particular piece is unknown.
46 Sir E. T. Cook, *The Press in Wartime* (Macmillan, 1920).
47 D. Brownrigg, *Indiscretions of the Naval Censor* (Cassell, 1920).
48 Hodder & Stoughton, 1920.
49 W. Fest, *Peace and Partition* (St. Martin's Press, 1978), p. 244.
50 Minutes of the Crewe House Committee, 29 October 1918, British Library, Northcliffe papers, vol. X.
51 *The Times*, 31 October 1917.
52 Pound and Hamsworth, *Northcliffe*, p. 669.
53 Ibid, p. 670.
54 P. Chalmers Mitchell, *My Fill of Days* (Murray, 1937), p. 295.

The Dawning of 'Public Diplomacy' in the age of Mass Communications, 1919–39

It is now widely appreciated that the Versailles peace treaties that concluded the Great War provided merely a 'twenty-year armistice' containing the seeds of future conflict. In Britain, on the domestic front, anti-German sentiment had been so whipped up by atrocity propaganda that calls to 'Hang the Kaiser' and 'Make Germany Pay' were prominent in the first post-war general election in December 1918. For its part, the 'War Guilt Clause' inserted into the Treaty of Versailles caused massive resentment in Germany, where the public had also been subjected to four years of propaganda that the war had been someone else's fault. However if the Great War was to prove the 'war to end all wars', as virtually everyone hoped it would be, then wartime recriminations would need to be quickly forgotten – not least so that Britain and Germany could resume their formerly lucrative trade links. In 1914 Britain and Germany had been each other's best customers. Moreover, post-war German economic recovery was in Britain's interests not least because of the need for Germany to pay its reparations to the victors – and the victors their war debts to the United States. A great deal of what might be termed psychological disarmament was required if the world was to enter a new and lasting era of peace. This was asking a great deal in light of the wartime climate of hatred – especially in France where much of the war had been fought.

The wartime propaganda experience had further consequences that were also to prove damaging to future peace. We have already seen how Hitler and others manipulated the alleged role of British propaganda to serve their own political purposes in the aftermath of the war. The role played by Crewe House in the creation of new states in Central and Eastern Europe – Poland, Austria, Czechoslovakia, Romania, Bulgaria – has evaded mainstream historical analysis. When President Wilson announced his Fourteen Points, he was making the most detailed statement of war aims of any allied leader to date. The Points nonetheless remained somewhat generalised, and when the subject nationalities pressed for more details, they were not exactly forthcoming. Although those somewhat general promises about national self-determination had provided wartime Allied propagandists, especially at Crewe House, with their best opportunities to date to offer real incentives to the 'oppressed nationalities', there was a longer-term price to be paid. This was because, in the process, the propagandists often made promises about the post-war settlement that were yet to be agreed in policy terms by the Allied governments.

This broke one of the fundamental tenets of effective propaganda: that policy and propaganda should be conducted hand in hand. Lord Northcliffe had been quite willing to force the government's hand with propaganda promises about polices that had yet to be decided in terms other than general statements of principle, and these particular chickens came home to roost at the Paris Peace Conference and in the years that followed. Slavs, Poles, Czechs and others all turned up in Paris demanding that those promises now be fulfilled, in other words that wartime propaganda should be translated into post-war policy. As a result, a series of newly created independent European nation states were born out of the remnants of the defeated Central Power empires in accordance with the principle of self-determination expounded by President Wilson. The problem was that these new states tended to be formed along ethnographic rather than sound strategic or economic lines. The rhetoric of wartime was hardly a sound basis on which to rebuild a peaceful Europe.

The Italians in particular were furious. They had entered the war on the Allied side in 1915 under the secret Treaty of London in return for the promise of post-war territorial gains in south-eastern Europe that were now being denied them because of self-determination for the Yugoslavs. They left Paris bitter and disillusioned, seized Fiume (Trieste) in a clash with the newly created Yugoslavia and, in a wave of national euphoria, began the swing to the right that saw Mussolini appointed as Prime Minister in 1922.

Since the October Revolution of 1917, the Bolsheviks had washed their hands of the 'imperialist' war, consolidated their political position with the formation of the Soviet Union, and promptly declared ideological warfare against the victorious powers that now sought to support their opponents in the Russian Civil War. Once that challenge had been successfully fought off, Moscow recognised that political support often lay in the minds of the masses, and began to sell the revolution to the people by using the new mass media of film and radio which required no levels of literacy to understand. Nor was this process to be confined to the Soviet Union and, since radio crossed borders without difficulty, the most powerful transmitter in the world was built by Radio Moscow in the 1920s to spread the word far and wide. The lessons were not lost on the Nazis once they came to power in Germany in 1933, and Hitler saw the role of radio as a means of keeping in touch with those Germans forcefully separated from the Reich by the terms of the Versailles treaty. In the climate of a mounting war of ideologies, international radio became a frontline weapon, and its use a far cry from the BBC's motto that 'Nation Shall Speak Peace Unto Nation'.

But international radio broadcasting was symptomatic of increased contact between countries and their peoples. The very fact that governments decided to embark upon such activity was a reflection of a 'shrinking world'. So also was increased access to foreign news, whether in national newspapers that were supplied by the international news agencies, or indeed by cinema newsreels that brought once-distant places into the local 'picture palaces' that were springing up everywhere. The European film industries, devastated by the Great

War, found themselves competing with the ever-growing power of 'Hollywood' films – which themselves became excellent advertisements for the American 'way of life' and the values that were cherished in the USA, including individualism, free market enterprise and the right to progress.

We have also seen how revelations about wartime propaganda served to alienate the United States, especially following the decision of the United States Senate not to ratify the Treaty of Versailles with Germany. Later, during the 1930s, when American support might have strengthened the hand of the European democracies in their dealings with the dictatorships, the use of propaganda as a means of gaining that support was largely denied the very countries who had pioneered its use. How the British re-entered the field in the face of the mounting totalitarian challenge is told in the subsequent chapters.

There was a further, more tragic consequence of the Great War propaganda experiment. The discrediting of wartime propaganda, and the revelations that few, if any, of the atrocity stories had been true, brought about a general disinclination on the part of the public in the 1930s and 1940s to believe real atrocity stories when they began to emerge from Nazi Germany. Corpse Conversion factories were the very stuff of Great War atrocity propaganda that came to be completely discredited after the war. The distortions of the First World War thus served to obscure the tragic realities of the Second.

Perhaps just as significant was the recognition between the wars that, thanks to communications technology, the conduct of inter-state relations was changed forever. Increasing economic, political and cultural interdependence meant that it was no longer possible for nations to stand aloof from the rest of the world. Coming to terms with this fact of life was frequently painful for a country such as Britain whose past Imperial achievement had spoken for itself. Seemingly at the height of its power, Britain was in fact in a process of relative and absolute decline. This, in turn, made the process of self-advertisement all the more essential if Britain's worldwide interests were to be protected from new types of dictatorial regimes which despised democratic values, but which readily embraced new communications technologies to achieve their objectives.

4

The Projection of Britain Between the Wars[1]

When the war ended, the British wanted to be rid not only of their propaganda machinery, but also of their reputation for how good at propaganda they were. But times had changed. Propaganda had become a proven weapon of war, and many believed that it could have valuable peacetime applications as well. While the British became a little precious about their wartime reputation, others less democratically inclined were far more imaginative. Before long, the manipulation of mass opinion through the new communications technologies became a characteristic of the Bolshevik regime in Russia, the new Fascist regime in Italy, and indeed of regimes of all different political persuasions throughout the world. Accordingly, barely a decade after the Great War, one Foreign Office official was found lamenting that propaganda was 'a good word gone wrong – debauched by the late Lord Northcliffe' and he wished it could be banished from the diplomatic vocabulary.[2] The author of this particular sentiment was Angus Fletcher. As Director of the British Library of Information at New York, Britain's only surviving official 'information service' in the USA, Fletcher was naturally keen to distance his work from wartime associations. What other nations were doing may have been 'propaganda', but the British told the truth.

This growing association of 'propaganda' with falsehood and the manipulation of opinion was why many British officials continued to dislike any form of publicity activity as a matter of principle. Nor did post-war enquiries into alleged German wartime atrocities help when they failed to come up with incontrovertible evidence that any such atrocities had taken place. 'Propaganda' was becoming well and truly discredited as a legitimate activity for the fair and decent minded, and a far cry from its pre-war definition as a process for the cultivation of ideas and beliefs. The value-neutral process of persuasion had become heavily loaded with pejorative connotations. Sir Horace Wilson, for example, writing in 1938, expressed the view that:

> Having been old fashioned for many years, I find myself unable to show enthusiasm for propaganda by this country and I still cannot bring myself to believe that it is a good substitute for calmly getting on with the business of Government, including a rational foreign policy.[3]

Yet, by 1938, the view that actions speak louder than words was itself becoming old-fashioned. Many officials were becoming increasingly alarmed at the way foreign governments had taken up in peacetime where the British had left off in 1918, and one warned that 'a sort of armament race in propaganda is developing, to which it is no easier to see finality than the armament race itself'.[4] At the Treasury, another official even suggested that:

> Armaments may be infinitely more expensive than propaganda but they, at least, have the virtue of being dumb and do not cause the same ill-will. From the point of view of appeasement, the propaganda race seems to me the more serious danger.[5]

Apart from the debatable assumption that words can in fact speak louder than even silent guns, the legacy of the past continued to haunt the propaganda needs of Britain's present and, to some extent, its likely future.

This is the context for how British foreign policy made the transformation from secret to public diplomacy in the information age. The transformation can be examined in three stages. First, it is important to recognise at the outset that although British propaganda was drastically reduced on the return of peace in 1918, it nonetheless did not cease entirely, even though it was to remain a constant victim of financial retrenchment and prejudice throughout the 1920s. Second, it was the Foreign Office that led that body of opinion which maintained that the virtual amputation of the 'fifth arm of defence' (as Steed called it)[6] had been a disastrous and short-sighted mistake, and argued that Britain must take positive steps to make herself more widely known and understood abroad. The most articulate exponent of this concept was Sir Stephen Tallents, who first coined the phrase 'the Projection of England' in an influential pamphlet published under that title in 1932.[7] Third, it is necessary to examine how what began as the projection of Britain gave way to a new phase of 'psychological rearmament' with the growing conviction that Britain might soon find itself involved in another major war.

4.1 Forfeiting the Initiative

The very idea of another major war seemed inconceivable in 1918. Propaganda, it was believed, had helped the British and their allies to victory, emerging in the process as an integrated wartime activity of government. Whereas the exact contribution made by British propaganda towards the Allied victory is ultimately impossible to measure, its role was nonetheless believed at the time to have been such that its use in any future war seemed guaranteed. Many agreed with Christopher Addison that 'this kind of thing is repugnant to the British spirit, but surely it is a weapon we ought to use in a struggle such as this'.[8] Had not prominent enemy personalities, including Ludendorff and later, of course, Hitler, confirmed this?[9] But with the war now over, grave reservations remained about the value of propaganda as an acceptable instrument of normal peacetime diplomacy.

At the end of the war, the automatic reaction of many British politicians and officials was to dismantle altogether the wartime propaganda machinery. This was not, however, the inclination of those with the most direct experience of it. In October 1918, for example, Lord Beaverbrook devised a scheme whereby his ministry would carry on working at least until after a peace treaty with Germany had been signed. 'The policy of the British Government at the Peace Conference will have to be explained to the world day by day if the solidarity of Allied opinion is to be maintained', he wrote. The aims and content of British propaganda would obviously have to be different, but there was a 'golden opportunity' to secure 'public support in all foreign countries for the view of the Imperial Government and to give the reason why the Imperial Government is justified in adopting a certain attitude towards the problems before the Conference'.[10]

Similar proposals were formulated at Crewe House, where Sir Campbell Stuart argued that the maintenance of Britain's post-war prestige 'demanded that our position in regard to the peace should be explained and justified by the widespread dissemination of news and views'.[11] Steed suggested that Crewe House should be converted into an 'agency of enlightenment on both sides'.[12] Northcliffe, not untypically, envisaged even grander plans for the re-education of the German people, converting Crewe House into an instrument for 'enabling the German people gradually to see why Germany had lost the war, and to understand the force of the moral ideals which had ranged practically the whole world against her'.[13]

These various schemes came to nothing. Relations between Northcliffe and Lloyd George, always erratic, were fast deteriorating and the question of the future role of propaganda became submerged beneath more immediate problems.[14] Lloyd George, fearful of the additional influence which Northcliffe might gain, thought his proposal 'dangerous in the extreme' and, he wrote, 'I curtly told him to go to Hades'.[15] Given the extensive re-educational propaganda used by the Allies at the end of the Second World War, Northcliffe's ideas were – not for the first time – way ahead of their time.[16] One can thus only speculate as to whether they might have changed the course of history. As it turned out, Northcliffe resigned on 12 November 1918, the day after the Armistice was signed. On the following day, the Cabinet hurriedly dismissed Beaverbrook's scheme,[17] although the Minister of Information had already effectively abandoned his plan by resigning a fortnight earlier. The 'golden opportunity' of which he had written was gone.

John Buchan was given the task of liquidating the wartime organisation. Most of the wartime machinery was promptly dismantled and responsibility for any remaining work, about which Buchan was either uncertain or which he considered it desirable to maintain, was transferred back into the hands of the Foreign Office, complete with staff and duties.[18] The Ministry of Information and Crewe House were officially closed down on 31 December 1918, but dismantlement took less time than originally anticipated, and the Foreign Office did, in fact, assume responsibility some weeks earlier.[19]

During the winter of 1918–19, the Foreign Office considered what to do with these inherited remnants. A 'Propaganda Department' had already been envisaged in at least one of its post-war reconstruction schemes.[20] Although the precise details of his decision remain vague, Foreign Secretary Balfour decided in December 1918 to reconstruct a smaller version of the Foreign Office News Department in order to carry on such work as was considered desirable to maintain in peacetime.[21] It was said that the objective was to retain 'a skeleton organisation at home and abroad which can be clothed with flesh and blood at short notice in case of need'.[22]

This decision to retain a department for the supervision of publicity and propaganda overseas within the overall diplomatic apparatus nonetheless marked a significant departure from established pre-war tradition. Opinions within the Foreign Office concerning the desirability of continuing such work, however, varied greatly. Lord Robert Cecil, despite his previous involvement in wartime propaganda, said that he now 'disliked the idea of propaganda in foreign countries on general principles, apart from commercial propaganda which was the real line to follow'.[23] On the other hand, the advocates of continuation, particularly former wartime propagandists, were vociferous in their support. George Beak, who as Consul General in Zurich had played a key role in distributing wartime material into Germany through neutral Switzerland, presented a particularly strong case. Beak argued that 'because the masses will now demand to know much more than previously of what is going on ... it would probably not only be futile but dangerous to attempt to keep knowledge from them'. 'The great thing', he continued, 'is to protect them from half-truths by letting them know as much as possible ... [and] it is, therefore, of the highest importance that only accurate news should get abroad'.[24] Furthermore, he wrote:

> It need hardly be said ... that the spirit of British propaganda would differ wholly and entirely from the German, in that it would not be aggressive in character. Germany's aim was to secure an Empire and dominate Europe; our aim is, presumably, to preserve and develop what we already have. The object of our propaganda, therefore, would be chiefly to make our institutions, mode of Government, arts and sciences, known and understood.[25]

S. A. Guest, Northcliffe's forerunner in psychological warfare activities, held similar views. He believed that propaganda was not merely desirable in the post-war world, but essential. His argument was that the build-up to war in 1914 demonstrated that diplomacy, 'by itself, is not enough for the maintenance of satisfactory international relations', and that foresight was needed 'to provide something further than diplomacy':

> Now that nations are taking a much larger share than hitherto in their own government, and international relations are being influenced by interests other than those of dynasties, we should be living in a Fools' Paradise if we were to expect that we should be able to maintain international equilibrium by means of a service which was originally designed to work under conditions which no longer exist.

Realistically, he continued:

> Commercial, financial, labour organisations and the Press, to which the
> officially accredited diplomat, as such, cannot obtain direct access may, at
> any given moment, exercise a far more powerful influence on international
> politics than that which can be exerted by any Foreign Office, and unless
> we have means of directly observing and affecting these and other agencies,
> we shall not be in a position either to obtain knowledge of the drift of
> affairs, or to intervene in time to forestall injurious tendencies. For this
> purpose we require a permanent organisation for Political Intelligence and
> 'Propaganda'.[26]

Because it was quickly apparent that the return of peace had been accompanied
by an increase in the use of propaganda by foreign governments to further their
national interests, often at the expense of British prestige, Guest believed that
it had become essential for the British Government to counter the false and
malevolent claims of others. 'It would be the most puerile folly on our part',
he wrote:

> To expect that henceforth a true version as to the policy, either internal
> or external, or the resources of the British Empire, will permeate every-
> where and will be maintained intact, and [that] erroneous and dangerous
> misconceptions will be obviated, without continuous effort on our part.[27]

The views of Guest and Beak reflected a growing body of opinion that regarded
publicity and propaganda as a necessary response to the new demands of the
twentieth century. Besides, they argued, it might even play a genuinely constructive role in promoting international understanding.

These ideas were considered at a departmental conference held on 20 March
1919. Lord Curzon, Acting Foreign Secretary in Balfour's absence, found it
necessary to lay down two fundamental premises in order to avoid further
dispute, namely '(1) that propaganda should continue, and (2) that it should
continue strictly in connection with, or under the control of, the Foreign
Office'.[28] Curzon was determined to ensure that any propaganda conducted
abroad would go hand in hand with British foreign policy, which – as we have
seen – had not always been the case following the transference of responsibility
for the work into the hands of Beaverbrook and Northcliffe early in 1918.
Accordingly, a circular despatch was transmitted to all diplomatic missions,
with the notable exception of the Embassy in Washington,[29] informing them
that 'British propaganda in Foreign Countries shall, in future, be regarded as
part of the regular work'. These instructions, signed by Curzon, ended with
the following note:

> I do not doubt that, from the experience of the past four years, you will
> have learned what forms of propaganda to encourage and what to avoid ...
> British interests would be ill-served by a blatant publicity of the kind
> associated with German agents abroad, official and unofficial, before and

during the war. On the other hand, a complete and contemptuous silence, however gratifying to our self-respect, is no longer a profitable policy in times when advertisement – whether of past achievement or future aims – is, perhaps unfortunately, almost a universal practice of nations as of individuals.[30]

Although the Foreign Office disclaimed 'all intention of conducting propaganda of the "Corpse Factory" type',[31] the Treasury didn't like what was being proposed. It was to be the start of an enduring difference of opinion. While acknowledging that it was not 'at the present moment practicable to terminate altogether the [remaining] system of propaganda' the Treasury nonetheless expected the Foreign Office 'to discontinue any type of propaganda as soon as experience shows that it is not productive of valuable results'.[32] Moreover, cultural propaganda was completely forbidden, while the Treasury took note of the policy of 'gradually converting British propaganda from a purely political aspect to largely commercial lines and assume[d] that, as a corollary, the work [would] pass to a great extent to the Department of Overseas Trade'.[33]

The general reluctance of the Treasury to authorise large-scale expenditure on propaganda stemmed, it was claimed, from an inability to justify or defend continuation in peacetime given the widespread suspicion concerning the use of government propaganda. This opposition had come to a head in 1918 when the Ministry of Information had been discussed in Parliament. From a political point of view, the ministry had been disliked because of its accountability to the Prime Minister, and not to Parliament or the Treasury. Indeed, given the nature of the Lloyd George government and of the premier's notorious flirtations with the publicity world, it was not beyond the imagination of many contemporaries to envisage the use of official propaganda by an unscrupulous government as a means of sustaining political power. This fear had largely motivated Austen Chamberlain's attack on the appointments of Beaverbrook and Northcliffe in February 1918.[34] The Ministry of Information had even been accused of putting out propaganda based on policy that had not previously been discussed in Parliament.[35] As we have seen, Crewe House had certainly been pushing in this direction. Hence, 'the manner of its creation gave the appearance of an extra-parliamentary power, and the fear that its propaganda activities might survive the war, had obviously combined to inspire a mood of deep suspicion'.[36] All propaganda, irrespective of the form it took, or the differences between its political, cultural or, to a lesser degree, economic variations, was viewed with distaste as an 'un-English' wartime expedient associated with secrecy, subversion and the activities of unscrupulous governments. As one observer wrote:

That the State should advertise itself was an idea which occurred to few before the war and which, had it been brought before the notice of the general public, would have seemed to them repellent; advertisement, apart from commercial advertisement, which through lapse of time had acquired respectability, was thought to be the work of the vulgarian: it was also thought useless.[37]

If propaganda was to continue at all, then, it was natural for the Treasury to express a preference for commercial propaganda, given its vocation and the economic preoccupation which characterised most contemporary political thought. It was far more acceptable to undertake, in effect, an advertising campaign on behalf of British trade and commerce than an uncharacteristic form of national self-glorification. A lasting peace, safeguarded by the League of Nations, would remain as a more than adequate testimony to the merits and achievements of British ideals and civilisation.

Whereas S. A. Guest had considered that it would be folly to expect the League of Nations to function successfully in an atmosphere which had not first been cleansed of all mutual suspicion by propaganda serving as an instrument of international understanding, the prevailing opinion was that international harmony would best be achieved in the halls of Geneva. In other words, the League, not propaganda, was a more acceptable method of securing international understanding and mutual respect. The result was that British overseas propaganda was severely reduced, and the reconstructed News Department was forced to operate under the constant threat of cuts. However, this was not simply a question of money, as undoubtedly the nature of the Foreign Office's work was frequently misunderstood. As one official explained:

> In reference to the work being done, the word 'propaganda' is a misnomer and the aim which we have put before us is rather that of correcting misapprehensions which arise abroad either through ignorance or as a result of the aggressive propaganda of other nations.[38]

Despite such assurances, suspicion remained. In the quest for normalcy, the carnage of the war with all its related nightmares haunted the national consciousness. Britain disarmed in the weapon of words, as it did in other more conventional forms of armaments. Yet the consequence of this was that the British case went largely unstated and was thus left open to deliberate misinterpretation by others less anxious about the dignity of courting public opinion.

Although the Foreign Office laboured hard to correct such false impressions as were created by state-subsidised foreign agencies, it had neither the financial resources nor the staff necessary for continuous effort. On receiving, for example, a request from Lord Allenby for permission to inaugurate British propaganda in Egypt, the News Department replied that it was unable to support the scheme on financial grounds, one of its officials reflecting that 'we shall have to rely on successful administration for propaganda in Egypt'.[39] That this was applicable to most areas of the world was a sorry reflection on the limited scope of Britain's overseas propaganda in the immediate post-war years.

Nevertheless, the fact remains that there was a department, however strait-jacketed, specifically concerned with information and propaganda, and that diplomats serving abroad, not just the press attachés, were instructed to regard propaganda as part of their normal duties. The wartime experiment had created not only an awareness of the power of propaganda, but also an appreciation, at least in the circles which had experience of it, of the role that it could play in the pursuit of national interests. The basic ground rules of British propaganda, such as the importance of news content, its dependence on clear policy and the effectiveness of the non-retaliatory approach, were thus appreciated long before they were really put to the test in the years that followed.

4.2 Re-entering the Field

The arguments and ideals that had led to the reduction of propaganda work in 1918–19 were soon to be exposed as illusory. If, on the return of peace, it was widely believed that British overseas propaganda was unnecessary, the subsequent growth in its use by rival governments made a reappraisal inevitable. Ironically, former wartime allies like France, Russia and Italy utilised the lessons of the British wartime experience, and combined them with technological advancements in such areas as broadcasting and the cinema, in order to mould propaganda into a powerful weapon of ideological and political expansion. Britain meanwhile remained a helpless and disarmed bystander.

The area in which British interests appeared to be suffering most was commerce. The challenge to Britain's domination of world markets, begun in earnest during the final decades of the nineteenth century, intensified with the search for post-war economic recovery. The Foreign Office argued that not only was Britain's somewhat limited commercial propaganda insufficient to counter the large-scale programmes of rivals, but also that commercial and cultural propaganda were mutually complementary. As foreign governments were proving at Britain's expense, the one was dependent for its success upon the other. Trade no longer followed merely the flag but now also followed the teaching of the English language, the schoolteacher and the textbook. This was a long-term strategy which could be designed to create an atmosphere of mutual respect and understanding that would in turn benefit not only Britain's commercial interests and prosperity, but would also serve to produce a background favourable to the peaceful conduct of diplomatic relations. To a more critical Treasury, however, such innovative ideas appeared to be an expensive substitute for good government and healthy competition. Even the short-term visible returns promised by commercial propaganda alone proved insufficient to prompt, say, greater official involvement in international exhibitions.[40] Rather, supreme acts of faith, such as the insertion of clauses relating to propaganda in the Anglo-Russian Trade Agreements of 1921 and 1930,[41] were indicative of general British reluctance to involve themselves in propaganda to any significant extent.

As a consequence, within a matter of years, both the Foreign Office and the Department of Overseas Trade were becoming increasingly alarmed at the frequency of disquieting reports received from overseas missions which generally made it clear that British interests and prestige were suffering from a lack of adequate explanation and representation abroad. Foreign propaganda was increasingly assuming an anti-British flavour and the limited scale of Britain's counteractivities was proving wholly inadequate. The battle for influence in 'neutral' countries, ably fought by Wellington House during the First World War, was gradually being lost in peacetime. Sir Roderick Jones, himself a former Director of Neutral Propaganda during the war, warned that Reuters, of which he was Managing Director, was finding it increasingly difficult to compete with the state-subsidised continental news agencies, with the result that British news was not gaining its fair share of distribution abroad.[42] Reinforced by such decisive evidence as that provided by the Report of the British Economic Mission to South America in 1929, which emphasised the interdependence of cultural and commercial propaganda,[43] the Foreign Office redoubled its efforts. In 1930 Labour Foreign Secretary Arthur Henderson succeeded in persuading the Treasury to reverse its embargo of 1919 preventing the conduct of cultural propaganda,[44] thus beginning the process which finally led to the creation of the British Council in 1934.[45]

Meanwhile, it was to the newly established Travel and Industrial Development Association of Great Britain and Northern Ireland, founded in December 1928, that the Department of Overseas Trade looked for help in rectifying the deficiencies in commercial propaganda. This body, which evolved from the privately sponsored 'Come to Britain Movement', was the initiative of several influential businessmen who managed to secure a small government grant to aid their efforts. Lord Derby, President of the Association, conceived a dual role for its work namely, 'the promotion of international understanding through personal contacts and – let us be honest about it – business'.[46] However, it was the former aim which attracted Derby's, and indeed the Government's, interest. In a speech that epitomised the mood of the early pioneers of national projection, Derby explained:

> We believe that people who visit these islands and see John Bull at home will discover that he is really a good natured person of simple tastes, who never harbours malice and only wishes to be friends with all the world. Having discovered this they will be slow to believe that John Bull is actuated by base motives such as are imputed to him, sometimes by his enemies, and sometimes through ignorance of his character. Similarly, it cannot but be good for John Bull at home to learn that there may be another point of view than his own, and that the stranger is a fellow much like himself. If at the same time the country is benefited by the expenditure of our visitors – well John Bull is a practical person and business is business.[47]

The Travel Association operated on two different, albeit related, levels. The first may be described as tourist information and publicity – providing details and advice concerning the various beauty spots and holiday resorts in the British Isles. Reflecting the growth in the tourist industry that piggybacked the development of commercial airlines, it was claimed that travel 'is world-wide, a great common idea'.[48] By utilising publicity to promote the British tourist industry, the Travel Association aimed to capture a proportion of the world's tourist market and thereby 'exert what may be called a human tidal pull towards these shores'.[49]

On the second level was the political and international aspect of its work. As Lord Derby pointed out, the Association's publicity was not merely confined to tourist promotion, 'but has set out to develop through travel a greater knowledge of, and interest in, British culture and British goods, thus bringing about, we are confident, an increase in our export trade, visible as well as invisible'.[50] It was further argued that:

> The visitor who comes over here, reads our newspapers, shares our recreations, talks with our people and makes friends, with many of whom he keeps in touch afterwards – such a person recognises the common interests of nations ... In fact, he becomes an ambassador for this country.[51]

Given that only the comparatively well off could enjoy holidays like this, and really only those who were educated enough to speak English, we are still looking at an elite target audience. Having said that, the Travel Association's publicity greatly benefited from some of the techniques of wider persuasion being pioneered by the Empire Marketing Board that was created in 1926, especially in the use of posters, pamphlets and, of course, documentary films.

The formation of the Travel Association was significant for three reasons. In the first place, it provided the first real recognition in peacetime of the need to conduct a national, permanently active publicity campaign abroad in an attempt to make Britain more widely known and understood. Second, it was recognition of the fact 'that the trade and commerce of any nation are enormously helped if potential customers can be persuaded to see and get to know that nation'.[52] Third, and perhaps more significantly, it provided testimony to the growing realisation that public opinion was becoming a determinant factor in the making of foreign policy. As one official wrote: 'the era when it was possible either to lead opinion in foreign politics by mere authority or tradition, or to ignore it from Olympian heights, has long since vanished'.[53] It was because these factors were beginning to infiltrate influential circles, both official and in the private sector, that support for more attention being given to national publicity was increasing.

By 1930, therefore, a start had been made on the projection of Britain abroad, albeit in a limited way. Both the Travel Association and, following a decision of the Imperial Conference that year, the Empire Marketing Board recognised the value of overseas propaganda as an instrument for promoting national interests and international goodwill. The Foreign Office embarked upon a small programme of cultural propaganda, beginning in Latin America.[54] Had it not been for the interruption of the economic crisis of the early 1930s, precipitated by the Wall Street Crash, progress may have been more dramatic. All too often at times of financial crisis, marketing and advertising budgets are among the first to be cut. The Empire Marketing Board was closed in 1933. Stephen Tallents, the Board's Secretary, was determined that recent advancements in the acceptance of the principle of national marketing should not suffer a similar fate.

Tallents was an unusual man with an unusual career, a curious blend of diplomacy and publicity. He is undoubtedly one of the most important figures in the development of British involvement in propaganda. His continuing influence in the field was to be reflected by his later appointments as Public Relations Officer at the GPO in 1933, and at the BBC in 1935, a post which he held simultaneously with that of Director-General Designate of the embryonic Ministry of Information.

In 1932, he set out his views concerning the importance of what he termed 'the Projection of England'. Essentially, his argument was that Britain no longer enjoyed that position of supremacy which had enabled it to remain aloof from world opinion for long periods in the past. Its worldwide responsibilities, as a European partner and as head of a great Empire, but also as a trading power with global interests, made it essential for it to project by all means available an accurate and representative picture of itself to the peoples of other countries. 'No civilised country', he wrote, 'can today afford either to neglect the projection of its national personality, or to resign its projection to others'.[55] Britain, he argued, must make a constructive effort to make herself more widely known and understood because 'peace itself may at any time depend on a clear understanding abroad of her actions and motives'.[56] The widespread currency of the English language provided an enormous advantage for such a task, language being the natural vehicle for the communication of ideas, as the work of such private organisations as the Pilgrims, the English Speaking Union and the All Peoples Association had clearly demonstrated. Yet Tallents wanted to see the creation, as he put it, 'in the borderland which lies between Government and private enterprise, [of] a school of national projection'[57] which would maintain close contact with the various existing publicity bodies and with the Press, the BBC, the news agencies and the film industry. Indeed, here was the basic outline of an organisation which resembled in almost too many ways to be mere coincidence that established in late 1934 under auspices of the Foreign Office: the British Council.

4.3 The British Council

The decision to establish an organisation specifically designed to conduct cultural propaganda injected a new dimension into the traditional conduct of British foreign policy – that of cultural diplomacy. The man chiefly responsible for converting the ideas of Tallents into reality was Reginald Leeper, who was to become the controversial head of the Foreign Office News Department in 1935. Following the demise of the Empire Marketing Board in 1933, Leeper devoted his considerable energy and imagination to the question of establishing an organisation under Foreign Office control to promote and co-ordinate Britain's long-term cultural relations, based on the French model of the Alliance Française. He was greatly aided in this task by Sir Robert Vansittart, permanent under-secretary of state for Foreign Affairs since 1930, who had, on his appointment, begun to take an active interest in the project.[58] Both men were galvanised further by a deep suspicion of the course of German events since Hitler's rise to power in 1933.

An indication of the extent to which the necessity for propaganda was coming to be admitted openly was revealed in *The Times*, which reassured its readers in 1935:

> Those who dislike publicity may dismiss the idea [of cultural diplomacy] on the plea that it is nothing but veiled propaganda, but none need fight shy of the word 'propaganda' so long as the work associated with it is openly performed and the principles spread are honestly held and are not insinuated into the minds of readers of listeners, but are provided as a contribution to thought and experience for those who wish to learn them.[59]

However, beneath such fine words and the public emphasis on the educational and cultural aspects of the work were the more practical as well as the more immediately political considerations. As Sir Samuel Hoare, the then Foreign Secretary, recognised:

> The commercial arguments in favour of intensifying the work of British cultural propaganda are no less strong than the political arguments. In all, the danger of German cultural and commercial penetration, which may be expected to increase as the power and wealth of Germany revive, makes it particularly desirable for British cultural propaganda to secure as firm a hold as possible on the minds and interests of the population, and particularly on the younger generation, before the counter-attraction becomes too strong.[60]

The British Council was therefore created in 1934–35 and developed as a democratic response to the new and urgent problems caused by the emergence of the totalitarian state in Europe. It was felt that to meet these problems a new outlook was required. The totalitarian use of propaganda, powerfully and deliberately directed against British interests abroad, forced Britain onto the defensive by offering foreign audiences an alternative ideology. Hence the Council's projection of British democratic institutions and indeed all that was considered best in the British way of life.

In 1936, Lord William Tyrrell, the British Council's first chairman, underlined an appeal for more funds with a significant new line of argument. He said:

> We have much to learn from others, but we also have much to teach them. If we do not do the teaching ourselves, we shall be misunderstood and misinterpreted. If you will regard us as a body able and willing to do this educational work abroad, may I ask you also to regard us as people who are assisting practically in our national defence. Modern defence consists not only in arms but in removing misunderstanding.[61]

Tyrrell was in an authoritative position to make such claims. Serving as Sir Edward Grey's Private Secretary before the First World War, he had been responsible for receiving journalists who called at the Foreign Office. His experience in this work was put to good use on the return of peace when he was made the first peacetime head of the News Department. In 1925, he succeeded Sir Eyre Crowe as permanent under-secretary and continued his support for propaganda work until becoming Ambassador in Paris in 1928. This appointment provided him with the opportunity of studying at first hand French democratic propaganda, always more extensive than Britain's, experience of which was put to good use on his retirement when he not only became Chairman of the British Council but also President of the British Board of Film Censors.

4.4 Moral Rearmament

The political importance of 'the projection of Britain' gained in significance with the growing conviction from 1935 onwards that Britain might have to face another war in the near future, and one in which, it was believed, morale, both at home and abroad, would play a decisive role. It was a conviction that assumed a greater sense of urgency with the announcement of German rearmament in March 1935 and the estrangement of Italy following the Abyssinian crisis in the year that followed. As Vansittart recognised, somewhat patronisingly, 'in the business, strict business, of "making eyes at" lesser but serviceable people, we have now very keen and efficient rivals who are already getting the better of us.'[62] Or, as one influential Foreign Office memorandum warned in February 1937:

> It is particularly important to spend now, before the danger has grown to unmanageable proportions, and we must row against the tide. It is no exaggeration to say that unless we are prepared to show our concern for the world to which modern development is binding us continually closer, we shall, when the need of them arises, find our present and potential friends the unwilling but helpless allies of those who have shown their intention of making every encroachment on our power that we can be forced, or deluded, into allowing.[63]

The Foreign Office was fully aware that, despite the start made in the long-term task of influencing perceptions, world events were moving at such a pace that there remained an urgent need to rectify the immediate deficiencies that hampered the short-term dissemination of British news and views. 'While visibility increases', wrote Leeper, 'vision lags behind'.[64]

If Britain's actions and policies were to be understood, they had first to become known. It was towards this goal that Leeper expanded the British Official News Service in 1935[65] and, in 1937, he negotiated an arrangement whereby the diplomatic correspondent of *The Times* enjoyed special privileges from the News Department.[66] The Foreign Office still saw opinion-makers as its initial target. But the new mass communications technologies provided opportunities to address public opinion more directly. When Leeper therefore next turned his attention to the question of broadcasting news in foreign languages, he found a sympathetic ally in Sir John Reith, the Director-General of the BBC, who had long been aware of the value of overseas transmissions, even before the inauguration of the Empire Service in 1932. Leeper and Reith had worked closely together on the high-powered CID Sub-Committee to Prepare Plans for the Establishment of a Ministry of Information in Time of War, which began its work in 1935[67] (see chapter five), and both had urged the importance of foreign-language broadcasts to the Ullswater Committee. The report of this Committee provided a further stimulus to the cause with its statement that:

> It is all the more important that what has been called 'the projection of England' should be effectively carried out by a steadily developing Empire service of our own ... In the interests of Britain prestige and influence in world affairs, we think that the appropriate use of languages other than English should be encouraged.[68]

This proposal took on added significance with the escalation of anti-British propaganda in the eastern Mediterranean and the Middle East, particularly the hostile broadcasts from the Bari radio station. Preliminary negotiations between the BBC and the Foreign Office began in the summer of 1936,[69] and a year later, Foreign Secretary Anthony Eden, prompted by the continued concern of Parliament,[70] informed the Cabinet that:

> The time has come when some more positive steps should be taken than that of asking the Italians to desist. Without attempting to imitate the tone or the methods of Bari, it is essential for His Majesty's Government to ensure the full and forcible presentation of the British view of events in a region of such vital importance.[71]

The Cabinet agreed, and decided to appoint a special committee for the purpose of examining the logistical problems.[72] It first met in September 1937 under the chairmanship of Sir Kingsley Wood.[73] Just over a month later, a report was produced which recommended that the BBC should begin broadcasting in Arabic as soon as possible.[74] The Cabinet accepted the report in its entirety,[75] and broadcasting began on 3 January 1938. Three months later, the service was extended to broadcasts in Spanish and Portuguese for South American audiences. Reith was triumphant; he described these momentous decisions in his memoirs under the subtitle: 'Projection at last'.[76]

Such was the obvious need for propaganda abroad by then, particularly in the Mediterranean area, that by the winter of 1937–8 there was little objection to the new measures. Indeed, as Prime Minister Chamberlain announced in the House of Commons:

> His Majesty's Government fully realise that ... the old stand-upon-your-dignity methods are no longer applicable to modern conditions and that, in the rough-and-tumble of international relations which we see today, it

is absolutely necessary that we should take measures to protect ourselves from constant misrepresentation.[77]

That said, there still remained an urgent need to co-ordinate the work of the various official and semi-official organisations engaged in the projection of Britain abroad with an effective utilisation of the available media. Having been forced to re-enter the field, piecemeal reactive measures were once again charac- teristic of the British penchant for 'muddling through'. Previous attempts at co-ordination had proved either unpractical, largely due to the diverse evolution of Britain's propaganda activities since the end of the last war, or half-hearted, because the necessary motivation had been absent. By 1938, the first of these problems remained a serious one to resolve; the second, however, no longer applied.

From the Treasury's point of view, familiarity with continuous requests for more money may well have served to breed contempt, but as Anthony Eden recognised during his first term as Foreign Secretary, propaganda had become an unavoidable fact of peacetime diplomatic life. He wrote in late 1937:

> It is perfectly true, of course, that good ... propaganda cannot remedy the damage done by a bad foreign policy, but it is no exaggeration to say that even the best of diplomatic policies may fail if it neglects the tasks of interpretation and persuasion which modern conditions impose. We have daily experience of what we may expect to suffer if we leave the field of foreign public opinion to our antagonists, and we must face the fact that these misinterpretations can only be countered by equally energetic actions on our part on behalf of the truth.[78]

This statement reveals the degree to which the Foreign Office had accepted the new facts of modern international life. It also reveals three of the basic assumptions on which the conduct of British overseas propaganda between the wars was based. In the first place, propaganda was designed to serve as an adjunct to normal diplomacy and not, as Sir Horace Wilson seemed to believe, as a 'substitute' for it, which was more often a characteristic of the totalitarian regimes.[79] Second, the British government, or more specifically the Foreign Office, had re-embarked upon such work as a response to the anti-British propaganda activities of other countries. It was more a reaction to external stimuli rather than the consequence of any desire to expand its responsibilities. And third, Eden's statement reveals his basic belief, held since the 1914–17 period, in the value of what Nicholas Pronay has termed 'propaganda with facts'.[80] It might also be remembered that the Foreign Office had always been inclined towards qualitative rather than quantitative propaganda, although the pressures of mass politics and the advent of the mass media were forcing it to re-evaluate the nature of its target audience. Having said that, this approach meant that the financial costs involved were slight when compared with the enormous expenditure on techniques of mass persuasion of its rivals. Just as its potential enemies were adopting the approach of Crewe House, the essential principles of Wellington House remained very much a part of Foreign Office thinking.

Nevertheless, it is also true to say that the depth of prejudice and suspicion about propaganda was decidedly less deep-rooted in the late 1930s than it had been at the end of the First World War. A simple illustration of the change which had taken place, at least in Parliamentary opinion, can be found in the contrast between the virtually unanimous hostility of the House of Commons towards the work of Lord Beaverbrook's Ministry of Information in 1918[81] and the equally unanimous support given by all parties to the propaganda work being done by various new British organisations during major debates on the subject in 1938[82] and 1939.[83] This was largely because the evidence and the kind of arguments that had prompted the creation of the British Council in 1934 continued to gather force and wider currency during the remaining five years of peace. Indeed, it was during this quinquennium that, both within official circles and beyond, the subject of propaganda received a measure of consideration in Britain unprecedented since the Great War. The issue was kept alive not only by the intensification of anti-British propaganda, and the steps taken by the government to counter it, but also by questions and debates in the House of Commons, regular debate in the Press, numerous articles published in learned journals,[84] and by the appearance of several influential books.[85] Nor was it a question of concern merely confined to the lower and middle levels of government administration. Quite the contrary, in fact; by the late 1930s, propaganda became a recurring topic of top-level and even Cabinet consideration. As one author observed in 1938, 'this generation is witnessing a boom in propaganda'.[86]

Leeper believed that increased centralisation was an essential prerequisite to further progress. He was 'strongly opposed' to the creation of a Ministry of Information in peacetime largely because such a body, as then envisaged by the Committee of Imperial Defence, would exercise special powers on the home front,[87] and would excite widespread political opposition. The process of influencing foreign public opinion, however, was considered to fall outside party politics. This became more apparent in February 1938 after a non-party debate on the subject on a motion tabled by a private member,[88] a debate which Herbert Morrison described as 'one of the most peaceful we have ever had in the House of Commons'.[89] On this occasion, the House enjoyed that rare event of unanimous support for the resolution which, in its final form, ran as follows: 'being of opinion that the evil effects of state propaganda of a tendentious or misleading character can best be countered, not by retaliation, but by the widespread dissemination of straightforward information and news based upon an enlightened and honest public policy', the government should devote the full weight of its moral and financial support to increasing Britain's overseas propaganda.[90]

In fact, the government had already acted. In January 1938, Leeper had proposed the creation of a Central Co-ordinating Committee under the Chairmanship of Sir Robert Vansittart who, to borrow Valentine Lawford's phrase, had recently been exiled to 'a sort of newly discovered Siberia known as Chief

Diplomatic Adviser'.[91] Eden had submitted the proposal to the Prime Minister on 18 January adding that it 'seems to me ... to be the natural outcome of the preliminary work done so far'.[92] Chamberlain agreed,[93] and the existence of the committee was announced three weeks later.[94] The announcement was received favourably by both the House of Commons and by the Press. *The Times*, for example, published a lengthy explanatory article justifying the need for the committee and expressing general support for its aims.[95] The German Press, however, predictably received the news with less enthusiasm. The *Völkischer Beobachter* led the chorus of hypocritical indignation, invoking memories of British propaganda during the First World War, but with the substitution of Vansittart for Northcliffe.[96] Such comparisons were, of course, misleading. The Vansittart Committee was not a propaganda department on the Crewe House model and had no executive powers; nor did it conduct propaganda itself. Its functions were purely advisory and aimed simply at the increased efficiency and co-ordination of the existing work abroad.

British overseas propaganda, as it had evolved since the last war, was organised by reference to its variable forms rather than by reference to media. Hence, the British Council was responsible for cultural propaganda, and the Travel Association for tourist propaganda. Vansittart's report, produced in May 1938, proposed that a major deficiency would be rectified if an organisation for trade propaganda were created,[97] but the Treasury opposed the suggestion on the grounds that such work should more properly be conducted by the private interests concerned.[98] Eventually, however, the opposition was overcome and in April 1939 an Industrial Publicity Unit was secretly established under the auspices of the Department of Overseas Trade on the condition that its propaganda would be designed 'to benefit the trade and industry of the United Kingdom as a whole and not particular trades or industries or individual concerns'.[99] Vansittart also suggested that much of the tension and rivalry which had characterised relations between the British Council and the Travel Association, despite the existence of joint committees on films and on broadcasting, could be avoided if Lord Lloyd, the Chairman of the Council since September 1937, also became President of the Travel Association on Lord Derby's retirement later in the year. When this occurred in December 1938, a great deal of overlapping and duplication of effort was avoided. Vansittart was also successful in persuading the Treasury to appoint an additional 15 press attachés to supervise the work abroad 'on the spot', bringing the total number to 20 by 1939. A further proposal to establish a National Film Council to co-ordinate the activities of government with the film industry in general proved less acceptable, and never really overcame the suspicion that it might also be used as an instrument for domestic film propaganda until the creation of the Crown Film Unit during the Second World War. Meanwhile, however, Lord Lloyd proved successful in securing a government grant of £160,000 for the Council's work in 1938–9 (it had been £5,000 in 1935) and Sir John Reith extended the foreign-language broadcasts to various European languages during the crisis of September 1938.

The Vansittart proposals were a major event in the evolution of Britain's involvement in peacetime propaganda abroad. They were, in many ways, the logical outcome of two decades of gradual, staggered and diversified growth in a controversial new area of governmental responsibility. They were a powerful, and not altogether unsuccessful, attempt not only to extend the existing work of national projection but also to rectify the more serious deficiencies so that the entire system would be more efficiently co-ordinated and adapted to meet the new conditions required for projecting Britain abroad. By this, the Foreign Office meant the containment of the spread of extremist ideologies in areas vital to British interests by the substitution of democratic ideals and the dissemination of confidence in an increasingly aggressive and totalitarian world. It was, in short, an attempt to reinforce Britain's search for peace by supplementary methods. If that search failed, plans were well under way for the creation of a Ministry of Information and various 'black' propaganda units such as Electra House and Section D.[100] And there was always the rearmament programmes.

British propaganda was less aggressive in character than its totalitarian counterparts, attempting rather to provide an opportunity for foreigners to learn more about Britain's actions and policies without forcing them to 'think British' if they had no desire to do so. It was, by nature, more 'pro-British' than 'anti-foreign'; while it engaged in self-explanation and self-justification, great care was taken to refrain from criticising the activities of other countries. Even so, propaganda continued to be regarded generally as a necessary evil rather than something constructive or positive. The British idea that propaganda could be used as an instrument for the promotion of international goodwill was gradually giving way to a perhaps more realistic appraisal of its value as an instrument of defence in a world threatened by the possibility of another war. However, the volatile combination of a controversial activity with such controversial figures as Reith, Tallents, Lloyd, Vansittart and Leeper ensured that the debate about what others were doing and what the British should do remained essentially within democratic perimeters. Propaganda may have been a good word gone wrong, but democracies, these men felt, needed to conduct it not only to protect themselves against the onslaught of its ideological enemies, but also for its own sake. For them, propaganda was about educating the British people as well as foreigners about what was right. In this respect, they were within the classical Platonic tradition of democratic thinking, whereby the guardians of society protected the people from themselves in order to save themselves from anarchy. The fact that a relatively recent political ideology, in the form of Marxist-Leninism, saw such thinking as 'oppressive', 'patronising' and 'imperialistic', especially since elements of that ideology had been embraced by the Labour Party which was now the official party of Opposition, merely placed the issue in party-political or class-based terms. Nervousness about attacks motivated by such thinking was at the root of the official reluctance to increase the propaganda activities of the state.

Whatever the validity of Leeper's own explanation as to why great official support for their new work had not been more readily forthcoming, namely that 'new ideas are anathema to the official mind',[101] it would be true to say that what these men meant by propaganda was often misunderstood by others less familiar with their work. Suspicion remained because no sooner had the word 'propaganda' escaped its dubious wartime connotations than it regained notoriety with the aggressive activities of the dictatorships. It was for this reason that Stephen Tallents went to great lengths to avoid using the word in his pamphlet *The Projection of England*. In fact, it does not appear once. But as one enlightened Member of Parliament said after a lengthy Commons debate on the subject in February 1939:

> We have heard much tonight about the projection of Britain and the British people. Well, what is that but propaganda? We may dislike the word because it has collected unpleasant associations. But the thing itself may be necessary and right. Let us not be ashamed or afraid of it.[102]

Had more people been prepared to admit this sooner, they might not have been so quick to seize upon one of the more sinister aspects of totalitarian ideology for their own definition.

Notes and References

1 This chapter is a revised version of a book chapter, 'British official attitudes to propaganda abroad, 1918–39' in N. Pronay and D. W. Spring, (eds), *Propaganda, Politics and Film, 1918–45* (Macmillan, 1982), pp. 23–49.

2 A. Fletcher to A. Willert, 10 May 1928, FO 395/437, P732/732/150.

3 Minute by H. Wilson, 18 January 1938, PREM 1/272.

4 Minute by E. Hale, 2 June 1938, T161/933, S42850/2.

5 Ibid.

6 H. Wickham Steed, *The Fifth Arm* (Constable, 1940).

7 S. Tallents, *The Projection of England* (Faber & Faber, 1932).

8 Memorandum by C. Addison, 17 December 1917, CAB 24/36, GT3031.

9 Northcliffe frequently cited such statements as a means of justifying the success of his work. See, for example, the enclosures in Northcliffe to J. T. Davies, 18 July 1918, FO800/213. *The Times History of the War*, written while Northcliffe was still at Printing House Square, also uses this approach to perpetuate the reputation for success.

10 Memorandum by Lord Beaverbrook, 'The functions of the Ministry of Information on the cessation of hostilities', 16 October 1918, CAB 24/67, GT6007.

11 Sir Campbell Stuart, *Secrets of Crewe House: The Story of a Famous Campaign* (Hodder & Stoughton, 1920), p. 202.

12 Steed, *Fifth Arm*, p. 41.

13 Steed, *Through Thirty Years* (2 vols, Heinemann, 1924), II, p. 248.

14 *The History of The Times, The 150th Anniversary and Beyond, 1912–48* (Printing House Square, 1952), Part I, pp. 384–98.

15 D. Lloyd George, *Memoirs of the Peace Conference* (2 vols, Yale University Press, 1939), vol. 1, p. 176.

16 See N. Pronay and K. Wilson (eds), *The Political Re-education of Germany and her Allies after World War Two* (Croom Helm, 1984).

17 CAB 23/8, 501(11) 13 November 1918.

18 In January 1919 the total staff of the News Department was estimated at 223, including 44 messengers and typists and 19 charwomen, of which 118 seem to have been inherited from the Ministry of Information. 'Notes on the liquidation of the Ministry of Information', INF 4/1B.

19 Minute by Sir Henry Newbolt, 17 January 1919, FO 395/301, 00346.

20 Memorandum by V. Wellesley, 'The reconstruction of the Foreign Office', 30 November, 1918, FO395/297, 001377.

21 W. Tyrrell to H. Batterbee, 30 December, 1918, FO 395/297, 0012.

22 Minute by S. Gaselee, 28 January, 1919, FO 395/301,00409.

23 Minute by J. Tilley, 31 January, 1919, FO 395/301, 00409.

24 Memorandum by G. B. Beak, 'Policy and propaganda', 2 December, 1918, FO 395/301, 00409.

25 Ibid.

26 Memorandum by S. A. Guest, 24 January, 1919, FO 395/301, 00409.

27 Ibid.

28 Note of proceedings at a meeting held on 20 March 1919 to consider the future of British propaganda abroad. FO 395/297, 001377.

29 British propaganda in the United States was something of an exceptional case. For further details see Philip M. Taylor, *The Projection of Britain; British overseas publicity and propaganda, 1914–39*, (Ph.D. thesis, University of Leeds, 1978), ch. 4, and Nicholas J. Cull, *Selling War* (Oxford University Press, 1995).

30 Circular despatch signed by Curzon, 19 May 1919, FO 395/304, 00848.

31 Note of proceedings of a conference held at the Treasury, 14 May 1919, FO 395/297, 002006.

32 T. C. Heath to Tyrrell, 31 May 1919, FO 366/787, 82638.

33 Ibid.

34 A. Chamberlain to Lords Curzon and Milner, 21 February, 1918. AC 15/7/7. Austen Chamberlain Papers, Birmingham University Library.

35 *Parliamentary Debates* (Commons), 5th series, vol. 109, 5 August, 1918, cols. 947–1035.

36 K. Middlemass and J. Barnes, *Baldwin: A Biography* (Weidenfeld and Nicolson, 1969), p. 68.

37 H. O. Lee, 'British propaganda during the Great War, 1914–18', undated (probably 1919) INF 4/4 A.

38 Memorandum by P. A. Koppel, 10 February, 1922. FO 366/783, 5.

39 Minute by J. Tilley, 24 October, 1919. FO 395/304, 00848.

40 Alfred Longden, 'British art exhibitions at home and abroad', 31 October, 1935, BT60/44/3, DOT 5215.

41 J. A. S. Grenville, *The Major International Treaties, 1914–73* (London, 1974).

42 A. Willert to E. F. Crowe, 18 December, 1928, FO 395/426, P1679/14/150.

43 Report of the British Economic Mission to South America led by Lord D'Abernon, 18 January, 1930, FO 371/14178, A1908/77/51.

44 Introductory memorandum, FO 431/1, no. 1.

45 Taylor, 'Cultural diplomacy and the British Council, 1934–39', *British Journal of International Studies* 4:3 (1978), 244–65.

46 Speech by the Earl of Derby at the Mansion House, 20 December, 1928, FO 395/435, P215/178/150.

47 Ibid.

48 Enclosed memorandum in L. A. de L. Meredith to R. Kenney, 1 August, 1929, FO 395/435, P1140/178/150.

49 Ibid.

50 Speech by Lord Derby, 20 December, 1929, Board of Trade BT 61/54/2 (Department of Overseas Trade), DOT E14888.

51 Enclosed memorandum in Meredith to Kenney, 1 August, 1929. FO 395/435, P1140/178/150.

52 Ibid.

53 Memorandum by J. D. Gregory, 21 February, 1925, FO 366/788, A ix (f).

54 Gaselee and Fletcher to Arthur Henderson, 15 July 1931, FO 395/449, P1140/178/150.

55 *The Projection of England*, p. 11.

56 Ibid, p. 17.

57 Ibid, pp. 41–4.

58 Vansittart to R. MacDonald, 28 April, 1931, Ramsay MacDonald Papers, PRO 30/69/1/287.

59 *The Times*, 20 March, 1935.

60 Hoare to Kennard, 8 November, 1935, FO 395/529, P3900/267/150.

61 Tyrrell's statement to the Chancellor of the Exchequer, 27 January, 1936, British Council Records, BCR BW2/109, F8412, GB/9/9.

62 Minute by Vansittart, 24 February, 1937, FO 395/554, P823/160/150.

63 Foreign Office memorandum, 'Foreign cultural propaganda and the threat to British interests abroad', 19 February 1937, FO 395/534, P823/160/150.

64 Memorandum by R. A. Leeper, 27 January, 1935, FO 395/541, P332/332/150.

65 R. A. Leeper to Treasury, 9 April, 1935; R. V. Nind Hopkins to Foreign Office, 8 May 1935, FO 395/522, P529/9/150.

66 D. McLachlan, *In the Chair: Barrington Ward of The Times* (Weidenfeld and Nicolson, 1971), pp. 128–9.

67 CAB 16/127, MIC1.

68 Report of the Broadcasting Committee, 1935. Cmd 5091 (1936) paras. 115–24.

69 A. Briggs, *The Golden Age of Wireless* (Oxford University Press, 1965), pp. 397–8.

70 *Parliamentary Debates* (Commons), 5th series, vol. 321, 2 March 1937, cols. 196–7; 3 March 1937, cols. 337–8; 25 March 1937, cols. 3170–8; vol. 327, 7 June 1937, cols. 1408–9; vol. 325, 23 June 1937, cols. 1177–8; vol. 325, 28 June 1937, cols. 1618–9.

71 Memorandum by Eden, 13 July 1937, CAB 24/270, CP185(37).

72 CAB 23/89, 31(37)6, 31 July 1937.

73 Cabinet Committee on Arabic Broadcasting, first meeting, 15 September, 1937, CAB 27/641, ABC (37).

74 Report of the Cabinet Committee on Arabic Broadcasting, 22 October, 1937, CAB 27/271, CP274(37).

75 CAB 23/90, 39(37)9, 27 October 1937.

76 Sir John Reith, *Into the Wind*, (Hodder & Stoughton, 1949), pp. 290–3.

77 *Parliamentary Debates* (Commons), 5th series, vol. 330, 21 December 1937, col. 1796.

78 Eden to Sir John Simon, 23 December 1937, T 161/907, S35581/03/38/1.

79 Z. A. B. Zeman, *Nazi Propaganda* (Oxford University Press, 1973), p. 65.

80 A phrase first used by the historian Nicholas Pronay in the presence of the author in 1973.

81 *Parliamentary Debates* (Commons), 5th series, vol. 109, 5 August 1918, cols. 947–1035.

82 *Parliamentary Debates* (Commons), 5th series, vol. 331, 16 February 1938, cols. 1909–69.

83 *Parliamentary Debates* (Commons), 5th series, vol. 343, 15 February 1939, cols. 1808–67.

84 It would be unpractical to cite all such examples, but see: W. E. Berchtold, 'The World Propaganda War', *North American Review*, 238 (1934), 421–30; M. Garnett, 'Propaganda', *The Contemporary Review*, 147 (1935), 574–81; Aldous Huxley, 'Notes on Propaganda', *Harper's Magazine*, 174 (1936), 32–41; A. Huxley, 'Dictators' Propaganda', *The Spectator*, 20 November 1936; A. Willert, 'British News Abroad', *The Round Table*, 27 (1937), 533–46; A. Willert, 'Publicity and Propaganda in International Affairs', *International Affairs*, 17 (1938), 809–26; S. N. Siegel, 'Radio and Propaganda', *Air Law Review*, 10 (1939); E. H. Carr, 'Propaganda in International Politics', *Oxford Pamphlets on World Affairs*, 16, (1939).

85 Of particular interest are: A. J. Mackenzie, *Propaganda Boom* (Gifford, 1938); S. Rogerson, *Propaganda in the Next War* (Bles, 1938); A. Blanco White, *The New Propaganda* (Gollancz, 1939).

86 Mackenzie, *Propaganda Boom*, p. 7.

87 Memorandum by R. A. Leeper, 13 July 1937, FO 395/546, P3261/1/150.

88 Mr Lees Jones, MP for Blackley.

89 *Parliamentary Debates* (Commons), 5th series, vol. 331, 16 February 1938, col. 1953.

90 Ibid, col. 1969.

91 V. Lawford, *Bound for Diplomacy* (Murray, 1963), p. 271.

92 Eden to Chamberlain, 18 January 1938, FO 395/596, P359/359/150.

93 Chamberlain to Eden, 19 January 1938, FO 395/596, P359/359/150.

94 *Parliamentary Debates* (Commons), 5th series, vol. 331, 7 February, 1938. cols. 670–1.

95 *The Times*, 8 February 1938.

96 N. Henderson to Foreign Office, 9 February 1938, FO 395/597, P786/359/150.

97 Report of the Co-ordinating Committee for British Publicity Abroad, 28 May 1938, FO 395/602, P1948/359/150.

98 Note by E. Hale, 'Publicity abroad', 2 June 1938, T 161/933, S42850/2.

99 E. Mullins to R. Williamson, 15 April 1939, BT 61/72/9, DOT E188773.

100 M. R. D. Foot, *S. O. E in France* (HMSO, 1966), pp. 1–3.

101 Minute by R. A. Leeper, 18 February 1937, FO 395/554, P823/160/150.

102 *Parliamentary Debates* (Commons), 5th series, vol. 343, 15 February 1939, cols. 1866–7. The speaker was Mr Emmot.

5

A Call to Arms: Psychological Rearmament[1]

The deepening inter-war crisis might not have been so serious had the British disarmed only in the weapon of propaganda at the end of the First World War. Profoundly affected by the bloody slaughter of the trenches, especially once the shock of what had actually happened set in,[2] most people in 1919 had entertained serious hopes of a lasting peace and of a universal rejection of war as a means of resolving international disputes. Retaining barely enough armed forces to protect some – though not all simultaneously – of its worldwide Imperial interests was a reflection of these hopes. Disarmament policies were pursued through the Washington and London Naval Treaties (1922 and 1930) until the lowest defence budget of the entire inter-war period was presented to Parliament in 1932.

The British also operated from 1919 onwards what they called a Ten-Year Rule as the basis of their defence planning, working under the assumption that they would not be involved in a war for the next ten years. It was renewed every year until March 1932. The ramifications, therefore, of the sudden Japanese attack on Manchuria some months earlier, followed by the advent of Hitler some months later, transformed these hopes into genuine fears, and essentially doomed to failure the world's first Disarmament Conference (1932–34) designed to implement the new and safer world order. Once again, therefore, a mere fifteen years after the 'war to end all wars', the British government found itself having to face up to the agonising possibility of waging another major conflagration.

5.1 The Politics of British Rearmament

George Canning's maxim was that nations should only issue threats if there was the military, economic or psychological capacity to actually carry them out. Until Britain was in such a position, it could not afford to bluff. The serious deficiencies in home and imperial defences therefore underlined the contemporary military imperatives to appease any potential enemies. It is important to stress, however, that appeasement was not born solely out of military expediency. It was a traditional aspect of British foreign policy, dating far back into the nineteenth century.[3] Although, like propaganda, it has subsequently become a pejorative term, appeasement is in many ways an admirable policy. Motivated by a hatred of war (or at least by a recognition that war affects adversely a nation's self-interests which, in Britain's case, this largely meant trade and Empire), appeasement signifies a preference for resolving disputes by peaceful negotiation rather than by force.

Appeasement as a policy in the 1930s has been criticised largely in retrospect, because the events of 1939 revealed – really for the first time – that Hitler was a man who could not be negotiated with, who could not be appeased. But to contemporaries, even those who regarded events within Nazi Germany from 1933 onwards with mounting distaste, this was not quite as apparent as it may be to us now. Hitler was particularly adept at disguising his true foreign policy objectives, in saying things his opponents wanted to hear, and at throwing out a series of psychological feints to wrong-foot them. Moreover, it has to be remembered that Germany was felt to have legitimate grievances against the Versailles Treaty: the principle of self-determination, for example, had been applied to just about everyone except the Germans themselves. In this respect, British policy-makers in the 1930s were paying the price for the idealism of the peacemakers of 1919 who had tried to draw up the new boundaries of Europe along ethnographic lines. The Saar Plebiscite of 1935, the reoccupation of the Rhineland in 1936, the colonial negotiations of 1937, the Anschluss and the Sudeten crises of 1938 were all examples of Germans being returned to Germany. It was not until March 1939, when Hitler seized the rump of Czechoslovakia, that Hitler incorporated non-Germans into the Third Reich for the first time. And when that happened, appeasement was dropped virtually overnight and replaced with a policy of security guarantees to those small powers of central, eastern and south-eastern Europe most immediately threatened by Hitler. We now know this was too little and too late. Yet it was, after all, the British (together with the French) who declared war on Germany in September 1939 when Poland was invaded, a country for which Neville Chamberlain's half-brother, Austen, had said just fifteen years earlier that Britain would not risk the bones of her grenadiers.

However, throughout the 1930s, while Britain continued to search for an agreement with Germany for sensible economic, military, strategic and even moral reasons, there was a need for an insurance policy in case that search failed. That fallback policy was rearmament. Again, it is too often forgotten that Britain was rearming for a war against Germany from 1935 onwards, a year in which Hitler as yet posed no serious threat to the peace of Europe. Indeed, the programmes that were initially laid down in that year were designed for completion by 1939. The reason why those programmes went uncompleted is a sorry tale of financial weakness, political infighting and industrial problems – not a lack of foresight. There was, for example, a serious shortage in 1930s Britain of the kind of skilled labour required to manufacture modern precision war equipment. Neville Chamberlain, both as Chancellor of the Exchequer (1931–37) and as Prime Minister (1937–40) was deeply concerned that Britain's preparations for war should not actually jeopardise her capacity to fight one.

Unfortunately, the kind of war for which Britain was preparing promoted bitter inter-service rivalry amongst its Armed Forces. The prevailing opinion was that, if the next war should come, there would be an initial 'knockout blow from the air'. Accordingly, if the British could survive this they would be able to engage successfully in a long war of attrition against Germany in which (as in 1914–18) the economy would serve as the 'fourth arm of defence' until enough men and equipment throughout the Empire–Commonwealth could be mobilised to defeat the German armies. Therefore, the RAF, Navy and Army competed ferociously for the limited amounts of money available as pre-war strategy underwent its tortuous shifts in planning.[5]

But these were the 'private' dilemmas of rearmament, mostly kept hidden from public view until historians began delving into the official records when they were opened after 1968. There was, however, a more 'public' element to British rearmament in the 1930s, one which was less apparent in terms of its management at the time but which is just as significant, namely the presentational elements of the rearmament programme to the British public. This in fact helps to explain why an overwhelmingly pacifist public opinion should in 1935 re-elect, albeit with a reduced but still sizeable majority, a National Government committed to a policy of rearmament. It also makes it easier to understand why that same public accepted, a mere four years later, seemingly without protest, a declaration of war against Germany, particularly when it was widely believed that the arrival of the bomber would signal the advent of Armageddon.

From the outset, propaganda – or publicity, as it was usually described outside government offices – thus played an integral role in the selling of rearmament. This process was known as psychological rearmament and it fell broadly into three phases. The first, which may be regarded as a preliminary stage, was between February 1934 (the date of the first Defence Requirements Committee (DRC) report) and November 1935 (the date of the General Election). In this period, the National Government recovered its composure on armaments matters, formulated its deficiency programmes, sold the idea of a bomber deterrent and won an election with a mandate for increased rearmament. The second phase ran from the election to just after the Munich crisis of 1938. In this period, psychological rearmament evoked co-operation and unity among the labour force, whose participation was vital to the progress of the rearmament programmes, while providing reassurance and reinforcement for the policy of appeasement. In the third phase, from after the Munich agreement to the outbreak of the Second World War, the call to arms continued alongside the promotion of national unity and co-operation, while emphasis was placed on defence against the bomber – i.e. that such a defence was possible. In this final period, emphasis was also given to the strength of Britain and of her allies (some real, some imagined) and to preparing the people for the prospect of an actual war in which they would be principal frontline actors.

5.2 Propaganda and Democracy, 1918–35

In the National Government's campaign to 're-educate' the British public about the need for rearmament, there were numerous obstacles to overcome. In a pluralistic and increasingly democratic society such as Britain, the conduct of government propaganda in time of peace, even the armed peace of the 1930s, was bound to raise objections. 'Propaganda' was now a dirty word; it was regarded as 'un-English', something foreigners did and democracies only resorted to in wartime. There may have been a growing acceptance of the need to project Britain abroad, but targeting the British people was quite another matter. However, beneath the surface of official disavowal and dis-approval, not to mention the official euphemisms for the P-word, such as 'publicity', 'national projection' and 'political education', lay an increasingly sophisticated appreciation of the role which propaganda could play in a peace-time democracy.

The rapid and enormous expansion in the size of the electorate since 1918 was regarded by many as necessary but alarming. It was necessary because the mass public needed some reward for its endeavours during the first Total War of 1914–18. The public had to channel their energies constructively into a pluralistic democracy rather than follow the example of the workers in the Russia of 1917 or the mass conscript armies in the mutinies of 1918–19 in France. It was alarming because of the belief that the mass electorate was still essentially ignorant and irrational and, if it embraced socialism on a large scale, posed an actual threat to democracy. As Neville Chamberlain put it in 1923, 'the new electorate contains an immense mass of ignorant voters, of both sexes, whose intelligence is low and who have no power of weighing evidence'.[6] In response, therefore, political parties in Britain on the one hand declared their commitment to 'political education' as a basis for effective democracy and, on the other, began to develop political propaganda techniques.

Because of the structure and ownership of the British press, the new media of broadcasting and film were seen as having a much greater potential for political communication in a mass democratic society. The creators of the BBC certainly believed that radio could provide as essential element of democratic education, and indeed worked towards that end. The BBC, after all, was born into a political system in the 1920s already very conscious of the potentially revolutionary implications of universal franchise, and increasingly aware of the power of mass opinion and the importance of mass persuasion. The ideal of an educated and enlightened democracy was in turn being embraced increasingly with the development of universal state education, and the expansion of public lending libraries and adult education. The founder of the British documentary film movement, John Grierson, who was initially employed by various gov-ernment departments in the late 1920s and 1930s, professed similar aspirations 'to use the cinema as an instrument of education and propaganda to assist that process of reconstruction which our modern society must undergo'.[7]

It was the Conservative Party that did most to develop modern political propaganda techniques in Britain. The inter-war period saw the dominant right fearful – at times terrified – of the threat of civil disorder, political upheaval and the overthrow of democratic institutions by a Moscow-inspired socialism. The predominantly Conservative governments of the era – for Labour was effectively in power for no more than four years throughout the entire twenty-year period – were increasingly alarmed at the extra-parliamentary activities of the left (particularly during the General Strike of 1926) and were correspondingly concerned to defend the established order against possible extreme alternatives. In the 1920s, this fear focused on the threat posed by Bolshevism. However, the dramatic rise of Labour as the party of opposition and the principles for which it stood – its identification with the working class and its use of Trade Union organisations for furthering its support – reinforced the fears of the Right. In the 1930s, these fears remained, but were largely subsumed by the creation of an all-party National Government and superseded by the external threat to democracy posed by Hitler's Germany.

Wireless and film were to prove powerful weapons in these struggles, for both sides. Their unique and apparently ethereal nature, penetrating the human mind beyond the level of conscious perception, gave these media a particular mystique. Their potency, interestingly, was rarely challenged and there was much talk of them being a 'magic bullet' for presenting any case desired and, by means of censorship, to pre-empt that of opponents. So when, in 1928, Stanley Baldwin wrote that 'democracy has arrived at a gallop in England and I feel all the time that it is a race for life' the challenge was seen in terms of: 'can we educate them before the crash comes?'[8] Senior Conservatives were in no doubt as to the solution. J. C. C. Davidson, Chairman of the Conservative Party from 1926 to 1930, informed Baldwin:

> If our strength in the country is to be maintained and we are to win over to our support the majority of the politically uneducated electorate, we must combine intensive political education with the appeal that the present Government pursues a policy which is in the interests of every class of the community, and is in fact national and imperial and not political.[9]

This at least was the aim, although the propaganda which resulted was often sectional and far from open. Sir Joseph Ball, for example, the Conservative Party's director of publicity, even managed to infiltrate his agents into Labour Party headquarters. Albert Clavering, director of the Conservative and Unionist Films Association (CFA) which had controlled the wartime Topical Budget News Film distribution, and the owner of a cinema and newsreel chain, was a close friend of Isodore Ostrer, President of the Gaumont British Newsreel Company, while his brother, Arthur, was a director of Pathé. Clavering not only prevented the commercial exhibition of Soviet films in Britain in 1929, he was also said to be the reason why, in 1935, 'we as a party are so far ahead of the other parties in the development of film propaganda'.[10] Two leading figures of British Movietone News (Sir Gordon Craig, its general manager, and Gerald Sanger, its editor) actually joined the CFA's central editorial committee. And the Conservative Party even secretly produced a film, *The Soul of a Nation*, a critical if not a commercial success.

In 1934, Baldwin revealed his sophisticated appreciation of the issues when he wrote:

The maintenance of an educated democracy depends on unceasing propaganda, pressed with vigour and enthusiasm, and at the same time directed
with a full and exact knowledge of the facts, towards clearly defined aims.
A confusion of aim or a lack of enthusiasm renders propaganda weak and
ineffectual.[11]

Shortly after this, the National Publicity Bureau (NPB) was formed – in October
1934, although its existence was not announced until March 1935. This body
was ostensibly designed to advertise the National Government's policies so that
it could be returned at the forthcoming election. Although it was, in many
respects, the culmination of Baldwin's national political philosophy, it was
disliked among some Conservative ranks for the room it gave to the left. In
reality, however, the NPB was Conservative-dominated – its Chairman was Sir
Kingsley Wood and its staff mainly drawn from Central Office. Joseph Ball
was its Director. Little is known about its work prior to the election of 1935
and one can only speculate concerning its role in securing the re-election of
the National Government. However, it did remain in existence until 1939 and
the experiment can be regarded as the direct forerunner of present-day election
propaganda techniques.[12]
    If the NPB can be regarded as a pioneer of direct political propaganda, there
were also indirect methods by which the Conservatives could influence the
electorate. It would, however, be fair to say that Labour never really achieved
comprehensive access to the mass media during this period. Despite the ideologically sympathetic group of documentary film-makers centred around Grierson
first at the Empire Marketing Board (1926–33) and later at the General Post
Office, the appeal of their films was far from widespread and they hardly offered
mass entertainment in the Depression years. The British Board of Film Censors
(BBFC) prohibited the making of films dealing, inter alia, with the conflict
between Labour and capital and played a major role in promoting an ideological
consensus in feature films of the inter-war period.[13] However, the Ostrer
brothers, who owned Gaumont British, were Labour Party supporters until the
1931 crisis and there was even a strong rumour that Isodore Ostrer offered the
family's controlling shares to the Party early in 1931. But the disastrous rout
of Labour later in the year and the breaking away of MacDonald to form a
separate National Labour Party brought the plan to an abrupt halt. In March
1935, Isodore Ostrer made an even more remarkable offer to the NPB 'to place
the entire organisation of Gaumont British and the "Sunday Referee" behind
the National Government'.[14] The support which Gaumont provided in the
years that followed is a central issue in the history of psychological rearmament.

5.3 Public Opinion, Rearmament and the Media

From the outset in 1934, the Defence Requirements Committee recognised
that, as a result of persistent and unopposed pacifist propaganda over the

previous fifteen years, the British public would have to be prepared for any sudden increases in defence expenditure and that public opinion would therefore require special attention. The July 1934 Cabinet decision to give priority to aerial rearmament was influenced greatly by what Baldwin called 'the semi-panic conditions which existed now about the Air'.[15] The final comment of the Cabinet on the DRC proposals stated:

> Although currents of more or less uninformed public opinion at home ought never to be a determining factor in defensive preparations, they have to be reckoned with in asking Parliament to approve a programme of expenditure. In the present case, it happened that the general trend of public opinion appeared to coincide with our own views as to the desirability of a considerable expansion of the RAF for home defence.[16]

General Pownall described the decision as the 'extraordinary' and 'inevitable' effect of public opinion, the press and of 'the Lord Lloyd-Churchill group'.[17] Hitler also helped. When British Foreign Secretary Sir John Simon visited Berlin in late March 1935, the Führer announced that Germany had already achieved air parity with Britain. This was absolute nonsense, of course, but the claim sparked off a renewal of 'semi-panic' about the bomber which in turn helped to prompt the announcement, on 22 May 1935, of a British air expansion scheme to be completed by 1937, not by 1939. Five days later, J. H. Thomas claimed: 'Public opinion was now fully alive to the air situation but was not prepared for expenditure in other directions'.[18] Large armies, after all, reminded people of trench warfare. Ships were expensive to build. Neither offered the prospect of protection against the bomber, and so the RAF held the day.

That public opinion should play an important part in shaping the government's early rearmament decisions was not without its political irony. For it was Baldwin himself who had done so much to add credibility to the fear of the bomber. In a famous speech to the Commons in 1932, Baldwin proclaimed:

> I think it well ... for the man in the street to realise that there is no power on earth that can protect him from being bombed. Whatever people may tell him, the bomber will always get through. The only defence is offence, which means that you will have to kill women and children more quickly than the enemy if you want to save yourselves.[19]

Just under two-and-a-half years later, when the government issued its rearmament White Paper in March 1935, a massive re-education campaign was under way. The White Paper itself stated:

> Hitherto ... public opinion is this country has tended to assume that nothing is required for the maintenance of peace except the existing international political machinery, and that the older methods of defence – navies, armies and air forces – on which we have hitherto depended for our security in the last resort are no longer required. The force of world events, however, has shown that this assumption is premature.[20]

From the propagandist point of view, the campaign presented particular difficulties. The German threat in 1935, despite recent events and Hitler's boasts,
was by no means plain for all to see. How real was the danger of another war?
For what purpose was rearmament required? To actually fight another war, or
to prevent one? Moreover, why should an overwhelmingly peace-loving and
battle-scarred British public sanction expenditure on armaments a mere 15 years
after 'the war to end all wars', particularly when that money could be used to
repair and rebuild British society in the aftermath of the Great Depression,
and particularly when it was believed that arms and arms races provoked war?
Furthermore, why should the Labour movement co-operate in such a venture
when its leaders were still advocating a policy of disarmament? In addition,
accepting the inevitability of war was a highly dangerous political stance in the
1930s. The next war would be radically different from previous wars. Next
time, entire peoples would be involved. Once the bomber got through, the
devastation it would invariably cause might well result in panic, defeatism,
anarchy, the breakdown of civil society and, some feared, possibly even a resort
to Bolshevism.

Because these fears were firmly entrenched in the consciousness of the
inter-war generation, they fuelled the desire to avoid another war, almost at
any price. The selling of rearmament was, therefore, a highly delicate issue
that would require skilful and professional handling. At home, a fine balance
had to be struck between the explanation for, and justification of, rearmament
on the one hand while avoiding fatalism and evoking public co-operation on
the other. Abroad, rearmament had to be presented as a peaceful measure so
as not to undermine appeasement while, at the same time, keeping concealed
the real extent of Britain's vulnerability. The Foreign Office supervised the
campaign abroad, its News Department working through the newly created
British Council and, from 1938, through the BBC's foreign language broadcasts.
In Britain itself, the government conducted a multimedia campaign, but was
to find its chief ally in the form of the five main newsreel companies.

5.4 The Newsreels

The newsreels operated within a commercial context of entertainment. This
was their political significance. Their attitude to news presentation was determined not by a charter and licence, as in the case of the BBC, but by an
understanding of what was good commercial practice or sense. And although
they repeatedly protested their impartiality, quite often their perception of
public opinion and the personal inclinations of their editors got the better of
their stories. There was a fine distinction to be drawn in their coverage of
foreign and defence matters between alienating their audience by constantly
pushing out propaganda – people in the 1930s went 'to the pictures' to be
entertained – and explaining the news.

In many respects, feature films could operate far more effectively insofar as domestic politics was concerned. After the 1936 Abdication crisis, it is no coincidence that several feature films were made relating to the subject of monarchy using a historical context in order to restore confidence in the institution – *Victoria the Great* and *Sixty Glorious Years* being the best examples (the latter even having had script contributions from Sir Robert Vansittart). The huge captive audience for such films in Britain – nearly four million cinema seats providing for an average weekly audience of between 18.5 and 21 million in the years 1934–39 – allowed an ideal opportunity for the newsreel companies to reach a predominantly working-class audience – the new electorate – in the 15–35 age bracket and to shape their view of the world.

Between 1934 and 1939 the newsreels were only too happy to inject items and commentaries into their issues which explained and justified the policies of the government, and with them the government was in the main well-pleased. We know of several occasions when the government asked the newsreels to delete certain material, but these incidents, revealed in the files of the Metropolitan Police, generally relate to labour unrest at home and abroad. There are one or two examples of censorship of contentious items relating to foreign and political affairs, the most notorious being British Paramount's critical newsreel issue of 22 September 1938 which caused a storm in Parliament. But the newsreels were not generally subject to censorship regulations, and for the most part their 'patriotism' meant that there was no need for them to be. The imported American *March of Time* series was, however, subject to BBFC regulations and was in fact frequently banned. As for the British-based companies, Conservative Central Office made frequent representations to either exclude undesirable material or, more commonly, to include desirable material such as ministerial statements. In 1934, Joseph Ball informed Chamberlain that, despite the film industry's opposition to political propaganda in cinemas, 'much has nevertheless been done without protest from the public by means of the newsreels'. And by 1938 he could inform Chamberlain with confidence that:

> I have cultivated some close personal contacts with the 'leaders' of the British Film Industry, and I am satisfied that I can count upon most of them for their full support to any reasonable degree ... We must devote the closest attention to the possibilities of exploiting screens of the ordinary cinema theatres throughout the country (seen by 20 million people weekly). I have already prepared the way for this with all the big circuits among exhibitors (including the all-powerful Cinematograph Exhibitors Association), with [Alexander] Korda among the producers, and with the chairmen of the five News Reel Companies.[21]

This network of governmental and Central Office contacts with the media explains why the head of the Foreign Office News Department could claim that the connections between his office and 'both the press and the BBC are now so close that it can conduct this work quietly and smoothly without giving the impression of propaganda'.[22] In practice, therefore, the news media accepted that they had a vital role to play in the preservation of the democratic system, forming an integral part of the unifying mass communications system which, in Reith's phrase, constituted the nervous system of the body politic.

5.5 The BBC

It is often assumed that the British government began to manipulate the media during or shortly after the Munich crisis in order to evoke popular support for its appeasement policy. Anthony Adamthwaite has demonstrated that this process began well before September 1938.[23] It perhaps helps to explain why public opinion at large supported the government's attempt to find agreement with Nazi Germany, why there was little protest at increased taxation for rearmament and why there was a remarkable degree of consensus during a period which has subsequently aroused bitter controversy.

In so far as broadcasting was concerned, the unique character of a centrally controlled, monopolistic and potentially all-pervasive broadcasting system in Britain guaranteed that, from its inception, the BBC would receive political consideration of its role in society and in the democratic process. Broadcasting was seen as one solution to the newly extended and 'ignorant' electorate whose uninformed and irresponsibly given vote would be, and indeed already was, regarded as a serious menace to the well-being of the country, 'the national interest'. Radio would provide the electorate with firsthand information and knowledge about the political process and serve as a unifying factor in the preservation of democracy, already on trial in Europe where in some cases it had been found guilty and replaced by other forms of government. As one official put it early on: 'From Palace to Slum, people are listening. It is the most democratic form of entertainment ever invented by man'.[24] Yet despite the idealism of the early broadcasters, inspired by the religious and puritanical zeal of Sir John Reith, their Director-General, the system was open to political manipulation. The General Strike of 1926 demonstrated both the BBC's potential as a purveyor of news and its limitations as an impartial and entirely apolitical organisation. It also showed the unashamed support of Reith and of the BBC for the principle of moderation over extremism and discussion over confrontation.

The potential of broadcasting as a mass political and educational influence also depended primarily upon its power as an entertainment medium. Its political and educational value, like that of the cinema, depended not on its actual ability to reach the entire electorate, nor even on its impartiality, but upon its power to attract a mass audience by the inducement of popular entertainment. In 1924, only 10 percent of British households had a licence. This figure rose to 30 percent in 1930 and 71 percent by 1939. The key role of broadcasting, therefore, lay not so much on the provision of information on which rational decisions could be made by its audience – although it also did this – but rather on its ability to arouse its audience's curiosity and to encourage in it a desire to make decisions, and to make them from a knowledgeable standpoint. As one of its officials appreciated:

Broadcasting is a powerful medium of propaganda. It is oracular and yet friendly. It is not what is said but the way in which it is said that influences its listeners. There is no need to say things directly over the air: the attitude of mind revealed in day-to-day behaviour is itself powerful propaganda. Political beliefs need not be imposed; they can be made to grow out of men's minds by suggestion.[25]

The BBC remained fundamentally committed to the idea of democratic education. In its political coverage, however, the government was a constraint, although not because it tried to restrict the BBC's independence or even because it tried to get the BBC to serve as an official propaganda mouthpiece. Rather, it was a question of the 'national interest' and this was particularly evident in the realm of foreign affairs.

The BBC's motto that 'Nation shall speak peace unto nation' reflected its profound concern for promoting an internationalist spirit both amongst its listeners and between states.[26] The BBC saw peace as depending to a large extent upon the elimination of national ignorance about international events and other nations. It therefore accepted as one of its primary duties the task of informing and educating its audience concerning the intricacies of foreign affairs, as well as providing numerous programmes and series on aspects of life in foreign countries. Initially, the BBC worked closely with the Foreign Office on the very first talks series to be broadcast, in 1931, on a specific and contentious overseas topic, 'Russia in the Melting Pot'. The BBC had wanted close consultancy on the matter of content, but the Foreign Office replied that:

[The BBC] is not entirely independent like a newspaper, as the government have a right to intervene and foreign governments are aware of this ... All I can suggest, if we are to attempt a liaison, is that our functions should be of a negative character, viz. that we should discourage anything of a controversial character and advise the omission of any passage which we considered likely to cause controversy in the press. In practice that would mean that we should confine ourselves to the omission of anything that might cause offence to a foreign government, or the correction of an obvious mis-statement of fact.[27]

It was, therefore, the government which initially resisted direct involvement in content control; and the experience of Vernon Bartlett's talks on foreign affairs in the early 1930s – which the Foreign Office considered excellent at first – appears to demonstrate that the BBC could be trusted to work for the nation as a whole.

Within two years, however, closer co-operation had become essential. Events in Europe, and the BBC's coverage of the rise of Hitler, the collapse of the disarmament conference and the withdrawal of Germany from the League of Nations, led to foreign politics assuming a more central position in the BBC's output. A taste of things to come occurred in early 1933 when the BBC informed the Foreign Office in advance that it was proposing to transmit a series of interviews held by Vernon Bartlett with various European leaders.

The Foreign Office was against the idea and made representations to replace the series with Bartlett summarising what had been said after the scripts had been submitted in advance for checking and amendment by the Foreign Office. In other words, despite increased public interest, foreign affairs was still regarded as an area in which the normal democratic freedoms could not be allowed an entirely free rein. The BBC was prepared to accept this even though it ran counter to its avowed aim to present politics, whether domestic of foreign, in an impartial and free manner. Besides, as Bartlett himself recognised:

> No foreign government is easily going to understand how a state concern like the BBC nevertheless retains a very great degree of autonomy. It will never believe that the Foreign Office is not expressing its views through the lips of the speaker on foreign affairs.[28]

It is clear therefore that it was the BBC's own sense of national duty and responsibility which brought it into closer contact with the Foreign Office, and thus made it more susceptible to Foreign Office influence.

Another talk in October 1933 by Vernon Bartlett brought matters to a head. It was in that month that Germany walked out of the League of Nations. Bartlett, a member of the League Secretariat in London, pleaded over the air for greater understanding of the German viewpoint and suggested that Britain and her allies were as much to blame for Germany's action as Hitler. The incident obviously had considerable international ramifications and sparked off a major debate over the role of the BBC in foreign affairs. The Germans were pleased; the French, however, were furious. Calls for stricter Foreign Office control were made; Bartlett had not consulted its News Department in advance. It was difficult for either side to resolve the issue without inviting criticism. But one thing was clear: greater Foreign Office-BBC contacts were essential in future. Bartlett was not sacked, but Reith did advise him to look for an outside job so that he could become one of a panel of occasional foreign affairs commentators. He joined the *News Chronicle* at the end of the year and continued to give a weekly talk until the end of March 1934, when his regular BBC contract was terminated. He did not broadcast for several years and harmony between the BBC and the Foreign Office was restored. Periodic misunderstandings did occur thereafter, but they tended to be settled in a comparatively smooth and co-operative manner.

Anthony Adamthwaite has argued that the absence in the late 1930s of a strong public challenge to the government's policies 'reflected in part the exercise of extensive official influence on the press, broadcasting and newsreels in the run-up to Munich.' 'In effect', he continues, 'the government restricted public debate and limited the ventilation of alternative views'.[29] The BBC played an important role in this process. Early in 1938, for example, the BBC was running a series of talks entitled 'The Way of Peace' covering such issues as isolationism, pacifism and the role of the League. When, however, Labour MP Josiah Wedgewood refused to delete references to Hitler and Mussolini's policy as one of 'persecution, militancy and inhumanity', the broadcast was cancelled. Again, on 2 and 16 September 1938, as the Czech crisis was mounting, the ill-fated Vernon Bartlett's talks on world affairs in *Children's Hour* were even cancelled 'at the request of the Foreign Office'. In these various, but very British, ways the political establishment was able to exercise not control, but rather influence, over the new media of mass communications. On matters of national interest – such as national survival – the links were in place to enable to government to disseminate its policies without the appearance of being in the nasty business of undertaking official direct propaganda.

5.6 The Preliminary Phase, 1934–35

This period was dominated by heightened anxieties concerning the air menace and worries concerning the resurrection of the German military phoenix. The newsreels reflected these anxieties and provided sympathetic coverage of the government's rearmament measures. On 7 February 1935, the newsreel Gaumont British ran an interview with Sir John Simon, then Foreign Secretary, who informed the audience:

> During the Anglo-French conversations, one of the subjects discussed between us has been the air peril, and it seems to us that the best way to insure against this risk in western Europe might be to provide a deterrent – by agreement between certain powers for immediate, combined air action against the wrongdoer which would make it too dangerous to attempt to commit the crime.
>
> It deserves consideration by all and its construction will benefit us all. Such a plan would give to us here in Britain, if we were thus attacked, the added protection of a continental air force.
>
> I invite my fellow countrymen to think over this plan for themselves. It is a plan to ensure peace and its object is to remove from our homes and ourselves a new and haunting terror.[30]

With the announcement of the Defence White Paper in March 1935, British Movietone ran an item entitled 'Is there to be an armaments race?' which used the rearmament of foreign powers to justify Britain's new expenditure. A week later on 14 March 1935 (the day before Hitler announced the reintroduction of conscription within Germany), Gaumont ran an interview with Prime Minister MacDonald about the White Paper. The Labour leader was clearly uneasy in front of the cameras, and perhaps also with his somewhat over- laboured argument about peace being the 'first declaration of the White Paper, peace is pursued in the proposals made in its middle part, peace is the road on which it ends'.[31] Despite the news from Germany the following day, the newsreels maintained their reassuring tone, with Paramount even running an explanation by George Bernard Shaw under the title 'No Need for Panic'. Shaw argued:

> Well, you may take it from me that the news from Germany is the very

best news that we have had since the war. Ever since 1918 we, like all other Powers, have been behaving just as badly as we possibly could. Well now, when Germany was defeated, when Germany fell, they went and sat on Germany's head although it was quite obvious, quite evident to any sensible person, that they couldn't go on like that forever. Then there came a very intelligent gentleman called Adolf Hitler and he, knowing perfectly well that the powers would not fight, he snapped his fingers at the Treaty of Versailles. That was what got him the votes of 95% of the whole population of Germany, even including the very people whom he'd been treating rather hardly. Just exactly as if we in England had been in the same position, as if the powers had beaten us and sat on our heads, then the first man who had the gumption to see that we might get up on our legs and defy all those old treaties, he would be the most popular man in England.

There can be no peace in this world until there is peace between England, France, Germany, Russia, the United States and all the big powers of the West. Now take that home and think about it and don't be frightened any more about the Germans.[32]

A study of the Armistice Day issues in the 1930s reveals the changes in attitudes towards rearmament and war. Until 1934, the solemn annual commemorations were as much about the celebration of victory and the mourning of the dead as they were about hopes for peace. But in 1934 a new element began to creep into the newsreels' coverage, as in Movietone's statement that 'once war seems inevitable again, a million martyrs will have died in vain'.[33] Pacifist sentiment was still high in 1935 and the newsreels gave it sufficient coverage, as in Gaumont's coverage of the Oxford Group's protest on the twenty-first anniversary of the Great War. But equally, in their coverage of the new rearmament measures, the message was that 'at last Britain is awakening to the knowledge that air preparedness is the surest guarantee of peace'.[34]

5.7 The Second Phase, 1936–38

Once the election had been won by the National Government, psychological rearmament entered a more vigorous phase. The predominant themes until late 1938 were, first reassurance that Britain was more than capable of protecting her worldwide interests (when, in reality, this was far from the prevailing official view kept hidden from the British people – and from foreign governments, particularly in Tokyo, Berlin and Rome). Second, increased sacrifices were required on the part of the British people, such as rising taxation, if peace was to be preserved. Reminders of what could happen used the Spanish Civil War and the renewal of hostilities in the Far East from 1937 as news hooks, to show what might happen if appeasement and rearmament failed to deter war and the bomber did get through. Third, there were constant calls for unity and co-operation amongst the people to prevent the unthinkable from happening.

The first half of 1936 saw an overlap with the justification theme of the preliminary phase of psychological rearmament. For example, Chamberlain (still Chancellor) informed Paramount's audiences that the new tax increases constituted an insurance policy for peace:

> In an armed and arming world, we couldn't be the only great country disarmed. We simply had to build our defence forces again, and we have to pay for it. But we mustn't take it too tragically ... When you come to look at it carefully, it isn't such a bad budget after all.[35]

However, whereas in 1935 the newsreels had still been prepared to provide an outlet for criticisms concerning the inadequacy of Britain's naval position – so vital in traditional psychological terms and for contemporary imperial defence concerns – they were in 1936 at pains to point out the strengths of the Royal Navy. For example, in October 1935, shortly after the outbreak of the Italo-Ethiopian war, Gaumont had carried an item entitled 'Jellicoe emphasises need for adequate navy' in which the former Great War sealord had warned:

> Under present conditions, the British Empire does not possess the sea power that is vital for its existence. What immediate steps are we going to take to put this matter right? The obvious necessity before us is that of starting to build up our navy, at once, to adequate strength ... The result is that the British Empire, the one power that is absolutely dependent upon the sea for its existence, is not now by any means in a satisfactory state of defence, and has certainly lost a great deal of its influence to boot in world affairs. The vote of a powerful nation carries strength; that of a weak one does not.[36]

Although this final sentence was fully in accord with the principles of psychological rearmament, this is almost the last blatant admission of Britain's weaknesses to appear in the newsreels for the next four years. More typically, emphasis was placed on Britain's strength, as in Gaumont's item of May 1936 quoting Sir Roger Keyes as saying:

> The Navy is still invincible, ready and willing to tackle any force that dares to challenge it. Nobody in Britain wants another war, but that is not because Britain is afraid. The Navy is still the greatest asset of Britain's safety and to the peace of the world.[37]

With the remilitarisation of the Rhineland in March 1936, the successful Italian conquest of Ethiopia by May and the outbreak of the Spanish Civil War in July of the same year, governmental and popular attention refocused on Europe, the continued German air menace and the fear of the bomber. It was the newsreels that attempted to provide continued reassurance.

In one of the most famous examples of newsreel propaganda in the 1930s, Gaumont British produced a masterly item in August 1936 entitled 'Britain's Trade Recovery and Prestige', more usually referred to by historians as 'Wonderful Britain'. Following an item on the Spanish Civil War, Gaumont ran the special issue under the caption 'The World Today – Britain leads the way to recovery', the commentary for which (spoken by Ted Emmett on one of his best days) went as follows:

> In the passage of time, it is no far cry back to Abyssinia, so recently racked with the torments of awful war. From Abyssinia, our review takes us to Palestine where racial factions clash unhappily day by day, where riots and slaughter crowd an all too complete programme of misery and despair. In a spirit not of boastfulness but rather of gratitude, we turn from these fitful scenes to Fortunate Britain, still with its tradition of sanity, the rock of steadying influence amidst the eddying streams of world affairs.
>
> Britain's industries have shaken off the chains that kept them fettered in the aftermath of the World War. They have risen from the slough which clogged the wheels of progress in the last decade. Trade returns are steadily improving. Weekly and monthly, the official statistics form a heartening accompaniment to the efforts alike of the small merchant and the big boss of giant industry to better times. Our railways today stand second to none. Shipbuilding yards, for many years hushed in the inertia of unemployment, have been given a lead by the triumphant completion of the Queen Mary, now unquestionably supreme upon the mercantile lanes of the sea. Frequently overlooked, but never to be forgotten, is the vital factor of British justice, the fairest in the world. The tradition of civil life and equity and incorruptibility has never been called into question. This honesty in the courts of evil and wrongdoing is a sure fortress against the social hatreds that foster revolution. The army, the navy and the airforce of this country have proved a sure protector and deterrent in the unrest that has prevailed abroad. Britain is taking her stand in the belief that a strong defence is a guarantee of peace. Statesmen who may have drawn upon themselves criticism from time to time, have nonetheless worked unremittingly for peace at home and abroad. As we look back, we realise that their efforts have brought this country safely through the innumerable crises that have beset it in the past few years. And, above all, we look to the head of this great nation, whose example and courage have won the admiration of envious nations less happy. Every member of the Royal Family works unselfishly and without stint in the cause of social service. The aim and the achievements of Queen Mary and the royal dukes and duchesses had been less to rule than to serve the country of which they stand head. For the King, already in the short time since his accession, has proved a worthy successor to his great father and to his grandfather, Edward the Peacemaker: 'Humanity cries out for peace and the assurance of peace'. Long may he continue to lead Britain from the chaos of world affairs closer to the day of lasting peace, prosperity and happiness.[38]

Setting aside the fact that King Edward VIII was to abdicate the throne a mere four months later, the newsreels frequently used the Monarchy in their coverage of political events as a means of evoking national unity and stability.

The co-operation of the workforce was vital to the continued progress of rearmament. The newsreels did all they could to encourage that co-operation, particularly at a time when the Labour Party remained opposed to the government's policy (although, in fact, the Trade Union movement was less truculent and even willing to discuss co-operation). In January 1937, the RAF proposed the conversion of rearmament Scheme F into Scheme H, which called for a further expansion of Britain's bomber deterrent force to keep pace with Germany's rearmament (600 more bombers and 50 additional fighters by April 1939). The government rejected the scheme on the grounds of cost; it had already had to borrow money to finance the existing programmes in February 1937. Gaumont followed an item on the fall of Malaga with a story entitled 'Britain's Rearmament Plan' which ran in part:

> Parliament has decided that Britain shall spend £1,500,000,000 on armaments in the next five years, not directed against any one country, said the Chancellor, but because of our vast responsibilities in all parts of the world, and as a measure for the preservation of peace. This means no remission in taxation, but it gives security. Even more than that, it will reduce the figures of unemployment. More ships mean more men at work ... Aircraft factories will be going at full production. Security will bring prosperity ... Every aeroplane, every tank, every ship, means more work and more safety. Even if it means an increase in taxation, what a great insurance! It is a life policy. Even if it does mean an increase, it also means security, more employment and the preservation of peace for this great country of ours, this British Empire.[39]

With the appointment of Neville Chamberlain as Prime Minister in May 1937 and the renewal of the Sino-Japanese conflict shortly afterwards, the newsreels maintained their support for the government's policies while reflecting for the last time, in their Armistice coverage of that year, the continuing hopes for peace. Gaumont's masterly issue asked 'Was it in Vain?', and provided an historical analysis of the previous twenty-five years, concluding 'It *Must Not* be in Vain'.[40] The Armistice Day coverage of the following year, the last such peacetime commemoration, was more concerned with preparations for war than it was any longer with hopes for peace.

Movietone's end-of-year review for 1937 was correct in its prediction that there would be 'no major war in 1938'.[41] But this was not without coming as close as it was possible to get to war. 1938 was the year of the Anschluss and Munich. It also saw the continuation of war in Spain and in the Far East. Both of these wars saw the indiscriminate bombing of innocent civilians and, in their coverage of them, the newsreels were at pains to point out what could happen to British homes if war should come between Britain and Germany. For example, Gaumont's item on the bombing of Guernica in May 1937 ended with the statement: 'This was a city, and these were homes – like yours'.[42] But towards the end of 1937, there began to emerge a challenge to the prevailing assumption that the bomber 'would always get through'. The development of radar and of new fighter aircraft (Spitfires and Hurricanes) offered new hopes for the air defence of Great Britain. It was also a financially convenient argument: fighters were much cheaper and easier to build than bombers and required fewer personnel to keep them operational. (Accordingly, in 1938, the emphasis of Britain's air rearmament was switched from bombers to fighters, while gas masks and air raid shelters were given greater prominence.) The message now was 'Be Prepared'. Calls were made to the workforce and to potential volunteers to the fighting services. Britain must be strong if peace was to be preserved. Following its coverage of the Anschluss in March 1938, Gaumont ran an item mischievously entitled 'Britain's Reply – Rearm on War Basis'. In fact Britain was in no position to 'reply' to Hitler's latest move even if it had wanted to, having long accepted the inevitability of the German action. However, in this item all the prevailing themes of psychological rearmament are evident. It ran as follows:

What is our position in Britain today? Mass meetings have been held in Trafalgar Square and the Prime Minister has made a statement in the House of Commons. Both make it clear that Britain's duty is to herself. Britain must be strong and even the present rearmament programme must be speeded up. An appeal to employers and workers of all kinds will be made to co-operate in the time of national emergency.

Shadow factories, where the production of aircraft is proceeding, must be able to produce at greater speed than hitherto. Production of armaments in all departments must be increased by national effort – not to take part in war, not to interfere in the wars of others, but to preserve the peace of our own Empire. These are the guarantees of our own national security, our independence, demanding expenditure down to the last shilling if necessary.

Sir Samuel Hoare, the Home Secretary, has called for a million air raid workers. Here again it is no alarmist call but a wise determination to be prepared. The Home Secretary said that the more disturbed is the continent of Europe, the more urgent it is for us to make every possible preparation against the most dangerous form of modern warfare. If Britain is prepared, then air raid terrors will be less formidable.

British morale and the personnel of the Empire's fighting forces are second to none. Our soldiers and sailors and airmen are unrivalled, but without the implements of war they would be helpless. A nation's fighting strength today depends almost as much upon the skill of the engineer and the scientist as it does upon those who carry arms. The spirit of Britain, backed by all the weight of armaments that she is capable of producing, will guarantee the safety of our people, not only now but also in the future. If a sacrifice is called for to provide those armaments, those aeroplanes and guns and tanks and battleships that comprise the grim paraphernalia of war, then let us make that sacrifice. What sacrifice could be too great to make in exchange for security, the safety of our homes and our own people? *Your* safety.[43]

But by the time the Czechoslovakian crisis threatened to plunge Europe into another major war in September 1938, it was clear that rearmament's principal enemy was time.

The Munich crisis seriously exposed the deficiencies that existed in Britain's defences. Although neither the public nor foreign opinion was informed of the extent of this weakness, military inadequacy was a major factor in Chamberlain's negotiations with Hitler in September 1938. Time had indeed caught up with the 1935 rearmament programmes. Britain was not yet sufficiently confident of her ability to fight a major war, either militarily or psychologically. At their first meeting at Berchtesgaden, Chamberlain had agreed in principle to the transfer of the Sudetenland from Czechoslovakia to Germany. It was a concession fully in accord with the principle of self-determination. But at their second meeting at Godesberg a week later, Hitler had set a deadline for the transfer, one that was unacceptable to the British government. And so, during the final week of September 1938, Britain found herself preparing for a war over a principle she had already conceded a war for which she had neither the conviction nor the means to fight.

It transpired that both ingredients were also absent in Germany. Hitler backed down from his Godesberg 'ultimatum' and agreed to a third meeting at Munich. While the Great Powers met once again to carve up the map of Europe, Britain's preparations involved a widespread series of improvisations (including the digging of trenches in Hyde Park) as described in Gaumont's item of 29 September 1938. The newsreels' call that 'Britain must be stronger' was also reflected in the British press. On the 27 September the *Daily Mirror* for example argued: 'Make Britain strong. Britain stands for peace, but she must be strong for war. It is your duty to give her strength. By joining your Defence Units. By growing all the food you can. By avoiding waste. By making aircraft, ammunition, ships. By keeping calm, cheerful, determined. To make the nation so strong that none may dare challenge the peace of the world'.[44]

The widespread sense of relief at the avoidance of war at Munich was reflected in the newsreels' coverage of the Four-Power Conference when they hailed 'Chamberlain the Peacemaker'. Gaumont's item ended with the statement: 'Posterity will thank God, as we do now that, in the time of need, our safety was guarded by such a man – Neville Chamberlain'.[45]

In the aftermath of the crisis, it was clear that, as one official put it, 'we must never again find ourselves in a position to the one we found ourselves in on 27 September'.[46] The existing rearmament programmes were accelerated; they were not yet replaced with new ones as that would merely indicate to public opinion at home and abroad that the government saw Munich as a time-buying device rather than an attempt to secure 'peace in our time'. Yet there is a problem here. If Chamberlain really did believe that his policy had succeeded, then why did he accelerate the existing programmes? On the other hand, if he felt that war with Germany was still a distinct possibility, then why did he not introduce new rearmament programmes sooner? Perhaps he felt that public opinion was not yet ready to deal with expansion; such a move would undermine the government's stance over Munich and may provoke Hitler. Perhaps the answer lies in the Prime Minister's statement to the Foreign Secretary, Lord Halifax, that 'we must hope for the best, while preparing for the worst'.

5.8 The Third Phase, 1938–39

Whatever the real reason, Hitler helped to determine the next phase of psychological rearmament. While the call to arms continued – calls for volunteers to the armed services, for air-raid workers and for continued sacrifices on the part of the British people – Hitler refused to follow up Munich with further negotiations. This, together with the enlightening evidence concerning the real nature of his regime after Kristallnacht (the 'Night of the Broken Glass'), a major anti-Jewish pogrom in November 1938, helped to dispel any last doubts as to the wisdom of rearmament. Hitler's seizure of the rump of Czechoslovakia in March 1939 settled the matter once and for all. It was in the intervening period that new rearmament programmes were introduced providing for a degree of fighter aircraft cover that was to prove vital – albeit barely sufficient – in 1940. The army was at last geared for involvement in a continental war whereas previously it was intended for imperial duties. Conscription was introduced for the first time ever in peacetime in May 1939. And, at last, Britain abandoned her go-it-alone approach to Germany, choosing instead to cultivate the French, and, more dramatically (if abortively), the Russians.

All this may justifiably be regarded as 'too little, too late'. But there were financial and economic constraints to unlimited rearmament that remained acute even in 1939. Moreover, there was a matter of perception to be tackled. Until the seizure of Prague, and the forcible incorporation of non-Germans into the Reich for the first time, Hitler was perceived to have legitimate grievances. It was his methods more than his objectives that had caused distaste. Chamberlain had, in fact, been extremely skilful in the publicity he allowed of the Munich agreement. That much maligned 'scrap of paper' effectively told the world (particularly the Americans although, notably, not the Russians): 'here are the limits of German expansion'. If Hitler kept to the agreement, then the world really would have 'peace in our time'. (The phrase 'Peace with Honour' was an unfortunate slip which Chamberlain regretted almost as soon as he said it.) If Hitler did not, then the world would see (as would the British people) that his goals were not limited and that he would have to be stopped for a 'just cause'. This was essential if a British government was to go to war risking the decimation by German bombers of its electorate (there was a General Election due in 1940) and all the risks which that was felt to entail. And, when all is said and done, the extra year of time bought for rearmament at Munich – though not Chamberlain's intention – did enable Britain to survive her 'finest hour' in 1940. True, the long-feared three-theatre war did not materialise until 1941 – Mussolini choosing to stay out until he thought the war was over after the fall of France, and Japan choosing to attack the Americans at Pearl Harbour in 1941. In September 1939, Germany was in no position to rain bombs over

London – that was not feasible until the fall of the Low Countries and France. But when it did happen, the Russians and United States were there to help.

Even so, British cinema audiences in 1939 could not have anticipated such events. Until March 1939, the newsreels continued their support for appeasement while maintaining their call to arms. For example, Gaumont's Armistice Day issue for 1938 included the lines:

> There need never be another cenotaph if Britain is strong enough to defy the threat of war. That is why all men and women, however their difference of opinions, should work together for the sake of our Empire. We in Britain have a hatred of war, but to fear war is to provoke it ... it is not sufficient today to live in the Empire; we must also serve it.
>
> Britain must be strong. If our fighting services are great, our youth may live in them today. If they are weak, our manhood must die in them tomorrow. Britain must be strong until the world returns to sanity and all men may live together in peace.[47]

Again, reflecting government policy, the repeated emphasis was placed on defence against the bomber in the form of fighters, air-raid precautions and Anderson shelters.

But a new element began to emerge in the psychological preparations, namely emphasis on the strength of Britain's 'allies'. Gaumont British, still the most supportive newsreel company and by now the most unashamedly propagandist, ran an entire series entitled 'The Defence of France' in which the ability of France to maintain her watch on the Rhine, behind the 'impenetrable' Maginot Line, was repeatedly stressed. (France's actual ability to safeguard this vital British interest was tested in 1940. But had the true extent of French weakness been revealed to British cinema audiences in the winter of 1938–9 it would merely have caused panic.) A further, and even more deceptive, element of the newsreels' coverage was the emphasis which they placed on the strength and solidarity of Anglo-American relations, as illustrated by Gaumont's brilliantly propagandistic yet wholly unreal coverage of Roosevelt's 'Sane call to Europe':

> The President's peace effort for Europe has aroused a wave of strong feeling in America. Mr Roosevelt's demand for a pledge of peace has fixed the responsibility. The diplomatic stroke from Washington is warmly welcomed by the government in Britain. France, too, lines up in complete and unreserved agreement with this effort to bring harmony out of the discord across the new map of Europe. Never before have so many nations stood united in the one common cause: Humanity. With some of these countries, Britain holds pacts of mutual assistance, and talks with the mighty forces of Soviet Russia proceed favourably towards the end of bringing tranquillity into this turbulent continent ... With the common ideal of peace and liberty, the world's democracies are standing shoulder to shoulder against the forces of tyranny and aggression.[48]

There are several points to note about this item, apart from the fact that it was almost entirely misleading. Roosevelt's peace appeal of 14 April, which was designed to divide German opinion from Hitler by proposing a peace conference that the Führer couldn't possibly accept, and thereby expose him as a warmonger (in both Germany and America), was given a significance out of all proportion to the reality of the international situation. Roosevelt was still trapped by isolationist American sentiment, and was to remain so until 1941. The emphasis placed on the 'Grand Alliance' of democratic nations was also misleading. Britain was in no position to aid France substantially, let alone Norway, Greece, Poland and the other states mentioned in the item. Moreover, the reference to Russia would be seen as hollow with the signing of the Nazi–Soviet Pact in August. Britain and France were essentially alone – and vulnerable. Even the item's reassurance about the speed with which anti-aircraft guns could be loaded and fired is manipulated by rapid editing. And the likening of Hitler's methods by Roosevelt to those of the Huns and the Visigoths was reminiscent of the stereotyping so essential to the war propaganda of 1914–18 and so characteristic of the coming conflict. To put it bluntly, the Big Lie had begun.

5.9 The Illusions Exposed

Interestingly, the pretext for the German invasion of Poland on 1 September was a fabricated attack on the German radio station at Gleiwitz, in which one German supposedly died and another was wounded. Two days later, the British people entered the Second World War with a unity and resigned acceptance that belies the fears and anxieties of the 1930s. They did not turn out in the streets to dance and cheer as they had done in 1914 with hopes that it would all be over by Christmas. But neither did they succumb to panic or despair. Instead, they listened calmly to Chamberlain on the wireless telling them that:

> We have a clear conscience, we have done all that any country could do to establish peace, but a situation in which no word given by Germany's ruler could be trusted, and no people or country could feel themselves safe, had become intolerable ... Now may God bless you all and may He defend the right. For it is evil things that we shall be fighting against, brute force, bad faith, injustice, oppression, and persecution. And against them I am certain the right will prevail.[49]

The British had declared war on Germany for just reasons. This was the only comfort they could feel on the eve of Armageddon, a mere generation after the war to end all wars. Appeasement had been tried and found wanting. It would remain to be seen how its counterpart, rearmament, would fare in the coming months.

In view of the long-feared threat of an aerial knockout blow and the anxieties concerning a possible three-theatre war, it is perhaps as well that neither materialised in 1939. But this in turn reveals two major pre-war illusions in what has been called an age of illusion. The Rome–Berlin Axis and the anti-comintern pact were by no means as coherent or as solid alliances as contemporaries believed. They were propaganda devices – highly effective ones – rather than genuine diplomatic alignments. They gave the impression that Germany, Italy and Japan were acting in concert when, in reality, this was rarely the case.[50] They were, rather, convenient and somewhat loose alignments based on a symbiotic relationship whereby the one power benefited from the distractions caused by the others. The Spanish Civil War was a case in point; it was in Hitler's interests to maintain tension in the Mediterranean not only to distract Britain's attention, but also to weaken Mussolini's grip on Austria. In 1934, the Duce had moved troops to the Brenner Pass to maintain Austrian independence threatened by a Nazi coup. Four years later, Mussolini had committed himself so heavily in Abyssinia and Spain (egged on by Hitler) that he was unable to repeat the exercise during the Anschluss. Similarly, in March 1936, Hitler had taken advantage of Anglo–French preoccupation with Mussolini during the Abyssinian crisis to march into the Rhineland. The renewal of the Sino–Japanese conflict in 1937 benefited Italy and Germany. And while Britain and France were recovering from the German seizure of Prague in March 1939, Mussolini seized Albania. In other words, the anti–comintern powers fed off each other all to Britain's disadvantage. They rarely acted in concert, rarely informed each other of their intentions but benefited enormously from the arrangement. Their peacetime marriage of convenience was designed to cripple the will to resist on the part of their opponents. And in the case of Britain, whose scattered worldwide interests were most directly affected, it served to do just that. And by the time Britain attempted to create an effective counter-bloc in 1939, Russia had been alienated, France had been surrounded by hostile fascist powers on all her land borders and the United States remained firmly isolationist. The war that erupted in September 1939 was a European war rather than a global conflict, but the global dimensions of Britain's Imperial dilemma in the 1930s had played a major role in defining the British response to the fascist challenge.

Similarly, the British had been working under the illusion that, if war should come, their cities and economic centres would be decimated within a matter of hours by German bombers. Once again, their opponents had played a masterly disinformation game designed to terrorise and debilitate. When, in 1935, Hitler claimed that he had already achieved parity in the air with Britain, it helped to shape the course of British rearmament in the years that followed. Germany was, in fact, nowhere near as powerful then – or later – in the air as its propagandists would have foreign observers believe. But the Nazi disinformation campaign about the Luftwaffe proved particularly effective in Britain, an island fortress now vulnerable to attack in a way that it had not been before, and still reeling under a wave of 'semi-panic conditions' about the bomber always getting through. The British response, the construction of a bomber deterrence force, was both psychologically and financially expedient. But until that deterrent became credible, which meant actually possessing a bomber force capable of dealing an equally destructive blow to German cities and factories – which

Britain was not expected to have until 1939 – the current state of British *relaying tactics* defences required that the government avoid issuing threats that may be called and therefore exposed as bluff. Thus was grafted onto the traditional policy of appeasement the new policy of rearmament. Deterrence would prevent war in the long run; the danger was in the present.

Hindsight has exposed these assumptions as illusory. We know now that Germany did not have sufficient bombers in 1935, or in 1939 for that matter, to launch its knockout blow. German bombers were designed for army support purposes as part of the overall Blitzkrieg strategy. Moreover, their long-range machines only had an acceptable chance of getting through to Britain's congested industrial and civilian centres if they were accompanied by adequate fighter protection. Bombers are slow and highly vulnerable to enemy fighters unless protected by their own such planes. For Germany, this meant conquering France and the Low Countries so that short-range fighter aircraft could afford some protection for their bombers as they passed over the Channel. Moreover, when the bombers did materialise over British cities in 1940, they often served to consolidate rather than shatter morale. The pre-war perception of the bomber as a doomsday machine, with all the exaggerated calculations concerning the potential damage it could do to life, limb, property and the fabric of British society, was far from the actual experience of the Blitz.

Nonetheless, in the 1930s, the air rearmament programmes served to allay many contemporary fears. In reality, however, the programmes only provided for what has been called a 'shop window deterrent', because German cities and factories were much farther away from British airfields than were British cities and factories from Germany's. As one historian has written:

> Torn between what it saw as its obligation to guide Britain out of the depression and back to prosperity (the task on which its political survival depended) and its obligation to provide for the national security, the Government responded by seeking to create the image of power without investing in its more costly substance. This was the rationale behind both the policy of 'showing tooth' in the Far East, and that of creating a 'shop window' deterrent against Germany. It was a policy recognised as involving risks, but the risks were considered far more acceptable than those to economic recovery in developing the substance of power.[51]

The fact that rearmament was not allowed to cripple the British economy was to reap rewards during the long war of attrition between 1939 and 1945. True, the United States also helped, and the long-term cost was the loss of much of the British Empire, but the economy did not collapse as it did in Germany and much of Europe.

When, in 1938–9, the need for urgency became increasingly apparent, the financial constraints which had done so much to affect the pace of British rearmament also helped to determine the nature of Britain's improvisations. Emphasis was switched from expensive bombers to cheaper fighters, from the construction of a bomber deterrent to the straightforward air defence of Great

Britain. A more realistic appraisal of British strategy manifested itself in the gearing of the British army from its imperial role to a continental commitment and in the introduction of conscription. Singapore was opened in 1938. Allies were cultivated: the Royal Family visited the United States in 1939; the French were welcomed on a State visit. All these measures were given maximum publicity in the British media and particularly in the newsreels. Despite the traumas of the Depression, the Abdication crisis and incessant foreign wars, national unity was preserved. The newsreels, through their skilful injection of persuasive and supportive items into their usually entertaining issues over the previous five years had played a significant role in achieving this goal amongst the very people who would be expected to fight the coming Total War.

Notes and References

1 This chapter is a truncated and revised version of a pamphlet written to accompany the film *A Call to Arms: Propaganda and Rearmament in the 1930s*, which I wrote and directed for the Inter-University History Film Consortium in 1984.

2 P. Fussell, *The Great War and Modern Memory* (New York, 1975).

3 P. M. Kennedy, 'The tradition of appeasement in British foreign policy, 1865–1939' in his *Strategy and Diplomacy* (Allen and Unwin, 1983).

4 R. A. C. Parker, 'British rearmament, 1936–39: treasury, Trade Unions and skilled labour', *English Historical Review*, 96:3 (1981), 306–43.

5 See R. P. Shay, *British Rearmament in the 1930s* (Princeton University Press, 1977); B. Bond, *British Military Policy between the Two World Wars* (Oxford University Press, 1980); S. W. Roskill, *Naval Policy between the Wars* (London, 1976); M. Smith, *British Air Strategy between the Wars* (Oxford University Press, 1982).

6 K. Feiling, *The Life of Neville Chamberlain* (Macmillan, 1946), p. 110.

7 For a detailed elaboration of these views, see F. Hardy (ed.), *Grierson on Documentary* (Collins, 1946).

8 K. Middlemas and J. Barnes, *Baldwin* (Weidenfeld and Nicolson, 1969), p. 503.

9 Quoted in T. Hollins, 'The Presentation of Politics: The place of party publicity, broadcasting and film in British politics, 1918–39', Ph.D. thesis, University of Leeds, (1981), p. 21.

10 Ibid, p. 64.

11 Ibid, p. 80.

12 For a recent evaluation, see Mariel Grant, *Propaganda and the Role of the State in Inter-war Britain* (Oxford, Clarendon Press, 1994) and D. L. Le Mahieu, *A Culture for Democracy: Mass Communications and the Cultivated Mind in Britain between the Wars* (Oxford, Clarendon Press, 1988).

13 N. Pronay, 'The first reality: film censorship in Liberal England' in K. R. M. Short (ed.), *Feature Films as History* (Croom Helm, 1981).

14 Hollins, 'Presentation of Politics', p. 677.

15 CAB 27/518, DCM (32).

16 CAB 24/45, CP 205(34).

17 B. Bond (ed.), *Chief of Staff: The Diaries of General Sir Henry Pownall* (Leo Cooper, 1972). Diary entry for 30 July 1934.

18 Cited in P. Kyba, *Covenants without the Sword: Public Opinion and Defence Policy, 1931–5* (Wilfred Laurier University Press, 1983), p. 143.
19 Parliamentary Debates (Commons), 5th series, vol. 285, 10 November 1932, col. 632.
20 Cmd. 4827 (1935).
21 Quoted in Hollins, 'Presentation of Politics', p. 664.
22 Quoted in Philip M. Taylor, *The Projection of Britain: British Overseas Publicity and Propaganda, 1919–39* (Cambridge University Press, 1982), p. 297.
23 A. P. Adamthwaite, 'The British government and the media, 1937–38', *Journal of Contemporary History*, 18:3 (1983), pp. 281–97.
24 P. P. Eckersley, *The Power behind the Microphone* (Cape, 1940), p. 154.
25 Ibid.
26 Hollins., 'Presentation of Politics, p. 551.
27 PRO, FO 395/453, P. 418/39/150.
28 V. Bartlett, *This is My Life* (Chatto and Windus, 1937), pp. 177–8.
29 Adamthwaite, 'British Government and the Media', p. 290.
30 Gaumont British 116, 7 February 1935. All subsequent newsreel references are to items logged in the Slade Film Register housed at the British Universities Film & Video Council in London. The newsreels themselves are owned by commercial companies, for example Gaumont's output is housed at the Reuters Library (now owned by ITN).
31 Gaumont British 126, 14 March 1935.
32 British Paramount 4281, 21 March 1935.
33 British Movietone 281, 11 November 1934.
34 Gaumont British, 146, 23 May 1935.
35 British Paramount 538, 24 April 1936.
36 Gaumont British 189, 21 October 1935.
37 Gaumont British 248, 14 May 1936.
38 Gaumont British 278, 27 August 1936.
39 Gaumont British 328, 18 February 1937.
40 Gaumont British 167, 5 August 1935.
41 British Movietone 447a, 2 December 1937.
42 Gaumont British 350, 6 May 1937.
43 Gaumont British 440, 17 March 1938.
44 *Daily Mirror*, 27 September 1938.
45 Gaumont British 497, 3 October 1938.
46 Brian Bond (ed.), *Chief of Staff: The Diaries of General Sir Henry Pownall* (Leo Cooper, 1972), diary entry for 3 October 1938.
47 Gaumont British 509, 14 November 1938.
48 Gaumont British 554, 20 April 1939.
49 K. Felling, *Neville Chamberlain*, P. 416.
50 D. C. Watt, 'The Rome-Berlin axis: myth and reality', *Review of Politics* 22:4 (1960), 519–43.
51 Shay, *British Rearmament in the 1930s*, p. 244.

6

Handling the Unavowable: Propaganda and Psychological Warfare, 1935–40[1]

When British representatives set off for Russia in September 1941 to attend the Moscow Conference, they went fully expecting the Soviets to enquire just exactly how Britain proposed to help them win the war against Nazi Germany. It would be a good question that would require a good answer. Given Britain's perilous war situation at that time, especially with Pearl Harbour and American involvement still some months in the future, Britain's negotiating position was far from strong. The reply the delegation was to provide was as follows:

> We shall undermine them by propaganda; depress them with the blockade; and, above all, bomb their homelands ceaselessly, ruthlessly, and with ever increasing weight of bombs.[2]

Two years earlier one of the British Cabinet's first decisions following the outbreak of the Second World War had in fact foreshadowed this statement. Within hours of the Anglo–French declaration of hostilities on 3 September 1939, authorisation was given for the Royal Air Force to initiate the psychological offensive against the Third Reich.[3] That same night, Whitley bombers from RAF 4 Group showered six million leaflets over selective targets on German soil. This exercise, the technical success of which helped to pave the way for Bomber Command's crippling nighttime bombing raids later in the war,[4] launched what was to become the most vociferous war of words ever waged by nation states.

That the government should have been prepared for propaganda in 1939 in a way that it had not been in 1914 was all the more remarkable in light of the situation which had existed during the Munich crisis merely twelve months earlier. On 5 September 1938, Stephen King-Hall, the distinguished publicist and expert on international affairs, wrote in an influential memorandum that:

> A moment might arrive when the whole situation might be saved by an immediate and nation-wide appeal to the German people. If we are involved in a war, a shower of pamphlets over Germany should precede a shower of bombs over the Ruhr.[5]

Almost as an afterthought, he added 'I hope we've got the bombers'. However, even if the bombers had then been available, the Air Ministry had still to be consulted as to its willingness to release the necessary men and machines for what would obviously be a highly dangerous mission. The idea of bombers being used as leaflet-delivery systems against the Germans, with memories of the way the enemy treated captured pilots in the last war, was unlikely to appeal to a Bomber Command sceptical of the value of 'bullshit bombs'. Moreover, there was no pamphlet, even in draft form let alone one fully translated and printed, ready for dissemination. There was thus a very real danger, as King-Hall warned, that 'if the crisis gets worse . . . we may be caught with our trousers down' in so far as propaganda was concerned.[6]

Despite some impressive improvisation in the weeks that followed, including the drafting of various leaflets[7] and some experimental leaflet-dropping raids carried out by the RAF in the north of England,[8] such an embarrassment was avoided only by Neville Chamberlain's third flight to Germany to bring Europe back from the brink of war by signing the Munich Agreement. In other words, the country that had pioneered the use of psychological warfare in the First World War was completely unprepared for its application in September 1938. As we shall see, an imaginative – if highly dangerous – exercise in 'black' radio propaganda was implemented. But clearly a great deal of planning and preparation had still to be done if Britain was to perform anything like as effectively in the next war as it had done in the last one.

6.1 Fears and Constraints

As we have seen in the previous chapter, the difference between the anticipated nature of a future war and the reality of experience is often very wide. When, for example, the long feared 'knockout blow' from the air failed to materialise in 1939, British propagandists had to deal with different kinds of problems – such as boredom – raised during the period of the 'phoney war'.[9] Equally, when the Luftwaffe did begin to appear over British skies in 1940, it was learned that the aerial bombardment of cities often served to consolidate rather than shatter civilian morale.

It is commonplace to plan for the next war by examining the lessons learned from the previous conflict. In the Great War, the use of the economic weapon, whether in the form of the Allied blockade of the Central Powers, or Germany's attempt to starve Britain into submission by the unrestricted U-boat campaign, had been designed to weaken the capacity of the other side to continue the struggle on the field of battle. From the British point of view, the successful application of the former, combined with her ability successfully to resist the stranglehold of the latter, was felt to have played a critical role in determining the final result. The cost of doing so, however, had been high. True, Britain in 1918 had emerged victorious, seemingly at the height of its power, but in reality Britain also emerged from the war in a process of decline. A repetition the next time might signal her complete collapse as a great world power.

But the blockade had not simply been designed to deprive the enemy's armed forces of their basic equipment and supplies. It was also directed towards the mass of the enemy population. The military could simply not afford to ignore events on the home front. When, therefore, in 1934–5, British defence planners were forced to consider the question of contingency plans for a future war, there was every reason to assume that propaganda would play an even greater role next time. There was also a significant new additional factor to be built into to the anticipated nature of the next war: the bomber. If the fear of the bomber and of an aerial knockout blow 'critically affected the making of British defence and foreign policy',[10] it also affected the propaganda planning. Quite simply, Britain's geographically insular position could no longer protect its people from direct involvement in a continental war as the bomber threatened to reduce still further the distance between soldier and civilian experience of Total War. British cities were vulnerable to attack in a way that they had not been before and newsreels showing the bombing of Guernica and Madrid during the Spanish Civil War could only have driven this 'reality' home.[11] It was therefore not unnaturally assumed that, if war should come, civilian morale was likely to prove a critical factor, and indeed it might be assumed that film would have a key role to play in helping to sustain the populace through the dark hours of saturation bombing. In fact, the overriding assumption that the bomber would 'always get through' led to the decision to close all cinemas in the event of war in an attempt to reduce the potential devastation and loss of life.[12] Clearly, Britain would need to survive the Luftwaffe's anticipated initial knockout strike before the fourth and fifth arms of defence could begin to play a decisive role. Even so, during that crucial initial phase, propaganda would still have an important role to play, both at home and abroad, and it was therefore felt that Britain would need to be sufficiently well-equipped to handle the resultant problems from the outset.

6.2 Propaganda by Committee

Significantly, the initiative came from the Air Ministry. The precise origins of the decision to begin planning for propaganda in the next war remain somewhat vague but it does appear that, during the summer of 1935, as the Committee of Imperial Defence (CID) was preparing for the impending clash with Italy in the Mediterranean over the Abyssinian affair, one of its subcommittees was deliberating over the delicate question of censorship in time of war. It was recognised that propaganda and censorship were closely related; some method of releasing news would be required to work in conjunction with the system for controlling it.[13] C. P. Robertson, press attaché at the Air Ministry, appears to have taken the initiative in proposing that plans for the establishment of a Ministry of Information should be set in motion so that 'we should not merely start off in the case of a future conflict where we ended in the last'.[14] In September 1935, Robertson produced a lengthy memorandum that argued that the wartime system had been deficient from an organisational point of view largely because of the multiplicity of bodies engaged in official propaganda. Robertson's point was that in any future war propaganda must be conducted from under one roof. Centralisation was, in his opinion, an essential precondition of success.

The CID considered Robertson's memorandum on 14 October 1935 when it was decided to establish a subcommittee to prepare plans for the establishment of a Ministry of Information on the outbreak of war.[15] The chairman and Minister of Information Designate was Sir John Colville, at that time Parliamentary Secretary to the Department of Overseas Trade, but shortly to become parliamentary under-secretary of state for Scotland. His subcommittee boasted an impressive membership: Sir Warren Fisher represented the Treasury and Sir Robert Vansittart the Foreign Office; Sir Russell Scott, the permanent under-secretary at the Home Office and his counterpart at the Dominions Office, Sir Edward Harding; J. A. G. Troup and Major-General J. G. Dill, respectively the Directors of Naval and Military Intelligence; Sir Donald Banks and Sir John Reith, the Directors-General of the GPO and of the BBC; and Sir Maurice Hankey, Secretary to the Cabinet and to the CID. Rex Leeper, head of the Foreign Office News Department, and Stephen Gaselee, the Foreign Office Librarian, were also present in view of their considerable experience of propaganda in war and peace. The government was certainly taking the whole business very seriously. Warren Fisher informed Reith, the only member who was not a government official, that this was 'as strong a CID committee as had ever been called'.[16] This may well have been so, but it was also true that few of its members had any detailed knowledge or experience of propaganda. This was presumably the reason why meetings of the subcommittee proved to be infrequent; only five full meetings were convened between 1935 and 1939, three of which were held within the first nine months of its creation. Rather, subordinate officials undertook the detailed planning.

Those officials were faced with a formidable task for an alarming eventuality. The defensive thinking which characterised all aspects of war preparations also permeated the planners of the Ministry of Information. For example, little time or thought appears to have been given to the question of psychological warfare until 1938, and the decision to close all cinemas on the outbreak of war was perhaps one reason why film also received relatively little attention until 1939. Because there was felt to be no effective form of defence against the bomber, the RAF devised the idea of a retaliatory strike against the Ruhr, a strategy that remained in force until after Munich when the emphasis was shifted more on to the Air Defence of Great Britain. Paradoxically, however, it was only then, when the RAF was concentrating upon the development of the fighter in conjunction with radar, that thoughts of a psychological offensive against the enemy began to determine an alternative use for the bomber.

A major problem for the planners was that although the march of technology meant that the character of the next war would almost certainly be radically different from that of the last, they had only the precedent of the Great War on which to model their new structure – unless of course they chose to model their organisation upon that of Goebbels. If that was effectively what happened, as Michael Balfour has argued, it created a ridiculous situation: 'in the war of words the British imagined that they were copying from the Germans something which the Germans imagined they had copied from the British!'[17] But, as Ian McLaine has pointed out, references to the German propaganda organisation are extremely rare in the records of the shadow Ministry of Information, and there is 'no reference whatsoever to Goebbels by name'.[18] The British were, after all, planning for an entirely different set of criteria, and a liberal democracy with its own peculiar historical idiosyncrasies required different propaganda techniques than that of a dictatorship.

If the lessons of the past were to prove of any real value for the future, they had first to be discovered. During the 1930s, this proved easier said than done because the records of the various wartime propaganda organisations had largely been destroyed in 1920, or else 'lost' in the years that followed. Detailed information on the wartime experiment was simply not available. Instead, the planners were forced to consult the memoirs of former participants.[19] This meant that the planning proceeded from a highly misleading premise because these works tended to exaggerate the role which British propaganda was believed to have played either in bringing the United States into the war on the Allied side in 1917 or in bringing Germany to its knees the following year. As a result, Robertson's initial warning went unheeded. The second Ministry of Information would, it seemed, merely turn out to be a more streamlined version of the first after all.

The outcome might well have been different, however, if the Foreign Office had originally been allowed to have its way. At the first meeting of the CID subcommittee on 25 October 1935, Leeper challenged the basic assumption of Robertson's memorandum that the Ministry should be an entirely separate entity. Alternatively, he argued, the Foreign Office News Department should constitute the nucleus of any future wartime organisation.[20] Leeper considered that the News Department's reservoir of resident experts, and links with the rapidly growing peacetime propaganda organisations such as the British Council, meant that there already existed an ideal basic structure capable of expansion and conversion to wartime requirements.[21] Under his scheme, it would merely be necessary to appoint a large advisory committee to maintain close contacts with the Foreign Office, the BBC and with other government departments. In effect, Leeper's proposal amounted to the reintroduction of the system which had existed in 1917 prior to the establishment of the Ministry of Information and Crewe House, a system which had enabled the Foreign Office to control the policy and direction of Britain's overseas propaganda before losing that control to the press barons.

The scheme divided the subcommittee. Hankey, Gaselee and, to a lesser extent, Colville, considered the peacetime apparatus capable and worthy of expansion and conversion if war should come. But theirs was a minority view. The powerful Warren Fisher considered Leeper's proposal 'too parochial and narrow' and dismissed it as beyond the subcommittee's terms of reference, which clearly called for the creation of a separate ministry. He also pointed out that the experience of the Foreign Office was limited to overseas propaganda in peacetime; there was no guarantee that its News Department could undertake home propaganda and censorship in time of war. Fisher's objections won the day, and it was decided that smoother running and greater efficiency would ensue if the Ministry was created as a unit apart from the existing machinery and free from the interference of Whitehall. The implication was that a return to the 1918 system was infinitely preferable to a return to 1917.

That the planners were subsequently prepared to accept the 1918 model as a blueprint was entirely understandable, particularly as their sources of information gave them little reason for starting afresh. It was also an easier option for already overworked civil servants who now had to take on an additional task on a part-time basis. Small wonder, therefore, that progress was slow. Moreover, their hands were tied to a considerable extent by the somewhat rigid conception of the Ministry laid down in a report of 27 July 1936 and accepted by the CID some months later.[22] They were also restricted by decisions made elsewhere. For example, in September 1935, another CID subcommittee had recommended that, in the event of war, a Ministry of Information should assume control over broadcasting and over the BBC.[23] This proposal was embodied in a report[24] and approved by the full CID on 14 October 1935 – nearly a fortnight before the first meeting of the subcommittee to establish a Ministry of Information. This decision meant that the planners devoted a disproportionate amount of time to working out the wartime structure of the BBC and its position in relation to the Ministry. Whereas broadcasting would undoubtedly prove an invaluable medium of wartime propaganda, there were other important instruments which demanded equal attention but which were denied their due consideration at first because of the determination of the BBC to be effectively exploited while, at the same time, preserving its autonomy and reputation.

The lack of co-ordination in the planning was epitomised by one official, who wrote after being forced to consult an article on propaganda in the *Encyclopaedia Britannica*, 'there must be experts somewhere'.[25] In fact, there were. In the first place, there was an abundant supply of experience and expertise within the existing peacetime propaganda machinery. For example, Lord William Tyrrell, the first chairman of the British Council, had not only served in the wartime propaganda organisation but had also been head of the News and Political Intelligence Department of the Foreign Office for a brief period after the war. He was also currently serving as President of the British Board of Film Censors. John Buchan (now Lord Tweedsmuir, the Governor General of Canada) had been in charge of the Department of Information in 1917. Lord Beaverbrook was still alive, as indeed was Sir Campbell Stuart, Northcliffe's right-hand man at Crewe House. Arthur Willert, head of the Foreign Office News Department from 1925 to 1934, had served in Britain's American propaganda organisation while working as Washington correspondent of *The Times*.[26] There were also many journalists working in Fleet Street who, at one time or another, had been connected with the wartime organisation, men such as Henry Wickham Steed, the former editor of *The Times*, and Sir

Roderick Jones, the Managing Director of Reuters. H. Noble Hall, the Travel Association's Paris representative, had worked in Wellington House. So had Arnold Toynbee and various other Chatham House experts. Rex Leeper, Willert's successor as head of the News Department, was the leading Foreign Office expert, being personally responsible for the foundation of the British Council to conduct cultural propaganda in 1934 and for persuading the BBC to inaugurate broadcasts in foreign languages in 1938. Leeper had, in fact, been appointed Assistant Director-General Designate of the proposed News Division of the Ministry, but was forced to withdraw his services in 1938 in order to concentrate upon his normal peacetime duties. Even Miles Lampson (Lord Killearn), Britain's ambassador in Egypt, had been involved in film propaganda work back in 1916.[27] This list goes on. Sir William Jury, head of the Cinema Department of Beaverbrook's Ministry of Information, was still alive. Sir Joseph Ball, who in 1939 was placed in charge of the Ministry's film work, was currently serving as deputy director of the National Publicity Bureau. In the private sector, there existed a growing body of industrial publicity experts such as Sidney Rogerson, the public relations officer at Imperial Chemical Industries, whose influential book, *Propaganda in the Next War*, was published in 1938.[28] But the only man, apart from Leeper, with any real idea of the problems involved who was directly involved in the planning before 1938 was Sir Stephen Tallents, who was appointed Director-General Designate in late 1936. Tallents took up his appointment in the shadow Ministry of Information after the complete acceptance by the CID of the July 1936 report.

Essentially, the principal reason why Tallents was unable to consult this considerable body of expertise derived from the intense secrecy that surrounded the planning. It was felt that, should the preparations become public knowledge, it might create a political outcry at home. Despite the enormous progress that had been made in so far as a peacetime propaganda machinery by Britain abroad was concerned, there remained widespread suspicion of official propaganda within Britain. Moreover, a Ministry of Information essentially meant war, and the government could not allow the impression to form that it had resigned itself to such a probability. Knowledge of the planning might also provoke Hitler. However, the effect of this policy of secrecy was to impose a severe brake upon the progress of the preparations.

By February 1938, a critical stage had been reached. Tallents warned that, although 'considerable progress' had been made, the time had now come for the planning process to be extended 'beyond the limits of government departments and the BBC, so as to enlist representatives of such interests as the press and the film industry in the discussion of the machinery appropriate to the changed conditions of 1938'.[29] He then warned that the planning was not sufficiently well advanced to enable the ministry to spring into existence in the event of a sudden emergency. He wrote:

> Even in a war in which the actual operations were geographically restricted, public opinion might come to be engaged on a world-wide front, and might

materially affect its issue. Our preparations for the conduct of war on land, by sea and in the air, are the concern of powerful existing departments, and their planning the subject of continuous study by specialised staffs. Our preparations for the conduct of wartime operations of great possible variety and extent in the field of public opinion have no comparable peacetime basis, and their planning is dependent on a handful of men, all, with one exception, very fully employed on other work.[30]

Both his subcommittee and the full CID agreed. With Hitler's annexation of Austria in March, the time had clearly arrived for a greater sense of urgency to be injected into the planning process.

6.3 The Munich Dress Rehearsal

When, however, a crisis did erupt over the question of the Sudetenland, the shadow Ministry of Information was partially mobilised on 26 September 1938 amidst chaos and confusion. Important decisions concerning appointments, accommodation and demarcation of duties still had to be resolved, while the Ministry's relationship with the peacetime propaganda machinery had still to be clarified. The planners had still not consulted the media and Tallents admitted to Leeper that the important foreign section of the proposed Publicity Division was 'not yet organised'.[31] Arrangements were accordingly made for the Foreign Office to transfer certain of its staff and facilities to the ministry, and on the 27 September the Foreign Office made arrangements with the Air Ministry and Stationery Office to print ten million leaflets in German which would be dropped by the RAF immediately war was declared, but not before.[32] The theme to be adopted was to be the same as in 1918 – the destruction of the German governing regime rather than of the German people.

These improvisations did, however, raise a serious problem. At precisely what point was the ministry to assume responsibility for propaganda from the Foreign Office? Before the outbreak of war? Or immediately after? If the ministry sprang into existence prior to a formal declaration of hostilities, it might provoke media opposition at home, particularly if war was averted at the last minute. Such action would also provide the enemy with advanced warning of what to expect insofar as psychological warfare was concerned, thereby providing an opportunity to prepare, say, for a leaflet raid, which in turn would merely serve to increase the considerable risks involved in such a mission. If, on the other hand, the Foreign Office was left in charge right up to the last minute, serious confusion might result from the wartime organisation suddenly taking over from established Whitehall departments without any advanced preparation.

But there was a further complication. The Ministry of Information was not the only organisation being prepared for the conduct of propaganda. In the wake of the Anschluss, two bodies came into being which were designed to conduct subversive activities against the enemy, including covert or 'black' propaganda (i.e. that emanating from an official source but claiming to come from somewhere else). The first of these, established under the auspices of MI6 and known as Section D, was set up 'to investigate every possibility of attacking potential enemies by means other than the preparation of military forces'.[33] Major Lawrence Grand was placed in charge of Section D's preparations in the fields of espionage, subversive propaganda designed to cause disaffection amongst the enemy, and what was described as 'moral sabotage'; it 'handled the unavowable'.[34] Together with another outfit known as GS(R), Section D was eventually to evolve into the Special Operations Executive (SOE).[35] The other organisation that came into existence at about the same time was known as Department EH, after the initials of its headquarters at the Imperial Communications Committee at Electra House on the Victoria Embankment. Established initially under the auspices of the Foreign Office, Department EH was eventually to evolve into the Political Warfare Executive.[36] During the penultimate week of September 1938 (the exact date remains vague, but on or about the 24th),[37] the old psywarrior Campbell Stuart was called in to take charge of Electra House and he began his work in complete secrecy, albeit too late to prove effective when the possible need of psychological operation arose at the height of the Munich crisis.

Whether Tallents knew of the existence of these two organisations is not certain. It was subsequently discovered, however, that on 26 September Major Grand had been instructed (by whom is not known) to secure the dissemination of leaflets in German 'through all channels outside this country' – presumably this meant the Secret Intelligence Service – 'and had apparently got a few of them into Germany'.[38] Confirmation of this event is not available. Nor is it known what Electra House was doing during those critical days, although it does appear that Campbell Stuart had hardly begun to gather his staff together when the Prime Minister 'felt that in the Munich meeting he had achieved world peace, and I was instructed to suspend my operations'.[39]

But there was one other remarkable initiative in this period. During the most critical days of the Munich Crisis, 26–30 September 1938, when peace or war hung in the balance, a clandestine 'political warfare' operation was carried out on the direct authority of Neville Chamberlain. This incident adds to our understanding of the Chamberlain government's surprisingly extensive and adroit use of media manipulation and other propaganda techniques in both domestic and international politics.[40] One reason why this story, and much of the background to it, remained unknown for so long is that the government understood surprisingly well how important it was for the success of 'informing the public' that it should be unaware of the source of that 'information'. Hence many of these exercises in what Baldwin preferred to call the 'education of the public' were in fact conducted through various branches of the Secret Services. This story, amongst other things, emphasises the basic inseparability of the spheres of 'intelligence' and 'information' in the modern state. We owe our knowledge of this particular story to a memorandum by Gerald Wellesley,[41] which found its way into the Additional Papers gathered as part of the Chamberlain Archive at the University of Birmingham.

6.4 'An Improper Use of Broadcasting'?

The actual story, as recorded by Wellesley, goes as follows. On the afternoon of Monday 26 September 1938 – the day when General Gamelin, the French Chief of Staff, flew to London to join Daladier and Bonnet in crisis discussions in the wake of Hitler's Godesberg 'ultimatum' (which both the British and the French cabinets felt impelled to reject), and the day after ARP was mobilised and the evacuation of children ordered – Gerald Wellesley telephoned Sir Joseph Ball 'with a view to placing the services of Wireless Publicity Ltd. and the Luxembourg Broadcasting Station at the disposal of H.M. Government'.[42] A meeting took place between them the following afternoon. Sir Joseph told Wellesley that 'information received from Germany indicated not only considerable discontent and unrest in that country, but also complete ignorance as to the true state of affairs, in particular the attitude of Great Britain and France'.[43] It was agreed that 'any steps taken to inform the German public of such matters, might prove of vital importance'.[44]

Sir Joseph asked whether it would be possible to arrange for Radio Luxembourg to broadcast, in German, 'such messages as Mr. Chamberlain's statement [published that morning] and Mr. Roosevelt's appeal to Herr Hitler, of which he believed the German public were in complete ignorance'.[45] He was assured that 'so far as our London organisation was concerned, this could be done at a moment's notice',[46] though he was warned that the 'Station itself is under the control of a French director who might require the authority of certain Officials of the Grand Duchy before the broadcasts could be made'.[47] Sir Joseph 'should immediately get in touch with Paris by telephone to arrange for the 'necessary pressure' to be brought to bear by the French members of the Board of Compagnie Luxembourgeoise de Radiodiffusion. Sir Joseph mentioned that similar broadcasts by the BBC were envisaged, but that the matter was still under consideration. 'In reply, [Wellesley] pointed out that the Luxembourg Station was in an entirely different position. In Germany 8 million wireless sets (out of a national total of 9 million) are "Volks Empfanger", i.e. "peoples [sic] sets", supplied by the government, and are incapable of receiving any but local broadcasts. Having regard to this, the Luxembourg Station, being only 10 miles from the German frontier, was exceedingly well placed'.[48] He also 'pointed out that since Luxembourg normally operates a daily news service in both French and German, it would not necessarily seem a very unusual departure if that service were to be developed [sic] on the lines under consideration'.[49]

Sir Joseph asked for preparations to be made for commencing the broadcasts 'immediately the scheme had been officially approved in London, explaining that no final decision could be taken until the return from Germany of Sir

Horace Wilson, who was due back that evening'. Sir Joseph concluded the meeting by pointing out that 'the whole business of the Station, and even its existence, might be jeopardised by the steps we were preparing to take'.[50]

After the meeting, the manager of Wireless Publicity Ltd. was told by Wellesley to arrange for staff to be on duty throughout the night and for the 'company 'plane to be ready to leave for Luxembourg at any moment', and Wellesley 'got into telephonic communication with Paris and arranged for the necessary representations to be made to the Luxembourg Director. By 7pm it was confirmed to [him] that this had been done'.[51] Fifteen minutes later Sir Joseph telephoned to say that the proposals had been approved and asked, with barely three-quarters of an hour left, for the setting-up of 'a direct relay from Luxembourg of the broadcast which Mr. Chamberlain was due to make at 8 pm'.[52] With five minutes to spare, the Post Office and the BBC succeeded in completing the connection with Luxembourg, for the first time ever – an impressive engineering feat as well as an extraordinary reversal of policy, as we shall see, and 'Mr. Chamberlain's speech was duly relayed commencing at 8 p.m.'.[53]

During the night, translations were made of six 'messages': Roosevelt's appeal; Chamberlain's, Daladier's and President Beneš' replies to it; Chamberlain's message to Hitler of 1 am, 27 September, and a summary of Chamberlain's broadcast to the nation in the evening of that day. The translations were then recorded on discs, and at 7.45 am the company's 'plane took off with them for Luxembourg. Radio Luxembourg broadcast these recordings at intervals throughout the day. During the morning of that day, Black Wednesday, 28 September, as mobilisation proceeded and anti-aircraft guns were being set up in the parks of London, Roosevelt's second appeal (which had only been received that morning) was translated, recorded and actually went out on the air at 2 pm that afternoon, to be repeated at intervals thereafter. On Wednesday night, between 9 pm and 2 am, a German translation of Chamberlain's House of Commons speech was prepared, recorded and put on a flight to Luxembourg by 5.45 am. On Thursday, Radio Luxembourg again broadcast all these recordings at frequent intervals, throughout the day. When news of the signing of the Munich Agreement arrived, 'on Friday morning I gave instructions for the German broadcasts to be discontinued'.[54]

Whatever the effectiveness of the operation on German public opinion might have been, this was an amazingly risky step for the British government to take. London was all too aware of Hitler's sensitivity to any form of propaganda against him, and the government fell over backwards to try and make British newspapers moderate their tone over Germany and to abstain from putting forward alternative ideas to appeasement. When Lord Halifax visited Berlin in November 1937, he listened to protests from Goebbels about 'attacks upon Hitler in the British Press and unfriendly reporting from British correspondents in Berlin', and Halifax responded by promising 'to do all he could to secure the "co-operation of the British Press"'.[55] On his return, he launched himself with vigour into a campaign of bringing pressure on the press which ran very close to, if not well beyond, the limits of constitutional propriety. Likewise, the BBC was told to 'bear in mind the extreme sensitiveness of both Hitler and Mussolini ... to "talks" and presentation of news'.[56] When the Czechoslovak crisis broke in September 1938, the government clamped such a comprehensive censorship on the BBC, to avoid upsetting what they took to be an unstable mind liable to fly into destructive rages, that even *Children's Hour* talks about world affairs were checked, indeed cancelled, at the request of the Foreign Office.[57] Given these perceptions of Hitler's sensitivity even to domestic media coverage, it is nothing short of amazing that Chamberlain chose to sanction the beaming of British propaganda directly into Germany – on wavelengths designed for reception by radio sets specially manufactured by the German authorities to prevent the reception of foreign stations. It was by any standard an overtly 'unfriendly' act towards another government, and particularly so in the middle of negotiations at the highest level, with Britain playing the role of honest broker. There could also be no doubt that the Nazi government regarded the direct beaming of propaganda into its own territory as a hostile act; its cessation was the prerequisite of any of the regime's treaties of friendship, for example in the German–Polish Treaty of Non-Aggression of 1934. Similar clauses were written into the Agreement for normalising relations with Austria in 1936.[58] Thus, when Chamberlain authorised the direct beaming into Germany of propaganda, in German, of a kind designed to drive a wedge between *Volk* and Führer, he authorised an act which the Nazis could have used to create an international *cause célèbre* amidst shouts of 'perfidious Albion'.

Moreover, there was the distinct possibility that in this case international law would have sided with the Germans. In May 1933, the Council of the International Broadcasting Union, of which Britain as well as Germany was a member, passed a resolution – proposed and drafted by the British! – which stated:[59]

> The Council ... holds that the systematic diffusion of programmes or communications which are specially intended for listeners in another country ... constitutes an inadmissible act from the point of view of good international relations. It calls upon all members of the International Broadcasting Union to avoid such transmissions, which constitute an improper use of broadcasting.

In March 1936, after extensive debate, the League of Nations passed the 'Convention on the Use of Broadcasting in the Cause of Peace'. It specifically outlawed the transmission of broadcast propaganda designed 'to incite the population of any territory to acts incompatible with the internal order or the security of a territory of a High Contracting Partner'.[60] Although Germany had not been a signatory to this Convention, having withdrawn from the League for the time being, Britain most certainly was.[61]

There was another, even more risky, dimension to this operation. A further potential danger lay in the political and propaganda opportunities that it might have presented to Hitler, should he have decided to break off his negotiations with Chamberlain on a suitable pretext. He could have claimed that Chamberlain had betrayed his good faith or that Germany was again being treated as an inferior against whom the British and the French still felt free to commit acts of humiliation or aggression. Furthermore, the operation could have revived all the barely dormant memories of Britain's wartime propaganda emanating from Lord Northcliffe's 'Ministry for the Destruction of German Confidence', touching upon the still-sensitive areas concerning Britain's previous propaganda, not only in Germany but also in the USA. There was, in addition, the ultimate risk that Hitler would react with all the word power of his own propaganda ministry, which would have had the most serious political repercussions for British foreign policy in general and for the policy of appeasement in particular. Chamberlain's own posture as 'the man of peace' would have been seriously undermined as, indeed, might have his own parliamentary position. In fact, Chamberlain was fully aware of all this. A little while later, when talking about this operation, he remarked to Wellesley, 'I do not know what this did to the Germans, but by God it frightened me'.[62]

6.5 Black Propaganda

How did such a sensitive and potentially explosive operation come about? The Cabinet Committee that had been set up in the autumn of 1937 to consider foreign language broadcasts by the BBC, under the chairmanship of Sir Kingsley Wood, did not disband once transmissions began in Arabic on 3 January 1938. It was reconstituted the following June under the chairmanship of Sir Thomas Inskip, the Minister for the Co-ordination of Defence, to examine the defence aspects of broadcasting and to consider a memorandum by the Postmaster General on 'Advertisement Broadcasting', which had been submitted to the Cabinet on 22 June.[63] Also, early in 1938, certain commercial concerns urged the government to reconsider its position in respect of advertisements on radio. They argued that such sponsored broadcasts could provide 'a welcome aid to commerce' and would serve to present 'a wide diffusion of British culture'. The Cabinet passed this question over to the reconstituted Committee on Overseas Broadcasting which, 'owing to pressure of more urgent business' (i.e. the negotiating of a complex agreement with Reuters to increase the supply of British news abroad) postponed discussion of this matter until early 1939.[64]

   In the meantime, the international crisis over Czechoslovakia prompted more urgent action. In his influential letter to Tallents of 5 September 1938, Stephen King-Hall wrote that, having 'recently received a good deal of reliable information from Germany ... there is no doubt that the home front is shaky'.[65] Any direct appeal to the German people might have a vital effect. The dropping of leaflets was of course an action that could only be taken once war had actually broken out; there remained an urgent need to increase the supply of British news and views to totalitarian Germany while peace prevailed. Radio provided the best opportunity for such a task. It was immediate, direct and difficult to prevent. As the crisis threatened to degenerate into war, following Chamberlain's return from Godesberg, the BBC had, on 24 September, begun to initiate its own arrangements for transmissions in German. Three days later, the Foreign Office informed the BBC that a translation of the Prime Minister's speech on the crisis would be required and, at very short notice, the speech was broadcast in German, French and Italian on the medium wave – at the expense of many regional programmes in the Home Service.[66] On the following day, the Foreign Office asked the BBC to continue the broadcasts.

However, transmitting on the domestic wavelengths allocated to Britain, even if in German, was one thing but infiltrating propaganda into Radio Luxembourg's wavelengths to be beamed by one of the most powerful transmitters in Europe, a bare ten miles from the German border, was quite another. This was 'black propaganda' or what the British termed 'political warfare'. The distinction between this and white propaganda was well understood, as already expressed in the deliberate organisational separation of the bodies concerned with planning the 'Ministry of Information' and those in Section D and Electra House planning 'enemy propaganda'. This organisational separation was due to a growing recognition that it was essential to separate overt or 'information' propaganda, that is output which officially represents the word of the government and which therefore needs to be 'truthful' in the sense of being factually accurate to maintain credibility, and those concerned with covert propaganda, which seeks to achieve immediate results by whatever means and where the essential requirement, apart from effectiveness, is that it should not be traceable back to the British government. There is no mention of the intention to use Radio Luxembourg amongst the records of either of the organisations that had been formally established for propaganda purposes since planning for the contingency of war began in 1935.

This fact may help to explain why Wellesley should have taken the initiative and proposed the use of Wireless Publicity Ltd, and through it the use of Radio Luxembourg, to the Prime Minister through Sir Joseph Ball, rather than that this should have come about the other way. After the Munich Crisis, when the lessons of the dry-run mobilisation of the propaganda agencies, alongside the other war-contingency organisations, came to be analysed, and planning was put onto a much more purposive footing, Radio Luxembourg was listed at the top of Section D's plans.[67] As we shall see, it also came high on the list of priorities for many others, including the Prime Minister. The use of Radio Luxembourg to beam covert propaganda into Germany during the crisis seems therefore, at first sight, to have been the result of a typically British reliance on private initiative and quick improvisation in a moment of crisis to make up for the lack of systematic planning before it broke. But if so, how was Gerald Wellesley, soon to succeed as the Seventh Duke of Wellington, with no apparent connections with Radio Luxembourg or indeed with broadcasting in any form, in a position to be able to put such an operation into effect 'at a moment's notice'? How could he get Radio Luxembourg to broadcast the material and be able to have it prepared in London so quickly and efficiently – and without evidently letting the cat out of the bag? For an answer we need to look to the fascinating, though little known, history of Radio Luxembourg and of Britain's, and the BBC's, relationship to it.[68]

6.6 International Broadcasting

In the 1920s when the technology of wireless transmission first reached the stage of practical application, the French government viewed the invention as simply a new technology for publishing, rather than looking at it in a totalitarian frame of mind as a means of propagandising, or 'educating', the population. Hence the French – like the Americans but unlike the British[69] – regarded publication in this new medium as a part of the constitutional right of every citizen, just as he had the right to print whatever he wished, subject only to the laws of libel, etc. But, unlike the USA, in France there was also a tradition by which the government possessed the same liberty to get its views conveyed to the public. The French government, therefore, had no objection to the establishment of local broadcasting stations, financed by whatever means might be found by those wishing to do so – and also proceeded to establish a national radio network, which put out the government viewpoint, without any pretence to fine distinctions between 'the voice of France' and the voice of the French government of the day. A number of local broadcasting stations did in fact come into being. Some of these, such as that at Fecamp in Normandy, lay close enough to the Channel for a substantial area of southern England to be able to pick up their broadcasts.

In 1931, one Captain Leonard Plugge[70] – a wealthy Englishman, socially well connected, a cross between a playboy-sportsman-buccaneer and a dilettante electrical experimenter – hit upon the idea of renting this transmitter after it had closed down for the night from midnight to 3am. His idea was to broadcast popular dance music interspersed with entertaining chat in English and, of course, with advertisements by British firms. The idea flourished, and Plugge soon extended his operations from Radio Normandy to Radio Toulouse, Radio Lyon, Radio Paris and Poste Parisienne, running the whole show through a grandly named International Broadcasting Company. The BBC was, naturally, furious because its policy of compulsory 'education' required, as Sir John Reith put it, 'the brute force of monopoly'. If the public had an alternative to tune in to, then the BBC's careful 'programming policy' of feeding the public with a diet of serious programmes, sweetened with some concessions to popular taste, would fail to work. People would turn the knob when the uplift came.

But stations such as these were limited in power and confined to the late hours, and were nothing compared to what was being built in Luxembourg. Here a band of radio enthusiasts, largely Belgian, obtained a concession from the Grand Duke to start a broadcasting service, which initially was meant to be an all-round service providing cultural and educational programmes as well as news.[71] The station was, however, to be financed by advertising. To raise the requisite capital for building it, a rather shady group of entrepreneurs moved in and converted the concession from a local station into a high-powered transmitter designed to cover an area bounded by the Alps in the south, Prague in the east, Biscay in the west – and Scotland in the north.[72] Captain Plugge was to sell its advertising space in England and arrange for suitable records and shows for its British listeners. As soon as news of the building of Radio Luxembourg reached Britain, the government, egged on by the BBC and its foster-parent the Postmaster General, began a massive campaign for throttling it. The International Broadcasting Union, a BBC foundation, refused to allocate it a suitable long-wave frequency – the 'pirates' simply seized one as a result – and passed resolutions calling upon their parent governments to take action, including the resolution quoted earlier denouncing broadcasting in other nations' languages. Early approaches for technical assistance and later for co-operation with Britain and the BBC were rebuffed.[73] The British Ambassador in Belgium, whose brief included the Grand Duchy of Luxembourg, made regular protestations to its government, which were met with evasion. The Grand Duke was mindful of the large tax revenue promised by the station and was attracted by the idea of Luxembourg becoming a household name on the airwaves alongside London and Paris.

By contrast, the French government looked on the fledgling station through the eyes of its propagandists and determined not so much to kill it – that it could have achieved, unlike Britain – but to gain effective, though secret, control of it. In typically French manner, this manoeuvre, in which Pierre Laval was involved, included the granting of the Légion d'Honneur to one Raoul Fernandez. This citizen of Luxembourg was one of the shady entrepreneurs behind the Société d'Etudes Radiophoniques SA which gained the original concession for, as the magazine *Wireless World* indignantly reported, 'bringing the Company in Luxembourg entirely under French control'.[74]

The French realised that such a station was eventually bound to broadcast not only music and shows, but news bulletins as well. Without investing the vast sums involved in building up a news organisation, it would need to buy a news service ready-made from an agency. Not surprisingly, that agency for Radio Luxembourg became Havas,[75] rather than Reuters or Wolffe (which became the Deutsches Nachrichtenbüro (DNB) under the Nazis).

The BBC kept on pressing the government for continued action against Radio Luxembourg long after it became an established fact. To support its case for taking action, it monitored Radio Luxembourg's broadcasts and presented, year after year, the results that showed the build-up of a vast European and British audience. By 1938, Radio Luxembourg reached peak audience figures of four million in Britain alone, which came close to fifty per cent of comparable BBC audience figures.[76]

British policy towards the kind of commercially-based overseas broadcasting stations pioneered by Captain Plugge had been sadly misguided. In the first half of the 1930s, when Sir John Reith was regarded as the government's expert advisor on matters of broadcasting, there was a failure to recognise Reith's

limitations when it came to matters where his mind was shielded from prac-
ticalities by his ethical convictions. By carrying out a futile crusade against
Radio Luxembourg in support of Reithian ideals which in the last resort were
politically as naive as he was himself, by consistently refusing technical co-
operation and even denying permission to provide a land-line connection, the
Foreign Office missed a great opportunity.

The Luxembourg station came on full power in January 1934. It was indeed
one of the most powerful and most universally receivable in Europe and, with
its vast potential for propaganda, it had been handed to the French on a plate.
But at another level, saner minds in Britain began to look at the implications
of the BBC's monitoring reports. One such was Isidore Ostrer, the head of
Gaumont British News. He had been the most skilful and clear-minded
manipulator of the propaganda potential of the newsreel, putting it at the
service of the National Government by a formal, though of course, secret
agreement with Ramsay MacDonald in 1935.[77] Working closely with Sir Joseph
Ball, Gaumont British News consistently played the most effective propaganda
role in selling the policies of the government, especially in respect of rearmament
and the projection of both Baldwin and Chamberlain. In 1934, Ostrer, in
defiance of the ban on press advertisements for Radio Luxembourg – one of
the Pyrrhic victories of the BBC/Post Office campaign – decided to allow
advertising in his own newspaper, the *Sunday Referee*,[78] which, incidentally,
he had also 'placed behind the National Government'. Furthermore, his studios
began to provide recordings for Radio Luxembourg of British variety shows
and other programmes, bringing some of the actual production work for the
station to Britain for the first time. Then in February 1936, the accedence of
King Edward VIII focused government attention on the propaganda potential
of Radio Luxembourg. It was thought that it would be a good idea to transmit
through Radio Luxembourg the King's speech, as it would give a much wider
circulation in Europe than the BBC could provide. The Postmaster General
was instructed by the Cabinet to seek the advice of the BBC and if it was in
the affirmative, to agree to the establishment of a landline to Luxembourg.
The BBC objected and the project was dropped, but attention having been
focused on the matter, realistic new steps were now taken to remedy the
consequences of a blindly antagonistic policy towards this powerful voice.

In March 1936, it was suddenly announced that a new company, called
Wireless Publicity Ltd, had taken over from Captain Plugge's International
Broadcasting Company the handling of Radio Luxembourg's business in England. The changeover was handled in an odd and secretive manner.[79] Captain
Plugge was given no notice nor reasons – he subsequently sued for breach of
contract but lost[80] – and the terms and personnel of the English service were
suddenly and completely changed. Wireless Publicity Ltd installed its own
presenter in Luxembourg and henceforth it was a condition of the contracts
signed by advertisers that first, the scripts of the programmes they sponsored
were to be edited by Wireless Publicity Ltd; second, the programmes were to
be made up in Britain; and third, Wireless Publicity Ltd was to arrange for

the preparation of all broadcast material sponsored by British firms.[81] At the same time, it was intimated that government disapproval of British firms sponsoring programmes had somehow vanished. Until then, such expenditure was regarded as legally being in an anomalous position and thus no formal advertising rates were published and no statement ever issued of how much money firms might have spent on sponsoring programmes. The International Broadcasting Company was registered off-shore, publishing no accounts. Wireless Publicity Ltd, a British-registered company, now published formal rates and contracts and yet evidently remained unmolested.[82] In addition, a large access of cash seemed to materialise with which J. Walter Thompson, the advertising agency, built what was soon reputed to be the most sophisticated recording studio in Europe. Here was produced, under the editorial direction of Wireless Publicity Ltd., an ever-increasing flow of notably more sophisticated and successful popular programmes, capitalising on the wealth of talent of the English musical stage and on the appeal of British dance music everywhere. As the *Advertisers Weekly* noted at the beginning of 1937, there were more stars appearing every Sunday on Radio Luxembourg than in a whole week of BBC programming.[83] Alongside the revitalised British popular film industry – with surreptitious government backing – Radio Luxembourg now began to be a useful part of British 'cultural propaganda', supplementing the more highbrow work of the British Council targeted at elites. Radio was of course a medium of mass communication, and the broadening of the target audience for cultural propaganda was also reflected in greater involvement, for example, in international soccer matches involving England and Germany in 1936 and 1938.[84] In 1936 a request for technical co-operation was once again turned down by the BBC, but Radio Luxembourg succeeded in mastering the new technology of short-wave transmission and in June 1938 began its 'World Service'.[85]

English dance-music-based programmes swept all before them in popularity. Furthermore, although dance music and variety were the fare most advertisers provided for attracting listeners to hear about the products they wished to sell, it was up to the customer to choose what he wished to have broadcast during the time which he bought at a rate of £400 an hour (plus the costs of making the programme, payable to Wireless Publicity Ltd, including even the fee of the disc jockey or presenter). The British Travel Association – ostensibly a branch of the government-funded cultural propaganda organisations created in the late 1920s – was one customer which seemed to have different taste. Through Wireless Publicity Ltd, it bought airtime to broadcast talks in *French* about British cultural achievements, by such well-known highbrow figures in the French-speaking world of Eastern Europe as Jean Cocteau and André Maurois.[86]

6.7 The Shadow World of Black Propaganda

Clearly, Wireless Publicity Ltd had done the nation an important service in repairing some of the damage caused by the silly policy of opposition 'tooth and nail', as Admiral Carpendale of the BBC had put it, which had allowed Radio Luxembourg to fall under French financial and, therefore, French news control. But who were 'Wireless Publicity Ltd'? Ostensibly it was a private company registered in March 1936, substantially owned by another private company, with which it shared a common address. This address and parent company help to explain its sterling work for the national interest both before and during the Munich Crisis. Wireless Publicity Ltd was located in Electra House, Victoria Embankment, London WC2. Electra House was no ordinary commercial building. It housed a group of those semi-secret organisations which provided Britain's background strength behind the rather feeble 'official' bodies concerned with the building-up of propaganda and subversive operations needed for a modern war. Wireless Publicity Ltd was a subsidiary of the principal tenant of Electra House – Cable and Wireless Ltd. Officially a private firm, government ownership of which was not admitted until the 1960s, Cable and Wireless Ltd. was in fact in charge of maintaining the 'Red Network', the undersea strategic cable-communications system of the Empire – since 1909 also a network of wireless stations – which had been built up originally by the Colonial Defence Committee.[87] The other main tenant of Electra House was the political counterpart of Cable and Wireless Ltd, also in a semi-official form, the Imperial Communications Committee (renamed 'Commonwealth Communications Council' after 1933). Both Cable and Wireless Ltd and the Imperial Communications Committee were effectively presided over by Sir Campbell Stuart for the whole of the inter-war period. Unsurprisingly, when the Foreign Office decided in 1938 to establish a secret propaganda department, from which grew the Political Warfare Executive, it chose Electra House as the appropriate location for it – hence its codename Department 'EH' – and the codename for the integrated organisation afterwards 'CS', i.e. Campbell Stuart.[88]

Cable and Wireless Ltd acted as a technical department and front-organisation for signal-intelligence, and as such was closely involved with the work of both MI6 and MI7(b). The latter had been established in 1916 for the compilation and distribution of propaganda by cables and by wireless and had been housed in neighbouring Adastral House. Wireless Publicity Ltd remained a subsidiary of Cable and Wireless Ltd until after the Second World War, when the position of Radio Luxembourg had changed and there was no further need for using it in this way. It was bought by Radio Luxembourg itself, and duly moved out of Electra House to Jermyn Street.[89] There is also some mystery surrounding those extremely modern and sophisticated broadcasting studios which were built after Wireless Publicity Ltd took over the handling of Radio Luxembourg's affairs in Britain. Did they belong to J. Walter Thompson or to Wireless Publicity Ltd? And who paid for them? It is most unlikely that it would have been J. Walter Thompson, for why should that company sink its money into recording studios for whatever work the continental stations might need, when there was ample spare recording capacity amongst London's film companies for any kind of recording work. But the studios were certainly not unemployed after the outbreak of war when Radio

Luxembourg closed down; in fact their address became known the world over: (Bush House, Aldwych, WC2.)

Common location, however, did not mean co-ordination, any more than being an 'official' agency entailed being part of a cohesive plan. In fact, one of the deplorable facts disclosed in the post-mortem which followed the dry-run mobilisation of September 1938 was the total lack of co-ordination among the three 'official' agencies engaged in planning for the hearts-and-minds aspects of war. The Ministry of Information, Section D and 'EH' learned of each other's work, and, as far as the documentation seems to imply, even of each other's existence, only after the Munich Crisis. Accordingly, a series of meetings was arranged to co-ordinate their activities, culminating in the establishment of a Joint Broadcasting Committee after the crisis was over. It seems that even this belated co-ordination did not include MI7(b), or what was left of it, for at the beginning of the war it recruited its own staff, headed by John Baker White, to conduct radio propaganda, only to be 'discovered' and, after a row, transferred to the Ministry of Information at the end of 1940.[90] Whether the fact that neither the nascent Political Warfare Executive nor the Ministry of Information appeared to know of the Luxembourg episode at the time indicates that Wireless Publicity Ltd was connected to MI6 or MI7 under the War Office is impossible to tell. According to one Soviet source, another body, the 'Travel Bureau', was set up with four staff to disseminate anti-Hitler propaganda to Germany, 'approved by Sir Warren Fisher and the Prime Minister after much discussion'.[91] Whether this was an MI6 front for one of these organisations is again not clear. We are equally in the dark as to what Wellesley's own position was in respect of Wireless Publicity Ltd, which allowed him both to offer its services to the government and to give instructions for the German broadcasts to be discontinued.

Gerald Wellesley had joined the Foreign Office in 1908 and served in it all through the war where, incidentally, he became Harold Nicolson's 'oldest' and 'dear friend'.[92] Having attained the rank of Second Secretary, he retired from the Foreign Office in 1919. From then until 1939, he appears to have had no official position, reappearing in 1939 as 'Second Lieutenant and acting Lieutenant Colonel' of the Grenadier Guards, serving subsequently in France, Egypt and Italy, until succeeding his uncle to the Dukedom forced his retirement to more honorific offices. He was a learned, cultured and wealthy man who wrote and edited several books in the 1930s and became Surveyor of the King's Works of Art and a most unlikely associate, on all accounts, of the lowbrow crowd of Radio Luxembourg and J. Walter Thompson. It is difficult to account for his involvement with them on grounds other than of duty – but in what capacity we do not know.

There is, on the other hand, a good deal more known about Sir Joseph Ball, which helps to explain the quite extraordinary fact that as far as Wellesley was concerned, Sir Joseph's word was all he had for launching such an immensely risky operation, the diplomatic consequences of which he, as a former Foreign Office man, was particularly well-qualified to understand. Ball was Director of the Research Department of Conservative Central Office and Deputy Chairman of the National Publicity Bureau, the publicity organisation of the so-called National government. Those posts scarcely qualified him to authorise a political warfare operation against another nation state, least of all in peacetime. But despite the fact that he held no official position, Sir Joseph was no stranger to the Secret Services. His role in this episode in fact helps to cast some light on him as one of the more mysterious characters behind Chamberlain, whose role had been noted by some of his contemporaries, as well as being commented upon by many historians since.[93] What is known of his career that he served in the First World War, apparently in military intelligence throughout, with the rank of Major, was awarded the OBE in 1919 and remained in MI6 after the war, rising to become civil assistant to the Director of Military Intelligence by 1921.

During the closing stages of the war, Ball came into contact with J. C. C. Davidson and Stanley Baldwin, and in 1924 was invited to become head of Central Office's newly formed Intelligence Department, which he at once renamed the Publicity Department. This had been created in response to universal male franchise and the fear that 'labour' might constitute a permanent political majority. He resigned his position in military intelligence, special arrangements being made to compensate him for lost pension rights. In March 1928, he was responsible for fixing up the 'amusing if not exemplary'[94] deal with Donald im Thurn, the German industrialist, which allowed Baldwin to avoid parliamentary inquiries into the authenticity of the Zinoviev letter. During the following year, Ball was asked to organise the newly formed Research Department at Central Office, where he effectively became full-time director under the political chairmanships of Lord Eustace Percy and Neville Chamberlain. One of his more remarkable achievements was that he succeeded regularly in obtaining copies of the confidential papers of the Labour Party's National Executive Committee, as well as those of Attlee's private office – quite unbeknown, of course, to the Labour Party. In April 1934, Ball proposed to Chamberlain the establishment of the National Publicity Bureau as separate from, and additional to, the Conservative Party's Central Office Publicity Department, for the purpose of creating a 'non-party' propaganda organisation, for which funds might be provided by executives of joint-stock companies which regarded themselves 'as precluded from subscribing to any party organisation'.[95] Following the 1935 election, it was generally accepted in the winning camp that the exceptionally progressive multimedia propaganda work, which the vast majority of funds thus obtained helped to finance in 330 constituencies, had a decisive impact on the overall result. Ball was awarded a KBE in the 1936 Honours List.

By that time, however, he had managed to develop singularly confidential relations with Neville Chamberlain, aided perhaps by a shared interest in fly-fishing.[96] He was almost the only person with an official or political relationship with Chamberlain who was also a regular visitor to his home (and Chamberlain to his), and the only one with whom Chamberlain spent many hours in the solitude of the riverbank. One effect of this close relationship was that, as Chamberlain began increasingly to conduct foreign policy personally, Sir Joseph Ball began to act as his private go-between and representative alongside Sir Horace Wilson, Chamberlain's other, though this time only political, confidant. The well-known story, told by Count Grandi, about Sir Joseph acting as Chamberlain's intermediary in the negotiations which Chamberlain was conducting behind his Foreign Secretary's back in the Anthony Eden affair, was denied by Sir Joseph before his death, though it is impossible to see why Grandi should have invented such a tale to put into an official despatch. But there is no doubt that Sir Joseph was one of the trio, with Sir Horace Wilson and Robert Hudson, whom Chamberlain sent to Berlin to conduct the highly secret negotiations for an economic 'appeasement' of Hitler in 1939,[97] a personal project fraught with extreme political danger.

But perhaps central to Sir Joseph's role was the shadowy connection with the Secret Services which he seems to have maintained throughout his career, after evidently resigning to take up his party-political career. The Donald im Thurn episode was just one of several odd tales betraying continued connections. In 1937, he held secret meetings with Señor Batista y Roca, representative of the Catalonian government, arranging equally confidential opportunities for him to contact Lord Halifax, and in March 1938 he came into possession of a dossier about communist subversion in Trinidad for which he was thanked by a friend in military intelligence.[98] Perhaps the most bizarre of these tell-tale stories was his admission during the war, in a post-prandial moment, that when, following Eden's resignation as Foreign Secretary, a group of Eden's supporters began to meet at the home of Ronald Tree MP, he had arranged for Tree's telephone to be tapped.[99] Given the technology of the time, that could only be done through the intelligence services which, considering the political implications, must have had complete trust in him. What perhaps clinches the argument for Sir Joseph being, and being known as, the Prime Minister's political go-between with the Secret Services and one who never, in fact, severed his relations with them, is the last position, this time official, which he held before retiring. Following a year as Head of the Films Division of the Ministry of Information, he was appointed Chairman of the Security Executive, the committee in control of MI5 and of home security matters in general. At the top, there is no division between 'intelligence' and 'propaganda', and Sir Joseph's career exemplifies this fact. He was clearly, though rather in the American manner, known to be the Prime Minister's personal agent for this area of government, and this explains why this operation, manifestly run in some way or another by the intelligence services, was conducted through him and under direct prime ministerial authority.

The decision to launch the Luxembourg operation must therefore have been taken ultimately by Chamberlain himself. And his personal knowledge of the operation evidently gave him, if he did not have it before, an interest in developing Radio Luxembourg for future use. For the broadcasts did not cease after the Munich Crisis. On the contrary, propaganda against Germany came

to be organised on an increasing scale, in accordance with the growing belief
that it would be an effective way of securing Hitler's compliance with his
promises, and if not, of preparing for stronger measures.

6.8 Gearing Up for War

In November 1938, Major Grand invited Hilda Matheson, former director of
talks and news at the BBC, to examine the possibility of broadcasting black
propaganda 'from stations outside Great Britain, primarily to Germany but also
to any other countries which proved available'.[100] The Joint Broadcasting Committee of Section D was the result. Following a fact-finding tour of European
radio stations, Matheson eventually suggested the discontinuation of the 'un-
profitable' arrangement with Radio Luxembourg and instead advised the
creation 'of a "good-will" committee to sponsor broadcasts arranged through
the broadcasting authorities of friendly countries, while the possibilities of
getting programmes into Germany were explored'.[101] Meanwhile, the Foreign
Office continued to examine the possibilities from its own point of view. As
Lord Halifax pointed out to the Cabinet in December 1938:[102]

> The programmes would be sponsored in the normal way by a commercial
> firm such as a travel agency and would contain a general news review
> amongst other items. A specimen copy of such a review had been prepared.
> The cost of six programmes a week for three months put out by one or
> other of these three stations (i.e. Luxembourg, Strasbourg and Liechten-
> stein) which normally broadcast in German is estimated at £6,000. The
> programmes would be submitted to the Foreign Office in advance and
> careful watch would be kept over them. Any participation by the British
> government in these programmes could effectively be concealed.

This indeed may have been the genesis of the Travel Bureau referred to above.

At the Cabinet meeting to discuss these proposals on 14 December 1938,
Chamberlain stated that his speech to the Foreign Press Association the previous
night 'had been specially relayed from the Luxembourg station'.[103] This was
a curious admission. Who had been responsible for the arrangement? The
Foreign Office was still at the stage of submitting its proposals for approval,
including financial sanction which was eventually granted on 21 December.[104] Miss Matheson had yet to start investigations for Major Grand.
Presumably, we are back with Sir Joseph Ball and Wellesley's activities at MI6.
In the discussions, Chamberlain also emphasised that he 'attached great importance to the broadcasts from the Luxembourg station which reached the popular
sets in Germany'.[105]

The Committee on Overseas Broadcasting under Inskip, now Dominions
Secretary, reconvened for its seventh meeting on 2 February 1939. Vansittart,
who for the past year had been co-ordinating the government's peacetime
propaganda overseas, explained the Foreign Office's special interest in the

Luxembourg broadcasts, which 'constituted an entirely new development. The Prime Minister had taken a great interest in it and had directed that every effort should be made to get the British point of view into Germany by wireless and that the possibility of making use of such stations as Luxembourg, Strasbourg and Liechtenstein etc. should be examined. With the approval of the Cabinet, plans had been laid for getting suitable material regularly broadcast from Luxembourg'.[106] He did not feel that the 'exceptional circumstances' of the Munich Crisis had ended: 'There was no doubt that we were in the presence of a continuing crisis and it was our duty by every means that came to our hand to convey the truth to the people of Germany'. The Post Office also recognised the value of the Luxembourg experiment and no longer pressed its initial objections to sponsored broadcasting from that station. However, it was unenthusiastic to see the project extended to Strasbourg or Liechtenstein, because of the dangers of this work becoming publicly known which in turn might cause the Luxembourg authorities to take fright. 'Once the fact leaked out that they had become instruments of British propaganda, the whole virtue of our foreign broadcasting policy would be gone'.[107]

Major Grand attended this meeting, but there is no record of his saying anything. Perhaps he was waiting for the results of Hilda Matheson's investigations. Meanwhile, the Foreign Office received reports from the Berlin Chancery concerning the impact of the broadcasts in Germany. One German journalist, for example, wrote:[108]

For some time now the British wireless has been causing a stir with its news service in German, and it is obviously trying to polish up the tarnished democratic escutcheons of Brothers Luxembourg and Strasbourg. Since the English voice, and this we frankly admit, sounds more truthful even when it is speaking in German, and since at the outset the news service was also more ingenious than its liberal relatives, great hopes were very likely set on its propagandistic efficacy.

But, he continued, the stations had defeated their own ends 'by sending lies and nothing but lies, and in Germany these stations are only tuned in from time to time in order to hear what particular lies are being circulated in the world at a given moment'.[109] The German minister in Luxembourg also protested to the government of the Grand Duchy, once after the initial broadcast of 27 September 1938 and again in April 1939 after transmission of a broadcast in German on the Italian occupation of Albania.[110] The British Ambassador in Germany, Sir Neville Henderson, also reported 'that the effectiveness of the broadcasting in German of accurate information regarding the views of HMG and the British outlook on the international situation might well in time of crisis make the difference between peace and war'.[111] The object of the broadcasts was clear. As a Foreign Office note records: 'Objective: – To divide German popular opinion from Hitler'.[112]

In conclusion, it can be said, therefore, that according to the terminology of the statements made about the international uses of broadcasting by the

British government – in the International Union of Broadcasting, in the League of Nations during the drafting of the Convention and in Parliament – the Luxembourg operation was indeed 'an improper use of broadcasting'. In the sense in which the Secret Services' propaganda activities 'handled the unavowable', it was also an 'inadmissible act'. Did it succeed? It certainly failed to divide German opinion over Hitler. Its only known effect was to have been noticed in Berlin, which thought it necessary to protest to Luxembourg about it. Was it then a mistake to launch it altogether? It certainly marked a new stage and a new willingness to take on Hitler on his terms, despite the risks of what he might do in retaliation – and with luck it might have helped to signify that new-found determination to Berlin. It came too late, as did other measures designed to warn him off – assuming that there was anything which would deter him – and that it failed in that sense too, the sequel to Munich, i.e. the seizure of Prague in March 1939, proves beyond doubt. But on the other hand, Britain got away with it. The Germans created no incident over it; in fact, their response was altogether encouraging to this application of a dose of their own medicine, however small.

From the point of view of the shadow Ministry of Information, the lessons of Munich were only too clear but, as Tallents wrote shortly afterwards, 'the sharpest and most urgent of them was the need of properly co-ordinated arrangements for the conveyance of information into enemy countries'.[113] On 5 October, he accordingly established contact with Section D, seemingly for the first time, in order to establish clear lines of demarcation and thus avoid the danger of overlapping. Grand informed the planners that there was no real problem, for his concern was largely with black propaganda.[114] In her Joint Broadcasting Committee, Matheson chose as her liaison officer with the Minister of Information's planners one Guy Burgess who, according to later-released Soviet documents, assisted Grand 'in producing anti-Hitler broadcasts under the ostensibly independent Joint Broadcasting Commission [sic] ... commissioned by MI6 for beaming to Germany from radio stations in Luxembourg and Liechtenstein'.[115]

Tallents meanwhile continued to establish contacts with other interested concerns, such as the Air Ministry, SIS and the War Office. On 6 October 1938, he met with Majors E. K. Page and W. T. Stephenson (later known as 'Intrepid') to establish a liaison with military intelligence.[116] But of the various Whitehall departments consulted, the Foreign Office proved the most reluctant to accept his demarcation lines and, in the aftermath of Munich, there developed a major inter-departmental struggle for control over propaganda. Although the 1936 report had specified that the Ministry of Information was to be responsible for all propaganda at home and abroad in time of war, the events of September 1938 had merely served to cloud the issue. Now there existed a separate organisation for black propaganda and one for enemy propaganda. The ministry, it seemed, was now to be in control only of overt or 'white' propaganda (i.e. that conducted from an attributable government agency). Moreover, on 27 September 1938, the Treasury had authorised the re-creation of the Foreign Office

Political Intelligence Department to supervise the collection and analysis of information of value to the propagandists and to the government as a whole.[117] (It was just like 1918 all over again.)

6.9 Déjà Vu

Leeper was keen to maintain the Foreign Office News Department as the nerve-centre of Britain's peacetime propaganda overseas, particularly as the government was devoting renewed attention to the subject, as reflected in the appointment of the Vansittart Co-ordinating Committee for British Publicity Abroad earlier in 1938.[118] He had lost the 1935 battle to ensure a central role for the Foreign Office in war propaganda planning, but when Tallents submitted a proposal in November 1938 to revise the Ministry's terms of reference so that it could come into being immediately prior to the outbreak of hostilities, Leeper was determined not to lose this one. Essentially, Tallents proposed a six-stage mobilisation process, the first three phases of which would take place in peacetime. Of the first stage, which he termed 'Undisturbed Peacetime Conditions', Tallents wrote:

> Nothing has struck me more forcibly in my recent exploration of this field than the emphasis spontaneously and separately laid by representatives of all three Service Departments on the need in present continental conditions, in which the boundaries between peace and war are so largely obliterated, of an efficient peacetime centre for the close study of 'enemy' public opinion, and the conveyance through channels appropriate in peace of truth about events and British policy to both 'enemy' and other foreign countries. They have recognised that the country needs specialised armament in the world of opinion not less than in that of munitions of war, and have bluntly remarked that such equipment might well make the difference between future war and peace.[119]

The second stage, which Tallents described as 'Peacetime Conditions Disturbed by Factors which might lead to War', provided for the establishment of machinery to conduct propaganda immediately prior to a possible explosion in a last-ditch attempt to save the peace while other forms of evasive action were being explored. Stage three would provide for complete mobilisation 'immediately preceding a decision for peace or war'.[120] Tallents further sought authorisation for the advanced preparation of propaganda material such as leaflets so that they would be ready for use at short notice.[121]

Leeper found these proposals completely unacceptable. He reminded the planners that not only was the Foreign Office the proper authority for the conduct of all official propaganda overseas in time of peace, it was also responsible for the study of foreign opinion. The News Department had already examined means of disseminating the British case into Germany in consultation with the Berlin Embassy, the British Council and the SIS and was about to submit its own proposals to the Cabinet. Besides, he added, propaganda material prepared well in advance might become obsolete by the time war did come.[122] He therefore requested that his objections to Tallents' proposals be formally recorded at the full meeting of the CID sub-committee scheduled to take place on 14 December.

On that same day, the Cabinet considered a memorandum signed by the Foreign Secretary, Lord Halifax (but almost certainly written by Leeper), in which the Foreign Office sought permission to increase its peacetime propaganda in Germany. The Nazi government, it was felt, feared counter-propaganda to such a degree that any British activity in this direction 'should be unobtrusive and unprovocative, as the German government will do their best to counteract it or even stop it, but it also means that our propaganda, if wisely done, may produce a big effect'.[123] Various specific proposals were made including the extension of the BBC's German news bulletins (which had begun on 27 September), increased personal contacts among businessmen, and the expansion of the British Council's long-term cultural and educational activities such as student exchanges, lecture tours and so on. 'Money so spent', it was argued, 'may rightly be regarded as an important item in our general defence programme.'[124]

It has been suggested that these proposals were 'a pitiful package of barrel-scrapings' and that the Foreign Office merely put them forward as the latest exchange in an inter-departmental battle. But that the Foreign Office wished to retain control over a system which it had championed since the end of the First World War in the face of continuous opposition was entirely reasonable. If war should come, it would surprise neither Leeper, who had been warning of the German danger since at least 1935, nor those few officials who supported his innovative ideas in the field of peacetime propaganda. Yet Leeper's success had very much been determined by the degree of acceptance which others, particularly in the Treasury, were prepared to allow in view of financial stringency and, at times, of overwhelming prejudice. In the aftermath of Munich, there was a real chance that his ideas would begin to gain much wider support.

Nevertheless, when the Cabinet discussed the Foreign Office proposals, strong doubts were expressed concerning the suitability of the News Department serving as the nucleus for any programme of increased peacetime propaganda because its press office 'had not always been in complete harmony with Government policy' – a reference to Leeper's recent behaviour during the Munich Crisis when he had been responsible for issuing the unfortunate communiqué of September 26.[125] Moreover, the financial implications of the proposals were severe, and the Cabinet decided to defer any decision pending further investigation by the Exchequer.[126]

Later that day, 14 December 1938, the CID subcommittee on the Ministry of Information convened to discuss Tallents' proposals. Grave concern was expressed at the lack of preparedness during the Munich Crisis, and Tallents attracted most of the criticism. Warren Fisher poured cold water over the six-stage mobilisation plan and warned that a shadow ministry must not be allowed to 'usurp in peacetime the functions of existing agencies or Departments, which should remain responsible for working out their own plans'.[127] In this interdepartmental struggle for control over propaganda in peacetime, Leeper's objections had won through while Tallents was chosen as the sacrificial lamb for the debacle of Munich as, shortly afterwards, he was dismissed as Director-General Designate and replaced by Sir Ernest Fass, the Public Trustee.

This was an astonishing decision. The only full-time planner with any real idea of the problems raised by Munich was replaced by a man with no prior experience of propaganda. Although the precise reasons for his dismissal remain unknown, it would appear that Tallents had upset enough influential people to warrant his replacement by a man who was less willing to rock the Whitehall boat. Nonetheless, the Foreign Office proposals for increased peacetime activity were approved by the Cabinet a week later.[128]

Not surprisingly, Fass proved not to be a success. He was certainly more willing than Tallents had been to accommodate the wishes of the established government departments. Sir Samuel Hoare, the Home Secretary, reluctantly assumed overall responsibility for the planning, although his level of commitment to the cause of propaganda in the next war was, as he himself admitted later, half-hearted to say the least.[129] In other words, both men were entirely unsuited to the enormous task of rectifying the serious deficiencies which had been exposed in the planning by the Munich dress-rehearsal.

Apart from the decision to increase the number of full-time planners working on the preparations from one to three, the only other satisfying outcome of the subcommittee's meeting of 14 December was a decision to appoint a new subcommittee under the chairmanship of Sir Campbell Stuart to re-examine the entire question of enemy propaganda in time of war. The first and only formal meeting of this body took place at Electra House on 26 January 1939. Discussion largely centred around a lengthy memorandum written by Leeper which revealed the considerable amount of propaganda currently being conducted by, or under the auspices of, the Foreign Office.[130] The Foreign Office was then confirmed as the proper authority in time of peace for the conduct of propaganda abroad and for the official study of foreign opinion.[131] Different arrangements would come into force on the outbreak of war, when Campbell Stuart would assume responsibility for the conduct of enemy propaganda. Meanwhile, Leeper was to ascertain the views of the British Council concerning the possible role of cultural propaganda in wartime, while negotiations with the BBC and with the Air Ministry concerning the role of broadcasting and leaflets in enemy propaganda were to be accelerated.[132]

Campbell Stuart continued his own preparations in complete secrecy. Arrangements were made to move his organisation from Electra House to Woburn Abbey on the outbreak of war.[133] He also began to recruit a small nucleus staff to establish contact with the service departments, the Foreign Office, the BBC and the shadow Ministry of Information, from which he was to be completely separate [134] (as in 1918). Alternative methods of distributing propaganda into enemy countries were also investigated but were not disclosed 'in the public interest'.[135]

Despite these improvements in the planning for enemy propaganda, the preparations for the Ministry of Information were still being conducted at a relatively leisurely pace. The German invasion of Prague in March 1939 was to provide the necessary injection of urgency and realism which had not always been evident before, even after Munich. In May 1939, the Prime Minister authorised the appointment of a special ministerial committee, composed of the Home and Foreign Secretaries and the Minister for the Co-ordination of Defence, to consider 'what steps should be taken during peace to counteract anti-British propaganda and to institute a more active policy of British publicity overseas'.[136] Although there appears to be no available record of any formal proceedings, the committee did submit a report to the Cabinet containing two major recommendations to expand the existing propaganda programme and to facilitate the planning for propaganda in war. Hoare proposed the removal of two of the principal obstacles which had hitherto tied the hands of the wartime planners, namely the obligation of strict secrecy and the lack of funds made available to the shadow organisation (which had up to now been carried on the Secret Service Vote). Moreover, because the Ministry of Information intended to assume responsibility for propaganda abroad from the Foreign Office in time of war, it had now become important to ensure 'continuity between the peacetime activities of the Foreign Office in relation to publicity abroad and the work that will in war fall upon the Ministry of Information'.[137]

This recognition was certainly long overdue, and Hoare's report produced two important results. The first was the reorganisation of the Foreign Office News Department. The purely propaganda side of the department's work was separated from the press work and placed under the auspices of a new body called the Foreign Publicity Department of the Foreign Office.[138] The head of this new department was to be Lord Perth, the recently retired Ambassador to Rome. Perth was also made Director-General Designate of the shadow Ministry of Information, replacing Fass. Hoare felt that this dual role would greatly ease the transition from peace to wartime arrangements, and the Cabinet agreed,[139] although not without causing a major scandal in the process.[140] Perth was certainly an unusual choice. Despite his enormously distinguished diplomatic career, like Fass he had little or no personal experience of propaganda matters, and many believed that Leeper should have got the job.[141] When announcing the decision in Parliament on 15 June, thereby revealing the existence of plans for a Ministry of Information for the first time publicly, Chamberlain was subjected to a series of difficult questions which failed to dispel the suspicion that Perth's appointment was 'a ramp of Sam Hoare's'.[142] The other major outcome of Hoare's report was the establishment by the Treasury of the Overseas and Emergency Publicity Expenditure Committee, known as OEPEC. This body was set up in late June 1939 under the chairmanship of Sir Alan Barlow, a senior Treasury official, assisted by Mr J. Cairncross as his secretary.[143] It was designed to cut across the normal time-consuming process of sanctioning expenditure for requests that required immediate action. For example, when the Foreign Office submitted to the Treasury a proposal to authorise its missions at Bucharest, Belgrade, Sofia, Athens and Budapest 'to spend up to £100 each, if necessary, to induce newspaper editors to print articles ... calculated to put across the British point of view', Cairncross's minutes on the proposed remarked: 'as we have already agreed to the "Operational Expense" (i.e. palm-greasing) ... I do not think we need boggle at this further analogous charge'.[144] But OEPEC was also designed to provide speedy decisions to requests from the planners of the shadow Ministry of Information and other wartime propaganda bodies. As the drift towards war increased during the summer of 1939, it naturally concerned itself more with propaganda in the coming war than with the conduct of propaganda during the final months of peace.

There can be no doubt that the Ministry of Information entered the Second World War hopelessly ill-prepared for the tasks which lay before it. Despite the considerable progress made during the final year of peace, there still remained much more preparatory work to be done, particularly in the areas of propaganda techniques and content. Small wonder that it should become something of a public joke, the subject of Evelyn Waugh's satire,[145] at least until Brendan Bracken took over in 1941. The same could not be said of the Enemy Propaganda Department, which had sufficiently prepared the ground to enable the RAF to conduct a leaflet raid on the opening night of the war. So why was it that, despite five years of pre-war planning, Britain entered the war of words in September 1939 not speechless, as it had effectively been in August 1914, but certainly inarticulate? It was not due simply to the fact that new machinery tends to need running-in before it can begin to operate smoothly and effectively, because Goebbels' Ministry of Propaganda, which after all had had six years of practice, also entered the war in chaos and confusion.[146] Nor would it be entirely accurate to attribute the planning deficiencies solely to inter-departmental rivalry and squabbling, although that undoubtedly played its part. Perhaps the answer lies in the fact that before Hitler's seizure of Prague in March 1939 few people in British governmental circles were prepared to accept the idea that a Ministry of Information or that psychological warfare would really be necessary. After all, they did mean war – and that was something everyone had been working so hard to avoid.

Notes and References

1 This chapter combines two revised articles: ' "If War Should Come": preparing the fifth arm for Total War, 1935–39', *Journal of Contemporary History*, 16:1 (1981), pp. 27–51; and ' "An Improper Use of Broadcasting ..." The British government and clandestine radio operations against Germany during the Munich Crisis and after', *Journal of Contemporary History*, 19:3 (1984), pp. 357–84 [co-authored with Nicholas Pronay]. I am grateful to Professor Pronay for allowing me to combine the latter into this book.

2 E. L. Woodward, *British Foreign Policy in the Second World War* (HMSO, 1971), II, p. 38.
3 CAB 65/1, 1 (39) 2, 3 September 1939.
4 C. Webster and N. Frankland, *The Strategic Air Offensive Against Germany, 1939–45* (London, 1961), I, pp. 201–4.
5 King-Hall to S. G. Tallents, 5 September 1938, FO 898/2.
6 Ibid.
7 They can be found in FO 898/1.
8 Memorandum by Tallents, 'Information in Enemy Countries', 7 November 1938, CAB 16/127, MIC 15.
9 Ian McLaine, *Ministry of Morale (Allen and Unwin, 1979), ch. 2.*
10 M. Howard, 'Total War in the twentieth century: participation and consensus in the Second World War' in B. Bond and I. Roy (eds), *War and Society: a Yearbook of Military History* (Croom Helm, 1975).
11 A. Aldgate, *Cinema and History: British Newsreels and the Spanish Civil War* (Scolar Press, 1979).
12 McLaine, *Ministry of Morale*, ch. 2.
13 M. Balfour, *Propaganda in War 1939–45* (Routledge & Kegan Paul, 1978), p. 53.
14 Memorandum by C. P. Robertson, 12 September 1935, CAB 16/127, MIC2.
15 CAB 16/127, MIC 1.
16 C. Stuart (ed.), *The Reith Diaries* (Collins, 1975), p. 122.
17 Balfour, *Propaganda in War*, p. 54.
18 McLaine, *Ministry of Morale*, pp. 12–13.
19 Such as E. T. Cook's *The Press in Wartime* (1920), Douglas Brownrigg's *Indiscretions of the Naval Censor* (1920) and Sir Campbell Stuart's *Secrets of Crewe House* (1920).
20 Although he failed to mention it, he did have the support of a CID decision made in October 1923 which inserted into the War Book a clause which stated that, in the event of another war or emergency, the Foreign Office should be responsible for propaganda 'or for recommending if and when a separate body for dealing with such work should be constituted'. Extract from the minutes of the CID's 177th meeting, 12 October 1923. FO 371/9405, W 8762/293/50.
21 First meeting of the CID subcommittee to prepare plans for the establishment of a Ministry of Information in time of war, 25 October 1935, CAB 16/127.
22 The report is paper number 12538, PREM 1/388. Its acceptance is recorded in CAB 16/129, MIC (CC) 1.
23 CID subcommittee on the general policy of broadcasting in time of war, 25 September 1935, CAB 16/120.
24 CAB 16/120, BW 14.
25 H. V. Rhodes to Tallents, 12 July 1938, INF 4/1A.
26 A. Willert, *Washington and Other Memories* (Boston, 1972).
27 Lampson to H. Montgomery, 28 July 1916, FO 371/2835, 184995.
28 S. Rogerson, Propaganda in the Next War, (Bles, 1938).
29 Progress report by Tallents, 23 February 1938, CAB 16/127, MIC 10.
30 Ibid.
31 Note of a discussion between Leeper and Tallents held on 27 September 1938, INF 1/442.
32 Minute by H. Knatchbull-Hugessen, 27 September 1938, FO 898/1.
33 M. R. D. Foot, *S. O. E in France* (HMSO, 1966), p. 2.
34 Ibid.
35 Ibid. See also B. Sweet-Escott, *Baker Street Irregular* (Methuen, 1965).

36 R. Bruce Lockhart, *Comes the Reckoning* (Arno Press, 1947).
37 See Tallents' account in his memorandum of 7 November 1938, CAB 16/127, MIC 15.
38 Ryan to Tallents, 5 October 1938, FO898/1.
39 C. Stuart, *Opportunity Knocks Once* (Collins, 1952), p. 185.
40 Anthony Adamthwaite, 'The British government and the media, 1937–38', *Journal of Contemporary History*, 18:2 (1983), 281–97.
41 Memorandum by Gerald Wellesley of Special Broadcasting Arrangements, 27–30 September 1938, Birmingham University Library, Chamberlain Papers, NC Add. 14.
42 Ibid.
43 Ibid.
44 Ibid.
45 Ibid.
46 Ibid.
47 Ibid.
48 Ibid.
49 Ibid.
50 Ibid.
51 Ibid.
52 Ibid.
53 Ibid.
54 Ibid.
55 Adamthwaite, 'British government and the media', p. 283.
56 Ibid., p. 285.
57 Ibid., p. 287.
58 'All factors for the formation of public opinion of both countries shall serve the purpose of re-establishing normal and friendly relations … both parties pledge themselves immediately to renounce any aggressive utilisation of radio … against the other party …' Agreement between Austria and Germany, 11 July 1936, Clause II. Similar agreements were made in respect of German-Polish relations. Hitler's view that radio was 'the most terrible weapon in the hands of those who know how to use it' was widely known and so, of course, were Goebbels' pronouncements on the subject. As late as 19 September 1938, just one week before this operation was launched against Germany, the Cabinet received a memorandum, 'Propaganda in Germany: The Dissemination of Ideas among the German People to Weaken their Fighting Power in War', which emphasised that the Nazi government had always regarded propaganda as a straightforward weapon of war and that 'its leaders have unlimited faith in the power of propaganda, which increases their fear of it as a potential weapon against themselves', CAB 16/127, MIC 14.
59 CAB 23/94 29 (38) 10. Here too, as recently as June 1938, the Cabinet Committee under Sir Thomas Inskip, established for considering the question of foreign-language broadcasts, was reminded of the whole of this resolution and this clause was actually quoted. See also A. Briggs, *The Golden Age of Wireless* (Oxford University Press, 1965) p. 360.
60 'League convention concerning the use of broadcasting in the cause of peace', 23 September 1936, League of Nations Documents, 1936–9.
61 Major Astor, a member of both Royal Commissions on Broadcasting, gave the official British understanding of this Clause in Parliament as 'no country should in the language of another broadcast matter which was not acceptable to that

country and contrary to its wishes' – a precise description of just what the Luxembourg broadcasts did do. *The Times*, 30 April 1936, p. 9.

62 The Seventh Duke of Wellington (Gerald Wellesley succeeded to the title in 1943) recalled this remark when consenting to deposit this Memorandum in the Chamberlain Papers. Information Dr. B. S. Benedikt.

63 Memorandum by the Postmaster General, 'Advertisement Broadcasting', 22 June 1937, CAB 24/29 CP 133 (39).

64 CAB 23/94, 29 (39) 10.

65 King-Hall to Tallents, 5 September 1938, FO 898/2.

66 Briggs, *Golden Age*, p. 645.

67 Major Lawrence Grand, Head of Section D, informed the Secretary of the CID subcommittee in charge of co-ordinating the planning of the Ministry of Information on 5 October 1938 that he had plans for four types of propaganda activity: 'a) Broadcasting: by broadcasting outside this country, e.g. Luxembourg ...'. A. P. Ryan to Stephen Tallents, FO 898/1.

68 For Radio Luxembourg see Briggs, *Golden Age*, ch. 4, Europe, cooperation and competition, which presents the BBC's view. For the other side, see Richard Nichols, *Radio Luxembourg: The Station of the Stars* (London 1983). There is little difference in the facts that appear in both books, but, of course, Nichols is both more up to date and more centrally concerned with Radio Luxembourg. The account here follows Nichols, with cross-reference to Briggs confined to points of divergence.

69 Lord Asa Briggs remarked that the evolution of 'few other institutions reveal[s] more clearly the differences between national traditions, national ways of life and national policies'. (Briggs, *The Birth of Broadcasting* (Oxford University Press, 1961), p. 26). It should have been added, 'dominant in a particular period'. It is curious how, in historical discussions of the British policy response to the arrival of broadcasting, there seems no recognition of the fact that the unique approach adopted in Britain only lasted for a very short time. By 1938, the Foreign Office had instructed the BBC to stop pressing the 'public service, no commercialism' line on the International Broadcasting Union, adopted in 1924, and in 1954, with the establishment of Independent Television, commercially funded and regionally based, the twin principles of non-commercial funding and 'a single national voice' had been abandoned. Although it took another twenty years before Britain acquired a pluralistic broadcasting system, with a large number of regionally based and commercially funded local radio stations in addition to some national networks as pioneered in the USA, the ideal, which had always baffled Europeans and Americans alike, of confining broadcasting to a public corporation in the name of 'integrating democracy' and seeking to create a single national voice for the better functioning of a democracy – which presumably has something to do with pluralism rather than totalitarianism – had, in fact, merely held up the development in Britain of the normal pattern and did so for less than a single generation.

70 Captain Plugge divided his time between a splendid Mediterranean yacht, a touring car, both fitted with what must have been one of the first 'portable' radios, and the London social scene, where his presence was regularly noted in *The Times*. In 1953 he became MP for Rochester/Chatham and in his first, and only, substantial speech – an extended question in fact – he attacked the blindness of the government in being unable to see the possibilities offered by pushing British ideals through non-British radio stations. He began, 'As the person who had initiated the first transmissions from an overseas station ...'. *The Times*, 30 April 1936, p. 8.

71 Sociéte d'Etudes Radiophoniques SA, founded in 1929. Nichols, *Radio Luxembourg*, p. 13.

72 Ibid. To cover the territory of the Duchy, four kilowatts would have been sufficient: the provision in the Ducal Charter stipulating that the concessionaires should build a 100-kw power station made it perfectly clear that it was the desire of the government of the Duchy to create an international station on its soil. The largest shareholder was the Compagnie Luxembourgeoise de Radiodiffusion (CLR), followed by the Banque de Paris et Pays-Bas. Nichols, *Radio Luxembourg*, p. 13.

73 The representative of Radio Paris and the French 'national' system on the International Broadcasting Union, R. Tabouis, offered the British, while the station was still being built, joint control, in effect, over it as a solution to the vehement British opposition to it, pointing to the 'utility of Radio Luxembourg as a neutral and impartial station'. Alas, this sensibly Gallic proposal for a deal over what was obviously going to be a powerful propaganda 'utility' went to Vice-Admiral Carpendale, Deputy Director-General under Reith, instead of someone like Vansittart. With sublime blindness to the real point, Carpendale rejected the offer, telling Tabouis that Luxembourg could not genuinely be an 'international neutral post' unless it was managed by a 'non-commerical and truly international committee'. The French might well have thought that the British must be living on another planet. See Briggs, *Golden Age*, p. 355. On the French side, it was Pierre Laval, the Minister of the Interior, who seems to have handled the matter of getting Luxembourg under French control.

74 'He has succeeded in agreement with the French Government in founding the most powerful station in Europe to be situated in Luxembourg, under absolute control of France'. *Journal Officiel*, quoted in Briggs, *Golden Age*, p. 354 and Nichols, *Radio Luxembourg*, p. 31.

75 Nichols, ibid.

76 Ibid, p. 47. Briggs, *Golden Age*, p. 364, gives fifty per cent. These figures need to be taken as approximations, since the techniques of audience research were still in their infancy.

77 T. J. Hollins, 'The Conservative Party and film propaganda between the wars', *English Historical Review*, 96:3 (1981), p. 367.

78 Nichols, *Radio Luxembourg*, p. 33.

79 Ibid, p. 39.

80 *All England Law Reports* 1936, vol. 2, 721 et seq., 2 May 1936, Chancery Division. The submission by Counsel for International Broadcasting Company makes it clear that Radio Publicity Ltd as mentioned in Briggs, *Golden Age*, p. 312, was in fact a British subsidiary of International Broadcasting Company.

81 Nichols, *Radio Luxembourg*, p. 43.

82 The first Scale of Rates was published on 1 August 1936, describing Wireless Publicity Ltd as 'sole agents for the United Kingdom'.

83 Quoted in Nichols, *Radio Luxembourg*, p. 42.

84 See Peter Beck's forthcoming book on this topic.

85 Nichols, *Radio Luxembourg*, p. 44.

86 Memorandum by H. Noble Hall, 28 February 1939, 'Note on Radio Luxembourg', enclosed in E. Phipps to Lord Halifax, 6 March 1939. FO 395/626, P 781/6/150.

87 For 'The Red Network'- undersea cables which only surface on territories marked red on the map, i.e. British possessions, thus ensuring that no-one else can interfere or listen into them – see P. M. Kennedy, 'Imperial Cable Communications and Strategy 1870–1914', *English Historical Review* 86:4 (1971), pp. 728–52.

See also J. Saxon Mills, *The Press and Communications of the Empire* (Heinemann, 1924).

88 Foot, *S. O. E. in France*, p. 2.

89 Radio Luxembourg was used by the Psychological Warfare Section of SHAEF 1944–46; some form of inter-allied, later NATO, supervision and use for cold-war purposes had been established before it was handed back, but details are not known. Influence commercially over the station thus became of no importance. Owing to austerity and strict control of foreign currency expenditure, British advertising was minimal. Once the barriers were removed, Wireless Publicity Ltd was wound up as a trade name and replaced by Radio Luxembourg, London, Ltd. Nichols, *Radio Luxembourg*, p. 83.

90 John Baker White, *The Big Lie* (George Mann, 1973), pp. 48–50. Baker White's own career exemplifies the inextricable connection at bottom between intelligence and propaganda, in his case inside the shadowy world of private organisations which grew up in the wake of the war-propaganda and communist agitation, some of which were covers for 'official' secret service work, while others were entirely privately funded and ploughed their own furrow, and the majority of which were somewhere in between. A good example of this kind of organisation was 'Section D', which came into being in 1923 to combat Bolshevik subversive propaganda and moved on to carry the good fight against the 'Nazi fifth column' (p. 12). By 1938 at the latest, it was directed by John Baker White, and worked by infiltrating agents into both fascist and communist propaganda organisations, supplying valuable information to MI5, as well as the Deuxieme Bureau, and ran its own 'white' propaganda operation under cover of the Economic League. In 1938, Baker White, presumably together with the services of his 'Section D', was recruited by 'EH' – the engagement interview being conducted by a trio consisting of Rex Leeper of the Foreign Office, Major Dallas Brook 'of the War Office' and Robert Bruce Lockhart, then apparently holding no official position. After this and his work for the DMI's radio propaganda until it was moved to the Political Warfare Executive, Baker White went on to work in the eastern Mediterranean theatre of war and in the Political Warfare Section, specialising in deception campaigns and ending the war a Lieutenant Colonel.

91 John Costello and Oleg Tsarev, *Deadly Illusions* (Century, 1993), p. 427.

92 Nigel Nicolson (ed.), *Harold Nicolson Diaries and Letters* (Collins, 19966–68), vol. 2, 262, note 2 and vol. 3, p. 140. It is odd that despite such extremely affectionate references, there is in fact nothing recorded of Wellesley's activities or opinions. Even where Nicolson describes a luncheon with Chamberlain, Churchill, Wellesley involving a heated political discussion, there is no record of Wellesley's contribution – if any.

93 For Sir Joseph Ball see J. Ramsden, *The Age of Balfour and Baldwin* (Longman, 1978), pp. 192–8, remarking on how Chamberlain relied on Sir Joseph's advice; F. Thorpe and N. Pronay, *British Official Films in The Second World War* (Clio Press, 1980), pp. 25–34; A. Beichman, 'Hugger Mugger in Old Queen Street', *Journal of Contemporary History*, 15:4 (1978), 671–88; R. R. James, *Memoirs of a Conservative* (Weidenfeld and Nicolson, 1969), containing much fascinating, though also cryptic, detail of Sir Joseph's work and character, including his 'intelligence' exploits concerning the confidential papers of the Labour Party which put Watergate into the small-beer category; and T. J. Hollins, 'The Presentation of Politics' (Ph.D. thesis, Leeds University, 1981). In Appendix A, Hollins lists the main references to what has been said about him in current historical literature,

and discusses the evidence which survives of him in the archives of the Conservative
Party. Dr Hollins' conclusion is that he both deserved and revelled in his reputation
as a sinister and conspiratorial figure deeply involved all through with the Secret
Services. Sir Joseph announced just before his death in 1961 that he had personally
burnt all his papers in preparation for it – there have been subsequent rumours,
characteristically, that he had not in fact done so.

94 Middlemas and Barnes, *Baldwin*, pp. 362–3.
95 Memorandum by Sir Joseph Ball to the Prime Minister, June 1938. Chamberlain
    Papers NC8/21/8, partly quoted in Hollins, 'Presentation of Politics', p. 36. In a
    letter to another of his closer associates, Lord Weir, Chamberlain reported on the
    development of the plans for the National Publicity Bureau, 'The great "facade"
    will make further progress on Monday next ... etc'. NC7/11/27/38, 11 May
    1934.
96 There are a number of private letters from Sir Joseph Ball to Chamberlain which
    help to shed light on the man as well as his relationship to Chamberlain: they
    normally manage to work in their mutual love of the sport as well as a heavy
    mixture of flattery and expressions of devotion on Ball's part. A rank example is
    NC7/11/32/8, sent 22 December 1939. It begins: 'I have managed to secure a
    small Christmas gift, a copy of one of Hereford's books about the development
    and use of his pattern of dry flies.' It then goes on to a page of flattery and
    concludes: 'Our position today is unassailable. It is indeed immense throughout
    the whole world. I shudder to think how much depends upon you personally. May
    you be given health and strength ... etc'. Little wonder that one of Sir Joseph's
    colleagues in the Research Department principally remembered him as a man who
    knew how to make friends at the top fast. Hollins, 'Presentation of Politics', p. 34.
97 Maurice Cowling, *The Impact of Hitler, British Politics and British Policy 1933–1939*
    (Cambridge University Press, 1975, paperback edition), p. 300.
98 Hollins. 'Presentation of Politics', pp. 3 6 and 110.
99 Ronald Tree, *When The Moon Was High* (Macmillan, 1975), p. 76.
100 Memorandum on the Joint Broadcasting Committee, 24 August 1939, Appendix
    to OEPEC paper 82, T 162/858, E 39140/4.
101 Ibid.
102 Memorandum by Lord Halifax, 'British Propaganda in Germany', 8 December
    1938, CAB 24/281, CP 284 (38).
103 CAB 23/96, 60 (38) 5.
104 CAB 23/96, 60 (38) 3.
105 Ibid.
106 CAB 27/641, ABC (37), seventh meeting.
107 Ibid.
108 Berlin Chancery to News Department, 10 March 1939, FO 395/626, P 920/6/150.
109 Ibid.
110 H. Noble Hall to Lord Lloyd, 3 May 1939, FO 395/628/1869/6/150.
111 Foreign Office memorandum, 'Government policy on broadcasting in English by
    Foreign Stations', 23 January 1939, CAB 27/641, ABC (37) 24.
112 Note on broadcasts to Germany, undated, unsigned. CO 395/630, P 2966/6/150.
113 Tallents to Sir Donald Banks, 4 October 1938, FO 898/1.
114 Ryan to Tallents, 5 October 1938, FO 898/1.
115 Costello and Tsarev, *Deadly Illustions*, p. 240.
116 Record of a meeting held at the BBC, 6 October 1938, FO 898/1.
117 Memorandum by Warner, 6 October 1938, FO 395/624, P 2853/2853/150.

118 Memorandum by Tallents, 7 November 1938, CAB 16/127, MIC 18.
119 Ibid.
120 Ibid.
121 Leeper to Ryan, 7 December 1938, CAB 16/127, MIC 18.
122 Ibid.
123 Memorandum by Halifax, 'British propaganda in Germany', 8 December 1938, CAB 24/281, CP 284 (38).
124 CAB 23/96, 59(38) 5.
125 CAB 23/96, 60 (38) 3.
126 Ibid.
127 Fifth meeting of the CID subcommittee to prepare plans for the establishment of a Ministry of Information in time of war, 14 December 1938, CAB 16/127.
128 CAB 23/96, 60 (38) 3, 21 December 1938.
129 Viscount Templewood, *Nine Troubled Years* (Collins, 1954), pp. 420–1.
130 Memorandum by Leeper, 'British Publicity Abroad', 20 January 1939, CAB 16/130, MIC (P) 2.
131 Undated draft report by Campbell Stuart. CAB 16/130, MIC (P) 5.
132 CID subcommittee on Propaganda in Foreign Countries in time of war, first meeting, 26 January 1939, CAB 16/130, MIC (P).
133 Balfour, *Propaganda in War*, 88–9.
134 Memorandum by Campbell Stuart, 8 February 1939, CAB 16/130, MIC (P) 3.
135 Undated draft report by Campbell Stuart, CAB 16/130, MIC (P) 5.
136 Memorandum by Hoare, 2 June 1939, CAB 24/287, CP 127 (39).
137 Ibid.
138 FO 366/1071.
139 CAB 23/99, 31 (39) 12, 7 June 1939; CAB 23/99, 32 (32) 9, 14 June 1939.
140 J. Harvey (ed.), *The Diplomatic Diaries of Oliver Harvey, 1937–40* (Collins, 1973).
141 Ibid, 294.
142 Ibid, 292.
143 T 162/858, E 39140/2.
144 Minute by Cairncross, 31 August 1939, T 162/858, E39140/2.
145 *Put Out More Flags* (Chapman and Hall, 1942).
146 R. E. Herzstein, *The War that Hitler Won* (Hamish Hamilton, 1979).

Total War and Total Propaganda, 1939–45

So much has already been written about propaganda in the Second World War that it might seem superfluous to add to the debate here. However, it remains a very rich vein for historical research, and good books continue to be published about it.[1] The three chapters in this section are amongst my own contributions to the literature, the third being a jointly authored piece based on recently released archival material.

What they demonstrate together is how adept, once again, the British were at wartime propaganda, censorship and psychological warfare. They were less good at learning the lessons of the past but instead had to reinvent certain wheels before the machinery was to run as effectively as it had done in the Great War. After two years of chaos, however, the system settled down to a remarkably effective process that aided the course of eventual victory. But the circumstances in which propaganda was conducted, at home and abroad, were vastly different in World War Two to what they had been in the Great War. Thanks especially to the bomber, this new war was a Total War in the proper sense of the phrase. Together with the arrival of truly mass media in the form of radio and cinema, it was unlikely that any square yard of Britain could remain untouched either by the war or by news about it. Radio meant that Britain's enemies could directly address the British people[2] – much as British broadcasters could address foreign peoples. This prompted Asa Briggs to describe the war as 'a war of words'. But it was also a war of images and sounds, with the cinema playing an important role in domestic propaganda and in campaigns for hearts, minds and allegiances in allied and neutral countries around the world.

As in the last war, by far the most important neutral country – at least up until the Japanese attack on Pearl Harbour in December 1941 – was the USA. But Britain had to be even more careful this time to avoid the appearance of exhorting Americans to join the war on its side. As the *New Statesman* pointed out the day before war was declared, 'Dr Goebbels had made truth Britain's greatest asset'.[3] And whereas the British laboured hard throughout to adhere to truthful principles, one person's truth is often another person's lie. Besides this was war, and the whole truth could not be told – at least until after it was all over. So the British convinced themselves that although they may been in the business of propaganda, it was a 'propaganda with facts' and therefore not really propaganda at all.

Notes and References

1 Most recently, see Sian Nichols, *The Echo of War: Home Front Propaganda and the Wartime BBC, 1939–45* (Manchester University Press, 1986) and Nicholas J. Cull, *Selling War: The British Campaign against American 'Neutrality' in World War II* (Oxford University Press, 1995).

2 See Martin Doherty, 'German wireless propaganda in English: an analysis of the organisation, content and effectiveness of National Socialist radio broadcasts for the UK, 1939–45' (Ph. D. thesis, University of Kent, School of History, 1998).

3 *New Statesman*, 2 September 1939.

7

Blue-Pencil Warriors: The British Wartime Censorship System, 1939–45[1]

(Censorship and propaganda are really different sides of the same medal: the manipulation of opinion) In democratic societies, including a Britain that could legitimately be said to be increasingly democratic, that medal is often felt to be out of place even alongside the various battle honours of a (pluralistic government at war.) Its apologists will argue that in the Second World War it was one of the essential expedients necessary for waging and winning the Total War against Nazi Germany. More normally, it is felt, it is something that democratic societies resort to only in time of war or crisis. However, 'a common cultural conceit in liberal democracies is the belief that the amount of censorship at any given time is decreasing and that speech is becoming increasingly free, while quite the opposite situation obtains'.[2] (In fact, as we have seen, Britain earned its propaganda and censorship honours long before 1939–45, and even long before Britain began to approach the semblance of a genuinely democratic system with the massive and dramatic expansion of the electorate between 1918 and 1928.) During the First World War, when positive means of persuasion – propaganda – was becoming an accepted feature of British governmental war-time responsibility, negative means – censorship – had already come of age.[3] But what distinguishes the British government's manipulation of opinion in the twentieth century from earlier periods, in peace and war, is not just the grafting of a positive propaganda machinery on to the already established censorship procedures. It is also the scale on which the official manipulation of opinion was conducted, the size and significance of the audience to be influenced and the means and media through which it operated. Never before had so much information been available to so many people with so many means open to them to express their point of view. Never before had their opinions counted for so much in the survival of the state or, conversely, in its destruction. Never before had there been such a need for governments of all kinds to devote themselves to the struggle for the hearts and minds of the politicised masses.

7.1 The Other Side of the Coin

Despite experience dating back to the early modern period, and despite con-siderable official attention given to censorship before 1914,[4] the censors employed at the Press Bureau during the First World War had encountered innumerable, and mostly avoidable, difficulties. Then the problem had been largely confined to the press. Sir Edward Cook, joint chief press censor for most of the war, recognised the inherent incompatibility of censors and journalists when he told pressmen in 1916:

> You should not, in kindness or for any other reason, speak too much good of the censorship. I don't suppose you are likely to do so, but it would be a terrible blow if you did. The enterprising newspaper or news agency and an official censorship are natural enemies; and if the day should ever come when the newspapers, British and Neutral, conspired to praise the Press Bureau, it would mean either the journalists had lost their 'go' or that our censors had been neglecting their duty.[5]

It would also mean something else. It is in the interests of a democratic government to have its censors criticised by the media as it gives the impression that the media are still operating freely and independently with only a minimum of wartime restrictions. The real extent of those restrictions is kept secret, for obvious reasons, but the result is not only a censorship system which appears to be more liberal than it is in reality, but also an effective method of disseminating official news and views through the media without actually revealing that it is propaganda. Cook was far too sophisticated a practitioner of his craft to inform the press that it was serving the interests of the government or that, through censorship, it had become an agent for the distribution of official propaganda. If the media spoke too kindly of the censorship, the game would be up.

The declared role of the Press Bureau was to provide the principal channel through which government departments released official war news to the press. The numerous problems that plagued the Bureau, particularly in the first two years of its existence, owed less to its own alleged inefficiency than to two factors, one of which was to recur in the Second World War. First, it was dominated by the War Office and Admiralty, whose principal concern, not unnaturally, was to prevent the publication of any information which might prove to be of value to the enemy. Initially, in both world wars, this preoccupation bordered upon an obsession and resulted in a dearth of news that merely fostered counter-productive speculation and rumour. It earned the official body the nickname 'Suppress Bureau'. Gradually however, the Service Departments' philosophy that 'no news is good news' gave way to an appreciation of the value of more positive forms of persuasion, especially after the war dragged on and morale began to emerge as an increasingly significant military asset.

Second, the Press Bureau encountered problems as a result of the procedures laid down for the censorship of news material. Technically, all press censorship was voluntary; editors were entitled to submit for consideration in advance any material that they suspected was likely to violate the Defence of the Realm Act (DORA). They were, however, under no compulsion to submit material beforehand although they were liable to prosecution for publishing anything which might subsequently be deemed to have violated the defence regulations.

Ignorance was no excuse. Nor indeed was the fact that the offending material might have been supplied by an official source – including the Press Bureau! A returned item marked 'Passed by the Censor' proved merely to be an expression of the Bureau's view that it did not contravene DORA. Because of this anomaly, which was rectified after the war, one would have to agree with Sir Edward Cook who remarked that the censorship between 1914 and 1918 only worked because of 'the genius of the British people for working a logically indefensible compromise'.[6]

The Press Bureau was closed down on 30 April 1919 and the official cable censorship was discontinued shortly afterwards.[7] The government hoped for a return to its normal peacetime relationship with the press, but the war had radically changed the nature of the relationship between governor and governed. The first experience of Total War, mutinies in the mass conscript armies, and the lessons of Bolshevik-inspired revolution in Russia and elsewhere, together with the continued implications of the communications revolution, all necessitated a new brand of post-war thinking concerning the manipulation of opinion. The British Board of Film Censors (BBFC), for example, which had been established in 1912 by the film industry with the active approval and involvement of the Liberal government, quietly retained and subsequently updated its supposedly temporary wartime rules concerning film coverage of, *inter alia*, industrial disputes and political unrest.[8] As the inter-war years progressed, the BBFC's role in political censorship became as significant as its task of moral guidance.[9] Similarly, the experience of the post-war popular unrest, and of the 1926 General Strike in particular, played a major part in the definition and establishment of a broadcasting monopoly in Britain when the BBC was granted its Charter in 1927.[10] The arrival of the first truly mass media in Britain was therefore accompanied by official measures designed to control their enormous potential for political and social exploitation. Instead of becoming liberating democratic instruments for the uninhibited expression of ideas, they became essential weapons of social engineering and of the manufacture of consensus in inter-war Britain.

In view of the threats which were perceived to have existed to the nascent British democracy, either from within, in the form of Bolshevik-inspired labour mob tyranny, or from without in the form of new totalitarian regimes dedicated to anti-democratic ideals, these measures were understandable and indeed essential from the establishment's point of view. Moreover, as the prospect of another major war became increasingly likely in the aftermath of the World Disarmament Conference, the Nazi revolution in Germany and mounting aggression in China, Africa and Spain, the National Government of the 1930s recognised that, just as in peace, the 'munitions of the mind' would play a significant role in determining the outcome of any future conflict.

As we have seen, planning for propaganda in the Second World War began in Britain as early as 1935. The integral 'organic' role of censorship in morale-forming was recognised from the outset. Indeed, such was felt to be its significance that it received more consideration from the planners of the future

Ministry of Information (MoI) than the other three intended functions of the Ministry, namely propaganda, production and distribution. Too often historians have seized upon early wartime criticisms of the MoI and upon inadequacies in the planning process to detract from the essential fact that British wartime censorship between 1939 and 1945 was a highly effective and successful operation.[11] Too little has it been appreciated that Britain went to war with a wealth of peacetime experience in censorship and with the basis of a censorship machinery that, once its wheels began to turn when the correct lubrication was added by 1941, was to run remarkably smoothly.

This is not to minimise the problems encountered by the pre-war planners. Despite the experience of the First World War and the existence of a shadow organisation since then 'ready to come into operation whenever required',[12] the planners were plagued by interdepartmental in-fighting and troubled by the conceptual aspects of democratic censorship. At their first meeting in October 1935, Major-General J. G. Dill, the Director of Military Intelligence, explained that the existing shadow censorship organisation consisted of four main divisions – telegraphic, postal, press and broadcasting – the first two of which were the direct responsibility of the War Office. In the event of war, a Press Bureau was to be established under the auspices of the Home Office to reproduce the functions of its Great War predecessor and to serve as the normal channel of communication between Whitehall and Fleet Street. A new, and key, element of future wartime activity – broadcasting – was the subject of separate negotiations between the government and the BBC, talks which predated the establishment of the MoI planning committee but which were to result in the recommendation that the Ministry would assume complete control over the BBC in wartime.[13] This decision was unfortunate. It meant that the planners devoted a considerable amount of time to working out the wartime relationship between the government and the BBC when they should have been taking a more rounded view. Moreover, most of that time was wasted; when war actually came, the terms of that relationship emerged naturally through expediency – some would say muddling through – rather than as a result of planning.

At their first meeting, Rear-Admiral J. A. G. Troup, the Director of Naval Intelligence, informed the MoI's planners that the Admiralty was particularly concerned with censorship in view of the recent breaches of intelligence during the Abyssinian crisis.[14] This was ominous. As in the First World War, the hyper-sensitivity of the service departments, and particularly of the Senior Service which succeeded in having its retired officers appointed to senior positions within the censorship organisation, to any security leaks was severely to debilitate the future efficiency of Britain's overall propaganda effort in the opening stages of the Second World War.[15] For just as propaganda and censorship are different sides of the same coin, so also are persuasion and intelligence. The one is the essential raw material of the other; the need for security has to be balanced against the needs of morale. In the Second World War, this realisation manifested itself in the work of the Political Warfare Executive (PWE) and the Special Operations Executive (SOE). But those organisations did not emerge properly until 1941; before then, the domination of the service departments in the propaganda activities of the MoI severely weakened the positive aspects of morale-forming.

The pre-war planning of the MoI censorship functions was thus devoted largely to the press and radio. This was to be the responsibility of the appropriately named Control Division. Postal and telegraphic censorship belonged to a slightly different category more directly concerned with the secret intelligence services, for which there was an organisation already in existence under the service departments' watchful eyes (and ears) and subject to the Committee of Imperial Defence's standing inter-departmental committee on censorship. If one of the major mistakes of the First World War experience was to conduct the whole business of propaganda, censorship and intelligence from a variety of different buildings, then the same mistake was about to be made in the opening phase of the Second World War.

As for the press, it was decided that censorship would again be on a 'voluntary' basis – at least to all outward appearances – with editors being invited to submit in advance any material which they though might infringe the defence regulations. These made it an offence 'to obtain, record, communicate or publish information which might be of military value to the enemy'.[16] The censors would have the right to pass material in full or in part, or to withhold it altogether but, in the next war, any material returned by the censors would absolve editors of any legal responsibility should it subsequently transpire to have benefited the enemy. Even if the press ignored suggested cuts, the government still had to prove that the offending publication had actually aided the enemy before prosecution could take place. This, at least, was the theory. It was logical and seemingly liberal. But, as will be seen, the key word in the regulation cited above was 'obtain' and such was the comprehensive nature of the censors' control over the news media's sources of information that very few ambiguities were left to chance. Having said that, the comparative clarity of these arrangements stands out in sharp contrast to the pre-war arrangements that existed for film and radio censorship.

In the case of broadcasting, the BBC was at one and the same time blessed and cursed in having one of its own officials appointed Director-General Designate of the MoI from 1936 to 1938. This was the remarkable Sir Stephen Tallents, public relations officer at the BBC and a leading pioneer of modern British governmental publicity and propaganda techniques. Tallents enjoyed the complete backing of his BBC chief, Sir John Reith, who warned in 1935:

> It is essential that the responsibility and reliability of the BBC's news service should be established beyond doubt, even though in practice accuracy could not amount to more than the nearest approach to absolute truth permitted by the overriding war conditions including censorship. On the lowest terms, a reputation for reliability is the only possible foundation for credibility – or for successful deceit, should such a course be necessary in the interests of the country.[17]

So indeed it proved. But until 1938, the MoI planners worked on the assumption that they would be responsible for all types of propaganda, domestic and foreign, black and white, positive and negative, press, radio and film. The emergence during the dress rehearsal of the Munich Crisis of various additional organisations to deal with psychological warfare, together with various other emergency arrangements, confused the entire planning process. Tallents was sacked shortly afterwards and by then Reith had already left the BBC. As a result, the BBC's role in wartime, remarkably, was still undecided by March 1939. A statement by the Home Secretary in July simply announced that the government would treat broadcasting 'as we treat the press and films and leave the BBC to carry on ... with a very close liaison with the Ministry of Information'.[18] This was followed in August by a decision that radio censorship would be 'indirect, informal and voluntary' although the fact remains that the BBC entered the Second World War with its position and role left largely undefined and unresolved.[19]

The Home Secretary's reference to film was not without its irony as, not unlike the BBC, preparations in that quarter were often conducted separately from the main planning process of the MoI. The topic had been raised at a planning committee in January 1936, and some preliminary investigations were carried out,[20] but it was decided a month later that detailed planning of film censorship lay outside the MoI's terms of reference. The existing defence regulations encompassed film in the same manner as other material that could prove useful to an enemy. The matter was therefore passed to the standing committee of the Committee for Imperial Defence on censorship, which then began to negotiate with film companies to work out a wartime system. This body decided that the MoI would concern itself with the suppression of film material 'inimical to the conduct of the war', of films showing the movement of troops and equipment and of exported film footage which might help the enemy. The BBFC would retain its existing position and functions concerning social and moral censorship, but political and security aspects of film would become the MoI's responsibility. The BBFC was thus expected to liaise closely with the MoI, with film producers and with other involved government departments. Although the existing peacetime arrangements were supposedly voluntary, the newsreels – the main area where film censorship was likely to prove most necessary in wartime – were not covered by BBFC guidelines. Indeed, it was only in July 1938 (at the very earliest) that the BBFC was informed that its wartime activities were to include compulsory newsreel censorship.[21]

The system that emerged eventually was somewhat different but the point was that, given the likely significance of film propaganda in wartime, this medium did not receive the concerted attention before the war that its persuasive powers and audience size deserved. The final absurdity concerning the lack of pre-war consideration was reflected in two early wartime decisions. The first was to close all cinemas on the outbreak of war. As we have seen, fear of the bomber, fuelled, it has to be said, by pre-war newsreels, outweighed the likely significance of film propaganda on morale. That decision was reversed after a fortnight. The second absurdity was not to allow film cameramen to accompany the British Expeditionary Force (BEF) to France. Even in 1914, film crews had accompanied the British army before having their permits revoked by the War Office following the retreat from Mons.[22] Indeed, the 1939 news blackout on the story was only lifted after a Paris radio announcement that the BEF had actually arrived in France, only to be reimposed once the newspapers had gone to press. This farce saw Fleet Street offices occupied and newspapers seized from dazed motorists and train commuters, with the blackout lifted again shortly afterwards.[23]

On the outbreak of war, therefore, all the pre-war planning problems suddenly erupted in a series of blunders which soon threatened the very existence of the MoI. Given that the Control Division, now renamed the Press and Censorship Division under retired Vice-Admiral C. V. Usborne (a former Director of Naval Intelligence) had received the most attention from the pre-war planners, the initial relationship between the press and the MoI was disastrous. If one considers the remarkable degree of support given by most of the media to government policy before the war, and the extent to which Chamberlain had placed such emphasis on this being a 'just war',[24] the British may as well have learned nothing since the previous conflict. Admittedly and undeniably, the early months of the Second World War were a difficult period, with most of the fighting taking place in distant countries about which the Service Departments seemed determined to ensure that the British people would continue to know nothing. However, the rigidity of their approach undoubtedly contributed to the mounting frustration of the British people during the 'phoney war' and to the popular impression that nothing much of significance was happening.

True, British military involvement during the first months of the war was limited chiefly to Naval matters. It was all the more unfortunate, therefore, that of all the service departments the Admiralty proved the most reluctant to part with news that might have had a positive bearing upon morale. As First Lord, Churchill (who should have known better as an ex-journalist and as a veteran of Gallipoli – or was it perhaps because of this experience?) was consistent in his refusal to co-operate with the MoI. He felt it was 'for the Admiralty or other departments to purvey to the Ministry the raw meat and vegetables and for the Ministry to cook and serve the dish to the public'.[25] Certainly, the MoI was only just beginning to learn its culinary skills but the Admiralty's offerings did not even constitute famine relief and that which did get through to news-starved journalists was distributed by a censorship staff largely made up of ex-naval personnel. The MoI was a new department whose precise relationship to Whitehall was as yet undefined, and news was emanating from a variety of different, and more established, official sources. The MoI wanted to see itself recognised as the sole provider and felt that the role of these older government departments was merely to supply it with 'meaty' news for distribution to the media, which could then garnish it according to the particular style of its editors. George Thomson, a Rear-Admiral who was first Deputy and then, from 1940, Chief Censor for the entirety of the war, felt that the press in particular did hold legitimate grievances. His atypical but ultimately sensible and accepted approach was that it was the censors' duty 'not only to try and prevent the enemy from gaining military information of value, but also to ensure that the press and the BBC should have complete freedom to inform the British people and the world at large of everything that was happening'.[26] When the latter clearly did not occur, the press responded in frustration by a somewhat misdirected but ferocious assault upon the MoI and its staff. This prompted Lord Macmillan, the first Minister of Information, to suggest in Cabinet that reform was essential. The outcome was a temporary disaster when, on 3 October 1939, the Prime Minister announced that henceforth a newly created Press and Censorship Bureau under the control of Sir Walter Monckton would conduct news censorship separately from the MoI.

This experiment lasted just over six months. The new Bureau harked back to the Great War system when censorship and propaganda had been conducted separately from one other. It was, moreover, doomed to failure because the service departments continued to dominate the censorship arrangements. In the meantime, the very existence of the MoI was jeopardised, having been divested of its principal *raison d'être*. But at least this period did allow the MoI to look to itself, set its own house in order and to define the positive role which it should play, particularly when John Reith became its minister in January 1940. For it was Reith who laid down two of the fundamental axioms of the MoI's work during the rest of the war, namely that 'news is the shock-troops of propaganda'[27] and that propaganda should tell 'the truth, nothing but the truth and, as near as possible, the whole truth'.[28]

Reith in turn fell victim to the fall of Chamberlain and his replacement by the Churchill government in April 1940. It was in that month, however, that the MoI reabsorbed the Press and Censorship Bureau. Up until that point, it has to be said, censorship had been a farce. The censors were over-preoccupied with detail and mechanical questions while the press had become so contemptuous of them that editors frequently ignored their rulings, thereby threatening the collapse of the 'voluntary' system and its replacement with straightforward compulsory censorship. But although the MoI was to remain the centre of organisational squabbling until after Brendan Bracken took over as Minister in 1941, its censorship functions began to settle down to a coherent pattern after April 1940 when the Ministry even gained responsibility for postal and telegraphic censorship from the War Office.[29] For the most part, this system operated remarkably well and efficiently for the rest of the war.

7.2 The Mechanics of British Censorship

How did that system work? The essential point about it was that all quick (or 'hot') news in Britain was censored at the source of its arrival. The British news media relied upon the news agencies for the overwhelming supply of its news. Before the First World War, the Post Office had rerouted Britain's worldwide cable network so that all the commercial cables came together at a single point. That point was in the London headquarters of the Press Association (which supplied the British press) which was also in the same building as Reuters (which supplied the overseas press). It was here that censors could control by far the best part of the news passing to Fleet Street, the provincial press, Broadcasting House and the foreign press before it reached them. It was pre-censorship in the case of the press and radio, although newsreels fell into a slightly different category and were subject to both pre- and post-censorship. As Nicholas Pronay has pointed out:

> This system allowed the news editors of the press as a whole, as well as the BBC, to exercise to the maximum effect their long-acquired skill in giving a great variety of form to what in fact was centrally released and thus reinforce their credibility through the illusion of many apparently independent presentations ... Members of the public could reassure themselves by comparing what they took to be instantaneous – hence uncensored – communication over the radio, with the variegated and elaborated version in the newspapers next morning and then with the newsreel supplying it for the public to see 'with their own eyes'.[30]

Censors from the War Office, Admiralty, Air Ministry, Foreign Office and Ministry of Home Security were housed in the MoI in Malet Street to advise on matters which related to their respective spheres of interest, before passing out official news and after they had monitored the agency messages. News passing overseas via Reuters was also censored at source, particularly that which was likely to create inter-allied disharmony. Slow (or 'cold') news, such as that found in books, magazines and the mail, could be dealt with at a much more leisurely pace.

By 1941, this system was in full flight. It operated so efficiently on a daily basis that many British and overseas observers were unaware that an effectively compulsory pre-censorship system was in fact operating. This helps to explain why Britain's wartime propaganda gained its reputation for telling the truth when, in fact, it could rarely tell the whole truth.

7.3 The MoI and Fleet Street: Press Censorship

In 1941, the MoI was charged with 'the creative function of providing a steady flow of facts and opinions calculated to further the policy of the government in the prosecution of the war'.[31] In order to achieve this, it was supposed 'to preserve intimate and cordial relations with the newspapers through their proprietors, editors and reporters'.[32] Much harm had already been done to those relations by the heavy-handed treatment which the censors had meted out to the journalists, partly because of their own predisposition and inexperience, partly because of the influence upon them of the service departments and partly because of the policy that security outweighed publicity. Once the MoI was given a 'creative' function, however, its work demanded the closer integration of its negative and positive activities. This became possible with the promotion of Thomson to Chief Censor, the appointment of Cyril Radcliffe in charge of news and censorship and the arrival of Bracken as Minister. 'We all thought alike', wrote Thomson.[33] Their philosophy was that the only reason for suppressing news was on security grounds and that once something had leaked out there was no point in maintaining a ban upon it.[34] This explains why the British press often carried enemy communiqués, thereby enhancing its reputation for objectivity and its credibility, a characteristic that even Goebbels admired. Moreover, Thomson, Radcliffe and Bracken all agreed that opinion was not to be censored; 'information covered facts, but not opinions, comments, speculation or the use which the enemy might make of such information to further his propaganda against us'.[35] This decision was not only sophisticated but skilful. Yet, it was made from the relative safety of knowing that all news released, on which the media could form its opinions, had already been censored at source. At the same time it suggested that a voluntary system was in place which provided an effective cover for official propaganda and a clearer conscience for a liberal democracy at war.

It was also a decision with which Churchill did not always agree, as on several celebrated occasions when the government clashed with the press. These clashes, it has to be said, were primarily between Churchill and individual newspapers rather than between MoI censors and Fleet Street. Before recounting them briefly, it is important to stress that the flare-ups that did occur were so few in number that they bear witness to the routine day-to-day efficiency of the censorship system. That there should be no more than half a dozen open breaches in six years of war – and most of those being in the difficult days of 1940 when the MoI was just beginning to settle down – was indeed a remarkable achievement. The Press and Censorship Division brought only four prosecutions in the entire war. And when all is said and done about the wartime anxieties of the press concerning the censorship, it was not so much what the MoI actually did but rather what it might do which most concerned journalists. The essential realisation that both Fleet Street and the MoI were part of the same business of winning the war, and that their partnership in shaping morale might help to determine its outcome, ultimately led to a mutual appreciation of the limits to which they could and could not go.

But there were some clashes. In May 1940, the government banned the export of Communist and Fascist journals. The ban on the former was only lifted after the Russian entry into the war or, rather, after the battle of Stalingrad. In July of the same year, the *Daily Worker* was warned that its pacifist line contravened defence regulation 2D, which made it an offence 'systematically to publish matter calculated to foment opposition to the prosecution of the war'.[36] The warning, however, was ignored and on 21 January 1941, the Home Secretary, Herbert Morrison, ordered Scotland Yard into the offices of the

Daily Worker, together with those of *The Week*, to stop the presses. They were only allowed to resume publication in August 1942 when a comprehensive re-educative campaign about 'Our Soviet Friends' was in full swing.[37]

Far more serious, by reason of the size and nature of its circulation, was the constant sniping of the *Daily Mirror*. The circulation of this newspaper rose from one-and-three-quarter million in 1939 to three million in 1946, and was particularly popular amongst the troops (no doubt attracted by the charms of its erotic comic-strip heroin 'Jane'). Together with its weekly counterpart, the *Sunday Pictorial*, the *Mirror* was more responsible than perhaps any other source for implanting into the popular psyche two of the most resilient myths about the 1930s, namely the existence of a German Fifth Column in Britain, and the 'Guilty Men' of Munich. Not surprisingly, that the two phenomena were related was a frequent suggestion. The *Mirror* conducted its acrimonious campaign against Chamberlain and his supporters throughout the first half of 1940 to the point where it even embarrassed Churchill, who felt the need to make representations to the paper and others that had since followed its lead.[38] But despite Chamberlain's departure, the attacks resumed and, on 25 January 1941, Churchill informed Cecil King that he felt his paper was promoting 'a spirit of hatred and malice against the government, which after all is not a Party Government but a National Government almost unanimously chosen, which spirit surpasses anything I have ever seen in English journalism. One might have thought that in these hard times some hatred might be kept for the enemy'.[39] The new Prime Minister then went on to turn the tables on the *Mirror*'s own arguments by suggesting that its attacks were fostering defeatism and thus serving the aims of the (in fact non-existent) Fifth Column movement which the paper loathed. It was as well that Churchill's inclination to suppress the *Mirror* was tempered by the Home Secretary and the MoI on the grounds that opinion must not be subjected to 'post-censorship'. For the moment, a personal interview was sufficient to abate the paper's attacks.

The period between February and November 1942 was as bleak for Britain in terms of morale, public as well as private, as any in the war. Barely had the country survived the shock of German battleships passing undetected through the Channel when the bastion of Britain's Far Eastern Empire at Singapore surrendered to the Japanese with the loss of 60,000 prisoners. German successes in the battle of the Atlantic continued; oil prices increased and the press, starved of victories, launched an attack against the military conduct of the war by 'bonehead generals'. So when, on 6 March 1942, the *Mirror* carried Philip Zec's infamous cartoon depicting a half-drowned oil-smeared merchant seaman clinging to a raft in a barren ocean, it was bound to cause trouble. The caption of the cartoon, written by 'Cassandra' (William Connor) ran: 'The price of petrol has been increased by one penny (official)'.[40] The implication was that heroic sailors were risking their lives for the benefit of black marketeers and higher profits with the government's connivance. The cartoon, together with the editorial that accompanied it, created a sensation. Churchill and many of his Cabinet colleagues were furious and, on 19 March, Morrison (who felt the cartoon 'worthy of Goebbels at his best'[41]) warned the *Mirror* that he might have to invoke defence regulation 2D. While the War Office (MI5) investigated the paper's ownership and staff, most of Fleet Street rallied to the *Mirror*'s defence in a way that could only have been hurtful to the staff of the *Daily Worker*, whose actual suspension had aroused comparatively little professional indignation. Now Fleet Street rallied behind its age-old battle cry of freedom of speech. Parliament rallied behind the government. When the storm subsided, however, it was clear that the warning had proved sufficient to place the *Mirror* as well as other newspapers on their guard for the rest of the war. The *Mirror* continued to champion the cause of the People's War and to provide what it saw as the voice of the people, whose fighting was hampered by the ineptitude of a generation of aged, upper-class, 'blimpish' appeasers. But it never went quite as far in its criticisms as it had done in March 1942 – although clearly still far enough to play a significant role in the defeat of the Conservative Party in 1945. Opinion had not actually been censored or punished, only threatened with it. And so, in 1945, Churchill must have rued the day when the MoI triumphed in its desire not to impose post-censorship on the press as he watched himself replaced by that very generation of 'younger' politicians which the *Mirror* championed so unashamedly. In the meantime, the short term advantages for the MoI were enormous. The episode had demonstrated the freedom of the British press in wartime and the merits of the 'voluntary' censorship system. Compulsory censorship had only been seen to be threatened, not imposed. That was excellent propaganda.

7.4 The MoI and Wardour Street: Film Censorship

It was another celebrated newspaper cartoon character who, when transferred to the cinema screen, prompted the single most notorious case of attempted film censorship in the Second World War. This was David Low's 'Sugar Candy', created for the *Evening Standard* in 1934, whom the eminent British film-making team, Michael Powell and Emeric Pressburger, portrayed in *The Life and Death of Colonel Blimp* (1943). Blimp represented all those values that the *Daily Mirror* despised about the British ruling class. In view of the storm over Zec's critical cartoon in the *Mirror*, any film designed to portray Colonel Blimp as 'the symbol of British procrastination and British regard for tradition – all the things which we knew and which were losing the war'[42] was bound to cause trouble, particularly with Churchill at a most difficult phase of the war. Low's character had been buried – literally – in late February 1942 when the government had passed certain measures designed to ensure an equality of sacrifice, although he was to be resurrected in the *Evening Standard* in June 1943. In the meantime, Powell and Pressburger's attempt to keep Blimp alive resulted in them approaching the MoI.

That they should approach the MoI, and not the BBFC, as they would have done before the war, reflected significant changes that taken place since the early chaotic days of September 1939 in the wartime film censorship and film production arrangements. At first, in addition to Usborne's press and censorship division at the MoI (which contained a film censorship section), a Films Division had been set up under the initial leadership of Sir Joseph Ball. Neither Ball nor Usborne were particularly concerned at that stage with feature films, choosing to leave the BBFC to exercise its discretionary powers in all matters that did not concern security. Newsreels, however, were a different matter, as Ball realised. He immediately encountered the unduly secretive tendencies of Usborne's staff when he proposed that the newsreel companies be provided with general guidelines and left thereafter to their own devices and editorial control.[43] Because of their pre-war track record over rearmament, Ball trusted the newsreel companies. Besides, all newsreel footage would, after all, be scrutinised by the censors prior to public release. But when Usborne refused, and propaganda opportunities to exploit the departure of the BEF and the sinking of the passenger liner *Athenia* by a German U-boat had been lost (particularly in the United States), Ball contemplated setting up the MoI's own newsreel and even had the War Office cinematographers shoot footage for it.[44] For sheer professionalism and expertise in the area of visual news communication, however, the existing companies could not be rivalled; nor, indeed, could their distribution network at home and abroad, especially in North America where it operated courtesy of their parent American companies. Further difficulties occurred when Walter Monckton's short-lived Press and Censorship Bureau was established separately from the MoI where the film censorship division remained until Reith rectified the anomaly in January 1940. It was only when negative and positive aspect of persuasion were reunited in the MoI's reorganisation of April 1940 that a more settled arrangement for film censorship was established.

The MoI decided, formally and wisely, to operate through the existing newsreel companies, which were placed on a compulsory rota system and given priority in film stock supplied to them and in personnel. In order to save time, so vital to the process of effective news communication, a liaison officer was appointed 'to convey our Do's and Don'ts to the newsreel companies'.[45] MoI censors would visit the offices of the newsreel companies to view in advance all material that they had filmed with the co-operation of the various government departments, and to scrutinise the proposed commentaries, and every Monday and Thursday, a final scrutiny session of the finished issue would take place at Malet Street at which further cuts could be ordered. These arrangements proved so efficient that comparatively few such final cuts were called for.[46] MoI censors were, moreover, always present when officials from the service departments viewed film intended for public release to provide them with consistency, continuity and reminders of the value of news as the shocktroops of propaganda.

If the newsreels 'bore the brunt of the propaganda war in Britain',[47] feature films were also to play an increasingly significant part. The MoI recognised that 'the film, being a popular medium, must be good entertainment if it is

to be good propaganda'.[48] Its Films Division, first under Ball then briefly under
Kenneth Clark, and finally, from 1940 to the end of the war, Jack Beddington,
was responsible for ensuring this. It supervised the production of official films
made by the government's own film units such as the GPO Film Unit, the
Crown Film Unit (the MoI's own) and the Service film units, but it also
commissioned films by private film companies and distributed any others which
served a morale-building purpose.[49] Its control was exercised in the first resort
through the granting of film permits and the licensing of film stock material
and, in the last resort, through the BBFC which provided a certificate of
exhibition. Before allocating film stock, which was now classified as a strategic
war material, the Board of Trade required the submission of a scenario which
the MoI's Films Division would advise upon. But the MoI also recognised
that the most effective form of film propaganda would be that in which the
government's involvement was kept hidden.[50] The original wartime BBFC
certificate which carried the words 'and complies with the requirements of the
Ministry of Information' was therefore dropped in October 1939. In all matters
which did not relate to security, the BBFC was theoretically left to its own
devices to work much as it had done before the war, scrutinising scenarios
submitted to it in advance and suggesting cuts in the scripts and the final
product prior to commercial release. In practice, however, its role and significance declined as the war progressed, not just because the MoI assumed
comprehensive censorship powers but also because most wartime films could
be interpreted as being related to security in some respect. Besides, many
film-makers preferred to deal directly with the MoI through which the BBFC
operated. Indeed, between 1943 and 1946, the BBFC was only called upon to
ban one film made during that period.[51] The MoI was normally able to prevent
films from reaching the stage of certification. Here again, as in the case of
press censorship, the essential feature was not the number of films that were
suppressed, but the number which were not.

When Powell and Pressburger called on the Films Division in 1942 to show
Beddington the script of their proposed film about Colonel Blimp (with Laurence
Olivier cast in the title role), they encountered some of the procedures by which
the MoI ensured such effective feature film pre-censorship while at the same
time exposing their limitations. Beddington and Bracken were not pleased with
what they saw. Powell recalled that they thought the script 'defeatist':

> They said: 'We don't think you should make this film. You can't have
> Laurence Olivier'. 'You're going to stop us making it?' 'Oh no, we're not
> going to stop you. After all, this is a democracy, but we advise you not to
> make it and you can't have Olivier because he's in the Fleet Air Arm and
> we're not going to release him to play your Colonel Blimp'.[52]

The reaction of Beddington and Bracken in fact says far more about their
particular sensitivity to any charges of 'blimpery' levelled against the government
than about the film script, which was far less critical or offensive than one
might assume from the ensuing fuss.[53] Even so, apart from not releasing Olivier

(whose part was eventually played by Roger Livesy), the MoI also refused to co-operate in the provision of uniforms, vehicles and other authentic military equipment needed by the film-makers. It was, again, not so much what the MoI did, but what it did not do which, on this occasion, was its primary method of attempted control.

Most film-makers would have been sufficiently deterred at this stage, but Powell and Pressburger went ahead with their project regardless. The War Office, most sensitive to charges of blimpery at that time, was deeply offended and James Grigg, Secretary of State for War, complained about the film to Churchill on 8 September 1942.[54] The Prime Minister rushed off a minute to Bracken: 'Pray propose to me the measures necessary to stop this foolish production before it gets any further. I am not prepared to allow propaganda detrimental to the morale of the Army, and I am sure the Cabinet will take all the necessary action'.[55] Bracken replied:

> The Ministry of Information has no powers to suppress the film. We have been unsuccessful in discouraging it by the only means open to us: that is, by withholding Government facilities for its production.
>
> I am advised that in order to stop it the Government would need to assume powers of a very far-reaching kind. These could hardly be less than powers to suppress all films, even those based on imaginary stories, on grounds not of their revealing information to the enemy but of their expressing harmful or misguided opinion. Moreover, it would be illogical for the government to insist upon a degree of control over films which it does not exercise over other means of expression, such as books or news-paper articles.[56]

Churchill, however, had the bit between his teeth and he raised the matter in Cabinet on 21 September. Here it was decided that the MoI and the War Office would view the film once it had reached the 'rough cut stage', that is before its final editing and release. If it was still deemed offensive, approaches would be made to the film's financiers, Joseph Rank's General Film Distributors Ltd, to have it withdrawn.[57] By May 1943, the censors had indeed scrutinised the film and concluded that 'it is unlikely to attract much attention or to have any undesirable effect on the discipline of the Army'.[58]

The film did, however, attract considerable attention, both at home and abroad, when it was released. Nicholas Pronay and Jeremy Croft have suggested, somewhat mischievously, that the entire episode was a covert propaganda exercise designed for American consumption. Their argument, essentially, is that the MoI could have prevented the film from ever being made – not least by preventing Powell and Pressburger's company from acquiring the rare and expensive colour film stock that is used for the film. Instead, the MoI was disguising its encouragement for a film about the merits of the new wartime British army as compared to its pre-war 'stuffy, undemocratic "red coats" image' for the benefit of American soldiers arriving in Britain at that time and for American civilian audiences who needed reassuring about the need for a

'Europe first' policy after Pearl Harbour. Olivier was not released and government co-operation refused in a deliberate attempt to draw attention to the film and to the fact that a democratic society at war did not censor its means of expression. Powell and Pressburger, they argue, were favoured MoI filmmakers, both before and after the incident.[59] In the absence of decisive evidence either way, it would appear that the clash, whether engineered or not, reflected the MoI's desire not to see opinion subjected to post-censorship on the grounds that it was counter-productive in propagandist terms. As in the case of the *Daily Mirror*, the MoI found itself having to curb the intuitive response of Churchill to ban any opinions that offended his personal core values. If it could not eradicate offensive opinions through its pre-censorship system – and for the most part it was able to do this by a combination of control and co-operation with the media – then they must be allowed free rein not just to provide the illusion of a liberal censorship system but also in the name of good propaganda. In the case of the Blimp film, Churchill succeeded in preventing the film going abroad through a series of measures which Bracken rightly considered illegal until August 1943, by which time the story had leaked to the press and crowds were flocking to 'see the banned film'.[60]

There were several means by which the export of undesirable films could be prevented. They first required a BBFC certificate that was, of course, issued on the 'advice' of the MoI. Second, the Board of Trade could refuse to grant a film an export license on the celluloid. Finally, the government could resort, as it did do in the case of the Blimp film, 'to the unorthodox expedient of refusing the normal facilities for transport abroad by air'.[61] In the case of foreign, and particularly after 1941, American, films coming into Britain, the Board of Trade could grant or withhold import licences, although the number of Hollywood films that we know were denied entry into wartime Britain was comparatively few (the pre-war film *Tobacco Road* being a rare example). In the case of the notorious Warner Brothers' *Objective Burma* (1945), which deeply offended British audiences by its presentation of American troops winning the war in Asia, it was the distributor that withdrew the film after one week, not the MoI.[62] Even the opinions of Britain's wartime allies were allowed considerable latitude; *Mission to Moscow* (1942), another Warner Brothers film which retold and reinterpreted Soviet foreign policy up to 1941, was not banned, despite the wishes of Conservative Central Office, which disliked especially its 'Guilty Men' thesis.[63]

7.5 The MoI and Broadcasting House: Radio Censorship

It was, technically at least, far simpler to prevent the import of foreign opinions via the airwaves by means of jamming. However, as in the case of Lord Haw-Haw, it was the MoI's policy not to support jamming of enemy broadcasts on the grounds that this would merely draw attention to them.[64] The BBC supported this view; a statement of May 1940 pointed out that:

Jamming is really an admission of a bad cause. The jammer has a bad conscience ... He is afraid of the influence of the truth ... In our country we have no such fears and to jam broadcasts in English by the enemy might even be bad propaganda.[65]

It was this kind of sophisticated appreciation of propaganda in the round that made the BBC such an essential component of the MoI's activities.

The significance of radio depended not just upon its universality or its immediacy. For the Nazis, 'in modern warfare, the belligerent does battle not only with armed force, but also with methods which can influence and wear down the minds of the people. One of these methods is Radio.'[66] As in the case of the newsreels, radio's potency as a medium of news communication and of propaganda rested on the entertainment context in which it operated. The BBC's role in the Second World War extended still further, from monitoring to overt and covert broadcasting and even to the air defence of Great Britain. By 1940, the BBC was broadcasting in 14 languages, as compared to Germany's 22. On the Home Front, however, the BBC began rather badly. It had anyway very little good news to report and it filled the gap with recorded music.[67] A public opinion survey at the end of September 1939 ascribed the paucity of news 'to the excessive strictness of the censorship' which in turn prompted an increase in audience figures for the German radio stations, which often broke news stories about Britain quicker than the BBC![68] That the first round of the radio war went to the Germans was partly due to the lack of preparedness with which the BBC went to war. The only ingredient present was a philosophy: that 'no permanent propaganda policy can in the modern world be based upon untruthfulness'.[69]

In September 1939, the BBC was still unclear as to the precise role it would play or its relationship with the MoI. Pre-war planners had anticipated that broadcasting would fall near enough under total government control while the BBC ostensibly remained constitutionally independent (despite the disappearance of most of its Board of Governors). In March 1939, it was agreed that the BBC's controller of programmes would serve as the MoI's censor for broadcasting. However, successful attempts at censorship and content control were made by the government in the critical days leading up to the war[70] (Usborne's section had been mobilised on 26 August). But the news blackout which greeted its outbreak produced a bleakness and dullness in radio broadcasting that was, before long, proving counter-productive in terms of morale. In the BBC's case, this was not due solely to the influence of the Service censors; great caution was exercised by the Air Ministry's preoccupation with the possible use of radio transmissions by enemy bombers as navigational aids. In an imminent air raid, for example, RAF Fighter Command would order the BBC by direct telephone to close down any transmitter serving as a beacon, whereupon the BBC would synchronise the introduction of another transmitter outside the target area with only a slight reduction in volume and quality. George Thomson prevented the publication of any letters in the press complaining about this.[71] As a result the

BBC was permitted a single home programme on two wavelengths (the Home Service) on which to serve up a much reduced diet of news amidst an endless stream of pep-talks and prerecorded gramophones.

It was not long before the advantages of leaving the BBC as independent as possible under the circumstances became apparent. The MoI soon learned that it was more profitable to leave news communication to the experienced professionals and that the credibility and integrity of their coverage could only be enhanced by an outward appearance of independence. Inwardly, the censors ensured that all news reaching the BBC had already been monitored at source.

This pattern, not surprisingly, first began to emerge when John Reith became Minister of Information in January 1940. By that time, the BBC had already begun to settle down to a recognisable pattern. It had livened up its programmes and had just begun its Armed Forces programme on two additional wavelengths. In the following six months, as the western European governments collapsed before the Nazi blitzkrieg, the BBC increased its external broadcasting and provided exiles with free access to its microphones, the Dutch Radio Orange being the first of what was to become a legendary source of morale-boosting and intelligence-serving news services amongst the occupied nations of Europe. When the Battle of Britain and the Blitz commenced, the decision to subordinate the BBC to the air defence of Great Britain proved to be more than justified. It was also during this period that the BBC provided facilities for American broadcasters such as Ed Murrow, who did so much to bring the war into neutral American homes distant from the bombing, and, with it, significant sympathy for the British during their finest hour.

Broadcasting to the enemy and to occupied countries – psychological warfare – was in the hands of a special unit, Department EH (the forerunner of the Political Warfare Executive), which was separate from the MoI and which operated courtesy of BBC transmitters. The MoI concerned itself only with broadcasting at home and in neutral countries. For all practical purposes, therefore, the BBC managed to retain its independence more by accident than by design. The MoI had wanted to take it over but the confusion in which it initially found itself, the connections of the BBC with other organisations involved in propaganda, and the BBC's development of an independent role for itself ensured both its short-term value as 'a working armament of war' and its long-term independence. Sir Kenneth Clark admitted that even when the MoI issued directives, the BBC would often 'pay no attention to them'.[72]

Neither Reith nor his successor as Minister of Information, Duff Cooper, were able to exercise greater MoI control over the BBC. By the time Bracken was appointed, it had little desire to do so. In January 1941 two MoI 'advisers' had been appointed to the BBC, one to supervise home affairs (A. P. Ryan) and one to deal with foreign broadcasting (Sir Ivone Kirkpatrick). The Board of Governors was even reconstituted in April 1941. The simple fact of the matter was that the BBC was involved with too many other, more established government departments such as the Foreign Office, the War Office and the Air Ministry for the MoI to bring broadcasting completely or solely under its auspices. Propaganda may have been the sole purpose of the MoI, but it was not the sole function of the BBC. When Bracken arrived, the value of the BBC retaining a large measure of independence was widely accepted within the MoI, so much so that it often served as a shield for the Corporation when demands for greater government control periodically recurred.

Even so, the MoI did exercise a measure of control over the BBC's output through its censorship functions. As George Thomson recalled:

> Many people had the idea that BBC broadcasts went out uncensored. This is quite incorrect, though it might seem at first sight an extraordinarily difficult problem to cope with ... Fortunately for the censorship however ... they depended almost entirely for their news bulletins on the news given on the news agency tape machines. And this news had, of course, already been submitted to, and passed by, the censorship.[73]

Slower news was scrutinised in a more leisurely way, although the four MoI censors stationed permanently at Broadcasting House would sit in the studios, finger at the ready on the cut-out button in the event of an unwitting slip, having already advised speakers on the do's and don'ts of their contributions in talks programmes. The resident censors also had the duty of scrutinising the scripts of the American broadcasters who used the studios of Broadcasting House every night. At Bush House, the home of the BBC's external broadcasts, Thomson installed ten censors each of whom was fluent in the languages for which they were responsible. Other censors were delegated to the various BBC stations around the country with instructions to clear any doubts by telephone with Malet Street. Once again, such was the effectiveness of these arrangements that, although there were numerous petty squabbles between censors and broadcasters chiefly over matters of detail, the BBC was able to gain its reputation for telling the truth when, in reality, the whole truth could not be told.

7.6 Unnatural Allies

Censors and journalists, we are told, are natural enemies in a liberal democracy; the role of the one is to prevent the unfettered activities of the other. But censors are also propagandists and official propagandists need the media if they are to conduct their work effectively. Official propaganda known to be such is of limited value; disguise is essential to its credibility. During the Second World War, censors and journalists became natural allies. By 1941, the MoI had developed a censorship system which not only appeared more liberal than it in fact was but which also provided a sophisticated means of disseminating official news and views through the media without revealing that Fleet Street, Wardour Street and Broadcasting House had become agents for the distribution of official propaganda.

This system required extremely skilful handling. In the first place, the 'free press' had to be reassured that, even in wartime, it was still comparatively free to formulate its own arguments and opinions. Otherwise it would be no different from, say, the captive press in the Third Reich. This was achieved by the so-called 'voluntary' system that allowed news editors to submit any material about which they were unsure to the MoI for advice. This process appeared to be based upon trust; the media was, after all, as patriotic as the next profession in its desire to see the war brought to a successful conclusion. Even when censors advised against publication, editors were under no compulsion to accept the MoI's ruling (unless they were newsreel editors) and, indeed, the onus was placed on the government to prove that the result had benefited the enemy. This was the fundamental difference from the system used during the Great War, which had placed the responsibility squarely in the hands of the press. The later system was not only more logical but also more sophisticated. Opinions and judgements, if they are to be authoritative and convincing, are based upon evidence – or 'facts'. Most 'facts' (i.e. news) reaching the media in the Second World War through the agency machines were monitored and censored at source. Little was being left to trust here. The government may, at any given time, have been in possession of the facts on which it could formulate its policies, but though the MoI's per-censorship system it ensured that the news media were rarely in a similar position. When the media were in such a position, it was because the government had allowed them to be. Few people in Britain, other than the American correspondents, challenged the wisdom of compulsory censorship of all news and views passing out beyond the country's shores. Fewer still realised that the same thing was happening with regard to news and views circulating within the country.

Second, if secrecy was the essence of the domestic pre-censorship system, publicity was the essence of its effectiveness. The system had to be seen to be voluntary if it was to serve effective propaganda purposes, and this required considerable latitude in the publication of opinions, even when they proved unpalatable to individuals within the government. The publicity afforded to the *Daily Mirror* and *Colonel Blimp* episodes suited the censors' purposes well. It reinforced the illusion that censorship of opinion was not taking place, which was an excellent propaganda line to adopt with former neutrals like the United States, enemies like Nazi Germany and new-found allies like the Soviet Union. If Churchill had been allowed to have his way, it would have constituted post-censorship which would not only have undermined the moral posture of a liberal democracy at war (as had occurred in France before its fall) but would also have given the propaganda game away. It was for this reason that we have the seemingly paradoxical situation of the MoI resisting periodic demands for tighter censorship controls with as much publicity as it could muster, safe in the knowledge that its control was already considerable.

The MoI recognised that it would probably be a temporary body whose existence would not survive the war. Its priority was the wartime condition of morale. Churchill, however, was a politician whose survival depended upon public opinion. It is somewhat ironic, therefore, to suggest that the MoI under one of his closest companions, Bracken, did much to allow the fostering of opinions during the war which were to do so much to bring about Churchill's defeat in 1945.[74] But that is in effect what happened: it forms the background of Lord Boothby's quip that the MoI did not win the war but it won the 1945 election for the Labour Party.[75] Churchill's attempts to censor, combined with his reluctance to publicise war aims, were made on the grounds that widespread publicity to criticisms of his wartime government lowered confidence and weakened morale. Despite his claims to have only provided the roar for the lion-hearted British people, his behaviour over the *Mirror* and *Blimp* affairs reflected the very same patronising attitudes of the British ruling elite that the public was beginning to reject, particularly the assumption that it could only stomach optimism and not bad news. Liberal democratic theory may have consisted of treating the public as adults who, if 'told the facts simply and frankly, will accept and co-operate in the consequences which follow',[76] but Churchill was not prepared to trust his political future to an electorate which had only been enfranchised for a generation. And the election of 1945 demonstrated that the British electorate was not prepared to entrust him with the task of building their New Jerusalem.

Notes and References

1 This chapter was originally published as 'Censorship in Britain in the Second World War: an overview' in A. C. Duke and C. A. Tamse (eds), *Too Mightly to Be Free: Censorship and the Press in Britain and the Netherlands* (De Walburg Press, 1987), pp. 157–178.
2 G. N. Gordon, *Persuasion: The Theory and Practice of Manipulative Communication* (Hastings House, 1971) p. 502.
3 M. L. Sanders and P. M. Taylor, *British Propaganda during the First World War* (Macmillan, 1982).
4 See P. Towle, 'The debate on wartime censorship in Britain, 1902–14' in B. Bond and I. Roy (eds) *War and Society* (Croom Halm, 1975); D. Hopkin, 'Domestic censorship in the First World War', *Journal of Contemporary History*, 5:4 (1970), pp. 151–69; C. Lovelace, 'British press censorship during the First World War' in G. Boyce, J. Curren and P. Wingate (eds), *Newspaper History: from the Seventeenth Century to the Present Day* (Constable, 1978).
5 Interview given by Sir Edward Cook to the Associated Press, April 1916, FO 371/2844.
6 E. T. Cook, *The Press in Wartime* (Macmillan, 1920), p. 44.
7 CAB 24/77, GT 7062 and CAB 23/11, 594(5), 16 July 1919.
8 J. C. Robertson, *The British Board of Film Censors* (Croom Helm, 1985), p. 19.
9 N. Pronay, 'The First Reality; film censorship in Liberal England' in K. R. M. Short (ed.), *Feature Films and History* (Croom Helm, 1981); J. Richards, 'The British Board of Film Censors and content control in the 1930s: I: Images of Britain; II: Foreign Affairs', *Historical Journal of Film, Radio and Television*, 1:2 (1981), and II, 2:1 (1982).
10 T. Hollins, 'The Presentation of Politics': the place of party publicity, broadcasting and film in British politics, 1918–39' (Ph.D. thesis, University of Leeds, 1981).

11 For the pre-war planning see: P. M. Taylor, '"If War should Come": preparing the fifth arm for Total War, 1935–39', *Journal of Contemporary History*, 16:1 (1981), 27–51; Temple Willcox, 'Projection or publicity? Rival concepts in the pre-war planning of the British Ministry of Information', *Journal of Contemporary History* 18:3 (1983), and 'Towards a Ministry of Information', *History*, 64 (1984); C. Robert Cole, 'The conflict within: Sir Stephen Tallents and planning propaganda overseas before the Second World War', *Albion*, 12 (1982).

12 CAB 16/127, MIC, 1st meeting, 25 October 1935.

13 CID subcommittee on the general policy of broadcasting in time of war, third meeting, 25 September 1935, CAB 16/120.

14 C. Andrew and D. Dilks (eds), *The Missing Dimension* (Macmillan, 1984), ch. 5.

15 The Admiralty's concern was most forcefully expressed at the second meeting of the MoI planning committee on 28 February 1936, CAB 16/127.

16 Memorandum on the press censorship, undated, unsigned, INF 1/75.

17 Memorandum by Sir John Reith on the position of the BBC in war, CAB 16/127, MIC 3.

18 Parliamentary Debates (Commons), 5th series, vol. 349, 18 July 1939.

19 A. Briggs, *The Golden Age of Wireless* (Oxford University Press, 1965), pp. 650–1.

20 CAB 16/128 and INF 1/178.

21 Robertson, *British Board*, p. 113.

22 Sanders and Taylor, *British Propaganda*, pp. 124–5.

23 The story is told in full in I. McLaine, *Ministry of Morale* (Allen & Unwin, 1979), p. 38. See also F. Williams, *Press, Parliament and People* (Heinemann, 1946), pp. 3–6.

24 F. R. Gannon, *The British Press and Germany* (Clarendon Press, 1971); A. P. Adamthwaite, 'The British government and the media, 1937–38', *Journal of Contemporary History*, 18:2 (1983), 281–97.

25 Note of a discussion between the MoI and Admiralty, 6 September 1939, INF 1/852.

26 G. P. Thomson, *Blue Pencil Admiral* (Sampson Low, 1949), pp. 3–6.

27 Sir John Reith, *Into the Wind* (Hodder & Stoughton, 1949), p. 354.

28 I. Kirkpatrick, *The Inner Circle* (St Martin's Press, 1959), p. 187.

29 Thomson recalled: 'In practice ... this branch of censorship conducted its work throughout the war quite independently, as a branch of the security services ... Its main purpose was to extract as much information from the enemy communications which might be helpful to the Allied cause. But it was also responsible for the censorship of private and commercial messages leaving Allied countries for destinations overseas'. *Blue Pencil Admiral*, p. 175.

30 N. Pronay, 'The news media at war' in N. Pronay and D. W. Spring (eds) *Propaganda, Politics and Film 1918–45* (Macmillan, 1982).

31 War Cabinet Minutes, WP (41) 142.

32 War Cabinet minutes, WP (41) 142.

33 Thomson, *Blue Pencil Admiral*, p. 31.

34 INF 1/73, 29 January 1941.

35 INF 1/73, 18 July 1941.

36 Defence of the Realm Act, 1911.

37 P. M. H. Bell, *John Bull and the Bear: British Public Opinion, Foreign Policy and the Soviet Union 1941–45* (Arnold, 1990).

38 S. Koss, *The Rise and Fall of the Political Press in Britain* (2 vols, Hamish Hamilton, 1981–4), II, p. 605.

39 Cited in M. Edelman, *The Mirror: A Political History* (Hamilton, 1966), pp. 104–5.
40 *Daily Mirror*, 6 March 1942.
41 Edelman, *The Mirror*, p. 118.
42 K. Gough-Yates, *Michael Powell: in Collaboration with Emeric Pressburger* (British Film Institute, 1970), p. 8.
43 Robertson, *British Board*, pp. 115–6.
44 Pronay, 'News Media at war', pp. 184–5.
45 Director's Order S 13 July 1941, INF 1/178.
46 See the figures cited by Pronay, 'News Media at War', p. 198.
47 Ibid, p. 202.
48 Programme for film propaganda (probably early 1940), INF 1/867.
49 F. Thorpe and N. Pronay, *British Official Films in the Second World War* (Clio, 1980).
50 Programme for film propaganda, INF 1/867.
51 Robertson, *British Board*, appendix 3.
52 Cited in I. Christie (ed.), *Powell, Pressburger and Others* (British Film Institute, 1978), pp. 105–6.
53 Jeffrey Richards and Anthony Aldgate, *Best of British: Cinema and Society 1930–1970* (Blackwell, 1983), ch. 5.
54 Grigg to Churchill, 8 September 1942, PREM 4 14/15.
55 Minute to Churchill, 10 September 1942, PREM 4 14/15.
56 Bracken to Churchill, 10 September 1942, PREM 4 14/15.
57 War Cabinet minutes, WP 126 (42), 21 September 1942.
58 War Cabinet minutes, WP 67 (43), 10 May 1943.
59 N. Pronay and J. Croft, 'British film censorship and propaganda policy during the Second World War' in J. Curran and V. Porter (eds), *British Cinema History* (Weidenfeld and Nicolson, 1983).
60 Christie, *Powell*, pp. 108–10.
61 Bracken to Churchill, 23 July 1943, PREM 4 14/15.
62 I. Jarvie, 'Fanning the flames: anti-American reaction to *Objective Burma* (1945)', *Historical Journal of Film, Radio and Television*, 1:1 (1981).
63 D. Culbert, *Mission to Moscow* (University of Wisconsin Press, 1980).
64 Policy committee minutes, 5 September 1940, INF 1/849.
65 Cited in Asa Briggs, *The War of Words* (Oxford University Press, 1970), p. 67.
66 Martin Docherty, 'German wireless propaganda in English: an analysis of the organisation, content and effectiveness of Nazi radio broadcasts for the UK, 1939–45' (Ph.D. thesis, University of Kent, 1998), p. 26.
67 Sian Nichols, *The Echo of War* (Manchester Univeristy Press, 1996).
68 Ibid, p. 133–4.
69 BBC Handbook, 1941, p. 30.
70 Briggs, *War of Words*, pp. 78–9.
71 Thomson, *Blue Pencil Admiral*, p. 164.
72 Lord Normanbrook to Director-General, 11 July 1941, INF 1/869.
73 Thomson, *Blue Pencil Admiral*, p. 165.
74 N. Pronay, '"The Land of Promise": the projection of peace aims in Britain' in K. R. M. Short (ed.), *Film and Radio Propaganda in World War Two* (Croom Helm, 1983).
75 Lord Boothby, *My Yesterday, Your Tomorrow* (Hutchinson, 1962), p. 147.
76 M. Balfour, *States and Mind* (Cresset Press, 1953), p. 74.

8

Film as a Weapon during
the Second World War[1]

The Second World War vastly increased the role and significance of film as a weapon in Britain's arsenal of 'Total War'. Like the tank and the aeroplane before it, however, this weapon needed time to become appreciated before it could be deployed to its greatest effect. Film had, of course, been used to some extent as an instrument of official propaganda and morale-boosting during the First World War.[2] Then, during the inter-war years, immense strides had been made in the area of official government publicity and documentary films by organisations such as the Empire Marketing Board and GPO Film Unit.[3] Yet in 1939, after five years of inter-departmental squabbles over propaganda in the next war, the overall place of film remained unresolved. Film was considerably distrusted by those who had traditionally taken up arms for their country, with the result that Whitehall's Service Ministries at first did all they could to hinder its effective deployment. This, the Service Ministries claimed, resulted in part from the need to avoid providing the enemy with valuable information – the time-honoured justification for military censorship – but it was just as much the result of ignorance concerning the positive impact which good propaganda films could have on morale both at home and in allied and neutral countries. The supporters of film in the Ministry of Information considered it a key instrument of wartime propaganda, which they maintained was the 'Fourth Arm' of defence.[4] It was, however, such a different kind of weapon, attacking the heart and mind rather than the physical body, that its full potential as an auxiliary to the fighting capability of a nation at war was not immediately appreciated. Only when the options of using other weapons, such as the Army, had been severely restricted following Dunkirk, and when the Strategic Air Offensive against Germany was fully underway, did the military mind really begin to see that potential. In short, until 1941–42 and the so-called 'end of the beginning', the service ministries tended to regard propaganda as 'a cheap-jack charlatan game',[5] unworthy of their serious consideration.

The antipathy of military men towards the media, from the Crimean War to the Persian Gulf War, is almost carved in stone. Ever since William Howard Russell's despatches from the Crimea to *The Times*, inaugurating not only the profession of war correspondent but also the practice of modern military censorship, the fear that the media might expose military inadequacies has lain beneath the paper-thin justification of the need to prevent valuable information from reaching the enemy and thereby to save the lives of servicemen. On the other hand, the Second World War was remarkably fluid in terms of information flow amongst the combatants. Hitler often watched Hollywood films captured from Allied sources. The British had cracked the 'Ultra secret'. Once a more sophisticated attitude towards propaganda evolved, the media gradually came to be recruited, often unwittingly, into the process of spreading disinformation.

Too often the military were over-defensive about opening up their activities to the prying gaze of the media, which were felt to be ill-equipped to judge those activities in their proper context. This in turn can be interpreted as reflecting a fear of the public, whose morale was deemed to be too fickle to accommodate setbacks – although, paradoxically, this in itself reflected a growing appreciation of the increasingly important role of public accountability in the age of democracy. It is also perhaps not too fanciful to suggest that, during the early years of the Second World War, the service departments had themselves become victims of official British propaganda concerning the 'spy menace' and the presence of a Nazi 'fifth column' within Britain. The fear that Nazi agents might be sitting in British cinemas scrutinising newsreels for clues to troop locations and equipment appealed to the military imagination.

8.1 Film Propaganda

The impact of a single film, like that of an artillery shell or a single bomb, was not in itself likely to prove decisive. Nobody in the MoI argued that. It was, rather, the totality of the campaign which mattered. If we stretch the analogy further, and liken the different kinds of film – feature films, documentaries, official short films and newsreels – to the various branches of the armed forces, the issue becomes clearer. A coherent strategy would be required if the cumulative impact of the messages conveyed by different types of film were to have a more significant effect over a longer period of time, especially in a long war of attrition. This would be particularly the case if the messages were reinforced by impressions made elsewhere in radio, posters, pamphlets and newspapers. It was this overall climate pervading all aspects of public life which, argued the professional propagandists, could determine the likely reception and impact of individual 'munitions of the mind'.[6] That the achievement of such a 'propaganda state' was being sought in a democracy, even a democracy at war, raises many difficult issues. But, by 1942, Britain was closer to this condition than at any time in her recent history. Yet, in order to achieve this climate of what may be termed 'Total Propaganda', considerable attention needed to be paid to each individual component, so that the sum of the parts added up to a coherent whole. In the case of the service ministries, this required a radical rethink of the way in which they conducted their activities, now that matters of operational security needed to be balanced alongside questions relating to publicity, information and civilian morale.

As the MoI got into its stride, courtesy of the respite provided by the 'Phoney War', three fundamental axioms of British wartime propaganda had emerged. These were that 'news is the shocktroops of propaganda', that it should tell 'the truth, nothing but the truth and, as near as possible,[7] the whole truth' and that for the 'film to be good propaganda it must also be good entertainment'.[8] These were to be the main principles on which the MoI evolved its own 'grand strategy' for the conduct of censorship and propaganda in a conflict which came to embrace civilian life to an unprecedented degree – a conflict in which it was felt that morale, however nebulously defined, might prove critical.

The problem lay not just with precise definitions of 'morale'. There were also debates about what actually constituted 'news' (good or bad, hot or cold, secret or public) and there was also the issue of war's often-stated first casualty, the truth. Fiercely resisting the temptation to be drawn here into postmodernist theories, I shall simply say that the essential problem in 1939–40 was that the news was bad and that was the truth. This was the propagandists' nightmare. The argument was not only that something had to be done, but that something indeed could be done to rectify the position, if only the service departments would give them – the propagandists – the tools they needed to finish the job.

Priority in official film propaganda at the start of the war had been given to the newsreel companies, which at least had a very good track record of packaging bad news in an entertaining and even cheerful way during the Depression years. Yet this annoyed the documentary makers, who felt that their achievements in film-making during the 1930s had more of a purpose, especially in portraying the very working man and woman who would now be called upon to fight this war. While the 'documentary boys' fumed that they were not being similarly enlisted, their problem had been that working men and women had not, in any significant numbers, wanted to see their films; the public had wanted escapist entertainment. This was still the case at the outbreak of war when all cinemas were, very short-sightedly, closed down for a time on grounds of safety (nitrate film was highly inflammable). Yet even when they were reopened, that champion of the British entertainment film of the 1930s, Alexander Korda, found that he had to make his first contribution to the war effort, *The Lion Has Wings* (1939),[9] without official support (although the project did have MoI approval). It was, in any case, American feature films which the British public most wanted to see, and Hollywood's record in projecting a positive, though not always realistic, image of Britain through 'historical' films such as *The Adventures of Robin Hood* (1938)[10] and *The Sea Hawk* (1940)[11] was second-to-none from a propagandist point of view. Even so, there was no way that the MoI could allow the film industry of a neutral, albeit Anglophile, country to do its film propaganda work for it – although, as we shall see, they did have plans for infiltrating the American film industry.

Despite the pioneering work of several historians,[12] much research remains to be done concerning the cumulative impact of feature films over a long period of time. Much more has been done, perhaps understandably, in the brave new world of using 'factual' film material as evidence.[13] Put at its simplest, the wartime role of official documentary films and newsreels, over which the government exercised a more immediate and direct control, was based upon an information-oriented approach to promoting certain messages at the expense of others. Any analysis of these messages can tell us much about contemporary official concerns, not just comparatively trivial ones such as 'digging for victory' or 'tittle-tattle losing the battle' but also more fundamental aspects of government policy which had long-term consequences for British society as a whole: the changing role of women; the relationship between Britain and its Commonwealth; the 'accuracy of strategic bombing'; the gallantry of 'Our Soviet Friends'; wartime visions of post-war society; and possibly even the political destiny in 1945 of Winston Churchill himself.

Historians of these large issues who have looked at film sources have learned much – not least what a rich and still relatively untapped vein of archival material such evidence provides. Yet it may be noted that a similar learning process was attempted by the MoI during the Second World War with a compilation film entitled *Film as a Weapon* (1941). This was never shown to a public audience but was designed to demonstrate to individuals in the service ministries, unconvinced of the power of the medium, what could be achieved if they extended their co-operation to the film-makers.

Before they examine any film as a text, historians need to be aware of its context. One of the first points to note is that the vast majority of feature films seen during the war dealt not with war themes – at least not directly – but with 'escapist' material. That said, what films do not convey is often just as significant as what they do project – an approach much loved by film scholars with their predisposition towards diegesis. However, feature films were but one course on the menu available to the cinemagoing public. That public was habitually fed on a diet that also included newsreels and documentaries which were not only a principal source of information and impressions for a good many people waging Total War, but which have also provided the meat of much historical research since that time. These more 'factual' films represented what might be described as the harder edge of British wartime propaganda, and they can tell us much about the overall climate of the 'People's War', not just for the three hours or so it took them to be viewed in one evening, but for the six years it took to win the war. But they were, to borrow some of Nicholas Pronay's many memorable phrases, 'illusions of reality' and very flawed 'windows on the world'. And one of course also needs also to remember the ever-present hand of the blue-pencil (or blue-scissored) censors.

Rarely visible, that hand was nonetheless crucial for, as Churchill once put it in a slightly different context, in successful propaganda there is no need to 'insert dots where the omissions have been made'.[14] No film exhibited publicly in Britain during the war escaped the eye of the censor; the corollary of this is that every film which the public saw had government approval. The scripts of feature films, for example, had to be submitted in advance of production to the British Board of Film Censorship, whereas newsreels were subjected to both pre- and post-censorship. Film propaganda was clearly too serious a business to be left solely to the film-makers.

Talking pictures had, of course, been in existence for a decade – but only that – before the outbreak of war. Politicians ignored the impact of film at their peril – both in the better-known case of the dictatorships and also in the newly evolving democratic systems such as Britain.[15] For, during the 1930s, as A. J. P. Taylor has reminded us, going to the pictures had become an 'essential social habit'[16] in Britain; it was 'far and away the most popular entertainment', especially for the very people who had recently been enfranchised and who were now most likely to be bombed – urban working-class people and their children between the ages of 15 and 35. By 1945, 30 million people – more than half the population – were attending a cinema in Britain every week, a figure which had risen from 19 million in 1939. After November 1939, there were, at any given time, no fewer than 4000 cinemas in operation, showing an average of 480 (mainly American) feature films per year,[17] as well as a wartime total of nearly 2,000 official films produced by the MoI and over 3,000 newsreel issues. It may well be that the Second World War was a 'war of words', but for a great many people it was also a war of images, or more precisely an audio-visual war.

Many factors appeared to be working against wartime film propaganda in Britain. Celluloid nitrate was classified as an essential war material; almost half the existing film studio space was requisitioned for war purposes, resulting in a drop in the number of operational film studios from 22 to 9; many essential personnel were called up; taxes affecting the industry were increased, with a consequential rise in seat prices; and urban cinemas were potential death-traps in bombing raids. Nevertheless, it is clear that the cinema was immensely popular, as was only too apparent to Britain's wartime morale managers. Given that almost every man, woman and child was likely to become involved in this conflict, and that, if victory came, nearly all adults would be able to demonstrate their reaction to the war's conduct at the electoral booth, the images and sounds in the cinema and the voices on the wireless in the home were likely to prove almost as vital as those which were not seen or heard as a result of the intervention of the censor.

8.2 'Gone with the Wind Up'?

At the top of the political command structure after 1940 was Winston Churchill – arguably British political history's greatest film fan – a man whose knowledge and enthusiasm for film was such that he instinctively recognised that his own greatest contribution would be not through the celluloid screen cinema but on the radio.[18] Beneath him in the ministerial hierarchy was Brendan Bracken, one of his closest confidants, and, after July 1941, the head of the most elaborate organisation for the conduct of propaganda, censorship and political warfare that Britain had yet experienced. Unfortunately, Bracken's inheritance was such that, on his appointment, Lord Beaverbrook, who had been Britain's first Minister of Information back in 1918, felt that it would be a 'sarcastic or even an unfriendly act' to offer him his congratulations.[19] The main reason for this quip was the early wartime history of acrimonious relations between the MoI and the Service Departments.

The production of *Film as a Weapon* was in part a response to the inadequacy of British propaganda, and of film propaganda in particular, in the early stages of the war. With the MoI in chaos and still lacking that most vital element of successful propaganda characteristics, consistency, as a result of four ministerial changes in its first two years of existence,[20] the lack of appropriate film material for cogent propaganda in neutral countries, and especially the USA, was a problem which demanded urgent attention.[21] The overwhelming tide of American isolationism, combined with a mistrust of foreign and especially British propaganda, created real problems, as is illustrated by a poster found in Chicago:

> ABSOLUTE NEUTRALITY – NOW AND FOREVER.
> BEWARE THE BRITISH SERPENT.
>
> Once more a boa constrictor – 'Perfidious Albion' – is crawling across the American landscape, spewing forth its unctuous lies. Its purpose is to lure this nation into the lair of war to make the world safe for international plunder. More than ever we Americans must evaluate this intruder into our Garden of Eden, appraising Britain down to the last penny weight of truth.[22]

True, the British had a colony of artists in Hollywood who, on Lord Lothian's instructions, had been told to stay where they were and work for the British war effort as a sort of fifth column, attacking the hearts and minds of the American cinemagoing public via feature films.[23] Their importance was fully appreciated by Lothian, who, in September 1939, wrote from Washington:

> It strikes me as being a great pity that the production side of the film industry should have been closed down in England ... for that means that within a short time all the films which will be shown will tend to be of American origin. It is therefore of the utmost importance that British actors, and still more British producers, who are operating in this country should be left to do so, partly because they ensure that the British point of view permeates the [film] industry, and partly because they keep alive the production of British or largely British films.[24]

As a result, directors such as Alfred Hitchcock and actors such as David Niven and Laurence Olivier, who were part of this highly secret brief, earned only public scorn in Britain for their alleged cowardice, greed and even treachery for not returning home to fight for King and Empire in their hour of greatest need, because they had supposedly 'Gone With the Wind Up'.[25] This in turn may have contributed, as the MoI believed, to the initial paucity of good feature film propaganda in Britain, as evidenced by the dreadful *The Lion Has Wings* (1939).[26] In fact, however, the main problem was the inadequacy of suitable newsfilm, capable of combating the impressions disseminated by the more effectively organised German propaganda machine and, especially, the German Weekly Newsreels, the *Deutsche Wochenschau*.[27]

This might seem odd in view of the fact that, under the influence of the MoI Film Division's first head, Joseph Ball, it was initially decided that the forward thrust of British wartime film propaganda, both at home and abroad, should be through the newsreels. After all, from the early 1930s onwards, the newsreels had done a magnificent job, *inter alia*, in selling the idea of rearmament to a largely anti-war audience, while simultaneously supporting appeasement. It was the five British newsreel companies that had evolved highly professional techniques of persuasion through their editing, their use of music and their commentary, in order to provide a 'clearer' window on the complicated and chaotic world of the 1930s. Why, therefore, was it that representatives of the British Information Services in the USA and other officials abroad complained that the British were losing the film propaganda war in neutral countries?

A significant explanation is to be found in the question of access. Unlike their German counterparts working in PK (*Propaganda Kompanie*) Units, British newsreel cameramen were initially denied the kind of access to military operations which made for exciting news footage. The same, incidentally, was also true of good war photographs. Frank Darvall, deputy director of the MoI's American division, pointed out that it was essential to maintain 'a constant supply of action photographs of real news value, of good technical quality and the kind calculated to give people the impression of the determination of the Allies and the efficiency of their Armed Forces'.[28] So preoccupied initially were the service departments with secrecy rather than publicity, and so steeped were they in a tradition of security which inspired a public relations philosophy of 'no news is good news', that no British newsreel cameramen were allowed to accompany the British Expeditionary Force to France. Even in 1914 film crews had been permitted to do that. The footage which was taken by the army film cameraman, Harry Rignold, who had been rapidly appointed at the outbreak of war, was found to be largely unusable by the newsreel companies. The companies had been placed on a rota, or pool, system, which meant that they were totally dependent on official sources for film from the fighting fronts.[29] It may well be that their dismissal of the footage shot by Rignold was part of a campaign to gain access to the front for themselves, which they were only permitted to do, after considerable MoI pressure, in October 1939. It is equally true that, given the attitude of the service ministries, the pool itself was invariably dry. That attitude helps to explain the astonishing paucity of footage recording Britain's 'miracle' at Dunkirk. The only newsreel cameraman present on that occasion, Charles Martin of Pathé, did shoot a little material but he was, perhaps not unnaturally, more preoccupied with helping the evacuation rather than filming it.[30]

8.3 Military Resistance

Apart from captured enemy footage, which they had used for training and for intelligence purposes, the service departments had, in the early stages of the war, displayed only limited enthusiasm for film. Their interest, in other words, as Frank Capra later put it describing a similar experience in the American context, was with 'the "hows" of war, not the "whys"'.[31] Their view of film as a double-edged weapon in the context of military intelligence was probably the main reason behind their refusal to allow greater access to British cameramen; the notion of using film for positive publicity reasons was almost completely alien to them. When one bears in mind that most official censors at the start of the war were retired naval officers, and that British involvement during the first months of the war was confined mainly to naval operations, it should come as no surprise to learn that the Admiralty was the most reluctant of the service departments to furnish the MoI with news which might have a positive bearing upon morale. What is more surprising is that the First Lord at that time was none other than the former war correspondent Winston Churchill, a film fan. As a Minister, Churchill was no doubt deeply conscious of his experience with the media over the Dardanelles Campaign in the Great War. He began World War Two as a member of the 'no news is good news' school of thought. When, for example, Churchill refused to admit that damage had been done to HMS Nelson and HMS Barham in February 1940, Lord Lothian wrote: 'I think Winston has made a fool of himself. He is always doing these things. That is why he never becomes Prime Minister'.[32]

But Churchill was by no means alone in this attitude. At the Air Ministry, the myth of the accuracy of strategic bombing was jealously sustained in the face of curious and sceptical eyes. In September 1940 Arthur Harris was of the view that 'much mischief has already been done by giving away valuable information to the enemy at the expense of our war effort and to the lives of our crews in order [to] make snappy paragraphs for the gutter press'.[33] Small wonder that, in such a climate of snippets and secrecy, exaggeration of British successes became the norm, with a corresponding increase in public scepticism recorded by Mass Observation in the first half of 1940.[34] The Navy's continuing reluctance to allow access, even during the battle of the Atlantic, was epitomised by the fact that it was left to a feature film, *In Which We Serve* (1941), starring Noël Coward, to carry the weight of public perception. This, moreover, was not until 1941. For the first fifteen months of the war, the MoI waged a running battle with the armed forces in an effort to extract stories which would cater for civilians who, having become combatants on the Home Front, had a vested interest in what was happening on other Fronts. It was this diminution of the traditional gap between soldier and civilian which called for greater mutual co-operation and understanding. Film could serve precisely this purpose in a way that no earlier medium could, and the MoI rightly felt that the Service Departments needed to be convinced of this fact.

A further – and in many ways the most critical – explanation, and one which will be considered in due course, was that British cameramen, even had they been allowed greater access, had hardly the kind of material to film which was likely to bolster morale at home and instil confidence abroad, at a time when the German war machine was blitzkrieging its way towards the English Channel.

But news footage is not necessarily the same thing as factual footage; news is a managed and packaged product that is subjected to a whole host of distortions involved in selection and sequential storytelling. The facts, in other words, may have been grim, but this did not automatically mean that the news needed to be. Nonetheless, as Churchill did recognise once he became Prime Minister, in wartime actions always speak louder than words, which is why he was hoping that British resistance on the beaches of southern England would stir American hearts. 'If we smash the Huns here', he wrote, 'we'll need no propaganda in the United States'.[35]

Churchill soon changed his mind. For example, before too long we can find him claiming that the redoubtable character of Mrs Miniver, immortalised in the book and the 1942 film, did more for the allied cause than a flotilla of battleships.[36] The fall of France in June 1940 had been such a shock that, in the absence of opportunities to fight the enemy by more conventional means, alternative weapons such as propaganda began to be given greater weight. This new receptivity to propaganda was evidenced by the appointment to the MoI of people like Jack Beddington from Shell as head of the Films Division and Sidney Bernstein from Granada to organise distribution. The GPO Film Unit was transferred to the MoI in the summer of 1940 and renamed the Crown Film Unit. Here the documentary movement was at last allowed its opportunity to make films about the 'whys'. Other significant developments were the appointments of Isaiah Berlin and William Stephenson to the American Propaganda organisation, the despatch to the USA of Alexander Korda, the replacement of Reith by Duff Cooper as Minister of Information, the BBC broadcast transmissions of J. B Priestley, and the commissioning of Powell and Pressburger's *Forty-Ninth Parallel* (1941) – made very much with United States opinion in mind, where it was released as *The Invaders*.[37]

At the Air Ministry, matters were greatly helped by the appointment of Air Commodore Peck as head of public relations. Under him a remarkable transformation took place, to the point where the RAF earned the nickname of the 'Royal Advertising Force'.[38] His collaboration with the film-makers at the MoI's Crown Film Unit culminated in the production of *Target for Tonight* (1941).[39] As Peck recognised:

In warfare today we cannot ... consider the release of information solely from the standpoint of absolute security. We must also take into account the maintenance of morale at home and among our allies, the maintenance of our prestige among neutral powers and the effective presentation of our case and our war effort to the world.[40]

During the Battle of Britain in the summer of 1940, the Air Ministry had seen the wisdom of granting greater access to the American press corps in London, which was centred upon Edward R. Murrow. Elsewhere, facilities for journalists, broadcasters and photographers (such as Cecil Beaton) were extended, and enormous strides were made in the improvement of documentary films such as *London Can Take It* (1940)[41] and *Christmas Under Fire* (1941).[42] Such developments all helped to demonstrate that positive projections could emerge from negative situations. As William Ridsdale of the Foreign Office News Department put it:

> To see British planes getting back, but only just getting back because they have been battered and riddled by the enemy, would provide the material for an impressive picture of the drain on our resources. These American correspondents would know the delicacy of such a position ... they could provide evidence of our spirit and our needs.[43]

Yet the shortcomings of the news-based approach to British propaganda continued to be revealed in the limited access to the fighting fronts provided by the service departments. The newsreels, as the second most topical form of information delivery after radio, still required attention. Combat footage was the final component in the transformation that was at last under way.

8.4 Film Projection

If there was a single point from which this change can be traced, it was June 1940. After the fall of France, German footage of the carefully stage-managed Armistice ceremony at Compiègne was widely seen around the world, and it became clear to all but the most blinkered that something needed to be done about improving access for British journalists and film camera crews. The situation was summed up by one official in the following terms:

> One regrets to say that the German system of placing camera-men (and killing them off) in the front line of every advance on land, sea and air has produced results out of all proportion superior in dramatic quality and propaganda value to anything achieved by British camera-men. The German newsreels concentrate solely on two things – first, the overwhelming superiority of German armaments and weapons of war, and secondly, by way of contrast, on the future of their people, healthier children and the beautiful land they are to inherit. British newsreels emphasise the reverse.[44]

This was one of the reasons why the compilation film entitled *Film as a Weapon* was put together by the MoI. Using captured German footage acquired by fair means and foul,[45] a special screening was arranged at the War Office on 19 March 1941. To place further pressure on Whitehall, this was accompanied by a Beddington-Bernstein inspired press campaign in the *Evening Standard* and *Daily Express*.

Obviously, it is impossible in print to recapture the force of the film. Kay Gladstone, of the Imperial War Museum where the film is now located, has in any case published a synopsis, with stills as illustrations, which can be consulted.[46] But a résumé of the inter-titles will serve to indicate the thrust of the film's argument:

Caption: The Nazis have four fighting services – Land, Air, Sea and PROPAGANDA. Propaganda has paved the way for many German victories. Much of this propaganda was conducted by FILM. The following excerpts from German newsreels show what was made possible by their wide and purposely organised facilities. Note: For purposes of economy most of this film is shown silent.

Caption: Part One. PEACETIME. The building of a Legend. CEREMONIAL. Note: Extensive coverage and careful placing of many cameras.

Caption: Fighting Services. Remarkable cooperative facilities given by Air and Navy.

Caption: Part Two. WARTIME. The selling of German Might. 1 – The camera with the NAVY. Showing that cameras are carried on many fighting ships.

Caption: 2 – The camera with the LUFTWAFFE. Note: The most striking example of this was of course *The Baptism of Fire*.

Caption: The end of a dogfight. Note: Only the posting of many cameras could have secured this lucky shot.

Caption: 3 – The Camera and WAR INDUSTRIES. U–Boat Factory. Note: These scenes betray no secrets but they give confidence to the German public.

Caption: 4 – The Camera in the FRONTLINE. Invasion of Holland, Belgium and France.

Caption: 5 – The visual recording of HISTORY. The March into Paris.

Caption: The signing of the Armistice at Compiègne. Note: This is no mere routine newsreel coverage – all was previously planned with official assistance.

End Caption: By Press, Radio and Film the legend of dictatorship was established. Press, Radio AND FILM can help our armed forces to kill that legend and reassert the message of democracy.

If there is such a thing as a single film that made a determinable propagandistic mark on its target audience, then this is almost certainly it. At its meeting on 19 May 1941, the Cabinet Defence Committee forced a more accessible approach to the media upon the Service Ministries.[47] Subsequent screenings of *Film as a Weapon* to the Air Ministry seem also to have had an impact, for in the second half of 1941 the RAF established its own Film Production Unit, while in October the hitherto under-resourced Army Film Unit was enlarged into the Army Film and Photographic Unit. These two bodies, as they grew in experience and recruited more and more people from the professional film-making community, such as Captain Roy Boulting, and photographers such as Bert Hardy, produced a series of documentary images which stand as a lasting testimony to the British military effort between 1942 and 1945, complementing the record of civilian bodies such as the Fire Brigade (*Fires Were Started*).[48] They also provided, via War Office censors and the MoI, millions of feet of film to the newsreel companies, which could at last provide a short-term indication of Britain's military achievement, as well as the kind of lasting historical record so evident in *The True Glory* (1945).[49] Such is the quality of the 'factual' film record of military activity after 1941 that it is barely recognisable when set against that which preceded it. The improved co-operation between the War Office and the Air Ministry was equally evident in the arrangements made to release personnel, actors and equipment for feature film production, thus ushering in what has been termed a 'golden age of British cinema'. In the words of Michael Powell, 'the film industry had become a war weapon'.[50]

8.5 The Golden Age of British Cinema

That this was at all possible was due in no small measure to pressure exerted by the MoI prior to the appointment of Brendan Bracken as minister in July 1941, though that appointment no doubt greatly assisted the process. It helps to explain the tremendous success of *Desert Victory*, the celebrated film account of the victory at El Alamein. Indeed, so successful was this product that it prompted inter-service competition in a scramble for recognition on film of the contribution being made by the various branches of the armed forces.[51] This created its own problems, so much so that the follow-up film, *Africa Freed*, was seriously delayed. The cause was, of course, inter-service rivalry between the Army and the Air Force. The 'Silent Service' remained largely unmoved, at least until 1944, when recording film of the Normandy invasion was finally taken by naval cameramen. Yet, even here, a discernible shift in attitude became apparent following proposals from Mountbatten, Chief of Combined Operations (upon whom Noel Coward based his character in the film *In Which We Serve*) and Stafford Cripps in 1942.[52]

Yet when all is said, perhaps the greatest single achievement of any service department's publicity unit during the war was not the actual production of any single film or body of films. Rather, three years of propaganda concerning the Strategic Bombing Offensive resulted, in Noble Frankland's words, in 'a more or less constant concealment of the aims and implications of the campaign which was being waged.'[53] Film was used as a weapon in this concealment, rather as videogame-type footage was used in the Gulf War, in order to deflect attention away from what was really going on at the sharper – and less accurate – end of conventional bombing. Given that British citizens had themselves suffered from bombing during the Blitz, the maintenance of the illusion that a strategic air offensive was being conducted by Bomber Command was all the more impressive. Harris, who disliked propaganda intensely and resented the use of his planes for dropping, as he put it, 'bits of bumph', was unsuccessful in his 1943 demand for a stark public statement 'that the aim is the destruction of German cities, the killing of German workers and the disruption of civilised community life throughout Germany'.[54] Instead, photographs and film footage of damage to industrial and military targets, rather than residential areas, were poured out from the Air Ministry, not just to provide a moral counterpoint to the activities of the Luftwaffe but also, until the offensive got fully under way in 1942–3, to show that Britain could not only 'Take It', she could also give it back – and that she could hit back with a high degree of accuracy, something which we now know to be patently untrue.

The improvement in British combat footage after 1941 nonetheless indicated a growing appreciation of the role of newsfilm as a weapon of war. In addition, of course, Britain was greatly helped after that date by the acquisition of propaganda-sensitive allies, who could also provide British newsreel distributors with the kind of spectacular footage supplied by Russian frontline cameramen or by hardened Hollywood professionals like William Wyler, who were prepared, and indeed allowed, to accompany the 'Memphis Belle' on 1,000-bomber raids over Germany.[55] This is not to suggest that the media professionals working for the newsreel companies ceased to complain about delays in receiving timely material from the combat cameramen. The minutes of the Newsreel Association of Great Britain bear witness to this. But both the quality and the quantity of the material with which they were now being provided had improved beyond all recognition from the early days of the war. Now, moreover, there was an even more compelling reason for this improvement. For if the British con- tribution to the war was to be placed in its proper perspective after 1941, comparable footage of British campaigns had now become essential, as much for the popular perception in allied countries as for its effect on domestic and neutral morale – the original reason behind MoI pressure for increased access for camera-men. In other words, the British war effort was competing for attention alongside the American and Russian war efforts.

Be that as it may, when Britain had stood alone in the war, with her back to the wall, it was perhaps just as well that her people were denied access to thrilling footage of Dunkirk or, later, of the fall of Singapore, and that they had to rely instead on the BBC transmitted oratory of Winston Churchill. Good propaganda, after all, loves a winner most of all, and effective propaganda does have to be rooted in reality. Despite the success of the British in dem- onstrating what could be done with bad news, the probability is that if Goebbels had been able to convert Stalingrad into a Dunkirk he would have needed to do so without the help of film.

Notes and References

1 This chapter originally appeared under the same title in David Dutton (ed.), *Statecraft and Diplomacy in the Twentieth Century: Essays Presented to P. M. H. Bell* (Liverpool University Press, 1995), pp. 134–54.

2 For a recent published analysis, see the special issue of *The Historical Journal of Film, Radio and Television* on 'Britain and the Cinema in the First World War', 13:2 (1993).

3 See Paul Swann, *The British Documentary Film Movement, 1926–46* (Cambridge University Press, 1989).

4 Henry Wickham Steed, in charge of propaganda to Austria-Hungary during 1918, described in 1940 how propaganda was a 'fifth arm' behind the Navy, Army, Air Force and economic warfare: 'the weapon of the mind for the battle of wits or, on a higher level, the sword of the spirit for the war of faiths': H. Wickham Steed, *The Fifth Arm* (Constable, 1940). Charles Cruickshank, in his *The Fourth Arm: Psychological Warfare 1938–1945* (Davis-Poynter, 1977), used the term 'fourth arm' of attack when describing wartime psychological warfare.

5 INF 1/857, Memorandum by A. P. Ryan 4 June 1941.

6 The phrase, as we have seen, was Lord Beaverbrook's, Britain's first Minister of Information in 1918. For a general historical overview see Philip M. Taylor, *Munitions of the Mind: War Propaganda from the Ancient World to the Nuclear Age* (Patrick Stephens Ltd, 1990).

7 Note that it does not say 'as far as possible'.

8 The respective sources for these three axioms are Sir John Reith, *Into the Wind* (Hodder & Stoughton, 1949), p. 354; a sign displayed in the depths of the MoI offices at the Senate House, University of London; and 'Programme for film propaganda', 1940, INF 1/867.

9 *The Lion Has Wings*, film, directed by Alexander Korda. London Films, 1939.

10 *The Adventures of Robin Hood*, film, directed by Michael Curtiz. Warner Brothers, 1938.

11 *The Sea Hawk*, film, directed by Michael Curtiz. Warner Brothers, 1940.

12 See, in particular, the contributions in K. R. M. Short (ed.), *Feature Films as History* (Croom Helm, 1981), and P. Sorlin, *The Film in History* (Blackwell, 1986).

13 In particular, see A. Aldgate, *Cinema and History: British Newsreels in the Spanish Civil War* (London, 1979), and N. Pronay, 'British newsreels in the 1930s: 1. Audiences and producers' and '2. Their policies and impact', in *History*, 56:4 (1971), pp. 411–8; and 57:1 (1972), pp. 63–72. See also Pronay, 'The news media at war' in N. Pronay and D. W. Spring (eds), *Propaganda, Politics and Film, 1918– 45* (Macmillan, 1982).

14 Minute by Churchill, 7 September 1941, PREM 3/476/3

15 T. Hollins, 'The Conservative Party and film propaganda between the wars', *English Historical Review*, 379:3 (1981), pp. 359–69.

16 A. J. P. Taylor, *English History, 1914–45* (Clarendon Press, 1965), p. 313.

17 I. C. Jarvie, *Hollywood's Overseas Campaign* (Cambridge University Press, 1992), p. 182.

18 For a discussion of Churchill's relationship with the medium of film, see D. J. Wenden and K. R. M. Short, 'Winston S. Churchill: film fan', *Historical Journal of Film, Radio and Television*, 11:3 (1991), pp. 197–214. By 1942, when Churchill's conversion had been achieved, he was still thinking of film as a historical record. This was his original intention for British Movietone's coverage of his first wartime meeting with Roosevelt. *Atlantic Charter* was released commercially by the MoI in October 1942. But the myth remains that Churchill was not interested in propaganda. In fact he frequently involved himself in the micro-management of its corollary, censorship, by personally stopping certain newsreel items. See, for

example, Brian Bond (ed.), *Chief of Staff: the Diaries of Lieutenant-General Sir Henry Pownall, Vol. 2: 1940–44* (London, 1974), diary entry for 20 October 1941.

19 Beaverbrook to Bracken, 21 July 1941, cited R. Cole, *Britain and the War of Words in Neutral Europe, 1939–45: the Art of the Possible* (Macmillan, 1990), p. 83.

20 The Ministry of Information is discussed by Ian McLaine, *Ministry of Morale* (Allen and Unwin, 1979), but curiously this study does not include film in its coverage.

21 For the USA., see N. J. Cull, 'The British campaign against American "neutrality": publicity and propaganda, 1939–41' (Ph.D. thesis, University of Leeds, 1992), published as *Selling War* (Oxford University Press, 1995).

22 Ibid, p. 64.

23 See H. Mark Glancy, 'The Hollywood "British" feature film, 1939–45', (Ph.D. thesis, University of East Anglia, 1993).

24 FO 371/22798, A6673, 11 September 1939.

25 J. R. Taylor, *Hitch: the Life and Work of Alfred Hitchcock* (Pantheon, 1978), p. 144; D. Niven, *The Moon's a Balloon* (Hamilton, 1971) and *Bring on the Empty Horses* (Coronet, 1983) p. 160. Lothian later relented with film people of military age. See Lothian to Eden, 8 June 1940, FO 371/24230, A3398/26/45.

26 Directed by Alexander Korda. London Films, 1939.

27 But, see K. Stamm, 'German wartime newsreels (*Deutsche Wochenschau*): the problem of "authenticity"', *Historical Journal of Film Radio and Television*, 7:3 (1987), pp. 239–248.

28 Darval to Perowne, 7 December 1939, FO 371/22841, A8608/7052/45.

29 See Ian Grant, *Cameramen at War* (Stephens, 1980), pp. 8–11.

30 C. Coultass, *Images for Battle: British Film and the Second World War* (Associated University Presses, 1989), pp. 39–40.

31 F. Capra, *The Name Above the Title: An Autobiography* (Da Capo Press, 1972), p. 329.

32 Scottish Record Office, Lothian Papers, GD 40/17, Box 405.

33 Harris to HQ, 12 September 1940, AIR 14/80.

34 See, for example, Mass Observation file report No. 142, 27 May 1940, and INF 1/292, Home Intelligence Report No. 27, week ending 9 April 1941.

35 PREM 4/25/8.

36 According to Valerie Grove in her introduction to Jan Struther, *Mrs Miniver* (Virago, 1989 reprint), p. xi.

37 *The Forty-Ninth Parallel*, film, directed by Michael Powell for the Ministry of Information, 1940. Powell recalled his meeting at the MoI when proposing the project: 'I want to make a film in Canada to scare the pants off the Americans, and bring them into the war sooner'. See his autobiography, M. Powell, *A Life in Movies* (Heinemann, 1986), pp. 347ff.

38 Undated, unsigned memorandum, 'Public relations and censorship – issue of communiqués and announcements', AIR 20/2950.

39 F. J. Assersohn, 'Policy and Propaganda: the presentation of the strategic air offensive in the British mass media, 1939–45' (MA thesis, University of Leeds, 1989).

40 Peck to CAS, 28 August 1941, AIR 20/2950.

41 *London Can Take It*, film, directed by Harry Watt for the Ministry of Information, 1940.

42 *Christmas Under Fire*, film, directed by C. Hasse for the Ministry of Information, 1941.

43 FO 371/24230, A3352/26/45, Ridsdale to Monckton, 30 May 1940.
44 INF 1/568.
45 One major source for acquiring German newsreel footage was the Iberian Penin-
    sula. In Portugal, the American representative of United Artists was approached
    by Sidney Bernstein to supply German films surreptitiously from December 1940
    onwards to the British Embassy for shipping to London and duplication. In Spain,
    Sir Samuel Hoare did manage to arrange an occasional exchange of Gaumont
    British newsreels for USA material. See also Cole, *Britain and the War of Words*.
46 K. Gladstone, 'British interception of German export newsreels and the develop-
    ment of British combat filming, 1939–42', *Imperial War Museum Review*, 2 (1987),
    pp. 30–40.
47 CAB 147/248.
48 *Fires Were Started*, film, directed by Humphrey Jennings. Crown Film Unit, 1943.
49 For the workings of Army photographers, see Jane Carmichael, 'Army photo-
    graphers in North-West Europe', *Imperial War Museum Review*, 7 (1994),
    pp. 15–22; and G. Casadio, 'Images of the war in Italy: the record made by the
    Army Film and Photographic Unit in Emilia Romagna, 1944–45', *Imperial War
    Museum Review*, 4 (1989), pp. 22–31.
50 Powell, *Life in Movies*, p. 236.
51 Anthony Aldgate, 'Creative tensions: *Desert Victory*, the Army Film Unit and
    Anglo-American rivalry, 1943–45', in Philip M. Taylor (ed.), *Britain and the
    Cinema in the Second World War* (Macmillan, 1988), pp. 144–67.
52 See the recommendations of the Cabinet Fighting Services Subcommittee, 25
    March 1943, INF 1/860.
53 N. Frankland, *The Bomber Offensive Against Germany* (HMSO, 1965), p. 97.
54 Harris to under-secretary of state for Air, 25 October 1943, AIR 14/843.
55 The National Archives in Washington today possess 13.5 million feet of uncut
    combat film from the Second World War: Jeanine Bassinger, *The World War II
    Combat Film: Anatomy of a Genre* (Columbia University Press, 1986), p. 125. It
    is worth pointing out the difficulties encountered by the Hollywood notable, Frank
    Capra, in securing frontline coverage from the US Signal Corps for his *Why We
    Fight* 'indoctrination' films. See F. Capra, *The Name above the Title*, pp. 328–34,
    and Tony Aldgate, 'Mr. Capra Goes to War: Frank Capra, the British Army Film
    Unit, and Anglo-American travails in the production of "Tunisian Victory"',
    Historical Journal of Film, Radio and Television, 11:1 (1991), pp. 24–5.

9

'Breaking the German Will to Resist': Allied Efforts to End the Second World War in Europe by Non-Military Means, 1944–45[1]

The British War Cabinet Committee on Methods of Breaking the German Will to Resist (GEN 52) was established on 22 November 1944, at the direction of the British Chiefs of Staff, in response to a personal request made two days earlier by General Eisenhower.[2] This committee held only three formal meetings (on 24 November 1944, 27 December 1944 and 30 March 1945) and issued two reports that have thus far attracted either minimal or somewhat dismissive attention from scholars. Its work was to devise methods for speeding up the end of the war in Europe at the intersection of subversion and psychological warfare. Wallace Carroll, who devoted a whole chapter of his insider's account of Second World War propaganda to the response to Eisenhower's initiative, chose to gloss over its activities. He instead spent most of his time chronicling the evolution of the policy of Unconditional Surrender, and developing his own arguments in support of that policy.[3] His verdict on GEN 52 was that the British failed to produce a good end-of-war psychological warfare plan because they 'were tired – after more than five years of war they had run out of ideas.'[4] Michael Balfour also dismissed the GEN 52 discussions as 'abortive'[5] while an official historian of the United States Army's European campaign formed the impression that GEN 52 did little because it 'could arrive at no satisfactory formula'.[6] Sir Robert Bruce Lockhart, who actually chaired the committee, offered the following assessment:

> I do not think that we accomplished very much more than the various propaganda agencies were already doing. At best the Committee helped to keep deception, subversion and propaganda on an even keel and to let the various experts feel that their views were being given consideration.[7]

Bruce Lockhart also expressed the opinion (not specifically connected with GEN 52) that 'political warfare did not noticeably weaken German resistance.'[8]

There are those who, on the other hand, believed the reverse to be true. Eisenhower himself, for example, felt 'that the expenditure of men and money in wielding the spoken and written word was an important contributing factor in undermining the enemy's will to resist.'[9] Likewise, Brigadier General Robert McClure, the Chief of the Political Warfare Division of the Supreme Head-quarters of the Allied Expeditionary Force (PWD/SHAEF) was convinced that psychological warfare helped to shorten the war.[10] Richard Crossman, a senior and legendary British figure within that organisation, was inclined to place subversive operations and black propaganda alongside strategic bombing as 'the only aspects of war at which ... the British ... achieved real pre-eminence.'[11]

These contradictory assertions do little to help us arrive at a balanced assessment of the actual historical record. Certainly, German morale did not crack to anything like the same extent as it had done in 1918 and, because the German people appeared to support the war to the bitter end (or at least not to oppose it) there is a temptation to judge Allied psychological warfare efforts in 1944–5 correspondingly as a failure. This chapter attempts a reassessment, and will challenge the commonly held hypothesis that it was impossible to reduce the German will to resist by other than purely military means. That hypothesis will be explored against the background of the political policy of Unconditional Surrender while eschewing speculation on the impact of alternative political policies. Although particular attention will be paid here to GEN 52's initiatives, one should also take note of other psywar activities taking place at the time which were already making a potential contribution to Eisenhower's requirements, as well as of other relevant initiatives which emerged subsequently without featuring on the agenda of GEN 52. The major conclusion is a heavily qualified rejection of the hypothesis that the German will to resist could only have been broken down by purely military means. It must be admitted, however, that this conclusion is not based exclusively on the actual progress and achievements of the various activities and initiatives described here. Rather, due consideration is taken of realistic alternative courses of action and outcomes that could have occurred within the constraints imposed by the political policy of Unconditional Surrender. This is possible in light of two factors. The rebirth of 'psychological operations' since Desert Storm in 1991 has brought with it a wider appreciation and debate about the role which psychological/informational weapons systems might play in determining the outcome of wars and, indeed, what are termed 'conflicts other than war'. Secondly, important new documents have been released into the public domain, especially David Garnett's 1947 Official History of the Political Warfare Executive, which is now available at the Public Record Office.[12] Perhaps for the first time, therefore, we can properly evaluate the actual role of psychological warfare in the ending of the Second World War and draw lessons for conflicts fought since then.

9.1 Eisenhower's Request

Following the breakthrough at Avranches at the end of July 1944, General Eisenhower's Allied Expeditionary Force made rapid progress towards Germany. American troops crossed the German frontier near Aachen on 11 September 1944 and it seemed possible that final victory in Europe might be achieved by the end of the year. Such hopes faded with the failure of Operation Market-Garden and the delay in seizing and opening the port of Antwerp. As a front line stabilised, it became apparent that the Germans still retained a formidable military capability and that their soldiers' will to fight was far from broken.

Eisenhower addressed this issue of German morale in a telegram to the Combined Chiefs of Staff (CCOS) on 20 November 1944. He wrote:

1. German morale on this front shows no sign of cracking at present. I am of the opinion that the enemy's continued stolid resistance is a main factor postponing final victory, which, in present circumstances, can only be achieved by prolonged and bitter fighting.

2. Factors which are compelling the enemy to continue strong resistance appear to be:

a. Overall iron discipline of the *Wehrmacht* and stranglehold by the Nazi party.

b. Successful Nazi propaganda which is convincing every German that unconditional surrender means the complete devastation of Germany and her elimination as a nation.

3. I consider it is of vital importance that we should redouble our efforts to find a solution to the problem of reducing the German will to resist and then to bring every appropriate weapon to bear to achieve this end. I have in mind particularly the employment of deception methods in addition to propaganda and other possible means.

4. Since any plan which aims at reducing the enemy's will to resist must affect the German Army in all theatres, this is not a subject which can be dealt with by Supreme Headquarters Allied Expeditionary Force, which is not in possession of the relevant information and does not control all the weapons to put such a plan into effect.[13]

He concluded by requesting that this issue be taken up 'as a matter of urgency' – which in one sense it was, as GEN 52 was formed two days later and met for the first time two days after that.

Some scholars and contemporary observers have interpreted this request by Eisenhower as an attempt to alter or revise the policy of Unconditional Surrender.[14] Certainly Eisenhower had displayed very little enthusiasm for the rigidity which that policy implied,[15] but the wording of his request is in fact entirely consistent with the development and implementation of appropriate deception, propaganda and other plans within those existing political constraints. Churchill for his part interpreted the request simply as a 'desire to get at German morale by underground methods'.[16]

Although Eisenhower's telegram was addressed to the Combined Chiefs of Staff in Washington, he asked that the matter be taken up in London. This was because London was the engine room of the Allied psychological warfare effort. This also supports the view that Eisenhower was seeking a specialist planning effort, not a political review of the policy of Unconditional Surrender.[17]

This was certainly the official interpretation placed on his telegram in London, where the Chiefs of Staff (COS) Committee jumped at the double to establish a new committee, comprising representatives of the existing specialist agencies and of relevant ministries. Its brief was to 'consider how far it was possible, by other than purely military means, to reduce the German will to resist.'[18] GEN 52 assumed stiffer wording in its title, namely Breaking[19] the German Will to Resist. It was chaired by the Director General of the Political Warfare Executive (PWE), Bruce Lockhart.

9.2 Allied Psywar Organisation and Capabilities in 1944

As well as propaganda and deception, Eisenhower's telegram contemplated the use of 'other possible means' to reduce the German will to resist. This appears to have been a euphemism for the subversion and sabotage capabilities of the British Special Operations Executive (SOE) and of the American Office of Strategic Services (OSS). SOE was certainly represented on GEN 52 and was to play a prominent role in the development of the Committee's initiatives. SOE, headed by Major General Colin Gubbins, was answerable to the Minister of Economic Warfare, Lord Selborne. It received a valuable temporary reinforcement on 22 November 1944 in the person of Major General Gerald Templer,[20] who was appointed to take charge of its German Section (Section X), and it was in this capacity that Templer became involved in the SOE contribution to GEN 52 until early March 1945.[21] However, the links between SOE and OSS had loosened during 1944 and the London organisation of OSS was not represented on GEN 52.[22]

Deception representation on GEN 52 was provided by the London Controlling Section (LCS). This agency planned and co-ordinated the dissemination of manipulated, distorted and falsified evidence to the enemy to induce key decision-makers to take decisions prejudicial to their interests. The LCS's outstanding achievement during 1944 had been Operation Fortitude South which had delayed the commitment of the 15th German Army from the Pas de Calais to Normandy after D-Day through the dissemination of evidence portraying the phantom 1st United States Army Group as being poised to make a major landing in the area of Calais. The scope for such deception activities in support of Eisenhower's requirement to reduce the German will to resist was not however immediately apparent to those concerned. Why, we don't know, but as a result, the LCS made only a limited contribution to the work of GEN 52 – which was perhaps to prove a significant mistake.

Propaganda representation on GEN 52 was assured through the appointment of Bruce Lockhart as chairman. The major British organisation directing propaganda to Germany and the German Armed Forces had been and remained the Political Warfare Executive. PWE propaganda that overtly proclaimed its British sponsorship (so-called 'white propaganda') was disseminated primarily through the broadcasts of the BBC's German Service and the dropping of leaflets by the RAF. The PWE's American counterpart in this area, the Office of War Information (OWI) had a strong presence in London.[23] OWI radio broadcasts to Europe had been dependent on the allocation of slots within the BBC's schedules until the American Broadcasting Station in Europe (ABSIE) was established in April 1944, thereby giving OWI a dedicated outlet for its own radio broadcasts for the first time. Similarly, OWI's leaflet-dissemination capability was also enhanced in June 1944, when the 8th USAAF dedicated a bomber squadron purely and uniquely to the leaflet role.[24] The British propagandists enjoyed no such luxury, although another means they had of delivering black printed material to Germany was available in the form of a dedicated balloon unit of the RAF.[25]

A separate area of PWE activity was headed by Sefton Delmer. As Director of Special Operations (Enemy and Satellites), Delmer was in charge of 'black propaganda'.[26] Such propaganda, disseminated both by radio and in the form of printed material, deliberately concealed its British origins and falsely claimed other sponsorship. For example, *Soldatensender West* claimed to be an official German radio station, while leaflets distributed within Germany purported to originate from non-existent German resistance organizations. Black propaganda, by definition, sought to deceive; the nature of the deception, generally aimed at mass targets, was somewhat different from the more specifically targeted leadership activities of the LCS. In addition, Delmer also produced 'grey propaganda', which carried no attribution whatsoever. An example was the air-delivered and highly praised newspaper for German troops, *Nachrichten für die Truppe*. The contents of this paper could not possibly be reconciled with official German sponsorship, but the failure to proclaim the true origin permitted the newspaper to express views that might have been embarrassing if attributed to an official British source. A further specialisation of Delmer's was the manufacture of 'sibs'[27] or rumours. As one might detect from this, the interface between Delmer's brand of propaganda and the subversive activities of SOE had become quite blurred in 1944. Delmer enjoyed a close working relationship with SOE, providing propaganda to support subversion and using SOE agents to disseminate his 'sibs' and black printed material. Responsibility for American black propaganda was vested in the Morale Operations Branch of the OSS. MO/OSS contributed to Delmer's *Soldatensender West* programmes, but developed a growing enthusiasm for independent activities during 1944.[28] MO/OSS was not represented on GEN52 although relevant MO/OSS activities are described later.

Both the Foreign Office and MoI were also represented on GEN 52. Ministerial responsibility for PWE was shared between the Foreign Secretary (Anthony Eden) and the Minister of Information (Brendan Bracken). The departmental interest of the Foreign Office in the response to Eisenhower's request was obvious; MoI's responsibilities for propaganda to neutral Europe and for the domestic broadcasting of the BBC made its involvement in GEN 52 sensible.[29] Representatives of the Joint Intelligence Sub-Committee (JISC) and the Joint Planning Staff (JPS) completed the British membership.[30] American representation on behalf of the Joint Chiefs of Staff (JCS) was requested, but the invitation was declined,[31] presumably because it was assumed that the final proposals would be sent to Washington anyway for endorsement and the JCS thus saw no reason to be drawn into the preliminary planning.

Finally, McClure was nominated to represent the Supreme Commander of the Allied Expeditionary Force (SCAEF) on GEN 52.[32] As Chief of PWD/SHAEF, McClure headed a sizeable propaganda organization that was becoming a central player in tactical psychological warfare.[33] His division was a combined Anglo-American enterprise, manned by a mix of military and civilian personnel. Most of the civilians had been seconded from OWI, MO/OSS, PWE or MoI. The senior British member of this organisation was Richard Crossman, an individual who was said to make 'whatever place or whatever organisation he is in the centre of the universe'[34] and whom Bruce Lockhart suspected of being behind Eisenhower's request of 20 November 1944.[35]

At the time of D-Day, PWD/SHAEF had been heavily reliant on PWE for assistance in mounting its propaganda campaigns. Its 'Voice of SHAEF'[36] broadcasts had been carried by the BBC and ABSIE, as it lacked its own studio and transmitter facilities. This deficiency was overcome with the capture of Radio Luxembourg in September 1944.[37] By November 1944, PWD/SHAEF was controlling a substantial propaganda effort independent of the London organisations, involving Radio Luxembourg, leaflets, newspapers and the co-ordination of the activities of the psychological warfare staffs and units at Army Group and Army levels. On the face of it, therefore, between them SOE, OSS, MO/OSS, LCS, PWE, the BBC German Service, OWI, ABSEI, PWD/SHAEF and Radio Luxembourg, together with RAF/USAAF support and the specialist expertise of Joint Intelligence Sub-Committee (JISC) and the Joint Planning Staff (JPS) appear to represent a formidable Allied capability, in terms of both human resources and technical assets, to develop and implement plans to reduce the German will to resist. The omens for meeting Eisenhower's request, at least from an organisational point of view, looked good.

Two special pieces of British equipment should be mentioned in addition. Aspidistra was a 500-kilowatt transmitter installed in an underground bunker at Crowborough in Sussex.[38] Its powerful capability was used for some BBC transmissions, for some of Sefton Delmer's black transmissions and for the spoiling or jamming of German air defence communications. Technical plans had been developed for Aspidistra to intrude into German domestic broadcasts. As it was known that German transmitters closed down during Allied air raids,[39] it would be possible for Aspidistra to capture the standard German home service broadcast from a transmitter in an area of Germany unaffected by air raids and re-transmit it to another area where the local transmitter had closed down. German listeners in the area of the actual air raid would thus receive their genuine home service via Crowborough until such time as the captured transmissions were suppressed and a spokesman of Sefton Delmer took over. The listeners would be unaware of this change and would continue to believe that they were receiving the genuine German home service. In November 1944, this plan had yet to be implemented.[40]

The other British piece of specialised equipment was a miniature delayed-action incendiary device, with instructions for its use printed in seven languages. SOE had prepared a plan, Operation Braddock II,[41] under which large quantities of these devices would be dropped over Germany in the hope that they would fall into the hands of foreign workers and persons hostile to the regime, who would in turn use them to commit arson. It was envisaged that this would place an enormous strain on the German security forces as they searched for amateur saboteurs and undetected devices and guarded vulnerable targets. Lord Selborne was especially keen on this plan, and regularly lobbied Churchill that the moment was opportune to implement Braddock II.[42] By July 1944, SOE had stockpiled some 3,750,000 incendiary devices. The COS, however, proved repeatedly reluctant to divert bomber assets to Braddock II, and in July 1944 it was decided that the best means of placating the ever-persistent Selborne was to refer the matter to the Supreme Commander.[43]

SHAEF's response was to propose the launching of Braddock II in conjunction with Aspidistra intrusion operations. The latter would broadcast purportedly official German warnings to the civilian population, thereby achieving maximum publicity for the arrival of the incendiary devices.[44] This proposal provoked a furious interdepartmental controversy in London because Brendan Bracken's views on the proposed use of Aspidistra were not consulted.[45] Black propaganda was a highly dangerous game and its players were temperamental types who revelled in their twilight world, with the result that personality clashes were the norm rather than the exception. Nor were tempers improved when Crossman admitted that SHAEF's ostensible enthusiasm for Braddock II was motivated by the prospect of PWB securing control over Aspidistra from the MoI.[46] In the event, only one significant Braddock operation was mounted on 25 September 1944 – but without Aspidistra support.[47] Other small drops, mainly for morale rather than sabotage purposes, continued until the end of April 1945.

Although the Braddock/Aspidistra saga exposed certain personal, organisational and procedural shortcomings within the Allied psychological warfare capability, it has to be said that the major limitation on that capability was imposed by the political policy of Unconditional Surrender. How could the psychological warfare experts offer classic inducements such as 'surrender or die' if enemy personnel believed they would be treated as war criminals if they did give themselves up? No better testimony to the handcuffing limitations of Unconditional Surrender can be made than Goebbels' delight at the policy. It provided him with an opportunity to unite the German people behind the Nazi Party (we will all be treated the same way, so we are all in this together) that no amount of his own propaganda had been able to create. It almost guaranteed that the success of Lord Northcliffe's Crewe House in 1918 in dividing the German people from its leadership could not be repeated.

Having said that, until D-Day, PWE and OWI had had little difficulty in conducting their business within these policy constraints. By November 1944, however, PWD/SHAEF had emerged as a significant additional contributor to the Allied propaganda effort, especially now that it was supporting troops already in occupation of some German territory. While the formula of Unconditional Surrender was simple – that there would be no negotiated peace – this simplicity offered little practical guidance on Allied policies and plans for the occupation of Germany. Indeed, these policies and plans were still being discussed in the European Advisory Commission and were not to emerge in final and definitive form until the Potsdam Conference in July and August 1945.

One historical analysis of the formula of Unconditional Surrender has correctly identified two of its essential components, namely a prohibition on negotiation with enemy leaders except to instruct them on the details of orderly capitulation, and a refusal post-capitulation to recognise the political authority of any enemy leader or indigenous body. The logic of this was that the resulting political vacuum post-capitulation would therefore have to be filled by military government.[48] While the formula of Unconditional Surrender itself did not prohibit advanced publicity on the policies which would be pursued by that military government, the fact remains that such policies could not be publicised until they had been formulated. This situation posed serious challenges for SHAEF in the pre-capitulation period, especially as its military government in the occupied areas of Germany was bound to be seen by Germans as indicative of the regime which would be applied to the whole of Germany after the war had ended. PWD/SHAEF's obvious inclination was to publicise the positive aspects of the pre-capitulation regime, and thereby attempt to counter Goebbels' domestic propaganda, while at the same time securing maximum co-operation from – and publicity for the consequences for – German civilians in the occupied areas. A further potential problem of this was that PWD/SHAEF propaganda along these lines might attract fierce Soviet criticism on the grounds that it was making commitments that had not yet been endorsed as tripartite policy. From the perspective of Washington, propaganda based on the temporary pre-capitulation regime might be embarrassing if the subsequent permanent regime failed to provide comparable basic conditions. While this dilemma was never satisfactorily resolved, the issues were raised by Eisenhower's political adviser, Robert Murphy, in conjunction with a controversial suggestion that, because of these dangers, all Allied propaganda (as distinct from straight news) to Germany should be suspended.[49]

Allied capability to reduce the German will to resist was also subject to some additional general moral constraints. Although falsehood was the hallmark of black propaganda, deception and subversion activities, there was a certain caution in London about embracing initiatives which might generate post-war legends in Germany of victory through trickery or involve the deception of Allied publics. These were, after all, people committed to democratic principles, people who broadly adhered to the ideology of the Atlantic Charter and the Four Freedoms. Fighting an enemy of the nature of Nazi Germany, especially in a 'Total War' situation, may have required some compromising of those principles, but there remained a reservation that the ends never quite justified the means. After all, that was precisely the kind of thinking which now drove the very regimes the Allies were fighting against in a war to the death. In 1944, the Allies could be pretty confident that they would win, but how this was done was beginning to impact on thinking about the future of Europe and whether democracy would prevail in the post-war era. As SHAEF's Standing Directive of June 1944 put it, Allied psychological warfare should make 'no suggestion that the Atlantic Charter applies to Germany by right'.[50]

9.3 The German Target

The Allied policy of Unconditional Surrender competed with the German policy of No Surrender, summarised within a British intelligence assessment issued on 14 July 1944:

21. All the elements for a collapse of Germany already exist ... The control, however, of the Nazi Party, which has nothing to hope for from any peace terms, is so deep-rooted and omnipotent that we are faced with an artificial situation. The Party will continue the struggle just so long as it can, by the most ruthless methods and skilful propaganda, compel the Armed Forces to fightand the Home Front to endure, regardless of the consequences for Germany's economy, hopes of revival as a military power or even as a country.

22. It is impossible therefore to predict how long this unprecedented state of affairs can last, since ordinary standards cannot be applied. It is, however, equally difficult to see how Germany can, if Allied attacks on the three major fronts are ceaselessly pressed home, prolong the struggle beyond December ...

24. When the collapse comes, it is likely to develop with startling rapidity. The only effective alternative to the Nazi Party would be the assumption of power by military leaders ...[51]

This assessment continued with observations on the low prospects for success of any attempt by the military leadership to wrestle power from the Party in advance of the final collapse. These observations would appear to have been vindicated by the failure of the 20 July plot six days later. Overall, therefore, apart from the suggestion that final collapse might occur by the end of 1944, this assessment was to prove remarkably accurate – in keeping with many of the PWE's intelligence assessments.[52]

The post-war United States Strategic Bombing Survey suggested that, by July 1944, 85 per cent of German civilians regarded the war as lost.[53] The Survey generally provides an extremely comprehensive range of statistics on the decline in German civilian morale. However, it records only limited evidence of the way in which defeatist attitudes translated into any actual behaviour that actively speeded up the final collapse. While the war-weariness, increasing levels of absenteeism and general lack of enthusiasm recorded in the Survey did have some adverse impact on the civilian contribution to the German war effort, very few overt acts of opposition to the conduct of the war were reported. On the contrary:

> As the destruction and dislocation grew, the people became more dependent than ever on the State – and thus on the Party – for the very essentials of life. Instead of rising in revolt against the Nazi regime, as the Allies had hoped, they were obliged to support it as the only authority capable of preserving order and continuing the supply of food, clothing, fuel and other necessities. They could not sabotage the war effort without endangering their own already precarious existence.[54]

Subsequent studies of German military morale tend to support the view that the will to fight was not seriously eroded until March 1945.[55] Yet Allied propaganda appealing to self-preservation through surrender (emphasising, *inter alia*, the good treatment accorded to Prisoners of War and thereby challenging the 'Victory or Siberia' and 'Strength through Fear' themes pursued by Nazi propaganda) does appear to have achieved considerable success in these combat situations in which German troops had been overrun or surrounded. Those responding, however, were generally individuals or small groups separated from their units and in imminent danger of being killed or captured. Such propaganda, it may therefore be argued, failed to generate widespread desertions by individuals not engaged in close combat and had only limited success in persuading commanders in hopeless situations to order group surrenders.[56] This in turn lent some weight to Goebbels' claims that German soldiers did not surrender but were only captured.

In light of this, Eisenhower's request of 20 November 1944 could be said to have posed a major intelligence and planning challenge. On the reasonable assumption that Hitler would maintain his policy of continued resistance and No Surrender, serious degradation of the German will to resist would depend critically on the identification of key but vulnerable targets within Germany and the German Armed Forces that were actually capable of active dissociation from Hitler's policy.

On an individual level, successful inducement of desertions by soldiers or acts of sabotage by civilians would contribute to the weakening of resistance. More spectacular results might be achieved if susceptible groups could be identified and prompted to take appropriate actions. The fostering of defeatist attitudes, in other words, would be insufficient to achieve the short-term impact required by Eisenhower. Rather, to have an impact, attitudes would have to be translated into actions. Thus the planning of a serious campaign to reduce the German will to resist would involve the identification of susceptible targets, selection of behavioural responses which the targets could realistically be expected to perform and the application of persuasion and pressure to induce the desired responses. As already noted, the people who were really qualified through experience to undertake this type of task, the staff of the LCS, were only tangentially involved in the deliberations of GEN 52. Instead, SHAEF seems to have become obsessed with quantity rather than quality, and its emphasis on the sheer bulk of material directed at its targets on a mass scale only served to make it lose sight of the significance of specific appeals to specifically vulnerable target groups.

Obviously, a further problem was that the policy of Unconditional Surrender imposed serious constraints on the manner in which targets could be approached and the inducements that could be offered. Enemy personnel who were prepared in principle to envisage an early end to the war could not be invited to discuss the nature of the post-war regime in Germany; nor could they be offered positions of political power within that regime. Equally, the Nazi security and propaganda organisations provided powerful disincentives and discouragements to individuals contemplating action that would degrade the German will to resist. This was driven home in the closing months of the war, when special German courts-martial dealt out exemplary punishments to persons found guilty of cowardice or defeatism. As Jay Baird has pointed out, the bodies of those executed were 'dangled from trees and lampposts' throughout the Reich 'as warnings to the rest of the population'. And Baird was right to remind us that 'traditional Nazi propaganda overlapped and merged with traditional German patriotism and the people's intuitive response to defend the Fatherland in danger ... even the most convinced anti-Nazis were ready to respond to the Party's propaganda motifs, a situation which Goebbels fully appreciated.'[57]

9.4 Ongoing Allied Psywar Activities

The natural gut-reaction by the specialists in London to Eisenhower's initial request was that because a great deal was already being done by the existing organisations – which SCAEF may or may not have known about – his desired result could be achieved by those bodies. GEN 52/1, the first report to emerge from the new committee, by implication suggested this by providing an annexe listing the objectives and themes of British white propaganda to Germany.[58] These were, however, almost exclusively concerned with the inducement of attitudinal responses that were being pursued through the broadcasts of the BBC's German Service and the dropping of leaflets. And because arrangements had been in place for some time for the harmonisation of British and American white propaganda from London, it was indeed reasonable for the OWI and ABSIE to feel that they were already pursuing similar objectives and themes. That they had a point is difficult to deny. It has been estimated that in the autumn of 1944, the BBC's German Service was attracting up to 15 million listeners (not all of them in Germany itself)[59] while leaflet dissemination from the United Kingdom by the 8th USAAF leaflet squadron in November 1944 achieved a monthly record of 466 tons.[60] Regular RAF and USAAF bombing missions disseminated further leaflets.

A second annexe to GEN 52/1 provided a summary of the ongoing activities of Delmer's black propaganda organisation.[61] The claim in this that black propaganda 'could achieve decisive ... effects in some sensational news operation'[62] was in fact to provide a taste of things to come. This was because, alongside Delmer's activities, MO/OSS had already launched two major black newspaper initiatives during 1944. *Das Neue Deutschland*, a newspaper sponsored by the MO/OSS organisation in Italy from April 1944, purported to be a clandestine publication of an underground German peace party.[63] Project Harvard was launched by the MO/OSS team in Stockholm in July 1944 and involved the production and dissemination of *Handel und Wandel*. Purportedly sponsored by German interests in Sweden, this newspaper was targeted at German industrialists and focused on their concerns for the future of German industry.[64]

PWD/SHAEF propaganda activities expanded in two important areas in December 1944. First, Eisenhower's receipt of national guidelines from Washington on pre-capitulation military government permitted him to authorise the initiation of a series of 'Voice of Military Government' broadcasts, starting on 4 December 1944. These were carried by the BBC, ABSIE and Radio Luxembourg and issued firm but fair instructions to the civilian population.[65] Although addressed to the occupied areas, the broadcasts were bound to achieve an impact in unoccupied Germany and to raise doubts about Goebbels' predictions on the harsh nature of the occupation regime being planned by the Allies. More significantly, in connection with these broadcasts and in anticipation of further advances into Germany, SHAEF adopted a 'stay put' policy for German civilians. The simple and practical advantages of this policy were perceived to be both that the roads would be kept clear of refugees, who might otherwise hinder military movements, and that military government in the newly occupied areas would retain the potential availability of skilled civilian labour. From the psychological viewpoint, it was known that the Germans intended to arrange evacuation of civilians from areas threatened by Allied advances, and so SHAEF's encouragement of completely opposite action would, it was hoped, create general confusion and cause resentment among those forced by the Nazis to leave their homes.[66]

The second inevitable expansion of PWD/SHAEF activities during this period was into the field of black broadcasting. From December 1944 onwards, the daytime white output of Radio Luxembourg was complemented by nighttime use of the transmitter by a station calling itself 'Radio 1212' (or 'Annie') that purported to be an underground station inside Germany.[67] Meanwhile, in the frontlines of the Allied Expeditionary Force, routine loudspeaker activities continued, supplemented by the dissemination of leaflets to the opposing German forces by artillery and aircraft. However, given the operational situation during November and early December 1944, there were felt to be no major or realistic opportunities for the encouragement of German surrenders on a significant scale.[68] It was therefore hoped that any initiatives in response to Eisenhower's request of 20 November 1944 would provide some kind of break-through for this already diverse range of propaganda activity. This was expecting a lot, and it certainly required some imaginative thinking.

9.5 New Initiatives: Periwig and Matchbox

As soon as the COS Committee established GEN 52 on 22 November 1944,[69] a one-page PWE appreciation on Eisenhower's requirements was pre-pared for its first meeting two days later. This document suggested that black propaganda might be used 'to give the Germans a plausible picture encouraging them to surrender whatever the actual truth may be as to our future intentions with regard to them'.[70] When GEN 52 first convened on 24 November, Un-conditional Surrender policy was disposed of as a high-level political matter[71] and there was 'fairly unanimous agreement that there was no propaganda short-cut to victory and that German morale could not be destroyed without fighting.' With this hypothesis accepted as a given at this stage of the war, various ideas were subsequently discussed and the departments represented were invited to develop these into memoranda for consideration at a future meeting.[72]

No such formal meeting in fact took place.[73] GEN 52/1 was taken by the COS Committee on 12 December 1944[74] and issued in its final revised form the same day. Although scrutiny and refinement of the proposals by a higher-level committee of ministers or officials was contemplated,[75] the paper appears to have been sent to Washington at the end of December without further substantial amendment.[76] JCS endorsement of the paper was notified on 24 January 1945.[77] The COS Committee simply noted this endorsement on 25 January[78] and instructions were sent to departments responsible for action the same day, informing them that the 'flag has dropped'.[79] The JCS, despite their previous endorsement of GEN 52/1, raised some belated comments on 31 January 1945,[80] which were merely noted by the COS Committee on 5 February and passed on to Bruce Lockhart.[81] So much for Eisenhower's exhortation that his request be taken up as a matter of urgency.

GEN 52/1 made 13 specific proposals,[82] most of them expressed in very general terms. Although described as a plan, it has to be said that it was little more than a list of uncoordinated ideas. Moreover, few of the ideas appear to have been pursued with vigour.[83] The proposed linking of Nazi leaders with funds in neutral countries, for example (of significance in light of late 1990s revelations about the fate of Nazi war treasures in Switzerland) was to be tackled initially by priming Lord Vansittart to ask an appropriate question in the Lords, to which a Government spokesman would reply that the possible existence of such Nazi funds was engaging the Government's closest attention.[84] However, action was delayed through Foreign Office insistence that the question be put in the Commons.[85] Other proposals do appear to have been incorporated

into routine PWE output.[86] The outcome of the proposals on German industrialists and POWs are not clear from the available primary sources. The
proposal to enlist the assistance of senior German POWs in broadcasting or
by work in the fighting line was eventually to result in a visit by General Sir
Andrew Throne to No. 11 POW Camp on 3 April 1945. The German generals
received his requests sympathetically, but quite understandably declined to
offer their services for fear of jeopardising the lives of their families in
Germany.[87]

The proposals on the harmonisation of Allied statements and on Austria
appear to have depended on anticipated discussions and decisions at the Yalta
Conference which did not, in the event, materialise. The unofficial approach
to the Vatican was made in February 1945; the Vatican was obviously anxious
to re-establish a strong role for the Church in post-war Germany. The British
Minister to the Holy See warned London against 'letting the Pope think that
he held any brief for the German people'.[88] In fact, the only proposals to
generate anything like a sustained campaign were those at Paragraphs 9 and
10, which were to merge into an operation codenamed Periwig.

Periwig was launched at an SOE/PWE meeting on 12 January 1945 and
was to involve the LCS, PWE and SIS under the direction of SOE.[89] As there
was felt to be little scope for developing the existing clandestine resistance
movements within Germany into a credible threat to the Nazi regime, Periwig
aimed to create imaginary resistance organisations, thereby putting maximum
strain on the Gestapo, developing a lack of confidence and feeling of insecurity
within Germany, increasing general suspicion and doubt, and eventually causing
a breakdown of the security services with consequent damage to the administrative machine.[90] As Garnett's recently released history of PWE put it:

> The plan was to behave as if we knew of the existence of a German
> Resistance Movement inside Germany which was willing to co-operate
> with us. The plan was therefore to dispatch stores and agents, to send
> code messages and to make open appeals to its members. It was obvious
> that the Gestapo would monitor the messages and a proportion of the
> stores and agents would fall into its hands and that it therefore might be
> convinced of the existence of a widespread resistance movement and make
> wholesale arrests and take other measures which would help to break the
> German Will to Resist. The main objective was to divert the energy of
> the police system into a wasteful activity. But once a belief in a Resistance
> movement became widespread in Germany it might soon become a
> reality.[91]

Such a frank admission of the risks which the plan posed to the lives of agents
perhaps helps to explain why this document remained closed until 1996! As
Garnett added starkly: 'Volunteers were asked for among anti-Nazi prisoners
of war, but very few came forward. Those that did were given four weeks
instruction by Instructors who were themselves deluded into the belief that the
German Resistance Movement existed'.[92] According to the same source, the

moral objection 'that the extremely cynical exploitation of genuine German anti-Nazis would have caused a wave of indignation, in Britain and America and in Germany itself, if the facts ever came out', 'does not seem to have been stated'.[93] Signs of desperation?

For Periwig, then, it was agreed that two months would be devoted to building up the credentials of imaginary organisations within the Armed Forces, the Nazi Party and the police and among German industrialists, mining workers, industrial workers, foreign workers, railway workers and religious groups. A Bavarian separatist organisation was to be added for good measure. During the initial period, no suggestion would be made that these organisations had links with the Allies. SOE proposals to bring the organisations to life included the compromising of innocent individuals, clandestine radio transmissions, rumours and the briefing of genuine agents despatched on separate SOE missions so that, if they were caught, they would impart information about Periwig which they believed to be true. After the preparatory two-month period, evidence was to be introduced linking the organisations with the Allies. The dropping of radio equipment, propaganda material, forged documents, arms, ammunition, explosives and rations would provide such evidence. Live pigeons would be dropped in cages, together with blank intelligence questionnaires for persons sympathetic to the resistance to complete and attach to the pigeons before releasing them for return to England. Additionally, a few uncaged dead pigeons with completed questionnaires attached would be dropped indiscriminately; according to Garnett, 'Pigeons continued to be dropped until 27.5.45 owing to Mr. Delmer's enthusiasm for the project'.[94]

A number of limited air drops certainly took place during March 1945, but the Secret Intelligence Services (SIS) proved reluctant to authorise drops which might attract unwelcome Gestapo security activity in areas in which its agents were located. SHAEF also imposed a ban on any drops within a 25-mile radius of any POW camp, for fear that it would be assumed that POWs were being tasked or encouraged to engage in espionage or sabotage activities. These restrictions in effect served to place most of Germany out of bounds to Periwig drops.

At the request of SOE's head Gubbins, these problems were referred to a special third meeting of GEN 52, chaired by Colonel John Bevan of LCS, on 30 March 1945. The meeting noted the views of those present and decided to let SHAEF decide whether the potential advantages of Periwig outweighed the potential dangers to SIS agents and POWs.[95] Unsurprisingly, SHAEF responded on 19 April 1945 to the effect that recent military developments rendered Periwig unnecessary. Incidentally and remarkably, the four agents who were parachuted into Germany as part of this highly dangerous operation all survived. One was picked up by the Russians, another by the British (after he had shot a Gestapo official who questioned his papers) and the other two by the Americans. The latter pair even claimed that 'they had succeeded in contacting subversive group, as instructed'. Garnett noted this, adding: 'this is an excellent example of how the imaginary can crystallise into the real. In this respect Periwig resembles the subject of many plays by Pirandello'.[96]

GEN 52/1 had refrained from making proposals for the use of Aspidistra, possibly because Bruce Lockhart had been forewarned that a (Crossman-backed) proposal was being prepared in SHAEF.[97] The SHAEF proposal was actually circulated in London on 19 December 1944.[98] The enclosures included a SHAEF (G–3 Division) paper recommending that an Aspidistra intrusion operation should be mounted in support of a future Allied breakthrough to broadcast an announcement of German capitulation. The announcement would be made either by a voice pretending to be Hitler,[99] or by an 'official German spokesman'. Also enclosed was a PWD/SHAEF paper, rejecting the G–3 Division recommendation for unspecified technical reasons[100] and substituting a suggestion that the announcement should purport to be made on behalf of von Runstedt to the effect that emissaries had been despatched to seek an armistice, but that units should fight on for the moment. After a pause of four minutes, the same announcer would then mysteriously withdraw the previous announcement, offering no explanation. PWD/SHAEF anticipated that this would create even greater confusion than the proposal to use a Hitlerian voice and would promote serious friction between von Runstedt and Himmler. As the broadcasts would be 'real', Allied broadcasting networks would certainly report what had been said, thereby giving the announcements rapid publicity throughout Europe. The Chief of Staff of SHAEF urged that it or some better plan on similar lines form part of the overall subversive strategy.

The COS Committee invited Bruce Lockhart to investigate the SHAEF proposals.[101] These were discussed at the second meeting of GEN 52, which directed Sefton Delmer to produce a plan on the basis of the PWD/SHAF proposal.[102] This emerged as GEN 52/2 on 4 January 1945. In the meantime, PWD/SHAEF had proposed a different plan, designated Matchbox, which was despatched direct to the CCS on 5 January.[103]

Matchbox involved a series of broadcasts purporting to be made from a mobile transmitter within Germany sponsored by military and industrial leaders opposed to the policy of No Surrender in general and to Himmler in particular. The reason for the submission of this second plan is not evident from the primary sources examined; it may have been intended as an alternative option if GEN 52/2 failed to secure approval. Garnett merely adds that GEN 52 responded 'favourably, although giving full weight to the dangerous results of failure and the post-war effect of providing Germans with the excuse that they had been defeated by a propaganda trick'.[104]

The COS Committee discussed both GEN 52/2 and Matchbox with Bruce Lockhart on 8 January 1945. The Committee expressed itself to be very uneasy over the 'victory through trickery' aspects of GEN 52/2 with its concomitant implicit deception of the British public. It was agreed to allow GEN 52/2 to be sent to Washington for JCS consideration, but with accompanying comment to the effect that the British COS were neither committed to nor attracted by the plan. The JCS were reminded that, should they press for the plan's adoption, they were dangerously close to political considerations and that it might therefore become necessary to consult British Ministers.[105] On 21 February 1945, the JCS notified their refusal to endorse GEN 52/2 and Matchbox. No reason was given beyond an assertion that implementation would be 'unacceptable under present conditions'.[106] Even though he quoted Brendan Bracken as saying that 'I am glad that this silly plan has been scrapped', Garnett himself added: 'The attempt on Hitler's life four months later [sic] showed, however, that Mr. Delmer's plan was not so silly after all'.[107] Garnett here reveals his PWE colours. True, he may have been thinking about the July 1944 plot, but the factual error does undermine his argument in support of Matchbox somewhat.

9.6 Other Initiatives: Casement and Capricorn

As has been suggested, any assessment of the actual and potential contribution of the GEN 52 initiatives to reducing the German will to resist must be considered alongside certain other concurrent initiatives. Eisenhower's request of 20 November 1944 prompted Roosevelt to propose to Churchill that they should join in a joint appeal to the German people and Army, assuring them that the Allies did not seek to devastate Germany or the German people, but wanted to save lives and save humanity.[108] Churchill was not convinced that such an appeal would be appropriate, particularly as Stalin contemplated demanding two or three million Germans for prolonged reparation work.[109] Eisenhower, in telegrams to Churchill and Marshall, supported Churchill's viewpoint.[110] Then, on 18 March 1945, Churchill proposed a similar appeal to the German Army but failed to convince Roosevelt, who took the view that propaganda should be left to the propaganda agencies.[111]

Churchill then decided to revive the question of Braddock II. Almost on cue, a further minute to Churchill from Selborne was referred to the COS Committee on 30 December 1944.[112] The COS avoided any direct response to this by adopting the view that it was SCAEF who should decide on the timing of any further initiation of Braddock II. They did, however, point out that such operations were unlikely to be of any use until such time as the German internal security services had lost control.[113] Then, on 23 January 1945, Templer sent Bruce Lockhart a detailed plan (prepared with Sefton Delmer and the technical experts) for future Braddock II operations. This favoured a large-scale but risky operation of the type long advocated by Selborne, adding that that if bombers could not be made available, a more modest operation could be mounted using the aircraft of the 8th USAAF leaflet squadron and the balloons of the RAF balloon unit.[114]

Small-scale deliveries from aircraft started in late February 1945 under the auspices of PWE.[115] Churchill, who had always as leader been interested in 'setting Europe ablaze', could now begin to do this literally, albeit as an arsonist on a modest scale. He did suggest more inflammatory operations in March 1945 [116] but this met with COS bureaucratic reservations. There were perceptions of an increased danger of reprisals on Allied POWs if incendiary devices were dropped near POW camps and it seemed inadvisable to drop devices anywhere in Germany at a time when the werewolf organisation was being set up.[117] Thus Braddock II was never launched on a large scale, and created a series of brush-fires rather than the inferno Churchill had long hoped for.

One further intervention by Churchill concerned SHAEF's 'stay put' policy towards German civilians, and resulted in the mounting of Aspidistra intrusion operations. During a visit to SHAEF on 4 March 1945, Churchill realised just how deep-rooted the 'stay put' policy had become, whereupon he adopted the view that there was much to be gained from forcing German civilians onto the roads in panic – as French civilians had done in 1940 much to the advantage of the advancing German armies. He therefore went about persuading Eisenhower to reverse the policy.[118] His success at this caused serious consternation in PWD/SHAEF, particularly as the 'stay put' policy had been promoted by white propaganda output.[119] Propagandists dedicated to a 'Strategy of Truth' were always nervous about changed minds for fear they would lose credibility. Black propaganda was different, and so PWE offered assistance in putting together a propaganda plan to support the new policy, and the opportunity was identified to use Aspidistra's intrusion capability.[120] The first bogus evacuation instructions were broadcast on the night of 24 March 1945 and there were six subsequent intrusion operations by Aspidistra.[121]

Apart from his contribution to Braddock II, it was Templer who was responsible for the production of another relevant plan in December 1944. He introduced Plan Casement with this homily:

It is submitted that unless HMG agrees to jettison former ideas about the ethics of deceiving friends, and adopts the general principle that 'the end justifies the means' – even to the extent of involving (by unacknowledgeable means) the government of a neutral state – no scheme for breaking the enemy's will to resist can be adopted with the rapidity now necessary; and that rather than a series of ingenious but unintegrated and somewhat long-term plans, a scheme should be put into operation which (a) is simple (b) can start within a few days (c) will be known to succeed or not within a few weeks (d) cannot lay HMG open to charges of complicity.[122]

Casement was devised on the assumption that it was necessary to expose to both the German Army and the German people plans purportedly made by Nazi leaders for escape to safety in Eire. By pure coincidence, a debate in the House of Commons publicised the recent refusal of the Eire Government to give assurances that German war criminals would not be granted asylum 'should justice, charity, or the honour or interest of the nation so desire'.[123] Over a month later, a PWE/SOE/LCS/Foreign Office Casement Committee decided to switch the destination to the Argentine for reasons of potential political sensitivities and plausibility. The SOE representative protested that Eire was a perfectly plausible destination, 'since criminals are known to hide near the scene of their crime.'[124] The project subsequently lost momentum and came to nothing, although Garnett was quick to point out in his history that PWE continued to sponsor sibs about the likely flight of Nazi leaders because of their capacity not to contradict or undermine 'a major theme of our political warfare to Germany – that Hitler was involving Germany in ruin by his decision to continue fighting after defeat was certain'.[125]

Another plan under discussion in January 1945 was Huguenot. This idea, apart from negating Wallace Carroll's assertion that the tired British had run out of ideas, sought to provoke irritating and complicated security measures in the German Air Force by suggesting that a few pilots had successfully defected to England in their aircraft. This plan, however, ran into difficulties when it was realised that it might actually induce defections and that, if that happened, further contingency plans would be needed to cater for the reception of any pilots who attempted to emulate the fictitious defectors.[126] 'The plan was yet another example of treating an imaginary situation as real and thus bringing it about', wrote Garnett. He added that in this instance only a covert operation could be attempted since any white messages to this effect would be in violation of the Geneva Convention of issuing false instruction on how to surrender. 'Mr Delmer accordingly went ahead with the black side of the operation. Instances of German Air Force pilots following the instructions and safely landing on Allied aerodromes followed'.[127] How this actually happened remains unclear, especially as no orders were issued to cease British anti-aircraft fire on enemy planes flying above UK air space. Having said that, as Garnett point out, this was not anyway a 'serious objection ... as the object of the plan was not to capture live German airmen'.[128] Fortune clearly favoured the brave, except on one known occasion when five German fighters attempted to wing-waggle as a friendly gesture three Mustangs from the All-Negro 332nd US Fighter Group. Four of the five were shot down.[129]

Interestingly, at the same time as GEN 52/1 was doing the restricted rounds in London, William Donovan (Director of OSS) decided to circulate a paper on black propaganda. This suggested inter alia that black media could be used to 'give the German people a vague and wholly spurious idea of the "terms" of Unconditional Surrender which the Allies will impose.'[130] This suggestion failed to gain enthusiasm in the State Department, although Assistant Secretary of State James Dunn did admit that the JCS had ultimate responsibility for black programmes in support of military operations.[131] Donovan's paper may indeed have influenced the launching of Operation Capricorn in late February 1945 which involved black broadcasting by a station purporting to be the voice of a Bavarian revolutionary movement. These broadcasts were developed from intelligence about a real clandestine resistance organisation in Bavaria headed by a Captain Gerngross.[132]

While Donovan focused on the potential of black propaganda to evade the constraints of the policy of Unconditional Surrender, PWD/SHAEF attempted to achieve greater flexibility for its white propaganda through an analysis of the policy itself. Robert Murphy alerted Washington to the evolution of a doctrine that:

> The policy of unconditional surrender was always meant to apply only to the German Government and High Command and to the ... Nazi Party ... but not to the German people as human beings and that even if this was not the intention at the outset it has since become the intention.[133]

Murphy's view was that there should be no compromise of the policy of Unconditional Surrender, and thus no propaganda statements which could be construed as commitments on the nature of the post-capitulation regime. This was upheld in Washington.[134] That Crossman was involved in this attempt to tamper with the policy of Unconditional Surrender was hinted at by Bruce Lockhart who warned Eden on 1 February 1945 that Crossman might have to be recalled in view of his status as the 'central figure of this controversy ... who enjoys the confidences of some of the generals and is suspect to the State Department.'[135] PWE was able to stay out of this controversy by the simple expedient of basing its white propaganda on statements made on the subject of Unconditional Surrender by Churchill, Eden, Roosevelt and Stalin.[136] PWE merely housed the OSS team conducting the black broadcasts. In passing, it is also of interest that Soviet propaganda to Germany through the National Committee of Free Germany and the associated League of German Officers openly pursued the proposed PWD/SHAEF doctrine, offering positive assessments of the consequences of surrender for the German people.[137]

9.7 The Capitulation of Germany

From late March 1945, German military resistance on all fronts began to disintegrate. On the 23rd, Goebbels noted in his diary:

> Among most sections of the German people faith in victory has totally vanished ... Admittedly the people are doing all they can to assist their leaders in further prosecution of the war – no one is failing to work or losing his will to fight; hardly anywhere, however, is there any hope of a happy ending to the war ... Enemy propaganda is beginning to have an uncomfortably noticeable effect on the German people. Anglo-American leaflets are now no longer carelessly thrown aside but are read attentively; British broadcasts have a grateful audience. By contrast, our propaganda has a difficult time making an impact.[138]

The process of capitulation culminated in the German High Command's authorisation of the signature of the final act of unconditional military surrender in Berlin on 8 May 1945. There is, however, little obvious evidence to link the German capitulation directly with the activities and initiatives described in this chapter. The statistics of Allied psywar performance at the point of conception were undoubtedly impressive. By March 1945, the Allies had taken 850,000 POWs, of whom 90 per cent claimed they had either seen or carried PWD leaflets. (In all, 4.9 million POWs were eventually taken by the Western Allies, and 1.9 million by the Soviets). This is not so startling in light of estimates that PWD distributed about six billion leaflets to continental Europe by the end of the war. But at the point of reception, the German armed forces and people, how these messages translated into behaviour remains a problem, especially as still they continued to work and still they fought on. Indeed, one near-contemporary estimate calculated that about 11 per cent of German troops still believed they were actually winning the war as late as March 1945.[139] So whereas Eisenhower's request of 20 November 1944 had contemplated the encouragement of capitulation without prolonged and bitter fighting, the final capitulation was actually to take place in response to events on the battlefields. It can be argued that Hitler's suicide on 30 April 1945 removed an important psychological constraint on military capitulation by the High Command. However, while his personal fate may have symbolised a wider disintegration of the German physical capacity to resist, any residual *will* to resist became increasingly irrelevant as the means of continued resistance were destroyed.

It is perhaps significant that as soon as the High Command ordered capitulation, the orders were obeyed; there were very few instances of units and individuals attempting to fight on. The werewolf organisation did not materialise and the attitude of German civilians towards the Allied military was characterised by a docility that had also been evident in the occupied areas of Germany before the capitulation. The statistics on the numbers of German soldiers being taken prisoner by the Allied Expeditionary Force during the final weeks of the war suggest that the military will to resist did in fact evaporate every bit as rapidly as the physical capacity to resist.[140] However, those statistics do not differentiate between those taken prisoner in hopeless military situations and those who seized opportunities to surrender in circumstances where it would have been possible to avoid capture. Nor do they reveal the numbers of *Volkssturm* and base troops within the overall totals – yet it was these categories of troops who generally surrendered more readily than veteran members of combat formations.

As hostilities drew to an end, the white propagandists of PWD/SHAEF discovered that one of their major themes had been compromised by their own governments. Amidst all the controversies over the interpretation of the policy of Unconditional Surrender, PWD/SHAEF had confidently assured its German military target audience that prisoners of war would be treated in accordance with the 1929 Geneva POW Convention.[141] However, an Anglo-American policy had meanwhile emerged, without the knowledge of PWD/SHAEF, under which Unconditional Surrender permitted the abandonment of the conditions imposed by the Convention.[142] In retrospect, it is difficult to understand this failure to co-ordinate propaganda output with policy – which could be said to be the heart of the problem ever since Unconditional Surrender had been announced – particularly in view of the political scrutiny and control of PWD/SHAEF statements on the nature of the post-capitulation military government regime.

The quality of Allied propaganda came under British parliamentary scrutiny on 28 March 1945. Questions in the House of Commons drew attention to 'anxiety amongst parents of soldiers fighting the Germans as to the character and adaptability of Allied publicity and propaganda ...'[143] and cited a leaked American military report as evidence that 'Allied propaganda, as at present devised, is failing to induce a tendency to surrender amongst German soldiers'.[144] Bracken[145] managed to disarm these criticisms by pointing out that Members had failed to study the truckloads of propaganda material supplied to the House of Commons Library since late 1944, although he agreed that 'the war, at this moment, is being decided by arms, and not by words'.[146]

The advance of the 7th United States Army towards Munich in late April 1945 triggered one incident which can actually be linked with an Allied propaganda initiative to reduce the German will to resist. In view of the tactical situation, the black broadcasts of Operation Capricorn were discontinued on 27 April 1945. That same evening, the real clandestine German resistance organisation which had inspired Capricorn seized key points in Munich. On the morning of 28 April, Radio Munich carried announcements calling for support for the anti-Nazi uprising of Captain Gerngross and the 'Freedom Movement of Bavaria'. Such an uprising had been advocated by Capricorn's 'Captain Hagadorn' since 26 February. Gerngross's *putsch* attracted some military and civilian support, but was suppressed by SS troops within 24 hours. Gerngross survived to see the Americans arrive in Munich on 29 April and, arguably, his diversion of SS troops facilitated the advance of the 7th Army. It is not clear if Gerngross had been aware of the true sponsorship of the Capricorn broadcasts, but he had listened to them and had found them 'marvellous'.[147]

9.8 Conclusions

We can now finally begin to assess the responses to Eisenhower's initiative against the hypothesis that it was impossible to reduce the German will to resist by other than purely military means. If the Munich *putsch* had been but one of a number of similar anti-Nazi uprisings, and if such uprisings could be linked with Allied propaganda, deception, sabotage and subversion initiatives, it would be possible to reject the hypothesis outright. In the event, the Munich *putsch* was an isolated incident and its links with Operation Capricorn were tenuous.

GEN 52 itself had been fairly unanimous 'that there was no propaganda short-cut to victory and that German morale could not be destroyed without fighting.'[148] Scrutiny of the somewhat ambiguous wording of Eisenhower's request of 20 November 1944 suggests that he was seeking an alternative to 'prolonged and bitter fighting' and believed that a non-military solution might be found to 'the problem of reducing the German will to resist'. It can thus be argued that Eisenhower's aspirations were viewed as unrealistic by GEN 52 from the outset. However, undue reliance should not be placed on the precise wording of telegrams and other documentation drafted under wartime pressures.

The response in London to Eisenhower's request can be criticised on several counts. First, the COS Committee failed to define an aim for GEN 52. The aim that it adopted for itself was to 'consider how far it was possible, by other than purely military means, to reduce the German will to resist'.[149] This aim did not appear in GEN 52/1, possibly because that paper failed to identify the extent to which other than purely military means might achieve this. Templer's remarks on 'a series of ingenious but unintegrated and somewhat long-term plans'[150] were obviously directed at GEN 52/1, which lacked a comprehensive assessment of the likely overall contribution of its various proposals to Eisenhower's requirements.

Ministerial involvement in GEN 52 was avoided on the grounds that such involvement would be premature until the Committee's proposals received CCS endorsement.[151] While the exclusion of ministers can be seen as an attempt to accelerate the development of a set of proposals, it may also have been indicative of the relatively low importance attached to GEN 52 in London.[152] But it did mean that the political issues constraining Allied psychological warfare were repeatedly dodged. Notwithstanding this, it was not until 25 January 1945 that executive instructions were issued in London for the implementation of GEN 52/1.[153] It is difficult to reconcile this ponderous staffing, and the subsequent lack of vigour in the implementation of GEN 52/1 and associated initiatives, with the urgency which Eisenhower attached to his initial request. Taken in conjunction with the quality of some of GEN 52/1's proposals, this lack of urgency could suggest that GEN 52 was seen in London as a token response to a request which implied that British propaganda, deception, sabotage and subversion agencies were not already doing all that was possible to hasten the defeat of Germany.

It is possible to speculate over two other explanations for the less-than-dynamic response of GEN 52. If Eisenhower's request was perceived in London as an indirect attempt to prompt a review of the political policy of Unconditional Surrender, the delegation of the response to a committee of officials subordinate to the COS Committee could have been seen as a diplomatic means of ensuring that political policy issues were ignored. The ambiguous wording of Eisenhower's request would have made it difficult for him to object subsequently to the course of action taken in London. The second possibility is that Bruce Lockhart substantiated his suspicions[154] that Richard Crossman was behind Eisenhower's request. Bruce Lockhart, for his part, was unlikely to have devoted enormous energy to an exercise prompted by Crossman that was possibly designed to enhance the prestige of PWD/SHAEF at the expense of the London agencies.

The only major initiative to emerge from GEN 52, therefore, was Operation Periwig. Gubbins saw this as 'the principal contribution which the various secret services, acting in combination, can make towards breaking the German will to resist' and considered that 'it can have really important results if pressed with vigour by all concerned . . .'[155] Periwig appears to have foundered because the various secret services did not act in combination. SOE's concern for the safety of its agents (together with SHAEF's concern for the safety of Allied POWs) challenged the assumption that the imposition of maximum strain on the German security services would be in the Allied interest. Nor is it clear how the confusion of the security services through air drops to imaginary resistance organisations and the scattering of live and dead pigeons would erode the German will to resist. While the Munich *putsch* can thus be cited as an example of the type of activity which PERIWIG sought to promote, it can also be seen as a demonstration of the ability of the German security services to maintain the upper hand right up to the end of the war.

Many of the initiatives described here – Braddock II, the Aspidistra intrusion operations, Huguenot and Capricorn – were similarly targeted at the German security services on the apparent assumption that degradation of their capabilities would prompt activities inside Germany which would hasten the final collapse. However, as it was to be events on the battlefields that brought final collapse increasingly closer, it seems certain that the inclination of individuals inside Germany to hazard their lives in the last weeks of the war was correspondingly reduced. Overall, then, there would appear to be little evidence to support the view that the initiatives emerging from GEN 52 and the associated initiatives made any meaningful contribution to the eventual collapse of German resistance. While those initiatives were hampered by procedural and organisational shortcomings, it is unlikely that improved procedures and organisations in London would have created exploitable targets in Germany. However, preoccupation with the German security services and perceived opportunities to promote disruptive activities within Germany could be explained through a failure to focus on the one obvious target that was critical to meeting Eisenhower's requirements.

This target was the German military opposition to the advance of the Allied Expeditionary Force into Germany. Although frontline propaganda to German troops on the battlefields has been dismissed by some historians as cutting down the cost of victory, but not accelerating it,[156] such statements cannot go unchallenged. It was the German Armed Forces – not the security services, the industrialists, organised religious groups, Bavarian separatists and the various other targets identified by GEN 52 and the associated initiatives – who deployed the physical means of delaying the Allied advance and prolonging hostilities. Every soldier who deserted or surrendered therefore reduced not only the cost of victory, but also increased the speed with which victory could be achieved. The real lost opportunity in the responses to Eisenhower's request thus appears to have been the failure to draw up an assessment of the scope for adjusting the output of propaganda to the opposing German forces.

The accepted wisdom within PWD/SHAEF was that Hitler should never be openly attacked for fear of antagonising the target audience.[157] PWE and OWI propaganda to Germany, on the other hand, openly ridiculed Hitler. It may therefore be worth scholars' while to re-examine the rationale for PWD/SHAEF's exclusion of such themes from its propaganda directed at the German military. Frontline propaganda undoubtedly achieved impressive results in inducing individual surrenders through appeals to self-preservation. The military situation in the closing months of the war should therefore have provided some scope for undermining residual loyalty to Hitler among frontline troops and encouraging large-scale group surrenders before the final disintegration of German military resistance. The fact that most German soldiers obeyed the final order to surrender when it came suggests that this particular target audience was far more vulnerable than has been commonly assumed.

In summary, the responses to Eisenhower's request provide an interesting case study of attempts to terminate hostilities by other than purely military means. The actual achievements of GEN 52 and the other responses underscored the subordination of propaganda, deception, sabotage and subversion activities to military operations and to political policy. They also demonstrated the importance of directing such activities to susceptible targets which can realistically be expected to perform appropriate actions. It was not impossible to reduce (as opposed to break) the German will to resist by other than purely military means. An analysis of the responses to Eisenhower's request suggests that the greatest scope for such contributions to final victory in Europe lay in the direction of appropriate propaganda to German troops on the battlefields. This opportunity appears to have been inadequately exploited through preoccupation with less susceptible and less effective targets within Germany. Greater attention should therefore have been paid to adjusting the output of Allied propaganda from those targets to German troops on the battlefields. Perhaps the Allies overestimated the morale of most German soldiers because they had swallowed Nazi propaganda about their invincibility. Perhaps it was due to the memory of Germany military successes in 1939–40. Perhaps they had even swallowed their own propaganda in 1944 about what a formidable opponent the German soldier was as an insurance policy against failure on D-Day. There was also a tendency to praise the enemy's fighting capability in order to make eventual Allied victory seem an even greater achievement. Whatever the reasons, the potential contribution of propaganda, deception, sabotage and subversion activities to reducing (as distinct from breaking) the German will to resist was not fully achieved because the right target was not identified. And so, while historians of the SOE are agreed that its work, especially Ultra, probably shortened the war by a couple of years, PWE and the other psywar organisations can boast no similar track record. Had they got their target audience right, however, who knows how many lives – German as well as Allied – might have been saved?

Notes and References

1 This article appeared first under virtually the same title in *The Historical Journal of Film, Radio and Television*, 18:1 (1998) pp. 5–48. It was co-written with N. C. F. Weekes, too whom I am grateful for allowing me to reproduce a version here. The original article contained several documents as annexes which can be consulted in the original but which are not reproduced here.

2 Minutes of first meeting of GEN 52, 24 November 1944, CAB 78/29.

3 Wallace Carroll, *Persuade or Perish* (Houghton Mifflin and Co., 1948), pp. 306–337 (Chapter 7 of Part II).

4 Ibid, p. 329. Carroll then lists four ideas which emerged from GEN 52 without offering any comment whatsoever.

5 M. Balfour, *Propaganda in War, 1939–1945* (Routledge & Kegan Paul, 1979), p. 399. He cites FO 371/46791 at the PRO in support of this verdict. Balfour served as a civilian intelligence officer in PWD/SHAEF, 1944–45.

6 Forrest C. Pogue, *United States Army in World War II – The European Theater of Operations: The Supreme Command* (Washington DC, Office of the Chief of Military History Department of the Army, 1954), p. 343. Pogue cites no sources in support of his statement and appears to be muddling GEN 52 with separate political discussions on war aims.

7 Sir Robert Bruce Lockhart, *Comes the Reckoning* (Arno Press, 1947), p. 330.

8 Sir Robert Bruce Lockhart, 'Political Warfare', *Journal of the Royal United Service Institution*, 95:578 (May 1950), p. 200.

9 Undated introductory letter by Eisenhower in Headquarters United States Forces European Theater, *The Psychological Warfare Division, Supreme Headquarters Allied Expeditionary Force: An Account of its Operations in the Western European Campaign, 1944–1945* (Bad Homburg, Germany, 1945 official publication, hereafter cited as *PWD/SHAEF Operations*).

10 Brigadier General Robert A. McClure, Foreword to Daniel Lerner, *Sykewar: Psychological Warfare Against Germany, D-Day to VE-Day* (G. W. Stewart, 1949), p. xviii. McClure was Chief of PWD/SHAEF throughout its existence.

11 R. H. S. Crossman, 'The Wartime Tactics that Led to Watergate', *The Times*, 16 May 1973, p. 18. Crossman served as the senior British member of PWD/SHAEF. Earlier in the war he had been Director of PWE's German and Austrian Regional Directorate.

12 D. Garnett, 'Political Warfare Activities carried out by the Departments EH and SOI and PWE from the Munich Crisis till the Surrender of Germany'. CAB 102/610.

13 CAB 105/158, SCAF 134, 20 November 1944. The telegram was copied to the British COS.

14 Stephen E. Ambrose, *The Supreme Commander: The War Years of General Dwight D. Eisenhower* (Doubleday, 1970), pp. 544–555; Bruce Lockhart, *Comes the Reckoning*, pp. 329–330; Carroll, *Persuade or Perish*, p. 306; Chester Wilmot, *The Struggle for Europe* (Harper, 1952), p. 570; Kenneth Young (ed.) *The Diaries of Sir Robert Bruce Lockhart: Vol. Two, 1939–1965* (St Martin's Press, 1974), diary entry for 23 November 1944. Bruce Lockhart was Director-General of the PWE, 1942–45. Carroll was Director of the London office of OWI until December 1943 and then assumed an OWI appointment in the United States in charge of propaganda to Europe.

15 See Ambrose, *Supreme Commander*, pp. 390–391 and Captain Harry C. Butcher, USNR, *Three Years with Eisenhower: The Personal Diary of Captain Harry C. Butcher USNR – Naval Aide to General Eisenhower, 1942 to 1945* (Simon & Schuster, 1946), pp. 443–444. See diary entry of 14 April 1944 for details of Eisenhower's unsuccessful attempts to modify the policy of Unconditional Surrender in April and May 1944.

16 Prime Minister to President, No 828, 24 November 1944, CAB 120/853.

17 It is possible, particularly in view of the wording of Paragraph 2b of SCAF 134,

that Eisenhower was hoping to prompt both a specialist planning effort and a political review of the policy of unconditional surrender.

18 CAB 79/83, COS 377(44)10(O), 22 November 1944; CAB 78/29, Minutes of first meeting of GEN 52, 24 November 1944. COS 377(44)10(O) merely directed that SCAF 134 'should be dealt with' by a committee and laid down the chairmanship and representation. The quoted aim appeared in the minutes of the Committee's first meeting; it seems likely that the detailed wording of this aim was developed by Bruce Lockhart through analysis of the text of SCAF 134. No evidence has been found to suggest that the wording was submitted to the COS Committee for endorsement.

19 Although the request from Eisenhower had spoken of reducing the German will to resist, the Committee's designation implied that it had the more ambitious aim of breaking the German will to resist. This implication was not reflected in the actual wording adopted as the aim of the Committee.

20 Colin Cloake, *Templer, Tiger of Malaya: The Life of Field Marshal Sir Gerald Templer* (Harrap, 1985) p. 142.

21 Templer then became Director of Civil Affairs and Military Government at Headquarters 21st Army Group.

22 Kermit Roosevelt (ed.), *War Report of the OSS* (Walker, 1976), vol. 2, pp. 6–7; Peter Wilkinson and Joan Bright Astley, *Gubbins and SOE* (I. B. Taurus, 1993), pp. 211–12.

23 General accounts of OWI's activities are provided by Charles A. H. Thomson, *Overseas Information Service of the United States Government* (Arno Press, 1948) and Alan M. Winkler, *The Politics of Propaganda: The Office of War Information, 1942–1945* (Yale University Press, 1978).

24 Pat Carty, *Secret Squadrons of the Eighth* (Brassey's, 1980), pp. 39–81 (Chapter IV) and James M. Erdmann, *Leaflet Operations in the Second World War* (Arno Press, 1969) provide details of the activities of the 8th USAAF leaflet squadron. Additional to its support to OWI, the squadron accepted taskings from PWE and PWD/SHAEF.

25 'Operations Record Book of "M" Balloon Unit RAF'; AIR 29/22; AIR 41/1, pp. 385–390.

26 Delmer's own account of his wartime activities is in *Black Boomerang* (Secker and Warburg, 1962). A more detailed account is provided by Ellic Howe, *The Black Game: British Subversive Operations Against the Germans During the Second World War* (Michael Joseph, 1972).

27 From the Latin *sibilare*: to hiss.

28 Roosevelt, *War Report*, vol. 1, p. 219 and Vol. 2, pp. 5–7 and 299–300. The MO/OSS contribution to *Soldatensender* was designated Project Muzak.

29 Bracken initially declined the invitation to be represented. See PRO, FO 898/355, undated notes by Bracken for Bruce Lockhart on the formation of GEN 52. The agenda for the second meeting of GEN 52 prompted the attendance of MoI's Director-General, Sir Cyril Radcliffe. See PRO, CAB 78/29, minutes of second meeting of GEN 52, 27 December 1944.

30 The full intended membership of GEN 52 is listed in PRO, CAB 79/83, COS 377(44)10(O), 22 November 1944.

31 CAB 105/48, JSM 401, 28 November 1944; CAB 79/83, COS 384(44)3(O), 29 November 1944.

32 Telegram from Smith (Chief of Staff, SHAEF) to Ismay (Secretary, COS Committee), 25 November 1944, WO 219/4778.

33 *PWD/SHAEF Operations* and Lerner's *Sykewar* provide the best accounts of PWD/SHAEF activities.

34 Young, *Diaries of RHBL*, p. 370 diary entry for 25 November 1944.

35 Ibid, p. 369 diary entry for 23 November 1944.

36 The PWE file on 'Voice of SHEAEF' is in FO 898/396.

37 The PWE file on Radio Luxembourg is FO 898/48.

38 The most detailed published account of Aspidistra is Mark Kenyon, 'Black Propaganda', *After the Battle*, 72 (1992), pp. 8–31. The PWE files on Aspidistra are in FO 898/42–47.

39 A fact which bewildered the Allies as they did not in fact use the broadcasts as directional navigation aids in bombing raids, even though the Germans suspected that this was the case.

40 Churchill had identified the potential for intruder operations of this type in 1940. See PREM 4/99/5, ff. 420–3. Aspidistra was purchased from an American manufacturer in 1941.

41 Operation Braddock I involved the dropping of small arms and explosives to organised resistance groups.

42 CAB 80/80, COS(44)157(O), 13 February 1944 records minutes from Selborne to Churchill on 13 April 1943, 4 October 1943 and 11 February 1944. CAB 80/85, COS(44)659(O), 26 July 1944, covers a further minute from Selborne to Churchill dated 25 July 1944. The PWE file on Braddock II is in FO 898/397.

43 CAB 79/78, COS 251(44)8(O), 28 July 1944.

44 CAB 80/86 – COS(44)743(O), 17 August 1944.

45 Bracken, quite incorrectly, declared himself to be the 'sole arbiter' on the employment of Aspidistra. The extensive and acrimonious correspondence is in FO 954/23, ff. 272–5, 277–9 and 281.

46 Young, *Diaries of RHBL*, p. 349 diary entry for 26 August 1944.

47 FO 898/397, f. 85.

48 Paul Kecskemeti, *Strategic Surrender: The Politics of Victory and Defeat* (Stanford University Press, 1958), pp. 218–19.

49 Telegram from Murphy to State Department, 17 October 1944, and replies of 20 November 1944 and 3 November 1944, US Department of State, Foreign Relations of the United States (hereafter FRUS) 44/I, pp. 560–2. Murphy's suggestion on the suspension of Allied propaganda was not agreed.

50 'Standing Directive for Psychological Warfare Against Members of the German Armed Forces', June 1944, Reproduced in Lerner, *Sykewar*.

51 CAB 119/137, JISC assessment JIC(44)302(O)(Final), 14 July 1944.

52 CAB 119/137 contains subsequent JISC assessments on German strategy and capacity to resist, none of which depart from the general thrust of the quoted extracts from the 14 July 1944 assessment. On the perceptiveness of PWE's intelligence reports, see Pauline Elkes, 'The Political Warfare Executive: a re-evaluation based on the intelligence work of the German Section.' (Ph.D. thesis, University of Sheffield, 1996).

53 United States Strategic Bombing Survey, *European Report No 64b: The Effects of Strategic Bombing on German Civilian Morale* (US GPO, 1946/7), vol. 1, p. 16.

54 Wilmot, *Struggle for Europe*, pp. 550–2.

55 The two major published studies are Murray I. Gurfein and Morris Janowitz, 'Trends in *Wehrmacht* Morale' in William E. Daugherty (editor), *A Psychological Warfare Casebook* (Arno Press, 1958), pp. 744–50; and Edward A. Shils and Morris Janowitz, 'Cohesion and disintegration in the *Wehrmacht*' in Morris Janowitz (ed.),

Military Conflict: Essays in the Institutional Analysis of War and Peace (Sage, 1975), pp. 177–220. Both draw on wartime research, including memoranda by Lieutenant Colonel Henry Dicks of the (British) Directorate of Army Psychiatry. Some of Dicks' memoranda are in WO 219/4716, WO 241/1–4 and WO 241/6. A general summary of Dicks' research appears in M. Balfour, *Four-Power Control in Germany and Austria: Part I – Germany* (Publisher unknown, 1956), pp. 51–64.

56 Kecskemeti, *Strategic Surrender*, p. 144 cites the example of Field Marshal Model, who avoided taking responsibility for surrender by the novel expedient of disbanding his command (Army Group B, surrounded in the Ruhr pocket in April 1945). Model's soldiers then surrendered as individuals; Model himself is believed to have committed suicide.

57 Jay W. Baird, *The Mythical World of Nazi War Propaganda, 1939–1945* (University of Minnesota Presss, 1974), pp. 251 and 258.

58 Annexe A to GEN 52/1.

59 Asa Briggs, *The War of Words* (Oxford University Press, 1970), p. 692.

60 Carty, *Secret Squadrons*, p. 107.

61 Annexe B to GEN 52/1.

62 Paragraph 1 of Annexe B to GEN 52/1.

63 Roosevelt, *War Report*, Vol. 1, p. 218 and Vol. 2, pp. 97–9.

64 Ibid, Vol. 1, pp. 218–19 and Vol. 2, p. 266.

65 Pogue, *Supreme Command*, pp. 344–345. The texts of the broadcasts are in *PWD/SHAEF Operations*, pp. 135–41. The broadcasts were reinforced through the dissemination of leaflets addressing similar themes.

66 Minute from McClure to Smith, 20 December 1944, WO 219/4719.

67 Erik Barnouw, 'Propaganda at Radio Luxembourg: 1944–1945' in K. R. M. Short (ed.), *Film and Radio Propaganda in World War II* (Croom Helm, 1983), pp. 192–7; Roosevelt, *War Report*, Vol. 2, p. 301; Laurence C. Soley, *Radio Warfare: OSS and CIA Subversive Propaganda* (Praeger, 1989), pp. 138–45. The PWD/SHAEF designation for this black station was 'Radio Annie'. The station was operated by 12th Army Group on behalf of PWD/SHAEF.

68 Events in the late December 1944 (i.e. the Ardennes offensive) offered even less scope for Allied frontline propaganda.

69 CAB 79/83, COS 377(44)10(O), 22 November 1944.

70 'Political warfare appreciation', 23 November 1944, FO 898/355.

71 At that time the subject of telegrams between Roosevelt and Churchill.

72 Minutes of first meeting of GEN 52, 24 November 1944, CAB 78/29 Young, *Diaries of RHBL*, pp. 369–70, diary entries for 23 and 24 November 1944.

73 By no means all the nominated departments were represented at the meeting on 24 November 1944. It seems that McClure visited London on 27 November 1944 and that GEN 52/1 was then drafted through circulation of memoranda and informal meetings.

74 CAB 79/84, COS 397(44)8(O), 12 December 1944, and attached Confidential Annexe.

75 Minute from Ismay to Radcliffe, 19 December 1944, FO 898/395.

76 CAB 119/122, f. 51.

77 CAB 105/48, JSM 537, 24 January 1945. The JCS notified agreement that 'the British COS and appropriate British departments in conjunction with SHAEF, should proceed to put it into effect'.

78 CAB 79/29, COS 27(45)12, 25 January 1945.

79 Minute from Capel-Dunn to Bruce Lockhart, 25 January 1945, FO 898/355.

80 JCS memorandum for CCS, 31 January 1945, FO 371/46791. The comments required that black propaganda only be used in support of the proposals at Paragraphs 7(a) and 7(b) of GEN 52/1 and that the wording of Paragraph 7(c) be softened.
81 CAB 79/29, COS 36(45)14, 5 February 1945.
82 Paragraphs 6(a), 6(b), 7(a), 7(b), 7(c), 7(d), 7(e), 7(f), 7(g), 8, 9, 10 and 11 of GEN 52/1.
83 Possible reasons for these shortcomings are discussed in the conclusions.
84 Minute to Harvey (originator not clear), 7 March 1945, FO 898/355.
85 Minute from Bevan to Sutton, 14 March 1945, FO 898/355.
86 Brief by Ryder for Bishop (Deputy Director-General of the PWE) 10 March 1945, FO 898/355.
87 CAB 119/122, JIC(45)123(O), 11 April 1945; PRO, CAB 79/32, COS 105(44)13, 20 April 1945. Extensive correspondence on the preliminary staffing of the approach is in PRO, WO 208/4210.
88 Telegram from Holy See to Foreign Office, 10 February 1945, FO 371/4679. German Catholics had been targeted by Sefton Delmer's organisation since 1945; See Paragraph IV. A (iii) of Annexe B to GEN 52/1 and Howe, Black Game, pp. 141–3, 151–5, 184 and 269.
89 Subsequent details on Periwig are drawn primarily from the two PWE files on Periwig: FO 898/354 and FO 898/356. The latter includes a folder on pigeon operations in support of Periwig. Sefton Delmer's personal recollections of the pigeon operations are in Delmer, Black Boomerang, pp. 210–212. Wilkinson and Astley, Gubbins, pp. 209–211 and p. 229, provides some detail on Periwig.
90 SOE paper on Periwig under cover of letter from Gubbins to Bruce Lockhart, both dated 26 March 1945, FO 898/354.
91 Garnett's history of PWE, CAB 102/610.
92 Ibid.
93 Ibid.
94 Ibid.
95 Minutes of third meeting of GEN 52, 30 March 1945, CAB 78/29.
96 Garnett's history of PWE, CAB 102/610.
97 Young, Diaries of RHBL, p. 371 diary entry for 28 November 1944.
98 CAB 79/84, COS(44)1039(O), 19 December 1944.
99 FRUS, 44/I, p. 522 documents State Department rejection of a similar proposal for a bogus Hitler announcement at the time of D-Day.
100 Sefton Delmer was cited as the source of the technical advice.
101 CAB 79/84, COS 407(44)10(O), 20 December 1944.
102 Minutes of second meeting of GEN 52, 27 December 1944, CAB 78/29. Delmer's account of the preparation of the plan appears in Delmer, Black Boomerang, pp. 195–9.
103 WO 219/4778, SCOFF 166, 5 January 1945. The page for SCAF 166 in CAB 105/158.
104 Garnett's history of PWE, CAB 102/610.
105 Confidential Annexe to COS 8(45)8, 8 January 1945, CAB 79/28, COS 8(45)8, Confidential Annexe to COS 8(45), 8 January 1945, CAB 79/90,
106 CAB 105/48, JSM 562, 21 February 1945.
107 Garnett's history of PWE, CAB 102/610.
108 President to PM, No. 655, 22 November 1944, CAB 120/856.
109 PM to President, No. 828, 24 November 1944, CAB 120/853.

110 Alfred D. Chandler, *The Papers of Dwight David Eisenhower – The War Years: Vol. IV* (Johns Hopkins Press, 1970), pp 2318–30 (Document No. 2140, cable to Churchill dated 26 November 1944; Document No. 2142 – cable to Marshall dated 27 November 1944).

111 PM to President, No. 915, 18 March 1945, CAB 120/853; President to PM, No. 721, 21 March 1945, CAB 120/856; PM to President, No. 919, 22 March 1945, CAB 120/853.

112 CAB 80/89, COS(44)1063(O), 30 December 1944.

113 CAB 79/28, COS 2(45)9, 2 January 1945.

114 Undated paper on Braddock under cover of letter from Templer to Bruce Lockhart, 23 January 1945, FO 898/397.

115 SOE report to Prime Minister for period 1 January to 31 March 1945, PREM 3/408/1; Carty, *Secret Squadrons*, p. 78. It appears that Templer's proposal for balloon dissemination was not pursued.

116 CAB 79/30, COS 65(45)2, 12 March 1945.

117 CAB 79/30, COS 66(45)3, 13 March 1945.

118 Churchill and Eisenhower appear to have been unaware of the difficulties encountered by the Germans in implementing their policy of civilian evacuation. The policy was abandoned on 3 March 1945, but reinstated at Hitler's insistence. See Hugh Trevor-Roper (ed.), *The Goebbels Diaries: The Last Days* (Secker and Warburg, 1978), pp. 32, 124 and 206, diary entries for 3 March, 13 March and 22 March 1945.

119 Memorandum from McLachlan to Bishop, 7 March 1945, FO 898/395; R. H. S. Crossman, Supplementary Essay in Daniel Lerner, *Sykewar*, pp. 325–6. Crossman described Churchill's intervention as 'infantile Machiavellianism'.

120 Internal minute from Bishop, 8 March 1945 FO 898/395; PWD/SHAEF Directive No. 2, 15 March 1945, FO 898/395; minutes of meeting (attended by *inter alia* Bishop, McClure, Crossman and Delmer) 15 March 1945, FO 898/395; PWE special directive, 15 March 1945, FO 898/296.

121 FO 898/47 contains details of all seven broadcasts.

122 Undated Casement plan under cover of letter from Capel-Dunn to Bruce Lockhart, 20 December 1944, FO 898/357. FO 898/357 is the PWE file on Casement.

123 Parliamentary Debates (Commons), 5th Series, 16 January 1945, Vol. 407, pp. 116–17.

124 Minutes of Casement meeting, 25 January 1945, FO 898/357.

125 Garnett's history of PWE, CAB 102/610.

126 Huguenot plan, 18 January 1945, and minute from McLachland to McClure, 31 January 1945, FO 898/399. FO 898/399 is the PWE file on Huguenot.

127 Garnett's history of PWE, CAB 102/610.

128 Ibid.

129 S. Sandler, *Segregated Skies: The All-Black Combat Squadrons of World War II* (Publisher unknown, 1992), p. 139.

130 'Black Propaganda Treatment of Unconditional Surrender' under cover of draft memorandum from Donovan to Secretary of State and letter from Donovan to Dunn, all dated 11 December 1944, FRUS 44/I, pp. 567–70.

131 Dunn to Buxton, 11 January 1945, FRUS 44/I, p. 579.

132 *PWD/SHAEF Operations*, p. 55; Soley, *Radio Warfare*, pp. 146–8.

133 Telegram from Murphy to State Department, 14 January 1945, FRUS *Diplomatic Papers 1945, Volume III – European Advisory Commission; Austria; Germany* (Washington DC, 1968) pp. 717–20,

134 Telegram from State Department to Murphy, 16 January 1945, ibid, p. 720.

135 Bruce Lockhart to Eden, 1 February 1945, FO 954/23. In the event, Crossman was not recalled; he remained with PWD/SHAEF until the end of the war in Europe, after which he resigned to launch himself on his political career.

136 Annexe I to Background Notes to PWE Central Directive for week beginning Thursday 25 January 1945, FO 898/296. This document comprises five pages of relevant quotations.

137 Extract from War Office Weekly Intelligence Review dated 27 December 1944 under cover of letter from Capel-Dunn to Bruce Lockhart, 6 January 1945, FO 898/355. ('It seems clear that the Russians are adopting exactly the policy that your Committee wish the British and American Governments to adopt.'). See also references to the 'Seydlitz movement' at Paragraph 11 of GEN 52/1 and Eric H. Boehm, 'The "Free Germans" in Soviet psychological warfare' in Daugherty (ed.), *A Psychological Warfare Case Book*, pp. 812–21.

138 Trevor-Roper, *The Goebbels Diaries*, diary entry for 23 March 1945.

139 M. Gurfein and M. Janowitz, 'Trends in *Wehrmacht* Morale', *Public Opinion Quarterly*, 10:43 (1946), 78–97.

140 *PWD/SHAEF Operations*. Exhibit 6 records figures of 75,000 for February 1945 and over 350,000 for March 1945. Between eighty-seven per cent and ninety per cent of these POWs had seen Allied combat propaganda leaflets.

141 Such assurances had to avoid giving the impression that German soldiers in Soviet hands would enjoy similar treatment; the Soviets were neither signatories of the Convention nor adherents to its principles.

142 McClure, Foreword to Lerner, *Sykewar*, pp. xvi–xvii; Brian Loring Villa, 'The diplomatic and political context of the POW camps tragedy' in Gunter Hischof and Stephen E. Ambrose (eds), *Eisenhower and the German POWs: Facts Against Falsehood* (Louisiana State University, 1992), pp. 52–77. The policy led to the creation of the categorizations of 'Surrendered Enemy Personnel' (British) and 'Disarmed Enemy Forces' (American); neither category enjoyed the protection of the Convention.

143 Parliamentary Debates (Commons), 5th series, 28 March 1945, vol. 409, pp. 1349–51.

144 Ibid.

145 Bracken's ministerial responsibilities for PWE included response to parliamentary questions on propaganda. For most of the war, such questions had been actively discouraged.

146 Parliamentary Debates (Commons), 5th series, 28 March 1945, vol. 409, pp. 1349–51.

147 Soley, *Radio Warfare*, pp. 146–8; PWD/SHAEF Weekly Intelligence Summary for Psychological Warfare, No. 33, 14 May 1945, FO 371/46894, pp. 3–5.

148 Young, *Diaries of RHBL*, pp. 369–70, diary entry for 24 November 1944. A similar reservation is recorded at Paragraph 3 of GEN 52/1.

149 Minutes of first meeting of GEN 52, 24 November 1944, CAB 78/29.

150 Undated Casement plan under cover of letter from Capel-Dunn to Bruce Lockhart, 20 December 1944, FO 898/357. Templer also emphasised the desirability of simple plans.

151 When CCS endorsement of GEN 52/1 was eventually notified, further endorsement by British ministers was found to be unnecessary.

152 Although Churchill had been briefed on the formation of GEN 52, eventual notification of CCS endorsement prompted the comment 'Surely we have already

refused to join this plan. Show me the file.' Minute from Churchill to Ismay, 27 January 1945, CAB 120/794.

153 Minute from Capel-Dunn to Bruce Lockhart, 25 January 1945, FO 898/355.

154 Young, *Diaries of RHBL*, p. 370, diary entry for 25 November 1944.

155 SOE paper on Periwig under cover of letter from Gubbins to Bruce Lockhart, both dated 26 March 1945, FO 898/354.

156 James P Warburg, *Unwritten Treaty* (Atheneum, 1946), p. 122.

157 Lerner, *Sykewar*, pp. 166–75.

Propaganda and Decline
in the Post-war World, 1945–91

A war that began with a cavalry charge in Poland and ended with atomic bombs on Hiroshima and Nagasaki saw a radical transformation of Britain's position in the world. Bombed, battered and bruised, Britain would never again be the engine-room of either world diplomacy or of global communications. The vulnerability of its Empire, epitomised by the fall of Singapore in 1942, required a new relationship with those scattered worldwide possessions that made Britain a truly global power. The losses of India, Palestine, Malaya and Kenya were not only the uncomfortable teething pains of the transition from Empire to Commonwealth; they were also the price to be paid for a country with a great future behind it. Like supporters of a once all-conquering soccer team that has seen better days, the British people found the post-war performance of its country, especially abroad, frustrating and disappointing. The past was always there to remind them of the inadequacies of the present.

It was small comfort that a former colony, the United States, became the inheritor of Britain's legacy to 'superpower' status – but at least it did ensure that an Anglo-Saxon perspective would continue to prevail around the word. It also meant that the English language would continue its advance as a universal language, the language of diplomacy and of popular culture. It was therefore inevitable that, once the damage of the war began to be repaired and Britain began to recover economically from its consequences, Britain should look to the United States for a 'special relationship' that stood firmly opposed to the perceived challenge posed by the Soviet Union in the evolving Cold War. Meanwhile, as Europe also recovered, Britain found itself torn between the drive for greater (western) European integration and Atlanticism.

It took several decades for these tensions to be resolved. In Eastern Europe, increased Soviet control, sometimes imposed by force as in Hungary in 1956 or in Czechoslovakia in 1968, helped to create a bipolar framework in which international relations operated right down to the early 1990s. The Cold War between East (Moscow) and West (Washington) sometimes flared up into 'hot' conflicts, as in Korea (1950–3) or Vietnam (c. 1963–75) but it remained an ever-present psychological framework for perceiving global events and knowing how to react to them. Within this psychological dimension, a global struggle for ideological allegiances was taking place alongside the more traditional military, economic and political competitions. This, together with the continued advance of communications technology, meant that cultural issues would be raised to the status of ideological battleground.

The advent of television, in particular, during the 1950s and 1960s helped to make this so. At first, television was largely a domestic phenomenon. With the extension of the nuclear arms race into outer space and the launching of communications satellites, it became an increasingly important factor in international affairs. In this respect, it combined the qualities of both radio and cinema and, once it had reached near-universal penetration in the First and Second Worlds (i.e. the West and in the Eastern Bloc) by the 1980s, it changed perceptions on a political, cultural and ideological spectrum that helped to end the Cold War.[1]

In the Third World, from which Britain was tortuously extricating itself, the press and radio remained the principal media through which ideological allegiance was sought. But the globalisation of communications in the post-war era made newly independent states vulnerable to the pressures of the Cold War. The British felt that rather than leaving a vacuum into which the United States or the Soviet Union might sneak, there remained a role for their continuing influence. It would be of a different nature and on different terms, as an adviser and friend rather than as a colonial overlord, but it would still require attention to matters of perception and presentation, and therefore to propaganda. Sometimes it worked and sometimes it didn't, and always it had to compete within the ideological framework of the Cold War and decolonisation. But the stakes were high for a country in irreversible decline which would need to survive by economic rather than by purely military means that Britain needed to sell itself now more than ever before. Selling democracy may now have become primarily the business of the United States, but Britain now needed to play its part for international and not just national imperatives. In this respect, the Cold War was as much a struggle for survival as either of the world wars had been.

Note and Reference

1 See Philip M. Taylor, *Global Communications, International Affairs and the Media since 1945* (Routledge, 1997).

10

Power, Public Opinion and the Propaganda of Decline: The British Information Services and the Cold War, 1945–57[1]

The Cold War provided Britain with a formidable propaganda challenge. As a Foreign Office document of December 1951 pointed out:

> The 'cold war' is a struggle for men's minds. It is a struggle to determine whether the mass of mankind shall look for hope towards the Soviet Union or towards the Western democracies. This struggle, however, is not solely a conflict between two sets of ideas. Power enters into it, and a third factor is that intangible product of power and ideas which is called prestige.[2]

This was not the kind of conflict that the British particularly relished. It had not been long since British power and prestige was held to be self-evident. Only two decades earlier, the Japanese invasion of Manchuria had set in train a series of events that was to expose the vulnerability of a worldwide empire that had seemed impregnable barely a decade before that. That vulnerability gave rise to a reluctant acceptance of the need to embark upon what the British preferred to call 'national self-advertisement' and what everybody else called 'propaganda'. During both world wars, the British had admittedly displayed an extraordinary talent for propaganda. But their attitude to propaganda in peacetime had always been less than enthusiastic. Yet the phenomenon of Britain's decline from being the only great global power at the start of the century to its position as a regional European power would, if anything, appear to merit a more positive and enthusiastic approach to public opinion and propaganda, not just at home, where the decline had to be explained or disguised, but also abroad where the business of 'national projection' on behalf both of British interests and of democracy itself was becoming increasingly essential in a world of competing ideologies.[3] Certainly, as the 1954 Drogheda Enquiry into the Overseas Information Services recognised:

> Propaganda is no substitute for policy; nor should it be regarded as a substitute for military strength, economic efficiency or financial stability. Propaganda may disguise weakness, but the assertion of strength will deceive nobody unless the strength is there.[4]

10.1 Challenges for Democracy

Propaganda may indeed ultimately fail to disguise weaknesses or the realities of decline, but it can also provide an illusion of strength and confidence that does serve to aid foreign policy objectives in most effective short-term ways. Hitler realised this in the 1930s with his highly effective disinformation campaign concerning the state of Germany's rearmament, which served to undermine the position of his potential adversaries. But democratic governments which purport to exist by consensus rather than by coercion delude themselves, or rather their people, into believing that the justness of a cause or the realities of a case will be self-evident to all concerned, and that little effort is therefore made to meddle in the democratic processes of freedom of speech, action and thought. John Grierson said of Britain that although her propaganda was 'not very scientific', 'she does believe, out of her liberal tradition, that telling the truth must command goodwill everywhere and, in the long run defeat the distortions and boastings of the enemy ... [in the] hope that an appeal to the Platonic principle of justice will triumph'.[5]

Plato, of course, also advocated that governors should employ censorship as a means of controlling opinion and morale and the British have always been less reticent about the use of this negative aspect of propaganda. But if propaganda is regarded as a process of persuasion it is just as essential for democratic regimes – perhaps even more so – to embrace the more positive aspects as it is for competing political systems. The history of the haphazard and 'unscientific' growth of Britain's overseas information services during the inter-war years undoubtedly reflected the dilemma of successive British governments whose inherent distaste for peacetime propaganda had to be balanced against the vital need to engage in at least some form of counteractivity. Not even the early years of the Cold War convinced them fully of this, for it was not until after the Suez crisis of 1956 that sufficient financial resources were provided to the essential business of 'projecting' Britain. The problem was that by the time the dilemma had been resolved, the British found that they were no longer the world's most powerful nation, that their ideological message carried less weight than that of the United States, that their propaganda was not backed up by the prestige of being the only world power and that, instead, their influence was being usurped by the superpowers.

The Cold War was indeed the apogee of the twentieth-century struggle for hearts and minds. It was by its very nature a global propaganda conflict, the alternative to real war. Machinery for the effective employment of propaganda, therefore, had become an essential weapon in any national arsenal, 'part of the normal apparatus of diplomacy of a Great Power'.[6] During the late 1940s, when the battle lines of the Cold War were being drawn, the Labour government in Britain found itself in possession of a permanent peacetime propaganda machinery that was increasingly ill-equipped to deal with the international circumstances of the post-war era. True, the problems facing it were formidable.

Not only did the government find itself presiding over Britain's declining position as a world and imperial power, but many of its supporters were also reluctantly abandoning their hopes of Anglo–Soviet friendship and grudgingly accepting Britain's role as an ally of the United States. Although by 1948 the Labour government had firmly taken sides in the Cold War, its worsening economic position, combined with events in Greece, India and Palestine, made it essential that Britain's case should not be allowed to go unexplained to the rest of the world.

As the Union Jack was hoisted down an increasing number of overseas flagpoles, the old 1920s adage that 'trade follows the film' (as indeed it follows all modern forms of marketing) became even more significant as war-crippled Britain competed in post-war world markets. It was equally important to ensure that, despite the increasing dependence of Britain's economy upon that of the United States, the national case would not similarly be allowed to become subsumed by the American. It was thus essential to embark upon the projection of Britain abroad in the widest possible sense, on the widest possible front and with the maximum effort. However, instead of increasing their national propaganda effort, the governments of Attlee (1945–51) and Churchill (1951–5) chose to whittle down expenditure on this vital area. As a result, just prior to the Suez crisis, overall expenditure on official information activity had reached its lowest-ever post-war level. Any correlation between this fact and the disastrous loss of prestige caused by that crisis awaits a historian, although the alienation of the media towards the government has now received attention.[7] However, even if the British Information Services had been provided with adequate support and funding to explain fully British foreign policy, it is likely that they would still have been fighting a losing battle.

10.2 A Permanent Information Policy

It is nonetheless important to identify the creation in 1946 of a permanent post-war organisation for the dissemination of official information both at home and abroad as a unique recognition in Britain of the need in peacetime to fuse national policy with propaganda. Naturally it drew on the experience of the inter-war precedents, such as the Empire Marketing Board's work between 1926 and 1933, the BBC Empire Service started in 1932, and the BBC's foreign language broadcasts begun in 1938–9. However, having entered the field relatively late in the day, Britain's peacetime propaganda before 1939 had largely been on the defensive. Perhaps democratic propaganda is inevitably, due to the very nature of a comparatively open society, defensive, but the failure to address adequately or positively foreign opinion was felt to be one more reason why Britain found herself so dangerously alone in the dark days of 1940. At least morale at home did not crack, as if was feared might happen, but how far this was due to the Luftwaffe rather than the initial misplaced exhortations of the Ministry of Information must remain a matter for speculation. What is certain is that sections of the wartime coalition government were determined that, on the return of peace, Britain must never again find herself in such an ill-equipped position from a propaganda point of view. Besides, for Labour it was one more way to argue for a break with the past and with the policies of the appeasers and the 'Guilty Men' of Munich. Labour could only have been impressed by the Conservatives' domination of the media in the 1930s and the way, for example, they had sold a policy of rearmament to a largely pacifist public through the National Government. They were even more affected by the unifying experience of the 'People's War'. A post-war national information agency would ensure more equal access to the public at home and a more coherent policy of centralised publicity abroad. In other words, for political reasons as much as perhaps for reasons of international competition, it was recognised that Britain must now engage seriously in an activity that rival powers found less unpalatable, not simply to defend her national interests but also to educate domestic and foreign opinion that Britain still had a major role to play in the post-war world.

The man who set in motion the train of events that resulted in the establishment of the Central Office of Information (COI) on April Fools' Day 1946 was no less a figure than Winston Churchill himself. This was not without its significance. In 1943, Churchill had created a committee of permanent officials and government ministers to consider the official machinery of government in post-war Britain.[8] The old Duff Cooper-inspired myth that Churchill was not interested in propaganda has survived even Martin Gilbert's mammoth biography. Yet nothing could be further from the truth. It had been on Churchill's own initiative, for example, that the Special Operations Executive had been created to 'set Europe ablaze' and although historical attention has tended to focus on SOE's sabotage and subversive activities it must not be forgotten that propaganda and disinformation were also part of its brief. Certainly, after 1941, Churchill was prepared to let his trusted Minister of Information, Brendan Bracken, handle the complicated day-to-day business of running the white propaganda machinery. But while Bracken often slept on the Prime Minister's sofa in the War Cabinet Rooms, many of his staff were projecting ideals about a New Jerusalem, ideals which were to manifest themselves in 1945.[9] In fact, apart from film, Churchill's real interest lay in negative propaganda, namely censorship. He had often taken time out during the hectic days of 1940–2 to involve himself personally in trying to suppress adverse criticism. And it must be remembered that Churchill himself was a supreme self-propagandist. A writer of great persuasive abilities, he also knew that radio was a more effective medium for his oratorial skills than was the medium he personally loved, namely film, and he deliberately avoided filmed interviews except where they were absolutely essential. During his wilderness years of the 1930s, Churchill had been squeezed out of the highly effective Central Office publicity machine, and he had had to resort to alternative private channels in order to ensure that his case about German rearmament was heard. As a wartime Prime Minister, like Lloyd George before him, he fully understood the importance of propaganda, but unlike Lloyd George he failed to exploit it for his own political purposes. And whereas Lloyd George had been quick to dismantle Britain's wartime propaganda machinery in 1918 for fear that it might be turned against him, Churchill returned to the wilderness in 1945 suspecting that his had done precisely that. This mistrust of official propaganda machinery was not to bode well for the information services during Churchill's second term as Premier.

Mindful of the traditional antipathy towards domestic propaganda and suspicious of the left-wing views of many of his staff, Bracken did not want to see the wartime propaganda machinery automatically converted for post-war use. The civil service officials, on the other hand, argued for some form of permanent peacetime machinery, feeling that:

> Though no doubt an elaborate or blatant Government publicity policy on the home front would in peacetime arouse suspicion and antagonism – more particularly after a return to Party Government – we take it as certain that Government public relations work, which was growing in importance before the war, will continue on a considerable scale in peace. On the other hand, since it is a subject on which Parliamentary opinion is extremely sensitive, the machinery must not be such as will lay Government open to political criticism.[10]

It was clear that, despite the potential political row that such a decision might provoke, Britain would at last begin to take seriously the business of peacetime propaganda on the domestic front. One has to remember that the first mass generation of enfranchised men and women had witnessed three disasters – the Great War, the Great Depression and the Second World War – which demanded that their participation in politics be channelled into democratic rather than alternative philosophies. That participation could be fostered through greater information; continuity of information policy was therefore essential.

Despite the politically sensitive issue of home publicity, however, it was clear to all concerned that the need for some form of representation overseas would be as important, if not more so, than it had ever been before. As the official committee on the machinery of government noted in April 1944 that:

> Whatever limitations may be placed on publicity at home by political and other factors, quite different considerations will apply to British publicity overseas and that, in the face of the efforts made by other countries, a positive British policy will command universal approval at home and pay handsome dividends abroad. In this as in other fields laissez faire is no longer regarded as good enough.[11]

Some form of professional post-war overseas propaganda, albeit on a reduced scale, was thus accepted by all parties – official and political – to be essential.[12] In other words, here the principle transcended party politics – as was quite right and proper given that the representation of Britain overseas was to be national and not sectional.

A major question, however, concerned bureaucratic responsibility for the work. It was essential that foreign publicity spoke the same language as domestic publicity. The Foreign Office, having pioneered government public relations before the war, was determined to reclaim its particular offspring. First Eden (who had been Foreign Secretary when the major pre-war expansion had taken place) and then Bevin, with the support of the Secretaries of State for the Colonies, India and Burma and of the President of the Board of Trade, promoted the idea of a post-war Government Information Agency (not the retention of the MoI but rather the creation of a new body) to co-ordinate the overseas publicity output of the various interested Whitehall Departments, so that British representatives abroad 'shall speak with one voice'.[13] Bracken's successor as Minister of Information disagreed, feeling that 'much the greater part of the subject matter of British publicity is the total British way of life, and in projecting this there is not the least likelihood of conflict with foreign policy as such'.[14] With such issues as the Beveridge Report and nationalisation on the new government's agenda, Foreign Office control over the new publicity apparatus would to his mind prove inappropriate, to say the least.

Prime Minister Attlee himself chaired a committee of a small group of ministers to look into this matter.[15] This committee concluded that:

> The projection of Britain abroad required the deliberate formulation of a comprehensive theme. Neither the Foreign Office alone, nor all the over- seas departments together could discharge this work. If followed that the formulation of policy for overseas publicity must be conducted inter- departmentally and under the direction of a Minister.[16]

Herbert Morrison, Lord President of the Council, also brought his considerable weight to bear in support of an independent Central Office of Information to serve as a co-ordinating centre for all government publicity at home and abroad, 'an organisation with ideas and a positive contribution of its own to make'.[17] On 6 December 1945 the Cabinet formally decided not to retain the MoI but to charge Morrison with the task of setting up a new organisation along the lines suggested by him.[18] The Foreign Office was able to ensure that respon- sibility for overseas publicity policy should revert back to the overseas departments concerned. And its established practice of rectifying misunder- standing, misrepresentation and misinterpretation abroad was to be continued, unlike in 1919 when the wartime propaganda machinery was shut down virtually lock, stock and barrel. The COI's role was restricted to that of a central national publicity agency serving the needs of Whitehall. This formula succeeded in defusing any potential political opposition at home while enabling the Foreign Office to conduct the projection of Britain abroad.

In 1946 it was stated that 'the basic object of British overseas information is to ensure the presentation overseas of a true and adequate picture of British policy, British institutions and the British way of life'.[19] This was, of course, the kind of area in which the British Council excelled. The Council had recently been the object of much criticism, and also of the internal Findlater Stewart Enquiry which recommended greater independence from government control but whose report was rejected by the Foreign Office for precisely that reason.[20] Its continued existence, at least for the moment, had been guaranteed by the Cabinet in February 1946.[21] By the end of the year the Foreign Office had determined the Council's role as follows:

> In strictly cultural subjects, which are defined as the English language, the British drama, Fine Arts, Literature and Music, the Council will undertake publicity and education directed towards any category of people and will use any medium for this purpose. In all other subjects the Council will undertake education rather than publicity and its operations will be directed not to the general public, but to certain defined groups.[22]

For this purpose it received a grant-in-aid of £2.8 million in 1945–6, restored to its wartime level of £3.5 million in the following year. It employed representatives in 46 overseas countries to target those 'certain defined groups', by which was meant elite opinion, the traditional target of the overseas information services.

10.3 Post-war Retrenchment

Even so, despite these decisions, the overseas information services continued to be regarded with suspicion by some, and seen as unnecessarily expensive by most, with the result that they were gradually reduced as peace wore on, the victim of annual cuts on 'a more or less arbitrary basis'.[23] The gross vote for the COI fell from nearly £4.5 million in 1947 to just over £1.6 million in 1955–6,[24] and although by that time the British Council's future had been assured following its five-year trial period, it too found its government grant reduced to not much more (£1.7 million in 1955). With the exception of 1953–4, when the figures were lower by a margin so small as to be irrelevant, the eve of the Suez crisis saw the lowest level of post-war government spending on the information services: about £10 million for the entire job, 90 per cent of which went on the overseas services and most of that on salaries. This, paradoxically, at a time when the need was for greater, not reduced, propaganda activity – both short- and long-term. The fact remained that many people unfamiliar with the day-to-day business of running a national publicity campaign continued to regard propaganda and even straight information work as an intangible, suspicious activity that could not produce clear results justifying the expenditure. British taxpayers were being asked to subsidise a campaign abroad, the results of which brought them no clear-cut returns or benefits. The overseas information services, operating as they do outside the experience of most British citizens, have always been a primary target for financial retrenchment and their vulnerability to political point-scoring at home, though perhaps inevitable, is enhanced at the hands of the uninitiated.

Perhaps because of this, the third annual report of the COI in 1950 chose to inject a sharper note of self-justification for its existence stating, for example:

> [The overseas services] are maintained in order that the people of other
> countries shall be kept aware of the kind of people the British are, and
> the kind of place they live in: in order also that the world shall learn more
> of the British Commonwealth as a whole, and especially of the Colonies.
> If accurate information of this kind is brought before the world, it is
> more difficult for misconceptions to arise of the kind that existed, for
> instance, on the Continent before the last war, and did something towards
> causing it.[25]

Using its more didactic tone, the report then went on to point out the four
main aims of the overseas services: 'to spread a knowledge of the things we
believe in, such as democracy, tolerance and social development'; 'to provide a
favourable background to the commercial selling of exports, by showing that
Britain is industrially and scientifically vigorous, that she makes reliable and
attractive goods, and that she has her share of new inventions'; 'the support of
British foreign policy'; and 'the great aim of spreading knowledge of the Commonwealth'.[26]

But now the development of the Cold War and the British role in the
Western Alliance meant that promotion was required not just at home but also
behind the Iron Curtain and in those Allied and neutral countries where the
British case had to be made or answered if economic and political influence
was not to be eroded. Moreover, Britain's position as an Imperial power, and
the transition from Empire to Commonwealth, had to be explained more adequately, both within the mounting bipolar context and in the colonies
themselves. After 1948 the British Council began to serve as the Colonial
Office's principal agent in the overseas possessions. The High Commissioners
were informed that the Council would help foster goodwill to Britain as the
dependencies moved towards greater independence, and that it could do 'valuable, positive work in countering Communist propaganda by showing that
Britain and the Western tradition for which Britain stands has something better
to offer than the Communist way of life'.[27] As Britain retreated from Empire,
it became even more important that the regimes which replaced London looked
to a democratic rather than a Communist model. In other words, cultural
propaganda was increasingly assuming a political dimension. The new Commonwealth Relations Office was only too conscious of this; Canada, for example,
refused to allow the British Council to open an office there until 1959. Added
to this was the element of marketing; Britain's post-war economic position
could be greatly aided by the use of propaganda. Explaining the British way
of life, so the theory ran, would cause exports to increase. Indeed, all the
essential characteristics of post-war national projection had already been established before 1939: qualitative rather than quantitative propaganda; defensive
rather than aggressive material; indirect rather than direct approaches with the
principal target audience being the opinion-makers rather than the opinion
itself; the emphasis on news and information as 'the shocktroops of propaganda'.[28] The work consisted essentially of long-term cultural activity, the

preserve of the British Council; and of day-to-day 'political' activity designed
to explain the government's position on any given national or international
issue, the type of work for which the BBC had inaugurated the foreign language
broadcasts.

In 1946, Sir Ivone Kirkpatrick informed the COI that 'the stage of winning
admirers and friends for Great Britain has now passed ... the time has come
to persuade each country to take specific action'.[29] However, although after
1948 the international situation required an increased use of both types of
propaganda, financial constraints meant that greater emphasis tended to be
placed upon the short-term, immediate counter-propagandist role of the information services at the expense of the long-term cultural activity of the British
Council. It seemed like the same old story. The information services as a whole
were constantly starved of adequate funding. The British Council was hit
particularly hard. As one official wrote in January 1951: 'We are engaged today
in a life struggle between two conflicting ideologies. The "cold war" is in
essence a battle for men's minds. The British Council is one of our chief
agencies for fighting it. Far from cutting down its activities, we should today
be thinking in terms of refurbishing its armour'.[30] Or as an investigatory
committee of officials noted in July 1952: 'in our view, the international situation, the Communist ideological onslaught on the free world, the need to
right the balance of payments and the necessity of maintaining Commonwealth
relationships, all demand an intensification of overseas information work'.[31]
The Foreign Office saw the role of information work as being to prepare the
ground continually for specific propaganda points, 'e.g. that the "Peace Campaign" is a fraud'.[32] But the government's overriding preoccupation was for
financial retrenchment. One Foreign Office official used an admirable analogy
in a most maladroit style when he argued that:

> The position of the British Information Services in 1951 may be compared
> to that of a football club which is trying to remain in the First Division
> with a team that has already had to be diluted with second-class players
> and has now begun to lose even these without replacement. The Club's
> prospects of success have dwindled much more than the percentage of
> money saved on first-class players, or the percentage of players lost. For
> such a team, concentration on the vital areas cannot mean concentration
> round the other side's goal. Further reduction of the side can hardly take
> place with safety unless the opposing team is willing to play some other
> game than football.[33]

Whatever this meant precisely, his point was clear. As another observer has stated
more eloquently of these cuts: 'it is impossible to estimate how much Britain
lost politically and commercially through this strange error of judgement'.[34]

Just as seriously affected, given that between them the British Council and
the BBC used up about three-quarters of the money voted for information
work overseas, were the BBC's External Services. The wartime reputation of
the BBC proved to be a major asset to the Overseas Services after 1945. Having

built up a large captive audience in Europe during the wartime Nazi occupation – by 1942 the BBC was transmitting in over forty-five languages – it was essential to continue the broadcasts not only in liberated countries but also behind the falling Iron Curtain. Moreover, as a Cabinet report of November 1945 pointed out: 'it is clear that both the Americans and the Russians intend to broadcast to Europe on an ambitious scale and we cannot afford to let the British view-point go by default'.[35] Nevertheless, it was urged that 'the BBC's reputation for telling the truth even when it hurts must be maintained, which means that the treatment of an item in overseas news bulletins must not differ in any material respect from its treatment on the current news bulletins for domestic listeners'.[36] This was the basis of the BBC's three-pronged approach to post-war overseas broadcasting: direct broadcasting in English and foreign languages from London (on medium-wave for Europe and short-wave for the rest of the world, including the Soviet Union); the re-transmission under licence of BBC domestic and overseas programmes; and the retransmission of London programmes on local wire broadcasting services. In short, the BBC principle was, as always, to let the British case speak for itself and not let the Foreign Office treat it like a ventriloquist's dummy. Indeed, so anxious was the BBC to regain its editorial independence that it even issued a directive to its newsroom to ignore all Foreign Office approaches unless they came from the News Department via the BBC diplomatic correspondent.[37]

10.4 Covert Propaganda

The BBC believed that what had proved an effective formula in wartime was good enough for the peace. The Foreign Office did not share this view, particularly in the context of the Cold War. In 1948, therefore, the Foreign Office sponsored a major departure from the accepted type of national projection with the establishment of a peacetime covert propaganda agency which was to prove less squeamish about irregular uses of radio: the Information Research Department (IRD). By early 1948 Bevin was more than ever convinced that 'the Russian and Communist Allies are threatening the whole fabric of Western civilisation' and called for the mobilisation 'of spiritual forces, as well as material and political, for its defence'.[38] The IRD was formed at the Foreign Office as a direct response to increasingly hostile Soviet propaganda in the wake of the communist coup in Prague, the escalating blockade of West Berlin and mounting pressure on Finland. Bevin wrote that:

> It is for us as Europeans and as a Social Democratic Government, and not the Americans, to give the lead in spiritual, moral and political sphere[s] to all the democratic elements in Western Europe which are anti-Communist and, at the same time, genuinely progressive and reformist, believing in freedom, planning and social justice – what one might call the "Third Force".[39]

This approach was to be secret, direct and aggressive, designed 'to pass over to the offensive and not leave the initiative to the enemy, but make them defend themselves'.[40] With all the force of Bevin's enthusiasm behind it, the IRD was in many respects a peacetime Political Warfare Executive; indeed, its first head was Ralph Murray who, together with several of his staff, had worked in the PWE during the war. Its job was not quite 'black' propaganda which, since the end of the war, had been the closely guarded and (still) highly secret preserve of MI6, but rather 'grey' propaganda, by which was meant the dissemination of biased information from an indeterminate source. The target was simpler to define: Communist Russia. As Bevin informed the Cabinet, the IRD would 'attack and expose Communism and offer something far better'.[41] 'Grey' was adopted because it was more direct and aggressive than white but unlikely to offend the Soviets quite so much as black. Even so, it was still a risky business for peacetime, and the riskiest use of radio in peacetime since the Munich Crisis.[42] The need for the IRD reflects the inadequate and essentially defensive nature of the Overseas Information Services in dealing with hostile Soviet propaganda, the impact of which was being most felt in the colonies. Bevin also wanted to target a different audience from that of the information services, namely 'the broad masses of workers and peasants in Europe and the Middle East' and although the IRD was not incapable of straying into black activities, particularly secret radio stations, it would appear that its work was initially largely 'grey' and directed at opinion-makers.

Information on the IRD is patchy indeed, but Wesley K. Wark has managed to extract some invaluable material from American sources. IRD material fell into two categories: the one consisted of 'secret and confidential studies re. Soviet policies and machinations which are designed for high-level consumption by heads of States, Cabinet Ministers etc.' and the other of 'less highly classified information suitable for careful dissemination by staff of British missions to suitable contacts (e.g. editors, professors, scientists, labour leaders etc) who can use it as factual background material in their general work without attributions'.[43] To distinguish its activities from those of the Americans, the IRD concentrated on areas threatened by Communism outside the USSR; 'wartime experience with resistance movements had shown it would be dangerous to encourage any premature development of subversive activities behind the Iron Curtain'.[44] Even so, as Wark has pointed out:

The very content of anti-Communist grey propaganda, in which Western values were set at a counterpoint against Soviet activities; the fact that the IRD had a mandate to respond to Soviet themes; and the pressures of the Cold War itself ruled out any such purely indirect approach. Although the IRD never attempted to construct anything like the orchestrated propaganda directed by the CIA against the Soviet Union, known inside the Agency as the 'mighty Wurlitzer', it was quite prepared to respond to Soviet targets as they presented themselves.[45]

Here again, then, Britain was on the defensive. Bevin's original idea had been to emphasise the weakness of Communism rather than its strength, that the IRD's work should constitute the nearest thing to psychological warfare in peacetime as befitting the conditions of the Cold War. His view was that American propaganda, by stressing the strength and aggressiveness of Communism, 'tends to scare and unbalance the anti-communists, while heartening the fellow-travellers and encouraging the communists to bluff more extravagantly'. British propaganda, on the other hand, 'by dwelling on Russia's poverty and backwardness, could be expected to relax rather than to raise the international tension'.[46] Whether or not it did this during the Suez crisis when the IRD appears to have been broadcasting black messages into Egypt must remain open to doubt.

This kind of work could not have been conducted by the BBC without blowing its cover as an impartial reporter of British news and views. Even the 1954 Drogheda Enquiry concluded that the BBC's popularity abroad 'depends above all on its high reputation for objective and honest news reporting'. It continued:

> We believe this to be a priceless asset which sets the BBC apart from other national broadcasting systems. This high reputation for objectivity must be maintained at all costs and we would deplore any attempt to use the BBC for anything in the way of direct propaganda of the more obvious kind. This is not to suggest that the BBC External Services are not, in fact, a weapon of propaganda. The best and most effective propaganda to many countries consists of a factual presentation of the news and of British views concerning the news.[47]

This was a rare giveaway. More usually the relationship between the government and the BBC, and between news and propaganda, was deliberately fudged in official public documents, as in the case of the July 1957 White Paper on the Overseas Information Services which stated:

> The BBC enjoys independence of programme content. In the Government's view the impartiality and objectivity of the BBC is a national asset of great value, and the independence which the Corporation now enjoys must be maintained. This independence is consistent with a close liaison between overseas departments and the BBC on the basis of mutual confidence and understanding.[48]

But as Beresford Clark was prepared to admit to a Chatham House audience that could not be fobbed off quite so easily in 1959: 'we do not pull our punches in offering explanation or interpretation of news ... our aim in all such comment is to serve the national interest'.[49] This often-used and deliberately vague phrase is of course written into the terms of the BBC's charter, indicating that the BBC sees its role in a different light to that of the Foreign Office. But the FO also recognises the value of a domestic insistence on the so-called independence of the BBC; it serves to reiterate to foreigners that the BBC is not HMG. It is slightly more difficult to explain the peculiarly British nature of the British

Council's relationship to the government – 'officially unofficial', in John Buchan's memorable phrase – and this was indeed the case in 1949 and 1950
following the defection to the Russians of two Council representatives, one in
Poland and one in Czechoslovakia, which coincided with the collapse of much
of the cultural programme in Eastern Europe.[50]

Thereafter, under Churchill's government, the British information services
were forced to concentrate their diminishing resources on areas chiefly outside
Europe – in Asia and Africa principally – that were principal battlegrounds in
the Cold War. 'Scarcely a country could be named where it is imperceptible
or whose capture by Communism could not affect the fortunes of the
west',[51] ran one 1951 review. Nearly everywhere, however, British efforts paled
into insignificance when compared to the extent of American activity and the
British case was frequently pushed into the background. Nor was Britain helped
by the closure of offices on the spot: 'the disappearance of evidence of British
interest in an area is all too liable to be interpreted as a sign that the United
Kingdom either is bankrupt or has "written off" the area in question, or both'.[52]
In South-East Asia, an area of expansion, all the problems of competing with
a louder and wealthier American voice were experienced during the Korean
War. In Western Europe, an area of contraction, the British case was likewise
being subsumed, but here the problem derived more from Britain's inability
to come to terms with herself either as a European Power or as an Atlantic
Power. If in the meantime Britain was to employ the Commonwealth as a
means of strengthening either role, decolonisation had to be carefully handled,
not just to ensure that some form of Commonwealth survived but also to
explain to American allies that it was not simply the old Imperialism in a new
disguise.

Considerable attention was therefore given by post-war governments to the
image of Britain in the United States. The problem for the British overseas
information services under the Labour government essentially derived from
the existence of a socialist administration committed to radical change presiding
over a crippled economy, while instructing its information machinery to
advocate continuity, tradition and vitality. However, if the reality of Britain's
post-war position was decline, no amount of propaganda could disguise that
reality. Britain's economic and political performance spoke for itself. The
'Britain Can Make It' Exhibition of 1946 reflected the Labour government's
belief that Britain could indeed make it back on the road to recovery while
building a 'New Jerusalem' for its citizens. But as the Festival of Britain
revealed to any with a discerning eye in 1951, Britain was quite obviously no
longer the workshop of the world. Propaganda, however effective it may have
proved in the short term, could not disguise that simple long-term fact. The
Labour government's failure was that it was committed to an information policy
designed to project an image abroad of confidence and economic recovery, but
the gap between that image and the reality was quite simply too wide for the
information services to achieve that goal.

Certainly the Conservative administration presided over a more prosperous period but the information services found initially that they had few friends in Churchill's cabinet. Even a sympathetic Eden could not protect the British Council or the BBC from continued cuts, and the Drogheda Enquiry of 1952–54, one suspects, was appointed to justify the policy of a report which advocated radical increases in expenditure. It took the Suez crisis finally to convince most in power of the wisdom of systematically cultivating the image of Britain abroad and of explaining seriously the day-to-day business of government policy. However, as Sir Ian Jacob, Director-General of the BBC, pointed out in 1957:

> You cannot create an illusion, at any rate for long. Our success ultimately depends upon the successful conduct and policy of this country, upon the achievements of British people and upon the maintenance of Britain as a world force.[53]

Here indeed was the heart of the problem. No matter how unpalatable it was for successive post-war British governments to swallow, the fact remained that Britain was indeed losing an Empire and had not yet found a role. True, it had acquired an atomic bomb that served to obscure to some degree the extent of its declining position in world affairs. But until that new role had been fully decided upon, until Britain finally defined its position between Europe and the United States, its information services would always be on the defensive. In the meantime, given that since there were fewer and fewer British ships on the high seas and more and more jars of Fortnum and Mason's jam in the department stores of New York, Paris and Rome, perhaps all was not quite lost. The Coronation of Queen Elizabeth II revealed that Britain did indeed have a genuinely marketable product in terms of national projection. But the product consisted of monarchy, ceremony, tradition and culture rather than a vital, forward-looking economy that could compete with the best across a broad range of manufactured goods. The past, or better still an illusion of the past, rather than the future provided Britain with its most profitable propaganda opportunity. So soon after the finest hour of 1940 and the euphoria of VE Day, this was perhaps too difficult for anyone to stomach, and the projection of Britain abroad was a casualty of this process of transition which only the Suez crisis could finally complete. It is axiomatic that policy and propaganda must work hand in hand. The failure of Britain's information services in the decade after the Second World War was not so much due to an actual divorce of policy from propaganda, but to the fact that policy was being determined without adequate consideration of the problems of presentation. In the climate of the Cold War, in the context of Britain's post-war decline, in the new rules governing Britain's role in international affairs and its retreat from Empire, this was simply inviting disaster.

Notes and References

1 This chapter was originally published under the same title in E. di Nolfo, *Power In Europe? II. Great Britain, France, Germany and Italy and the Origins of the EEC, 1952–57* (Vol. 2, Walter de Gruyter, 1992), pp. 445–61.

2 Unsigned memorandum, 'Information, Propaganda and the Cold War', 10 December 1951. FO 953/1051.

3 Philip M. Taylor, *The Projection of Britain, 1919–39* (Cambridge University Press, 1981).

4 Summary of the Report of the Independent Committee of Enquiry into the Overseas Information Services, April 1954, Cmd 9138.

5 F. Hardy (ed.), *Grierson on Documentary* (Collins, 1946), p. 170.

6 Summary of the Report of the Independent Committee of Enquiry into the Overseas Information Services, April 1954, Cmd 9138.

7 See Tony Shaw, *Eden, Suez and the Mass Media: Propaganda and Persuasion during the Suez Crisis* (I. B. Taurus, 1996).

8 CAB 66/42, WP (43) 476, 23 August 1943.

9 N. Pronay, '"The Land of Promise": the projection of peace aims in Britain' in K. R. M. Short (ed.), *Film and Radio Propaganda in World War Two* (Croom Helm, 1983).

10 Further report by the official committee on the machinery of government, 24 April 1944. PRO CAB 87/74, WP (44) 482, MGO 47.

11 Ibid.

12 See the memorandum by the Minister of Information, September 1945. PRO CAB 129/5, CP (45) 316, Annexe IV.

13 Note by E. Bevin, undated. PRO CAB 129/5, CP (45) 316, Annexe II.

14 Note by the Minister of Information, 13 November 1945, CAB 129/5, CP (45) 316, Annexe III.

15 Note by C. R. Attlee, 30 November 1945, CAB 129/5, CP (45) 316.

16 Minutes of a meeting of the Cabinet committee on the post-war organisation of government publicity, 18 September 1945, CAB 78/37, GEN 85/1.

17 Report by Herbert Morrison, 23 November 1945, in CAB 129/5, CP (45) 316.

18 CAB 128/, CM (45) 60th meeting, conclusion 6.

19 Report of the committee on government information services, 9 February 1946, CAB 129/7, CP (46) 54.

20 F. Donaldson, *The British Council: The First Fifty Years* (Cape, 1984), p. 132.

21 CAB 128, 21 February 1946. See also 'The future of the British Council', CAB 128/5, CM (17) 46.

22 'Definition of the work of the British Council', 3 December 1946. BW 1/27, P 802/718/907.

23 Summary of the Report of the Independent Committee of Enquiry into the Overseas Information Services, April 1954. Cmd 9138.

24 Sir F. Clark, *The Central Office of Information* (Allen and Unwin, 1970), p. 172.

25 Third annual report of the Central Office of Information for the year 1949–50 (HMSO, 1950).

26 Ibid.

27 Colonial Office circular from Sir Charles Jeffries, 28 November 1949, British Council archives, GEN/682/6.

28 Sir John Reith, *Into the Wind* (Hodder and Stoughton, 1949), p. 354.
29 Minutes of the ninth meeting of the Overseas Production Conference at the COI, 9 July 1946, INF 12/61, OP (46).
30 Sir J. Troutbeck to E. Davies, 27 February 1951, FO 924/892, CRA 20/28/51.
31 Cited in Summary of the Report of the Independent Committee of Enquiry into the Overseas Information Services, April 1954. Cmd 9138.
32 Unsigned memorandum, Information, Propaganda and the Cold War, 10 December 1951, FO 953/1051.
33 Ibid.
34 Cited in Donaldson, *British Council* p. 177.
35 Report on Broadcasting Policy by the Lord President of the Council, the Minister of Information, the Postmaster General and the Minister of State, 20 November 1945, CAB 129/4, CP (45) 293.
36 Ibid.
37 T. Barnam, *Diplomatic Correspondent* (Hamish Hamilton, 1968), p. 192.
38 See E. Bevin, 'The first aim of British foreign policy', CAB 129/23, CP (48) 6.
39 Ibid.
40 Ibid.
41 Ibid.
42 N. Pronay and Philip M. Taylor, '"An improper use of broadcasting ..." The British government and clandestine radio operations against Germany during the Munich crisis', *Journal of Contemporary History*, 19:3 (1984), 357–84.
43 W. K. Wark, 'Coming in from the Cold: British propaganda and Red Army defectors, 1945–52', *International History Review*, 9:1 (1987), 48–72.
44 Ad-Hoc committee on anti-Communist propaganda, 19 December 1949, CAB 130/37, GEN 231, 3rd meeting.
45 Wark, 'Coming in from the cold', p. 54.
46 CAB 129/23, CP (48) 8.
47 Summary of the Report of the Independent Committee of Enquiry into the Overseas Information Services, April 1954, Cmd 9133.
48 Overseas Information Services, Cmd 236, July 1957.
49 B. Clark, 'The BBC's External Services', *International Affairs*, 35:2 (1959). The myth – or self-delusion – that the BBC overseas services are not an arm of government propaganda continues to be perpetuated by BBC staff. See Peter Fraenkel, 'The BBC External Services: Broadcasting to the USSR and Eastern Europe', in K. R. M. Short, (ed.) *Western Broadcasting Over the Iron Curtain* (Croom Helm, 1986), pp. 139–57.
50 Donaldson, *British Council*, pp. 151–2.
51 Unsigned memorandum, 'Information, Propaganda and the Cold War', 10 December 1951, FO 9523/1051.
52 Ibid.
53 I. Jacob, 'The BBC a national and an international force', an address to the 8th annual conference of the Institute of Public Relations, 18 May 1957.

11

The Enduring Tensions of Democratic Propaganda in the Information Age

This book has in part sought to redress the neglect of propaganda and psychological warfare as significant instruments of British foreign policy in the twentieth century. There has been a tendency in the literature of mainstream diplomacy to dismiss targeted information activity as a simple sideshow or, at best, as an interesting adjunct to the political, military or economic strategies of the period. Certainly, in wartime, propaganda assumes a more visible position, but with the evolution of the British parliamentary system into a full democracy – in which all adult men and women had the birthright to vote once they reached a certain age – it also took a central, if less blatant, role as a function of the state. Debates about the House of Lords and proportional representation notwithstanding, Britain at the end of the twentieth century is a much more democratic society than at its start. Information aplenty flows from government to people, and in the opposite direction.

Although government now feels that it is obligatory to provide information about its workings, this is often taken for granted. Few people today, for example, are actually aware of the existence of the Central Office of Information or, if they are, they associate its activity with road traffic or domestic safety campaigns. This is regarded as pretty harmless from a propaganda point of view, if indeed it is regarded as 'propaganda' at all. Its officials are 'information officers' who prefer the word 'publicity', which has less perjorative connotations and implies that the motivation is designed to benefit not the source but the recipient. As such, it is seen as a useful and indeed important activity of a state functioning responsibly in the democratic context of informing its citizens primarily for their own benefit.

11.1 The Advertising Age and Popular Culture

This is, of course, a carefully cultivated self-delusion. If we take an exaggerated example to illustrate this, the argument runs as follows. The seasonal drink–drive campaigns paid for by the government out of the tax revenue of its citizens are designed to save the lives of the innocent at the hands of the irresponsible. Any 'publicity' which exerts psychological pressure on the irresponsible not to drink and drive benefits the innocent and is therefore a 'good thing' for the state to do to protect its citizens. Persuasion is infinitely preferable to coercion.

However, in reality, if road casualties are reduced in the process, this puts less pressure on the state-run National Health Service, which thus means that it really benefits the state, the source of the 'publicity' in the first place. Government publicity thus assumes the posture of benefiting both sides, which means it cannot be 'propaganda' at all.

The fiction is exposed by the parallel example of anti-smoking campaigns. Cigarette advertising is banned in certain places (such as on television) but not in the print media or on billboards. Why, given the pressure which smokers also place on the National Health Service? Essentially because the revenue from taxes on cigarette smoking is higher than the cost to the Health Service, and therefore it benefits the source more not to ban advertising on cigarettes. The official conscience is cleared by the introduction of a 'government health warning' on each packet and on each advertisement. Once again, the value of cumulative campaigns is illustrated by this example. In the 1950s, when smoking was still regarded as a 'glamorous' activity, the sort of thing that Hollywood film stars did, there began to emerge medical evidence that it may be prejudicial to health. But it took thirty years of gradual medical evidence, including later revelations about 'passive smoking', to transform attitudes towards smoking to the point where it was seen as an anti-social activity. The rights of the (albeit sizeable) minority who chose to smoke were put under increasing pressure to the point where the dangers of smoking causing hypothermia were almost as great as its contribution towards lung cancer!

Advertising has become the acceptable propaganda of late twentieth-century free market enterprise democracies. In Britain, as elsewhere, there are standards by which it has to operate, regulated by the Advertising Standards Authority. Some advertisements can – and do – cause offence, but generally advertising is felt to be 'harmless' because the people have the choice whether or not to buy the product. It is also upfront about what it is. In the 1950s, when experiments with subliminal advertising threatened to make it something else (something, perhaps, more akin to the alleged 'brainwashing' attempts of the Chinese in the Korean War?) that type of trick on the mind was banned. But what still makes it propaganda, let us call it economic propaganda, is that expenditure is made to benefit the source of the product, a benefit measured by profit. It is curious indeed that levels of tolerance towards this particular form of propaganda are much higher than towards 'political propaganda' which is why the latter seeks euphemistic aliases such as 'political advertising', 'information policy' and, more recently, 'spin doctoring'.

To some extent, advertising has acquired respectability over time. But it is also linked to capitalism. In the 1950s and 1960s, Britain's post-war economic recovery, which saw mounting affluence penetrate into much wider levels of society than before, was in a sense symbolised by the acquisition of three consumable items: the automobile, the refrigerator and the television set. Such phenomena prompted one writer as early as 1958 to suggest that 'entire brackets of professions and industries are in the "opinion business", impersonally manipulating the public'.[1] With the founding of Independent Television in

1954, the BBC's monopoly on broadcasting in Britain was broken and advertising was able to penetrate every home in possession of a TV set. This prompted Raymond Williams to write in 1962 that 'the organisation of communication is for profit, and we seem to have passed the stage in which there has to be any pretense that things are otherwise'.[2] Propaganda in the form of advertising also appeared more respectable because it was being conducted by private enterprise, and not by the state.

But state propaganda remained significant, as did other forms. For example, the growing number of imported television programmes from the United States, not to mention Hollywood films screened on television, provided unprecedented access to American values and the American way of life. Many scholars in the then-new disciplines of communications and media studies saw this as a form of 'cultural imperialism', a theme which was taken up by many Third World countries to demonstrate the continuing dominance of, and their continued dependence on, the West in terms of news, information and entertainment.[3] This debate, in turn, became caught up in the Cold War. Indeed, academic disciplines such as psychology, psychiatry, physics, international relations and communications owe a great deal to government-subsidised research into Cold War characteristics and applications.[4] And, in turn, this growing realisation of the centrality of cultural movements and developments, especially after the 'youth revolution' and the arrival of popular music in the 1950s and 1960s, gave rise to new academic disciplines such as sociology and cultural studies. Marshall McLuhan and his concept of the 'global village' became extremely fashionable, while western academic research focused on communications as a great force for liberating and empowering the individual. 'Knowledge is power' became almost a synonym for democracy.

By way of contrast, the Soviet Union and its Communist allies positioned 'propaganda' at the centre of their domestic and foreign policies. Looking back, it is possible to see that this fitted in well with the self-delusion of people in western liberal democracies that propaganda was something that only the enemy engaged in. It was also itself a major western propaganda theme of the Cold War. Regimes so devious that they were prepared to engage in such dirty tricks as propaganda and brainwashing fuelled the fear of 'the enemy', especially once that enemy acquired the bomb, and therefore the need for consistently high defence budgets to act as a deterrent against its use. Popular culture reflected and reinforced this climate by producing films and programmes for the new medium of television that exploited fear of the enemy through the genres of science fiction, spy fiction and even the western. One theme of this cultural output was that the enemy without was possibly also an enemy within. Alien invaders deviously adopted human forms to secure control over individual will, as in *The Invasion of the Body Snatchers*,[5] a Hollywood movie in which the society under attack looked suspiciously like an American view of America facing a Soviet invasion. Elsewhere, spies were traitors who looked like us but who hid under the bed, while savages besieging wagon trains ran in menacing circles around pioneers of the new frontiers of individualism and universalism.

So soon after the Second World War and the legacy of Dr. Goebbels, the word 'propaganda' was already inextricably linked to totalitarianism by the time the Cold War erupted. Indeed, words came to mean a great deal in a conflict which was, after all, seen by its architects as fundamentally ideological. At least, that is how policy-makers chose first to rationalise it, and then to present and thereby justify it, to their publics. One can detect in the official documents a considerable amount of nervousness about the rights and wrongs of this. Policy-makers first had to convince themselves that there was a genuine threat, and then they had to convince the wider public. Until certain key documents defined the nature of the enemy for them, and even afterwards, they hesitated in their convictions. Consequently, events would be seized upon in retrospect to justify arriving at that position in the first place and, to this extent, the prolonging of the Cold War became a self-fulfilling prophecy.[6]

If enormous amounts of money had been needed to explain 'why we fight' Germany, Italy and Japan during the war, then it should come as no surprise that massive amounts were expended on justifying not only fighting the Soviet Union on the ideological front of the Cold War era, but also massive expenditure on 'defence' against not just an imagined enemy, but a real one. If the West was to fight a genuine ideological enemy which threatened its very way of life, then that way of life would need to be articulated as never before in order to order to add substance to the shadow of a 'war' which wasn't really a war at all in any conventional terms.

Vigorous efforts to project western ideology, culture and America's role as the leader of the free world and the bastion of anti-communism would lead to later accusations of Americanisation, 'cultural imperialism' and 'coca-colonialism'. Indeed, in the 'megaphone diplomacy' of the Cold War, post-war debates about 'freedom', and especially 'freedom of information', became struggles to define the ideological framework by which heroes and villains could be clearly identified. While the Marxist-Leninist concept of information was that it should, by omission and commission, serve the best interests of the Soviet State, the West could label this simply as 'propaganda'. Interestingly, the Soviet authorities made no pretence about what they were doing; nor did they balk from using the word. Instead, they charged the West with hypocrisy, arguing that because information was a commercial commodity in the West, its supposed free flow was in fact market-driven, which merely made it a servant of capitalism and imperialism. Nor were these purely semantic arguments; they were fundamental to the global struggle for hearts and minds about which system offered the best way forward. They were also at the root over later debates concerning the creation of a New World Information and Communications Order.

With Nazi Germany defeated, it did not take much for the West to transform Allied wartime propaganda themes about the conflict being one between the 'Free World' and the 'Slave World' within a post-war bipolar framework. Even before the Truman Doctrine and the infamous NSC 68 document, the scaffolding for this framework had already been erected in key international agreements. The preamble to the United Nations Charter, for example, reaffirmed 'faith in fundamental human rights, in the dignity and worth of the human person, in the equal rights of men and women and of nations large and small'.[7] Its very first Article declared the UN's aims to be the promotion and encouragement of 'respect for human rights and for fundamental freedoms for all without distinction as to race, sex, language, or religion'.[8] The underlying philosophy was based upon an Anglo-American ideology that had first been defined by the Atlantic Charter in 1942 – from which the Soviets had been excluded.

The notion, therefore, that propaganda and democracy are incompatible is just as misguided as Northcliffe's notion that propaganda and diplomacy were incompatible. Democratic propaganda takes a different form, even in wartime, to propaganda conducted by authoritarian regimes. It has different rules of operation – such as its adherence to 'truth' – but when all is said and done, its motivations are the same. Propaganda is the deliberate attempt to induce opinions and actions desired by the source. But in more open societies, including in Britain itself, adherents of democratic pluralism pointed to the potential vulnerability of western public opinion to competing influences, including foreign propaganda. Certainly, the Soviet Union appeared to enjoy a considerable advantage insofar as competing ideologies were concerned quite simply because, within its own borders at least, it allowed no competition. For Moscow it was already becoming clear that the Cold War 'seriously impedes, if not completely rules out, the flow of truthful information about socialism and breeds negative stereotypes of the Soviet Union'.[9] This forced the Soviets to rethink tactics for controlling the terms of the debates in international affairs and to set the agenda of international discourse as a counter to the western-inspired declarations and organisations set up after 1945. For this the Soviets needed separate organisations of their own, and numerous 'front' associations were established. Perhaps the most famous of these was the World Peace Council, founded in 1949, which supported the North Korean invasion of South Korea in June 1950 and which was responsible for disseminating fabricated charges of US germ warfare during that conflict. 'Agents of influence', such as sympathetic journalists, academics and even intelligence officers operating in the West were also cultivated by Moscow in an attempt to get western opinion-formers to speak on the USSR's behalf and in its defence. The KGB conducted widespread *dezinformatsia* (disinformation) through what it later termed 'active measures' in an attempt to discredit western governments and alienate popular support for their policies *vis à vis* the Soviet Union, for example through supporting western anti-nuclear peace movements.[10] Overt and covert, the Soviets integrated active measures into their foreign policy at all levels. As Schultz and Godson have explained, 'as is the case with military, economic and diplomatic instruments, the Kremlin designs and employs these measures to support Soviet strategic objectives and operations'.[11]

The western concept of peace was an absence of war whereas the Marxist-Leninist tradition saw war as a continuation of politics by other means. The result of this was to see international affairs in terms of conflict, struggle and competition against any adversaries who did not share the same historical destiny. To this end, the media, instruments of communications and the messages they carried were all part of the same strategy, not separate from it, and thus were much more closely integrated in the Soviet machinery of state than they ever were in the West.

Of course, the authoritarian nature of the Soviet system greatly facilitated this central co-ordination and integration. In pluralistic western democracies, the establishment of state machinery for the conduct of international communications and propaganda made co-ordination a difficult problem. Hence bodies established to conduct external communications were barred from directing their messages at domestic audiences. In Britain, the BBC World Service was paid for largely by the Foreign Office, while the British Council conducted its cultural diplomacy also from British taxpayers' money. But the scale on which they operated was beginning to pale into insignificance when compared to the propaganda expenditure of the superpowers.

In Egypt, for example, the Soviets began to promote their influence in 1955 and supported General Nasser's decision to seize the Suez Canal in the following year. When the British and French colluded with the Israelis to attack Egypt so that they had a pretext to invade in order to protect the canal, it seemed that Soviet arguments about imperialist aggression carried some weight. However, US disapproval caused Britain to suspend the operation, seriously damaging her position – and self-confidence – in the Middle East while simultaneously underlining America's leadership of the Western Alliance. France, for its part, turned more and more away from Empire to concentrate on Europe. Third World governments saw the extent to which strong nationalism, in this case Arab nationalism, could defeat former Imperialist overlords, and watched with interest Nasser's employment of radio, in the form of the 'Voice of the Arabs', to achieve these aims. For their part, the British feared the destabilising potential of radio in the 'wrong' hands, and it was noted that with every broadcast which 'boomed forth from the Voice of the Arabs transmitter the British government desperately tried to tighten its grip upon those countries where its writ still ran'.[12]

The humiliation of the British and French over Suez, together with the rift it caused within the NATO Alliance, and the emergence worldwide of nationalist movements with Communist inclinations, therefore encouraged the Soviets to step up their propaganda offensive, especially now that order had been restored within the Eastern Bloc following the Hungarian uprising. The British, working through public and cultural diplomacy, did what they could to ensure that British interests were projected abroad in a general sense and, through their intelligence organisations, countered Soviet propaganda on its own covert terms. Militarily, there was a need for propaganda and psychological warfare in the wars of insurgency, in Malaya and Kenya for example.[13] But it was not really until the outbreak of the Troubles in Northern Ireland at the end of the 1960s that the central problem facing democratic propaganda in the age of television came to a head.

11.2 Northern Ireland

Because of the Thirty-Year Rule which operates in Britain, by which government files remain closed for three decades after an event, British historians become nervous when writing about 'contemporary history'. In the case of Northern Ireland, around which more propaganda involving the British has been waged than perhaps in any conflict since the Second World War, it becomes extremely difficult to separate fact from fiction, myth from reality, news from propaganda. But one thing is clear. The propaganda war surrounding the Troubles in Ulster has been waged chiefly through the mass media. In this sense, Northern Ireland presented a challenge for the British government not dissimilar to that presented by the Vietnam war for Washington. Could a democratic state which deployed its troops in the full glare of modern media attention succeed in achieving its objectives? Vietnam appeared to demonstrate that wars are nasty, brutal affairs which create situations that, if filmed, repel and offend television audiences. The problem in Northern Ireland was compounded by the fact that not only were British troops being deployed on British soil, albeit across the Irish Sea, but that their principal opponents were dressed as civilians. No matter how much British official spokesmen tried to demonise the IRA as 'terrorists' or to explain the military presence in terms of protecting Northern Ireland from itself, the sight of heavily armed British troops confronting stone-throwing children in the streets of Belfast looked bad. And it not only looked bad on the evening news bulletins in the living rooms of mainland Britain, it looked worse in living rooms across the Atlantic Ocean in cities with large expatriate Irish populations such as Boston, Chicago and New York. In short, this was a public relations disaster for Britain insofar as projecting British democracy abroad was concerned.

Initially, the British government sought to treat the Troubles as a 'domestic' problem which concerned no one else, and especially not Dublin or Washington. According to one critic, 'like a cancer Ulster has eroded freedoms and constantly revealed the hollowness of British claims to be the champion of democracy and free speech, or indeed, to run an open society'.[14] Certainly, the introduction of internment and trial without jury in 1971 seemed to reinforce this view, but the problem for Britain was that it was engaged in a struggle chiefly with a 'terrorist' organisation. As other terrorist activities around the world – from the Munich Olympics in 1972 to the Lockerbie incident of 1988 – have demonstrated repeatedly, democracies cannot overtly fight terrorists on their own terms. Hence the terrorist bomber invariably holds the advantage and, in the age of the mass media, thrives on publicity. Put simply and brutally, it would have been inconceivable for terrorists to operate the same way in Nazi Germany. This was what lay behind Alan Clark's controversial contention in 1997 that one of his solutions to the Northern Ireland problem would be to 'take out' around 500 people in Ulster overnight.[15] However, no British government could be seen to behave in this way. Attempts to combat 'the men of violence' had to be made through the secret services, intelligence-gathering, the law (i.e. the Prevention of Terrorism Act) and, as initiated by Margaret Thatcher in the 1980s, efforts to starve terrorists of 'the oxygen of publicity'.

Many of these efforts aroused considerable controversy. The extension of the IRA's campaign to mainland Britain saw controversial trials surrounding the alleged perpetrators of bombings in Birmingham and Guildford. Even Lord Chancellor Gardiner felt that the summary measures in Ulster itself were 'illegal, not morally justifiable and alien to the traditions of what I still believe to be the greatest democracy in the world'.[16] This type of inner anguish prompted Airey Neave, himself to be a victim of an IRA bomb in the car park of Parliament itself, to claim that 'we are losing the propaganda war in Northern Ireland' partly because the British media, with its tradition of impartiality, was not alerting the British people to the 'true dangers'.[17] The broadcasting ban on IRA spokesmen introduced by Margaret Thatcher was an indication of how the government attempted censorship as a weapon in the propaganda war, but the ridiculous sight (and sound) of IRA spokesmen having their statements read out on air by actors with Irish accents undermined this attempt to muzzle them. The process of banning television programmes on Northern Ireland (over thirty between 1971 and 1984) came to a head in 1988 when Thames Television made a programme about alleged IRA terrorists being shot by British special forces on Gibraltar.

This programme was *Death on the Rock*,[18] and it claimed the existence of a 'shoot-to-kill' policy operating in Ulster. Had the British government resorted to tactics that would have been more at home in Nazi Germany? This suggestion is what made the government so furious, and it attempted unsuccessfully to prevent the programme from being aired. This revealed the limitations of the government when dealing with a free and independent media, although it had proved more successful in persuading the governors of the BBC to cancel the programme *Real Lives*.[19] And when John Stalker, Deputy Chief Constable of the Greater Manchester Police Force, began to investigate the alleged 'shoot-to-kill' policy, he was dropped from the enquiry after two years, the suspicion remaining that he was getting too close to the 'truth'. Once again, we shall have to wait until the archives are opened thirty years after the event before historians can begin evaluating fully these events. In the meantime, we merely have snippets of information relating to the propaganda war.

One such tantalising snapshot emerged from the Colin Wallace affair. In the 1980s, rumours began to surface that that Wallace, who claimed to be responsible for the 'dirty tricks' or disinformation campaign in Northern Ireland, had organised 'Operation Clockwork Orange'[20] between 1968 and 1975. Wallace was a part of the Army's Information Policy Unit, that is its psychological warfare unit. Wallace threatened to go public because his 'black' propaganda activities also embraced intelligence service activities against British politicians such as Harold Wilson and Edward Heath. Accordingly he was dismissed from the civil service in 1975. His claims reveal the extent to which the British government was attempting to combat 'terrorism' on its own terms, including the covert insertion of articles discrediting leading IRA figures in the British press.[21] In this respect, Wallace's unit was within the tradition of the Foreign Office's Information Research Department, which had attempted similar techniques with Communist sympathisers until it was closed down in 1978.

11.3 The Falklands War of 1982

By way of contrast to the 'dirty war' in Ulster, the Falklands war of 1982 between Britain and Argentina allowed to London again pose as the champion of self-determination. This time, 1800 inhabitants of the Falklands Islands who wanted to remain 'British' appealed to the British government for help following the unprovoked Argentinian invasion of the islands they called the 'Malvinas'. London was helped by the fact that the government in Buenos Aires was a right-wing military dictatorship under the leadership of General Galtieri, whose track-record in suppressing human rights internally earned it near-universal condemnation, and therefore made 'bad guy' stereotyping of the regime and its 'dirty war' against its own domestic dissidents that little bit easier. The problem diplomatically was that Margaret Thatcher's staunchest ally, President Ronald Reagan, had earmarked Argentina as the spearhead of his anti-Communist drive in Latin America (known as the Caribbean Basin policy). Prime Minister Thatcher therefore knew that asking the United States to choose Britain over Argentina was asking a great deal, while President Reagan recognised that he needed the British as a loyal NATO ally in his new Cold War against the Soviet 'Evil Empire'. It will be fascinating to examine the archives to discover how the British diplomatic corps in Washington and at United Nations headquarters in New York managed to persuade the Americans once again to 'take a right view' of this British war, and to see how this process compares to the efforts made between 1914 and 1917 and between 1939 and 1941.

As for the American media, there was a sense of disbelief that the British seemed willing to go to war 8000 miles from home over 1800 sheep farmers in the South Atlantic ocean. *Time* magazine carried its story about the mobilisation of Task Force South under the cover story 'The Empire Strikes Back'. But once the Royal Navy Task Force passed Ascension Island, as British politicians talked of their resolve not to 'appease' the Argentinians, and as the British tabloid media excelled themselves with such excesses as 'ARGIE BARGIE' and 'UP YOURS GALTIERI', British propaganda emphasised the justness of Britain's cause and secured United Nations' approval to remove the Argentinian invaders by force before any negotiations over sovereignty could take place. Indeed, having the approval of the United Nations was becoming the moral yardstick by which nation-states felt that they could justify deploying their forces into military actions, not just internationally but at home as well.

The British had learned a great deal not only from their Northern Ireland experience but also from the American experience of the 'first television war' in Vietnam. It was widely (if wrongly [22]) believed that the media were responsible for turning American public opinion against the war in Vietnam, and the British were resolved that this would not happen in the Falklands. Accordingly, only 30 journalists and crew – all British – were allowed to accompany the troops to the South Atlantic and they were to be heavily dependent on the military for information and communications back to Britain. All the old military suspicions about the media being a potential enemy within resurfaced, as the 'no news is good news' philosophy described at the start of this book held sway. Of course, by the early 1980s, thanks to developments in international communications and satellite television, there was an argument that it was even more important to prevent news about the war's progress from reaching the enemy. But the fact remains that military-media relations were at an all-time low, and the censorship imperative outweighed the need to 'inform the public'.

The result was that, once the fighting broke out, news of events often took days to reach the British – and world – public. The military's near-total control of information flowing out of the war zone, combined with the media-unfriendly briefings by the Ministry of Defence back in London, meant that the British had found a way to wage war in the information age. The Americans watched with interest and, following their attempt to exclude the press altogether during the invasion of Grenada the following year, they began to develop the system of the 'news pool' that was first tried during the invasion of Panama in 1989 and put to the full test in the Gulf War of 1991. But the Falklands campaign was probably the last time that a democracy at war could be guaranteed a near-monopoly over the flow of information from a war zone. Developments in communications technologies in the 1980s, from the fax machine to the portable satellite phone and video camera, would mean that, in future, newly created live television news stations such as Cable News Network (CNN) would be everywhere.

The Falklands campaign revealed some further tensions for democracies at war in the information age. The tradition of impartiality in the British media, which carries with it an imperative to report both sides of an argument or case, is put to its firmest test when the nation is at war. In 1982, the press, and the tabloid press in particular, was highly supportive of the war to the point of hysterical jingoism. But the broadcast media, and the BBC in particular, came under fire for using such terms as 'the British forces' (instead of 'our troops') and when, starved of British footage, it carried material from Argentinian sources, it was attacked in Parliament for being 'unacceptably even-handed'. Clearly patriotism and propaganda are more acceptable in wartime, and the criticism in 1982 was a bit rich since the track record of British war correspondents in all wars fought since 1914 was as patriotic and propagandistic as anyone else's.[23]

A second element that came to the fore in the Falklands war was the issue of speed. As the media were becoming increasingly competitive, greater emphasis was being placed on getting the story first. The military, on the other hand, were prepared to see the story told, but not as it was happening. Rather, they preferred to delay the news long enough for it not to be of any use to the enemy. This was too long for the media, since old news is no news at all.[24] The irony of all this, as the Gulf War was to reveal, was that the public agreed with the military.

11.4 The Gulf War of 1991

Although Britain's military contribution to the multinational effort to expel Iraq from Kuwait in January and February 1991 only in fact constituted about 5% of the total forces available to the American-led coalition operating under United Nations' auspices, Britain's war in the Gulf was characterised by several unique features. Perhaps the most notable was the degree to which public opinion was overwhelmingly behind the war effort, as revealed repeatedly by public opinion polls and surveys. Moreover, thanks to the role which television, and especially live television, was to play, the British public were able to feel that they themselves were actually part of a war that was being enacted in their name. John Major, the Prime Minister who had replaced Margaret Thatcher in November 1990, was even reported to be channel-hopping as coalition aircraft launched Operation Desert Storm on the night of 16 January. The arrangements made for the release of information about the progress of the war to the world's media gave the British a central position, thereby providing what was essentially a media profile that was disproportionate to their actual contribution. Finally, Britain's government and people were considered by the Americans leading the coalition to be their staunchest allies, consolidating still further the 'special relationship' that had flourished under the predecessors of President Bush and Prime Minister Major.

Although the coalition was unequivocally American-led, the military contributions made by British forces in both the air and land phases of Desert Storm were important. RAF Tornados flew dangerous low-flying missions against Iraqi targets at the start of the war, and suffered comparatively heavy losses in the process. Equally, British regiments made significant contributions to what General Schwarzkopf described as his 'Hail Mary Play' as allied forces swung rapidly to the west of Kuwait and moved swiftly into southern Iraq during the 100-hour ground war. Codenamed Operation Granby, the British contribution also included 4 warships, 3 minesweepers and 6 supply vessels playing their part in the deception campaign to lead Saddam Hussein into believing that the coalition was planning a direct seaborne assault as part of the campaign to liberate Kuwait. The known cost to British lives for both the six-month-long Operation Desert Shield and the two-month long war was 44 dead (25 in action) and 43 wounded. In total less than 400 coalition soldiers lost their lives compared to an estimated 20,000–100,000 Iraqis.

Until the official archives are opened for public scrutiny, much will remain unknown about the Gulf War. This might seem surprising in view of the fact that the war appeared to be fought out in full view of global television audiences.

The war was certainly a major television event, in Britain and elsewhere, with an estimated 20 million viewers per night tuning into the main evening news bulletins, as compared to about 16 million daily newspaper sales. The British press, with the marginal exception of *The Guardian* and the obvious exception of *The Morning Star*, was overwhelmingly pro-war, although the quality papers such as *The Independent* often carried articles by such journalists as Robert Fisk and Richard Dowden who refused to participate in the newspool arrangements drawn up by a Vietnam-influenced American military in conjunction with the censorship-minded Saudi Arabian authorities. Such journalists became known as the 'unilaterals' and their copy provided stories which were not always in harmony with the line being put out by Central Command in Riyadh.

Another source of information for British audiences hungry for news about the war was the unique presence of journalists from coalition countries in the enemy capital under fire. Apart from again providing an illusion of a war being enacted for television audiences, the Iraqis permitted western journalists to remain behind after war's outbreak in the hope that they would be able to utilise western television for propaganda purposes. CNN's ability to keep transmitting live audio reports throughout the first night of coalition raids mesmerised audiences. However, because the coalition had deployed only precision-guided 'smart' weaponry in the form of cruise missiles and radar-evading F117A Stealth bombers, journalists were able to report only on pinpoint hits on strategic targets rather than upon massive civilian destruction. Western journalists were for the most part, therefore, told to leave on 19th January, leaving behind only CNN's crew and a few print journalists from countries such as Spain and Japan.

Throughout the first week of the war, the media event continued with the Iraqis firing their Scud missiles at Israel and Saudi Arabia, the American Patriot anti-missile missile performing heroics in intercepting them, the release of spectacular videogame-type footage by the coalition demonstrating the accuracy of their hi-tech weaponry, the parading of captured coalition pilots on Iraqi TV (with CNN duly retransmitting the pictures around the world, causing outrage) and the release of a massive oil spill into the Gulf waters. Moreover, as the coalition extended its air offensive against Iraq's NBC (nuclear, biological and chemical) installations, stories of increased civilian damage began to emerge from Iraq, including the infamous 'baby milk plant' at Abu Gurhaid. By the end of January, the Iraqis permitted the re-entry of western journalists into Iraq, operating under the careful supervision of Iraqi Ministry of Information 'minders'. In the first ten days of February, crews from BBC, ITN and from other national broadcasting companies were escorted to alleged bombed civilian sites at Nassiriyah, Najaf, Fallujah and Kirkuk.

Increased coalition concern about the question of 'collateral damage' came to a head on 13 February when two laser-guided bombs smashed through the roof of an installation in the Al-Amiriya suburb of Baghdad, killing nearly 400 people. The coalition insisted that it had hit what it had been aiming at, namely a command and control bunker that had been emanating signals to Iraqi troops in Kuwait. The television pictures, however, showed horrific scenes of carnage and the charred corpses of mainly women and children. The pictures were so graphic that many broadcasters, including those in Britain, chose to self-censor the images on grounds of 'taste and decency'. Nonetheless, even the sanitised images caused outrage in both the USA and in Britain – with CNN's reporter Peter Arnett being labelled the 'Lord Haw Haw' of the Gulf conflict and the BBC being described in the House of Commons as the 'Baghdad Broadcasting Corporation'. Even so, the pictures failed to shake public support for the war in those countries.[25]

Two days after the Al-Amiriya bombing, the world was momentarily relieved as Iraqi radio announced that it was prepared to withdraw from Kuwait. However, it quickly emerged that it was only willing to do so on certain conditions – including the withdrawal of Israel from the occupied territories. President Bush described the 'peace offer' as a 'cruel hoax' while Prime Minister Major followed suite by terming it a 'bogus sham'. On the same day, the countdown to the ground war began.

Coalition ground forces had already clashed with the Iraqis at the end of January at the Saudi border town of Ras Al-Khafji. Although the battle had eventually resulted in a coalition victory, with General Schwarzkopf dismissing its military significance as a 'mosquito on an elephant', it was heralded by Baghdad Radio as a great victory. From a propaganda point of view, it almost certainly was, with even BBC radio announcing that 'the day belonged to Iraq'. Given that the very same day the coalition had proclaimed air superiority over Iraq and Kuwait – greatly aided by the fact that almost 200 Iraqi air force planes had fled to Iran the previous week – how was it, journalists asked, that the supposedly battered, poorly-fed and badly led Iraqi conscript forces were able to launch an offensive into Saudi territory? The coalition accordingly stepped up its air offensive against Iraqi troop positions in the Kuwaiti Theatre of Operations and against supply lines and bridges in an effort to reduce coalition casualties once the ground war began.

In spite of a number of diplomatic initiatives to call a halt to the fight, by the Iranians and the Soviets amongst others, the ground war was launched at 04:00 local time on 24 February 1991. Coalition forces moved swiftly into Kuwait and southern Iraq, the latter move including American, British and French mechanised divisions which would swing right in an enveloping ma- nouver to trap the Iraqi forces who had been ordered to evacuate Kuwait early the next morning. Despite a coalition news blackout, the Allied advance went much better than expected and the news was simply too good to suppress. Even though advancing coalition forces were encountering minimal resistance, they were beginning to witness the consequences of a scorched-earth policy adopted by the Iraqis with the firing of Kuwait's 600 or so oil wells.

Kuwait City was 'liberated' on 26 February. To the north, General Schwarz- kopf announced that all the gates to southern Iraq had been closed. Three days later, television pictures were able to reveal what he had meant by this as the first footage of a massive convoy attempting to escape through the

Mutlah Gap was transmitted around the world. Caught in a trap, the convoy fell victim to Allied air forces who laid down an aerial barrage that one US pilot described as 'like shooting fish in a barrel'. By that time, however the story had moved on. On 27 February, possibly in an effort to salvage what he could from what was proving to be a 'mother of all defeats', Saddam Hussein agreed to adhere to all United Nations Resolutions concerning Kuwait, and President Bush declared 'a unilateral cessation of hostilities' – not a ceasefire, as the Iraqis were quick to argue as a device for proclaiming victory – and a halt was called to the fighting at 8am local time on 27 February. General Schwarzkopf met with Iraqi commanders at Safwan airbase to lay down the coalition's terms on Sunday 3 March. The enemy commanders had no choice but to accede.

So what issues emerged from the war that we can evaluate with some degree of authority? First, it is important to stress that there were essentially two wars taking place: the war as fought by the coalition's combined air, land and sea forces against the army of Iraq, and the war as portrayed by the media. The latter did not necessarily accurately reflect the former, and we will not know precisely how well it did this until the archives are opened. On the other hand, the media's war record is 'fixed', captured forever in print and on videotape. In a sense, the media were the story of this war in that they provided an illusion of open coverage in a climate of controlled information environments and censorship. The media reflected popular support for the war effort, and those few journalists who worried that the press corps had been caught up in the military arrangements and were thus serving the interests of Allied propaganda were themselves out of step with their audiences. It is these same people who are concerned that the public saw only a sanitised war, with the real horror not appearing on television. But all wars in the twentieth century – with the single exception of Vietnam – have been fought thus. The old cliché that 'truth is the first casualty of war' is also in fact the first reality of war fought out in the information age in which we currently live.

No one could argue that the Gulf War was about democracy. Kuwait was an authoritarian regime with values far removed from such western concepts. But western societies had become dependent on oil and so, in a sense, they were fighting to protect their way of life – which was how the war was 'sold' to the public in the United States.[26] In Britain, the press helped to sustain public support by personalising the conflict as a war against Saddam Hussein rather than the Iraqi people – which was in fact the line adopted by the government following the American lead. It was, moreover, portrayed as a 'just war' because the coalition was backed by UN resolutions authorising, in the words of one propaganda video, the 'Nations of the World [to] Take a Stand'. Saddam Hussein was the aggressor against 'poor little Kuwait', a 'new Hitler' who must be stopped by all 'freedom-loving' nations. And so, the war 'to liberate Kuwait' was stopped precisely when that objective had been achieved. Saddam proclaimed victory because he had taken on the west and survived. And so, as his principal protagonists Bush and Major fought and lost their next elections, he remains as an enduring reminder not just to the fickleness of democratic electorates but also to the stoicism of brutal authoritarianism.

Notes and References

1 C. Wright Mills, *The Power Elite* (Oxford University Press, 1958), p. 305.
2 Rayomond Williams, *Communications* (Penguin, 1962), p. 24.
3 For further details see Philip M. Taylor, *Global Communications, International Affairs and the Media since 1945* (Routledge, 1997).
4 C. Simpson, *Science of Coercion: Communications research and Psychological Warfare* (Oxford University Press, 1994).
5 *Invasion of the Body Snatchers*, film, directed by Don Siegel. Allied Artists, 1955.
6 For further elaboration of this argument see Philip M. Taylor, 'Through a glass darkly: propaganda and psychological warfare in the 1950s' in Gary Rawnsley (ed.), *The Sword and the Pen: Propaganda and the Cold War in the 1950s* (Macmillan, 1999).
7 The charter can be found at www.un.org.
8 Ibid.
9 V. Artemov, *Information Abused: Critical Essays* (Progress Publishers, 1981), pp. 8–9.
10 Richard H. Shultz and Roy Godson, *Dezinformatsia: Active Measures in Soviet Strategy* (Pergamon-Brassey's, 1984).
11 Ibid, p. 3.
12 Anthony Nutting, *No End of a Lesson* (C. N. Potter, 1967), p. 101.
13 Susan Carruthers, *Winning Hearts and Minds: British Government, the Media and Colonial Counter-insurgency 1944–60* (Leicester University Press, 1995).
14 Guy Arnold, *Brainwash: the Cover-up Society* (Virgin Books, 1992), p. 233.
15 *The Times*, 26 May 1998.
16 Cited in Patricia Hewitt, *The Abuse of Power* (Martin Robinson, 1982), p. 158.
17 Roger Bolton, *Death on the Rock and Other Stories* (W. H. Allen, 1990), p. 25.
18 *Death on the Rock*, TV programme, directed by Roger Bolton. Thames Television, 1988.
19 *Real Lives*, TV programme, directed by Michael Zander. BBC, 1985.
20 See Paul Lashmar and James Oliver, *Britain's Secret Propaganda War, 1948–77* (Sutton, 1998).
21 For further details, see Martin Dillon, *The Dirty War* (Hutchinson, 1988), pp. 197–208.
22 D. Hallin, *The Uncensored War: the Media and Vietnam* (Oxford University Press, 1986).
23 Philip Knightly, *The First Casualty: The War Correspondent as Hero, Myth-maker and Propagandist* (Harcourt Brace Jovanovich, 1975).
24 This issue is highlighted by Derek Mercer et al. *The Fog of War* (Heinemann, 1987).
25 David E. Morrison, *Television and the Gulf War* (John Libbey, 1992).
26 For further details on the propaganda war, see Philip M. Taylor, *War and the Media: Propaganda and Persuasion in the Gulf War* (Manchester University Press, 1992).

CONCLUSION

The New Propaganda: Psychological and Information Operations

Since the Gulf War, propaganda in the form of 'psychological operations' (or, in this jargon-ridden world of acronymphomania, PSYOPs) has undergone a tremendous transformation. During the 1991 war, PSYOPs was conducted extensively by the coalition against the Iraqi forces. Largely an American effort, what was once called psychological warfare was felt to have been responsible for actually saving the lives of 60,000 or so Iraqi soldiers who chose to surrender rather than fight. Thus more lives may have been saved by communications than were lost by the organised violence of war. Messages to 'surrender or die' were issued by coalition radio stations and by the dropping of 30 million leaflets. As a consequence, and especially in light of the arrival of a 'New World Order' in which wars between states have seemingly been replaced by wars within states, new applications are being tried for the targeted use of information in the brutal circumstances in which civilians increasingly find themselves.

This first became apparent in Somalia in 1992, when American forces forcibly entered the country on a 'humanitarian' mission authorised by UN resolutions. In fact PSYOP units had also been active in the aftermath of the Gulf War during Operation Provide Comfort, which attempted to supply humanitarian relief to the Kurds in Northern Iraq. But in Somalia, PSYOP units were essentially responsible for setting up a communications network between the intervening American forces and the local people they were trying to help, in a country whose societal infrastructure had all but collapsed as a consequence of a civil war between competing warlords. The experience convinced many that PSYOPs was not just a 'combat force multiplier' in times of war, but was also an essential adjunct to the activities of military forces in international crises where civilians rather than soldiers were the most significant target audience.

The most striking example of this newly emerging form of propaganda was in Bosnia after the Dayton Peace Agreement finally called a halt to the brutal fighting that followed the collapse of Yugoslavia. Posters, magazines, and radio and television programmes were used by the multinational forces under the umbrella of first IFOR (Implementation Force) and subsequently SFOR (Supplementary Force). As part of attempts at 'democracy building' after 1996, messages on how to return home safely, on the importance of informing on war criminals, and even on how to vote, were supplemented by mine-awareness campaigns and explanations about why international forces were present – not as invaders but as friends who were there to help.

Here at last was propaganda that democracies could be proud of. Other nations, including the Germans and the British, felt likewise and began to expand their capabilities – although they remained nervous about using the 'P'-word. Hence the Germans labelled their activity 'information operations' and even SFOR, under American leadership, conceded that a better label for what they labelled a POTF (Psychological Operations Task Force) was the 'Joint Combined Information Operations Task Force'. Nervousness about the historical connotations of propaganda notwithstanding, there emerged as the 1990s unfolded a realisation that information flow was vital in what were now being termed 'operations other than war'.

In such situations, especially, civilians were involved and this gave rise to a widespread debate first about 'information warfare' and subsequently about 'information operations'. Firmly entrenched within the democratic tradition of a 'strategy of truth', this type of activity was becoming more acceptable morally than at any time in the past. 'Our motto is electrons, not bullets', claimed one military official who clearly felt that persuasion was infinitely preferable to killing people.[1] In a dangerous world, where many threats were perceived to be transnational – such as terrorism, drug trafficking and organised crime – the battle for hearts and minds suddenly became an international issue, and one that apparently had greater significance than it had ever had before. As more and more nations became democratic, there evolved an appreciation that democratic nations tend not to go to war with other democracies – or at least they haven't done yet.

Yet certain states, especially those which are ideologically unstable such as Bosnia or Albania, continue to pose a threat to international stability once they collapse internally or become subject to ethnic or factional struggles for power. The brutality of such processes, including genocide – as in Rwanda and also in Bosnia – is made all the more alarming because its consequences can be seen on television around the world. The sight of suffering civilians, especially the 'innocent women and children' of time-honoured propaganda tradition, is felt by some observers to increase pressure on policy-makers to 'do something' to stop the horror before the eyes of a global audience. In these respects, the media become agents of propaganda on behalf of the damned.

When all else is said and done about such situations, watching democracies have a simple choice. They can intervene in such crises for 'humanitarian' reasons, or they can leave the competing factions to butcher each other and their peoples. If the pressure on the home front to intervene is sufficient to prompt the deployment of 'our boys', then there is a need to explain to the indigenous population of the target countries that 'our boys' are not in fact 'invading' – as the propaganda of the warring factions will undoubtedly proclaim. This requires communication.

Of course, as soon as someone with a vested interest starts communicating, they will do so in accordance with those vested interests. Democracies may delude themselves into thinking that this is not propaganda but is rather 'information', but they should have the courage of their convictions that, having made the right choice, their propaganda is in the right tradition, the democratic tradition that has formed the subject of this book. Democracies should not be ashamed of selling democracy. Democracies purport to represent consensus through persuasion, they respect individual human rights, freedom of opinion and freedom of expression and, when they have the courage of their convictions, they oppose those who would deny those rights. They are not faultless, nor, as we have seen, are they beyond using 'dirty tricks' – especially in wars against their enemies. But since their enemies are invariably non-democracies or non-democratic factions, they sometimes have to fight fire with fire. In the last resort, it is essential to remember what Neville Chamberlain said to the British people when declaring war on Nazi Germany in 1939: 'for it is evil things that we shall be fighting against, brute force, bad faith, injustice, oppression, and persecution'.[2]

Notes and References

1 For further details, see the chapter on PSYOPs in Philip M. Taylor, *Global Communications, International Affairs and the Media since 1945* (Routledge, 1997).
2 K. Feiling, *Neville Chamberlain* (Macmillan, 1946), p. 416.

Bibliography

A Note on Primary Sources

Because this book examines contemporary themes as well as historical evidence, a combination of historical and social science methodology has been required to acquire evidence. Straightforward archival research has been carried out in a variety of archives, but the Public Record Office at Kew remains the single most important source of material relating to government propaganda. Here, the archives of the Foreign Office, Cabinet Office, Ministries of Information and Central Office of Information, together with the files of the Political Warfare Executive and the British Council, have been supplemented with work undertaken in Washington, Paris and on published documentation. Work on less 'traditional' sources, such as newsreel material, has been undertaken over the years in the commercial organisations which now own this important 'record' of Britain's past, although alas the costs involved of working in such archives are often prohibitive for academic researchers.

For more recent activity, interviews and published articles remain essential. I have been fortunate in having privileged access to contemporary NATO personnel and journalists through my work on communications and media studies, particularly in the context of military–media relations. This has informed my findings on aspects of this book which extend beyond the confines of the Thirty-Year Rule. But, with the drive towards more 'open government', together with increasing amounts of information being made available on the World Wide Web, it is certainly easier than in the past to access information about what is going on all around us now. This, plus the archives of the Institute of Communications Studies at the University of Leeds, especially relating to the Gulf War Archive of worldwide broadcast output, empowers the historian to apply historical methodology on more recent sources. Media output, though often very unreliable, thus becomes an essential source of information – but it does have to be handled carefully and supplemented by other sources. These include not only newspapers and radio and television programmes but also interviews and the kind of audience research conducted by Dr David Morrison's research unit at the Institute. In short, although embedded in historical method, this book is based upon a multi-disciplinary approach to a subject that is, after all, multi-disciplinary.

Secondary Sources

Adams, J. C., *Seated with the Mighty: a Biography of Sir Gilbert Parker* (Borealis Press, 1979).

Adamthwaite, A. P., 'The British Government and the Media, 1937–38', *Journal of Contemporary History*, 18 (1983), 281–97.

Aldgate, Anthony, *Cinema and History: British Newsreels and the Spanish Civil War* (Scolar Press, 1979).

Aldgate, Anthony, 'Creative tensions: *Desert Victory*, the Army Film Unit and Anglo-American rivalry, 1943–45', in Philip M. Taylor (ed.), *Britain and the Cinema in the Second World War* (Macmillan, 1988), pp. 144–67.

Aldgate, Anthony, 'Mr. Capra goes to war: Frank Capra, the British Army Film Unit, and Anglo-American travails in the production of "Tunisian Victory"', *Historical Journal of Film, Radio and Television*, 11 (1991), pp. 24–5.

Ambrose, Stephen E., *The Supreme Commander: The War Years of General Dwight D. Eisenhower* (Doubleday, 1970).

Andrew, C., *Secret Service* (Heinemann, 1985).

Andrew, C. and D. Dilks (eds), *The Missing Dimension* (Macmillan, 1984).

Arnold, Guy, *Brainwash: The Cover-up Society* (Virgin Books, 1992).

Artemov, V., *Information Abused: Critical Essays* (Progress Publishers, 1981).

Assersohn, F. J., 'Policy and Propaganda: the presentation of the Strategic Air Offensive in the British Mass Media, 1939–45' (MA thesis, University of Leeds, 1989).

Baird, Jay W., *The Mythical World of Nazi War Propaganda, 1939–1945* (University of Minnesota Press, 1974).

Baker White, John, *The Big Lie* (George Mann, 1973).

Balfour, M., *States and Mind* (Publisher unknown, 1953).

Balfour Michael, *Four-Power Control in Germany and Austria: Part I – Germany* (Publisher unknown, 1956).

Balfour, Michael, *Propaganda in War, 1939–1945: Organisations, Policies and Publics in Britain and Germany* (Routledge & Kegan Paul, 1979).

Barnam, T., *Diplomatic Correspondent* (Hamish Hamilton, 1968).

Barnouw, Erik, 'Propaganda at Radio Luxembourg: 1944–1945' in K. R. M. Short (ed.), *Film and Radio Propaganda in World War Two* (Croom Helm, 1983).

Bartlett, V., *This is My Life* (Chatto and Windus, 1937).

Bassinger, Jeanine, *The World War II Combat Film: Anatomy of a Genre* (Columbia University Press, 1986).

Beaverbrook, Lord, *Men and Power, 1917–18* (Collins, 1956).

Beichman, A., 'Hugger mugger in Old Queen Street', *Journal of Contemporary History*, 15:4 (1978).

Bell, P. M. H., *John Bull and the Bear: British Public Opinion, Foreign Policy and the Soviet Union, 1941–45* (Arnold, 1990).

Berchtold, W. E., 'The world propaganda war', *North American Review*, 238 (1934), 421–30.

Blanco White, A., *The New Propaganda* (Gollancz, 1939).

Bolton, Roger, *Death on the Rock and Other Stories* (W. H. Allen, 1990).

Bond, B., *British Military Policy between the Two World Wars* (Oxford University Press, 1980).

Bond, B. (ed.), *Chief of Staff: the Diaries of Lieutenant-General Sir Henry Pownall, Vol. 2, 1940–44* (Leo Cooper, 1974).

Briggs, A., *The Birth of Broadcasting* (Oxford University Press, 1961).

Briggs, A., *The Golden Age of Wireless* (Oxford University Press, 1965).

Briggs, A., *The War of Words* (Oxford University Press, 1970).

Brownrigg, Rear-Admiral Sir Douglas, *Indiscretions of the Naval Censor* (Cassell, 1920).

Bruce Lockhart, Robert, *Comes the Reckoning* (Arno Press, 1947).

Bruce Lockhart, Robert, 'Political Warfare', *Journal of the Royal United Service Institution*, 95:578 (May 1950).

Bruntz, G. C., *Allied Propaganda and the Collapse of the German Empire in 1918* (Stanford University Press, 1938).

Buitenhuis, P., *The Great War of Words* (Batsford, 1989).

Butcher, Captain Harry C., *Three Years with Eisenhower: The Personal Diary of Captain Harry C Butcher USNR – Naval Aide to General Eisenhower, 1942 to 1945* (Simon & Schuster, 1946).

Calder, K. J., *Britain and the Origins of the New Europe, 1914–18* (Cambridge University Press, 1976).

Capra, F., *The Name Above the Title: An Autobiography* (Da Capo Press, 1972).

Carmichael, Jane, 'Army photographers in North-West Europe', *Imperial War Museum Review*, 7 (1994).

Carr, E. H., 'Propaganda in international politics', *Oxford Pamphlets on World Affairs*, 16, (1939).

Carroll, Wallace, *Persuade or Perish* (Houghton Mifflin & Co., 1948).

Carruthers, Susan, *Winning Hearts and Minds* (Leicester University Press, 1995).

Carty, Pat, *Secret Squadrons of the Eighth* (Brassey's, 1980).

Casadio, G., 'Images of the war in Italy: the record made by the Army Film and Photographic Unit in Emilia Romagna, 1944–45', *Imperial War Museum Review*, 4 (1989).

Chalmers Mitchell, P., *My Fill of Days* (Murray, 1937).

Chandler, Alfred D, *The Papers of Dwight David Eisenhower – The War Years: Vol. IV* (Johns Hopkins Press, 1970).

Charteris, Brig-Gen. J., *At G. H. Q.* (Cassell, 1931.)

Christie, I. (ed.), *Powell, Pressburger and Others* (British Film Institute, 1978).

Clark, B., 'The BBC's External Services', *International Affairs*, 35:2 (1959).

Clark, Sir F., *The Central Office of Information* (Allen and Unwin, 1970).

Cloake, Colin, *Templer, Tiger of Malaya: The Life of Field Marshal Sir Gerald Templer* (Harrap, 1985).

Cockerill, Sir George, *What Fools We Were* (Hutchinson, 1944).

Cole, C. Robert, 'The conflict within: Sir Stephen Tallents and planning propaganda overseas before the Second World War', *Albion*, 12 (1982).

Cole, C. Robert, *Britain and the War of Words in Neutral Europe, 1939–45: The Art of the Possible* (Macmillan, 1990).

Cook, Sir Edward, *The Press in Wartime* (Macmillan, 1920).

Costello, John & Oleg Tsarev, *Deadly Illusions* (Century, 1993).

Coultass, C., *Images for Battle: British Film and the Second World War* (Associated University Press, 1989).

Cowling, Maurice, *The Impact of Hitler, British Politics and British Policy 1933–1939* (Cambridge University Press 1975, paperback edition).

Crossman, R. H. S., 'The wartime tactics that led to Watergate', *The Times*, 16 May 1973.

Cruickshank, Charles, *The Fourth Arm: Psychological Warfare 1938–1945* (Davis-Poynter, 1977).

Cudlipp, Hugh, *The Prerogative of the Harlot* (Bodley Head, 1980).

Culbert, D., *Mission to Moscow* (University of Wisconsin Press, 1980).

Cull, N. J., *Selling War: The British Propaganda Campaign against American 'Neutrality' in World War Two* (Oxford University Press, 1995).

Delmer, Sefton, *Black Boomerang* (Secker & Warburg, 1962).

di Nolfo, E., *Power In Europe? II. Great Britain, France, Germany and Italy and the Origins of the EEC, 1952–57* (Walter de Gruyter, 1992).

Dibbets, K. and B. Hogenkamp (eds), *Film and the First World War* (Amsterdam University Press, 1995).

Dillon, Martin, *The Dirty War* (Hutchinson, 1988).

Docherty, Martin, 'German wireless propaganda in English: an analysis of the organisation, content and effectiveness of Nazi radio broadcasts for the UK, 1939–45' (Ph.D. thesis, University of Kent School of History, 1998, (2 vols).

Donaldson, F., *The British Council: the first fifty years* (Cape, 1984).

Duke, A. C. and C. A. Tamse, *Too Mightly to Be Free: Censorship and the Press in Britain and the Netherlands* (De Walburg Press, 1987).

Dutton, David (ed.), *Statecraft and Diplomacy in the Twentieth Century: Essays Presented to P. M. H. Bell* (Liverpool University Press, 1995).

Eckersley, P. P., *The Power behind the Microphone* (Cape, 1940).

Edelman, M., *The Mirror: A Political History* (Hamilton, 1966).

Elkes, Pauline, 'The Political Warfare Executive: a re-evaluation based on the intelligence work of the German Section' (Ph.D. thesis, University of Sheffield School of History, 1996).

Erdmann, James M., *Leaflet Operations in the Second World War* (Arno Press, 1969).

Feiling, K., *The Life of Neville Chamberlain* (Macmillan, 1946).

Fest, W., *Peace and Partition* (St. Martin's Press, 1978).

Foot M. R. D., *S. O. E in France* (HMSO, 1966).

Fraenkel, Peter, 'The BBC's External Services: broadcasting to the USSR and Eastern Europe' in K. R. M. Short (ed.), *Western Broadcasting Over the Iron Curtain* (Croom Helm, 1986).

Frankland, N., *The Bomber Offensive Against Germany* (HMSO, 1965).

Fussell, P., *The Great War and Modern Memory* (Oxfrod University Press, 1975).

Gannon, F. R., *The British Press and Germany* (Claredon Press, 1971).

Garnett, M., 'Propaganda', *The Contemporary Review*, 147 (1935), 574–81.

Gladstone, K., 'British Interception of German Export Newsreels and the Development of British Combat Filming, 1939–42', *Imperial War Museum Review*, 2 (1987), pp. 30–40.

Glancy, H. Mark, 'The Hollywood "British" feature film, 1939–45' (Ph.D. thesis, University of East Anglia, 1993).

Gordon, G. N., *Persuasion: The Theory and Practice of Manipulative Communication* (Hastings House, 1971).

Gough-Yates, K., *Michael Powell: in Collaboration with Emeric Pressburger* (British Film Institute, 1970).

Grant, Ian, *Cameramen at War* (Stephens, 1980).

Grant, Mariel, *Propaganda and the Role of the State in Inter-war Britain* (Clarendon Press, 1994).

Grenville, J. A. S., *The Major International Treaties, 1914–73* (Methuen, 1974).

Gurfein, Murray I. and Morris Janowitz, 'Trends in *Wehrmacht* Morale' in William E. Daugherty (ed.), *A Psychological Warfare Casebook* (Arno Press, 1958).

Hallin, D., *Vietnam: The Uncensored War* (Oxford University Press, 1976).

Hardy, F. (ed.), *Grierson on Documentary* (Collins, 1946).

Harmsworth, G. and R. Pound, *Northcliffe* (Cassell, 1959).

Harvey, J. (ed.), *The Diplomatic Diaries of Oliver Harvey, 1937–40* (Collins, 1973).

Haste, Cate, *Keep the Home Fires Burning* (Allen Lane, 1977).

Hazlehurst, C., *Politicians at War* (Cape, 1971).

Herzstein, R. E., *The War that Hitler Won* (Hamish Hamilton, 1979).

Hewitt, Patricia, *The Abuse of Power* (Martin Robinson, 1982).

Hiley, N. 'Cinema, spectatorship and propaganda: *Battle of the Somme* (1916) and its contemporary audience', *Historical Journal of Film, Radio and Television*, 17:1, (March 1997), pp. 5–28.

Hischof, Gunter and Stephen E. Ambrose (eds), *Eisenhower and the German POWs: Facts Against Falsehood* (Louisiana State University Press, 1992).

Hollins, T., 'The Conservative Party and Film Propaganda between the wars', *English Historical Review*, 379 (1981), pp. 359–69.

Hollins, T., 'The presentation of politics: the place of party publicity, broadcasting and film in British Politics, 1918–39' (Ph.D. thesis, University of Leeds, 1981).

Hopkin, D. "Domestic Censorship in the First World War", *Journal of Contemporary History*, 5 (1970), pp. 151–69.

Howard, M., 'Total War in the twentieth century: participation and consensus in the Second World War' in B. Bond and I. Roy (eds), *War and Society: a Yearbook of Military History* (Croom Helm, 1975).

Howe, Ellic, *The Black Game: British Subversive Operations Against the Germans during the Second World War* (Michael Joseph, 1972).

Howells, Richard, *The Myth of the Titanic* (Macmillan, 1999).

Huxley Aldous, 'Dictators' Propaganda', *The Spectator*, 20 November 1936.

Huxley, Aldous, 'Notes on Propaganda', *Harper's Magazine*, 174 (1936), 32–41.

Jacob, I., 'The BBC: a national and an international force', an address to the 8th Annual Conference of the Institute of Public Relations, 18 May 1957.

James, R. R., *Memoirs of a Conservative* (Weidenfield and Nicolson, 1969).

Jarvie, I. C., 'Fanning the Flames: anti-American reaction to *Objective Burma* (1945)', *Historical Journal of Film, Radio and Television*, 1 (1981).

Jarvie, I. C., *Hollywood's Overseas Campaign* (Cambridge University Press, 1992).

Kecskemeti, Paul, *Strategic Surrender: The Politics of Victory and Defeat* (Stanford University Press, 1958).

Kennedy, P. M., 'Imperial Cable Communications and Strategy, 1870–1914', *English Historical Review*, 86 (1971), pp. 725–52.

Kennedy, P. M., *Strategy and Diplomacy* (Allen and Unwin, 1983).

Kenyon, Mark, 'Black Propaganda', *After the Battle*, 72 (1992), 8–31.

Knightley, P., *The First Casualty; the War Correspondent as Hero, Propagandist and Myth-maker from the Crimea to Vietnam* (Harcourt Bruce Jovanovich, 1975).

Koss, S., *The Rise and Fall of the Political Press in Britain* (2 vols, Hamish Hamilton, 1981–4).

Lasswell, H., *Propaganda Technique in the World War* (MIT press reprint, 1971).

Lawford, V., *Bound for Diplomacy* (Murray, 1963).

Le Mahieu, D. L., *A Culture for Democracy: Mass Communications and the Cultivated Mind in Britain between the Wars* (Clarendon Press, 1988).

Lerner, Daniel, *Sykewar: Psychological Warfare Against Germany, D-Day to VE-Day* (G. W. Stewart, 1949).

Lloyd George, D., *Memoirs of the Peace Conference* (2 vols, Yale University Press, 1939).

Lovelace, C., 'British press censorship during the First World War' in G. Boyce, J. Curren and P. Wingate (eds), *Newspaper History: from the Seventeenth Century to the Present Day* (Constable, 1978).

Lutz, Ralph, *The Fall of the German Empire, 1914–18* (Stanford University Press, 1932).

Mackenzie, A. J., *Propaganda Boom* (Gifford, 1938).

Masterman, Lucy, *C. F. C. Masterman, A Biography* (Cassell, 1968).

May, A. J., *The Passing of the Habsburg Monarchy 1914–18* (2 vols, University of Pennsylvania Press, 1966).

McEwan, J. M., "Northcliffe and Lloyd George at war, 1914–18", *Historical Journal*, 24 (1981) pp. 651–72.

McLachlan, D., *In the Chair: Barrington Ward of The Times* (Weidenfield and Nicolson, 1971).

McLaine, Ian, *Ministry of Morale: Home Front Morale and the Ministry of Information in World War II* (Allen and Unwin, 1979).

Mercer, Derek et. al., *The Fog of War* (Heinemann, 1987).

Messenger, G. S., *British Propaganda and the State in the First World War* (Manchester University Press, 1992).

Middlemass, K. and J. Barnes, *Baldwin: A Biography* (Weidenfield and Nicolson, 1969).

Morrison, David, *Television and the Gulf War* (John Libbey, 1992).

Neilson, K., '"Joy Rides"? British Intelligence and Propaganda in Russia 1914–17", *Historical Journal*, 24 (1981), 885–906.

Newton, Lord, *Retrospection* (Murray, 1941).

Nichols, Richard, *Radio Luxembourg: The Station of the Stars* (Allen, 1986).

Nichols, Sian, *The Echo of War* (Manchester University Press, 1996).

Niven, D., *The Moon's a Balloon* (Hamilton, 1971) and *Bring on the Empty Horses* (Coronet, 1983).

Nock, J., 'A New Dose of Britain Propaganda', *American Mercury*, 42 (December 1937).

Nutting, Anthony, *No End of a Lesson* (C. N. Potter, 1967).

Owen, F., *Tempestuous Journey* (Hutchinson, 1954).

Parker, R. A. C., 'British rearmament, 1936–39: treasury, Trade Unions and skilled labour', *English Historical Review*, 96 (1981), 306–43.

Pogue, Forrest C., *United States Army in World War II – The European Theater of Operations: The Supreme Command* (Washington DC Office of the Chief of Military History Department of the Army, 1954).

Powell, M., *A Life in Movies* (Heinemann, 1986).

Pronay, N., 'British newsreels in the 1930s: 1. Audiences and producers' and '2. Their policies and impact', *History*, 56 (1971) pp. 411–18; and 57 (1972) pp. 63–72.

Pronay N., 'The First Reality: Film Censorship in Liberal England' in K. R. M. Short (ed.), *Feature Films as History* (Croom Helm, 1981).

Pronay, N., '"The Land of Promise": the projection of peace aims in Britain' in K. R. M. Short (ed.), *Film and Radio Propaganda in World War Two* (Croom Helm, 1983).

Pronay, N. and Croft, J., 'British Film Censorship and Propaganda Policy during the Second World War' in J. Curran and V. Porter (eds), *British Cinema History* (London, 1983).

Pronay, N. and D. W. Spring (eds), *Propaganda, Politics and Film 1918–45* (Macmillan, 1982).

Pronay, N. and K. Wilson (eds), *The Political Re-education of Germany and her Allies after World War Two* (Croom Helm, 1984).

Ramsden, J., *The Age of Balfour and Baldwin* (Longman, 1978).

Reeves, N., *Official Film Propaganda during the First World War* (Croom Helm, 1986).

Reith, Sir John, *Into the Wind* (Hodder & Stoughton, 1949).

Richards, J., 'The British Board of Film Censors and content control in the 1930s: 1 Images of Britain; 2 Foreign Affairs', *Historical Journal of Film, Radio and Television*, 1:2 (1981) and 2:1 (1982).

Richards, Jeffrey and Aldgate, Anthony, *Best of British: Cinema and Society 1930–1970* (Blackwell, 1983).

Robertson, J. C., *The British Board of Film Censors* (Croom Helm, 1985).

Rogerson S., *Propaganda in the Next War* (Bles, 1938).

Roosevelt, Kermit (ed.), *War Report of the OSS* (Walker, 1976).

Roskill, S. W., *Naval Policy between the Wars* (Collins, 1976).

Salmon, L. M., *The Newspaper and Authority* (Oxford University Press, 1923).

Sanders, M. L., 'Wellington House and British propaganda during the First World War', *Historical Journal*, 18:1 (1975), 119–46.

Sanders, M. L. and Philip M. Taylor, *British Propaganda during the First World War* (Macmillan, 1982).

Sandler, S., *Segregated Skies: The All-Black Combat Squadrons of World War II* (Publisher unknown, 1992).

Saxon Mills, J., *The Press and Communications of the Empire* (Heinemann, 1924).

Shaw, Tony, *Eden, Suez and the Mass Media: Propaganda and Persuasion during the Suez Crisis* (I. B. Taurus, 1996).

Shay, R. P., *British Rearmament in the 1930s* (Princeton University Press, 1977).

Shils, Edward A. and Morris Janowitz, 'Cohesion and Disintegration in the *Wehrmacht*' in Morris Janowitz (ed.), *Military Conflict: Essays in the Institutional Analysis of War and Peace* (Sage, 1975).

Short, K. R. M. (ed.), *Feature Films as History* (Croom Helm, 1981).

Shultz, Richard H. and Roy Godson, *Dezinformatsia: Active Measures in Soviet Strategy* (Pergamon-Brassey's, 1984).

Siegel, S. N., 'Radio and Propaganda', *Air Law Review*, 10 (1939).

Simpson, C., *Science of Coercion: Communications Research and Psychological Warfare* (Oxford University Press, 1994).

Smith, M., *British Air Strategy between the Wars* (Oxford University Press, 1982).

Soley, Laurence C., *Radio Warfare: OSS and CIA Subversive Propaganda* (Praeger, 1989).

Sorlin, P., *The Film in History* (Blackwell, 1986).

Spaight, J. M., *Air Power and War Rights* (Longman, 1924).

Squires, J. D., *British Propaganda at Home and in the United States from 1914 to 1917* (Harvard University Press, 1935).

Stamm, K., 'German wartime newsreels (Deutsche Wochenschau): the problem of "authenticity"', *Historical Journal of Film, Radio and Television*, 7 (1987), pp. 239–48.

Struther, Jan, *Mrs Miniver* (Virago, 1989 reprint).

Stuart, C. (ed.), *The Reith Diaries* (Collins, 1975).

Stuart, Sir Campbell, *Secrets of Crewe House: The Story of a Famous Campaign* (Hodder & Stoughton, 1920).

Stuart, Sir Campbell, *Opportunity Knocks Once* (Collins, 1952).

Swann, Paul, *The British Documentary Film Movement, 1926–46* (Cambridge University Press, 1989).

Sweet-Escott, B., *Baker Street Irregular* (Methuen, 1965).

Taylor, A. J. P., *English History, 1914–45* (Clarendon Press, 1965).

Taylor, A. J. P., *Beaverbrook* (Simon and Schuster, 1972).

Taylor, J. R., *Hitch: the Life and Work of Alfred Hitchcock* (Pantheon, 1978)

Taylor, Philip M. "The Foreign Office and British propaganda during the First World War", *Historical Journal*, 15 (1972), pp. 113–59.

Taylor, Philip M., '"If War should Come": preparing the Fifth Arm for Total War, 1935–39', *Journal of Contemporary History*, 16 (1981).

Taylor, Philip M., *The Projection of Britain: British Overseas Publicity and Propaganda, 1919–39* (Cambridge University Press, 1981).

Taylor, Philip M., *Munitions of the Mind: War Propaganda from the Ancient World to the Nuclear Age* (Patrick Stephens Ltd, 1990).

Taylor, Philip M., *War and the Media: Propaganda and Persuasion in the Gulf War* (Manchester University Press, 1992).

Taylor, Philip M., *Global Communications, International Affairs and the Media since 1945* (Routledge, 1997).

Taylor, Philip M., 'Through a glass darkly: propaganda and psychological warfare in the 1950s' in Gary Rawnsley (ed.), *The Sword and the Pen: Propaganda and the Cold War in the 1950s* (Macmillan, 1999).

Taylor, Philip M. and Badsey, Steven, 'Images of Battle: The Press, Propaganda and Passchendaele' in Peter Liddle (ed.), *Passchendaele in Perspective* (Pen and Sword Press, 1997), pp. 371–89.

Templewood, Viscount, *Nine Troubled Years* (Collins, 1954).

The Times, History of, The 150th Anniversary and Beyond, 1912–48 (Printing House Square, 1952).

Thomson, Charles A. H., *Overseas Information Service of the United States Government* (Arno Press, 1948).

Thomson, G. P., *Blue Pencil Admiral* (Sampson Low, 1949).

Thorpe, F. and N. Pronay, *British Official Films in The Second World War* (Clio Press, 1980).

Tilley, J. and S. Gaselee, *The Foreign Office* (Putnam, 1933).

Towle, P., 'The debate on wartime censorship in Britain, 1902–14' in B. Bond and I. Roy (eds), *War and Society: A Yearbook of Military History* (Croom Helm, 1975).

Tree, Ronald, *When The Moon Was High* (Macmillan, 1975).

Trevor-Roper, Hugh (ed.), *The Goebbels Diaries: The Last Days* (Secker and Warburg, 1978).

United States Strategic Bombing Survey, *European Report No. 64b: The Effects of Strategic Bombing on German Civilian Morale* (US GPO, 1946–7).

Valiani, Leo, *The End of Austria-Hungary* (Secker & Warburg, 1973).

Voska, E. V. and Irwin, Will, *Spy and Counter-Spy* (G. G. Harrap & Co., 1940).

Warburg, James P., *Unwritten Treaty* (Atheneum, 1946).

Wark, W. K., 'Coming in from the Cold: British propaganda and Red Army defectors, 1945–52', *International History Review*, 9:1 (1987), 48–72.

Warman, Roberta, "The erosion of Foreign Office influence in the making of foreign policy, 1916–18", *Historical Journal*, 15:2 (1972), pp. 113–59.

Webster, C. and N. Frankland, *The Strategic Air Offensive Against Germany, 1939–45* (HMSO, 1961).

Wenden, D. J. and Short, K. R. M., 'Winston S. Churchill: film fan' in *Historical Journal of Film, Radio and Television*, 11 (1991), pp. 197–214.

Wickham Steed, H., *Through Thirty Years* (2 vols, Heinemann, 1924).

Wickham Steed, H., *The Fifth Arm* (Constable, 1940).

Wilkinson, Peter and Joan Bright Astley, *Gubbins and SOE* (I. B. Taurus, 1993).

Willcox, Temple, 'Projection or publicity? Rival concepts in the pre-war planning of the British Ministry of Information', *Journal of Contemporary History* 18 (1983).

Willcox, Temple, 'Towards a Ministry of Information', *History*, 69 (1984).

Willert, A., 'British news abroad', *The Round Table*, (1937), 533–46.

Willert, A., 'Publicity and propaganda in international affairs', *International Affairs*, 17 (1938), 809–26.

Willert, A., *Washington and Other Memories* (Houghton and Mifflin, 1972).

Williams, F., *Press, Parliament and People* (Heinemann, 1946).

Williams, Raymond, *Communications* (Penguin, 1962).

Wilmot, Chester, *The Struggle for Europe* (Harper, 1952).

Wilson, T. (ed.), *The Political Diaries of C. P. Scott, 1911–28* (Collins, 1970).

Wilson, T., *The Myriad Faces of War* (Polity, 1986).

Winkler, Alan M., *The Politics of Propaganda: The Office of War Information, 1942–1945* (Yale University Press, 1978).

Woodward E. L., *British Foreign Policy in the Second World War* (HMSO, 1971).

Wright Mills, C., *The Power Elite* (Oxford University Press, 1958).

Young, Harry F., *Prince Lichnowsky and the War* (University of Georgia Press, 1970).

Young, Kenneth (ed.), *The Diaries of Sir Robert Bruce Lockhart: Vol. Two, 1939–1965* (St. Martin's Press, 1974).

Index